South Tipperary, 1570–1841

South Tipperary, 1570–1841

Religion, Land and Rivalry

DAVID J. BUTLER

FOUR COURTS PRESS

Set in 10.5 pt on 12 pt Bembo for
FOUR COURTS PRESS LTD
7 Malpas Street, Dublin 8, Ireland
e-mail: info@four-courts-press.ie
http://www.four-courts-press.ie
and in North America by
FOUR COURTS PRESS
c/o ISBS, 920 N.E. 58th Avenue, Suite 300, Portland, OR 97213.

A catalogue record for this title
is available from the British Library.

ISBN 1–85182–891–5

Printed in England
by MPG Books, Bodmin, Cornwall.

For my mother,
and
in memory of my father

Hegemony is actually a process of struggle, a permanent striving, a ceaseless endeavour to maintain control over the 'hearts and minds' of subordinate classes. The work of hegemony, so to speak, is never done.

R. Miliband, *Capitalist democracy in Britain* (1984), 76

Contents

Illustrations

Maps

Tables

Acknowledgments

The researching and writing of this book would have been difficult without the support and advice of Professor William J. Smyth, affectionately known as 'Prof', whose abundant encouragement, impromptu maps and diagrams have guided me over many years and whose knowledge of the historical and cultural geography of Ireland has proved truly inspirational. The department of Geography, UCC was most generous in providing me with extended after-hours access to its GIS computer laboratory and facilities, integral to the completion of this research and for this I am very grateful. I also wish to acknowledge the experience in teaching and administration gathered in the department in staff-related and lectureship roles.

I am especially grateful to the many individuals who have helped me along the way; while apologizing to any whose names I may have omitted inadvertently, I wish to record my indebtedness to the following: Dr Gerry Kearns, department of Geography, University of Cambridge; Professor David Livingstone, department of Geography, QUB; Dr A.P.W. Malcomson; Dr Frank O'Brien; Dr Mervyn O'Driscoll and Dr John Tyrrell, department of Geography, UCC, for their reading of earlier drafts and most helpful comments thereon; Professor Bruce Campbell of the department of Geography, QUB, and Mr Kenneth Nicholls of the department of History, UCC, for their sage comments and pronouncements; Dr Andy Bielenberg and Dr Hiram Morgan of the department of History, UCC, and Dr Jacinta Prunty of the department of History, NUI Maynooth for their generosity in drawing my attention toward additional source material; David Joyce, for his extremely thoughtful GIS tutorials, which enabled me master drawing and redrafting the maps included in this work and his invaluable work in converting them to a format suitable for publication; Helen Bradley, GIS Officer of the department of Geography, UCC, whose good humour and availability will always be remembered and appreciated; the ever-patient Rose Walsh, Brendan Dockery and the other administrative staff of the department of Geography, UCC for processing my many research related requests – indeed, my friendship with Brendan, Rose and Joan Walsh over the years provided a refreshing change from my focus on the computer screen and interesting perspectives both on academia and 'the university of life' outside of it.

The staff of the various research depositories I have visited were most helpful: *in Belfast*, Robert Bonar and Andrew MacMillan, successively assistant secretary of the Presbyterian Historical Society of Ireland; Revd Robin Roddie, archivist, Wesley Historical Society; Maureen McMaw, Baptist Union of Ireland; David Scott, Grand Orange Lodge of Ireland; Public Record Office of Northern Ireland; *in Cork*, Pastor Ted Price, Cork Baptist Church; Revd John Faris, Trinity Presbyterian Church; *in Dublin*, Friends Historical Library, particularly Verity Murdoch and Mary Shackleton; Grand Lodge of Freemasons; Irish Architectural Archive; National Archives of Ireland; National Library of Ireland; Registry of Deeds; Representative Church Body Library, particularly Dr Raymond Refaussé and Dr Susan Hood; Royal Irish Academy; Trinity College manuscripts department; Revd Bill Darlison, Unitarian Church; *in South Tipperary*, Very Revd Dr P.J. Knowles, dean and archivist, Bolton Library, Cashel; Revd G.A. Knowd, Clonmel; Revd I. Knox, Clonmel; Very Revd Dr R.B. MacCarthy, dean of St Patrick's cathedral; Canon B.Y. Fryday, Kilcooley; Tipperary (S.R.) County Museum, Clonmel; Ann Hallinan, county registrar; *in North Tipperary*, Mary Guinan-Darmody, Local Studies department of the Joint County Library, Thurles; *in Waterford*, Fr Uinseann Ó Maidin, archivist, Mount Melleray abbey; staff of Municipal Library, Waterford. The staff of the oft-visited Special Collections, Boole Library, UCC deserve special mention: Peadar Cranitch, Ann Cronin, Teresina Flynn, Catherine Horgan, Mary Lombard, Margaret Fitzpatrick and particularly Julian Walton, who is in a class of his own regarding the sourcing of obscure publications relating to Irish ecclesiastical history. Also those individuals who entered into correspondence with me, particularly Revd A.S. Cromie, Presbyterian Historical Society of Ireland; Revd Dudley Levistone-Cooney, President, Wesley Historical Society (Irish Branch); Steven ffeary-Smyrl concerning dissenter meeting-houses; Ruth Illingsworth and Dr Martin Pulbrook concerning Unitarian congregations; Revd Andrew M. Hill and Christopher Stell of the Unitarian Historical Society; Pastor Robert Dunlop and the late Dr H.D. Gribbon, Baptist Historical Society of Ireland; and the late Tom Walsh, Bolton Street, Clonmel, whose initiation of contact with Cyril McIntyre and Eugene Field of the Irish Railway Record Society on my behalf proved invaluable, opening an almost forgotten door on Clonmel Unitarianism.

My membership of the UCC Choral Society greatly aided the preservation of my sanity over the years and has provided much worthwhile diversion, both in Cork and overseas, from the hours spent working on this research. The memories of participation in the *Musica Mundi* International Choral Festivals in Budapest, Hungary (2001) and Grado, Italy (2002) will long remain with me and I am thankful for the friends I have made through the society and serving on the committee, both from Ireland: Sinéad Allen, Andrew Deering, JB Harrington, Sarah Kendall, Michael Keohane, Claire Mansfield, Aoife Miskelly, Grace Power, Drew Ruttle, and from overseas: Olivier Bopp, Halvor Dahl, Boaz Fuchs, Oldrich Janda, Danny McNamara and Hayo Schapp. Outside of Choral – although still in the world of music – my friends (and fellow organists!) Melvin Beamish, Paul Beecher, Roy Buttimer, Brian McCarthy, Carmel O'Shea and Pádraig Wallace aided and abetted in this welcome diversion through coffee breaks and conversations, at various stages in the research, parallel to my musical education at the hands of Maggie Davis and Colin Nicholls. And of course, from my postgraduate days, there are memories of great conversations and social evenings in the company of Millie Glennon and Katelijne Rouffa and fellowship with Patricia Atkins, William Brady, Richard Browne, Aoife Curtin, Georgina Ferris, Joanne McCarthy, Xóan Parades, Conor Ryan and Mark Rylands; also continuing links to my undergraduate days through Brian O'Donovan, Sinéad Power and Richard McMahon.

I am grateful to the Higher Education Authority (HEA) and the Irish Research Council for the Humanities and Social Sciences (IRCHSS) for the Government of Ireland doctoral scholarship in the Humanities and Social Sciences, of which I had tenure for portion of my postgraduate career. The publication of this research was generously aided by a subvention from the National University of Ireland (NUI) Publications Fund, for which I am most thankful to the university and its registrar, Dr Attracta Halpin. In addition, the Cashel, Waterford and Lismore Diocesan Board of Education (Church of Ireland) generously supported the expense of preparing the index – so central to this book – for publication and I am most grateful to Revd Arthur E. Carter, secretary to the board, for his kindness in this matter.

I wish to acknowledge the generous permission of Lord Egremont, for permission to publish the image of the village of Cullen (1703) taken from a manuscript estate map in the Petworth House Collection, and the efficiency of the staff of the West Sussex Record Office in processing the material, particularly Alison McCann, assistant county archivist. I also acknowledge the gracious permission of the National Library of Ireland to publish images from the Lawrence Collection, 'down survey' and their manuscript collections, especially the courtesy of Collette O'Flaherty, assistant keeper.

I am, indeed, fortunate to have encountered so considerate a publisher as Four Courts Press and I am most grateful to the staff – particularly Michael Adams, Martin Fanning and Anthony Tierney – for their most helpful advice on a variety of fronts from the outset.

The final word goes to my mother, who has supported this work throughout at a whole series of levels and, consequently, this work is jointly dedicated to her and to the memory of my father.

Abbreviations

BL Add. MSS	British Library Additional Manuscripts
CAI	Cork Archives Institute
'civil survey'	The Civil Survey, A.D. 1654–56, County of Tipperary
'down survey'	The Down Survey of the baronies of Ireland
FHL	Friends Historical Library, Dublin
GIS	Geographical Information Systems
GO	Genealogical Office, National Library of Ireland, Dublin
HC	House of Commons
IHS	*Irish Historical Studies*
JCHAS	*Journal of the Cork Historical and Archaeological Society*
JRSAI	*Journal of the Royal Society of Antiquaries of Ireland*
JWSEIAS	*Journal of the Waterford and South East of Ireland Archaeological Society*
LOL	Loyal Orange Lodge
NAI	National Archives of Ireland, Dublin
NLI	National Library of Ireland, Dublin
PRIA	*Proceedings of the Royal Irish Academy*
PRO	Public Record Office, London
PRONI	Public Record Office of Northern Ireland, Belfast
QUB	Queen's University, Belfast
RCB	Representative Church Body Library, Dublin
RD	Registry of Deeds, Dublin
RIA	Royal Irish Academy, Dublin
TCD	Trinity College, Dublin
UCC	University College, Cork
UCD	University College, Dublin
WO	War Office, London

Introduction

A long street down which some cattle stray; barrack-like houses with jack-
daws on their roofs; a Catholic church, new, with high spires; a Protestant
church, old, that looks as if it had defencefully huddled itself away ...[1]

'A Munster town in 1926'

Growing up in South Tipperary, I was aware from a comparatively early age of the
large number of ruined and disused churches and gate lodges in the locality, particularly in the hinterland between the county town of Clonmel and my home-
town of Cahir, ten miles distant. One of my earliest memories, travelling by car to
Clonmel with my parents, aged about four years, is of having landmarks pointed
out to me en route, in order to retain my interest and avoid a bout of travel sickness. These landmarks – the ruined Board of First Fruits church at Derrygrath
(Woodrooffe) and the gate lodge and trees on the Watson estate at Ballingarrane,
near Clonmel – must have made an indelible impression, for by my early teenage
years I was already displaying interest in local studies, particularly in the history of
churches and big houses. As I did so and as our travels expanded throughout rural
Ireland, I also noticed the often detached, visibly older sites of Anglican churches,
whether in ruins or in use, and the contrast provided by visibly newer, larger, often
more modern Roman Catholic churches.

In my native place, the historic former estate, garrison and milling town of
Cahir, I was aware from an early age of different Christian traditions, in that the
town possessed (and still possesses) a church of each of the three main Christian
denominations on the island of Ireland: Roman Catholic, Anglican and Presbyterian.
This diversity (when compared with other small towns in the south of Ireland in
the early 1980s), was often remarked upon, as significantly larger population centres often did not possess two Protestant churches. While the majority of the townspeople were Roman Catholic, there was a significant Protestant minority spread
through town and district. However, with seven of fifteen households' Protestant,
ours was the most multi-denominational neighbourhood in the town. The main
reason for this religious diversity lay in the building, c.1910, of a pair of semi-
detached villas and a terrace of six cottages in cut-sandstone by the Going and Smith
milling company for its workers and administrators on a site opposite our house.
These families – converts to Anglicanism from the Society of Friends – formed the
company by joining Suir mills (Going) with Cahir mills (Smith) and by purchasing the Abbey mills (Grubb) from the remnant of that Quaker dynasty in 1893.[2]
The firm promoted employment among Protestants, at manual and particularly at
administrative level, with the result that a disproportionate number of Protestants
inhabited these dwellings. Following the closure of the mill in 1967, their descendants bought out their leases; five of these houses contained Anglicans or Presby-

1 P. Colum, *The road round Ireland* (1926), 426. 2 D.J. Butler, *Cahir: a guide to heritage town and district* (1999).

terians by the early 1980s. My interest in the study of religious diversity, community distribution, territorial organization and interaction results in great part from my immersion in this inter-church neighbourhood.

Throughout the centuries, Christians have expressed their understandings in different ways – in essential belief, in ways of expressing their faith, in manner of worship and in the form and structures of church life – reflecting different understandings of authority. The various divisions of Christianity have often led to considerable bitterness and conflict. In particular, the rupture in medieval Christendom created by the Reformation meant that the churches that emerged from it defined themselves over and against each other, especially the Protestant denominations over and against the Roman Catholic Church; the emphasis was placed on doctrinal and liturgical differences, rather than things that were still held in common. This was later also the case among the Protestant denominations, where differences, rifts and splits have long been a prominent feature. The history of Protestantism reveals much inter- and intra-denominational conflict, on a national and international scale.

When dealing with historical and cultural issues in Ireland, one is inevitably dealing with religion as well, for religion applies not only to the beliefs, practices and organizations associated with formal religion, but is the name by which the Irish people have called their ethnic differences. Religion has been the single most important way in which Irish people have defined themselves since the last quarter of the sixteenth century, when cultural divisions and differences between the Irish and the English led to religious animosity between the Protestant and Roman Catholic religious communities in Ireland and the development of opposing identities. It mattered not if an individual entered their church only to be baptized and to be buried; the life they lived between those two events was, in the eyes of those with whom they dealt, the life of either a Protestant or a Roman Catholic. In this sort of environment, it was natural that religious differences should be associated strongly with political differences and it followed that religion would become heavily politicized.

This book aims, during the course of the empirical chapters, to identify the formation and interaction of implicit and explicit spatial strategies that define cultural identity and territorial management in a colonial context. Through a case study examination of South Tipperary it examines those strategies employed by the ruling Protestant minority in Ireland to gain and retain power and maintain hegemonic spaces *vis-à-vis* the ruled Roman Catholic majority. It further seeks to establish how the 'underground' Roman Catholic majority population first accommodated itself to this ruled situation and then progressively challenged and devised counter-strategies of resistance that increasingly dominated and undermined the minority-ruling establishment. The intention is to explore the processes, experiences and intrinsic ambiguities of colonialism on the people of South Tipperary and, in this way, further enhance understanding of the dialectic between these communities in early modern Ireland.

There is a distinct lack of both geographical and historic writing and research at county level, of the dialectic between the Protestant and Roman Catholic communities in Ireland, *c.*1570 to *c.*1841. Papers delivered and books written to date tend to focus on the study of Christian denominations in a nationwide context, occasionally in a diocesan or regional context. Research at county level avoids one of the characteristics that undermines so many studies involving religion, namely the tendency to make over-generalizations, for it is 'only by performing the tedious task of tallying activities and arrangements parish-by-parish, and clergyman by clergyman can one simultaneously arrive at justifiable generalizations and at an appreciation of the range of divergence'.[3] At the same time, a study area of this size avoids the insufficient diversity that a study at a smaller territorial level – such as a barony or parish – would invariably encounter.

The study of an Irish county, such as South Tipperary, opens up many interesting perspectives and aims to contribute to the literature by combining geographic concepts with archival work and interdisciplinary material. In examining the changing relationship between Protestants and Roman Catholics, this study looks beyond the largest Protestant denomination in the study area, Anglicanism, to the smaller Protestant dissenting denominations, little known and less understood by the Irish people in general. The suitability of the study area for this type of research lies in the fact that South Tipperary contained a greater than average religious diversity, particularly in and around the county town of Clonmel, which was bettered outside the province of Ulster only by the largest cities in Ireland. In light of the spirit of Christian ecumenism and the ongoing northern Irish peace process – both set against centuries of inter-denominational bitterness and the politicization of religion – it is vitally important to promote an understanding of the workings, beliefs, practices and organization of these denominations, present throughout the island of Ireland.

Although South Tipperary has only been in existence as an administrative unit since 1839 through the creation of a North Riding and South Riding in that year, Co. Tipperary had existed as a shire of the English colonial administration in Ireland since the first-half of the thirteenth century.[4] It is a county that has been described as 'hybrid [in] physical, economic and cultural terms',[5] and 'an area of convergence where major strands in Ireland's history have met'.[6] South Tipperary – which possesses all the diversities and characteristics of a medium-sized Irish county, with the added benefit of a dynamic position at the crossroads of south-central Ireland – is divided into five baronies, viz. Iffa and Offa; Middlethird; Clanwilliam; Kilnamanagh and Slieveardagh. It comprises 115 civil parishes and consists of two main areas: the southern portion that lies on either side of Clonmel, ancient capital of the entire county, contained within the diocese of Waterford and Lismore; and the northern portion, comprising the greater portion of the archdiocese of Cashel and Emly, centred on Cashel, the ecclesiastical capital of the province of Munster. The feature that unites both parts of South Tipperary, as also the North and South Ridings, is the river Suir, whose partly-tidal aspect positioned it as the primary artery of regional transport into the nineteenth century, and enabled considerable trade between the inland port-towns of Clonmel and Carrick-on-Suir and the regional seaport of Waterford.

3 D.H. Akenson, *The Church of Ireland: ecclesiastical reform and revolution, 1800–85* (1971), 12. **4** D.A. Murphy, *The two Tipperarys* (1994). **5** W.J. Smyth, 'Landholding changes, kinship networks and class transformation in rural Ireland: a case-study from Co. Tipperary' (1983), 16. **6** T. Jones-Hughes, 'Landholding and settlement in Co. Tipperary in the nineteenth century' (1985), 339.

The key to power in South Tipperary and beyond has always been landed property, and an examination of its topography provides some explanation for the subsequent distribution of both Anglo-Norman and post-Reformation English settlers. The northern-half of South Tipperary is rich and fertile, from the Galtee Mountains in the south-west to the border with North Tipperary and from Slievenamon in the south-east to the Slieveardagh Hills in the north-east. As may be seen in map 1, the more urbanized southern-half contains fertile plains dominated by mountains: the Knockmealdowns on the southern boundary run parallel to the Galtees on the west, while Slievenamon to the east end faces the Comeragh Mountains in Co. Waterford, just across the Suir valley. The extensive fertility of the county led to its being highly attractive to settlers, both in the Norman and Cromwellian periods of conquest. The most extensive soil type covering the area is the grey-brown podzolic found on undulating lowlands and overlying carboniferous limestone. Broadly speaking, these soils cover western Iffa and Offa, Middlethird, and Clanwilliam. This soil has a wide agricultural usage, being alternatively capable of supporting rich grassland, as in the Golden Vale, or cereal and other crops. There are two areas of exception to this soil type in South Tipperary. The first, in the north-east, is the acid brown earth associated with the Slieveardagh Hills and the podzolic soils found in the upland hill terrain east of Slievenamon, covering much of eastern Iffa and Offa and Slieveardagh baronies. The second extends to the west of Cahir, and forms an area of peaty podzols and blanket peat, centring on the Galtee Mountains. These two areas have limitations deriving from their soil type, which make their range of agricultural uses more restricted than the area covered with grey-brown podzolics. The significance of these features has been recognised in a number of publications.[7]

The question I would like to pose here, however, is how writing about this compact and centrally located area of southern Ireland informs, and is informed by, wider perspectives on the nature of colonialism. In South Tipperary, through the course of the early modern period, existing cultural settings were encountered and contested by the wider practices of English colonial expansion. Such research needs to dissect 'the norms and forms of colonial dominance … through a variegated account of the strategies and spaces of resistance'.[8] It is hoped this study will demonstrate the extent to which the Roman Catholic colonized population in South Tipperary drew on 'multiple strategies of resistance to resist exclusionary definitions, to fend off the intrusive mechanisms of bureaucratic power and to advance their own claims'.[9]

Recent research has shown the slow and uneven efforts to integrate Ireland into English political, legal and cultural structures in the later sixteenth and early seventeenth centuries to have been part of the English 'Atlantic empire'.[10] The placing of this study on a European scale and in a contemporary context is therefore crucial, for it was merciless intolerance by Roman Catholic monarchs toward their

---

7 M.J. Gardiner and T. Radford, *Soil associations of Ireland* (1980); F.N.A. Allen et al. (eds), *Atlas of the Irish rural landscape* (1997); P.C. Power, *History of South Tipperary* (1989). 8 D. Arnold cited in B.E.S. Yeoh, 'Historical geographies of the colonized world' (2000), 163. 9 Yeoh, ibid. 10 T. Barnard, 'The origins of Empire' (1998); N.P. Canny, 'Identity formation in Ireland' (1987); idem, *Making Ireland British, 1580–1650* (2001).

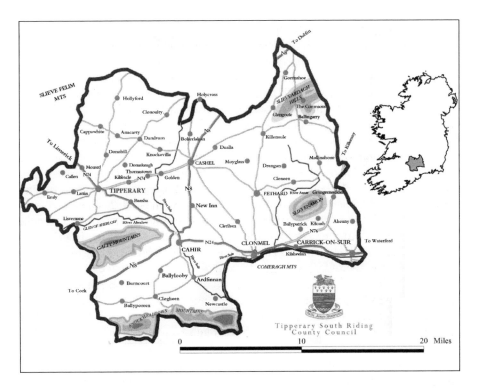

Map 1: South Tipperary topography and settlement

Protestant minorities on the European Continent, alongside their support of the ousted Stuart dynasty, which led the New English Protestant settler community to fear, and take steps to curtail the socio-political advancement of the Irish Roman Catholic population, and their centuries-old linkages with Roman Catholic countries such as France and Spain. Protestants in Britain and Ireland were made greatly fearful of events on the European Continent.

Throughout the course of this study, the aim is to detail the inconsistencies and ambiguities of New English colonial expansion and contraction in South Tipperary, for 'practices of resistance cannot be separated from practices of domination ... they are always entangled in some configuration'.[11] South Tipperary is an example of a space where disparate cultures met, clashed, and grappled with each other 'in highly asymmetrical relations of domination and subordination'.[12] Recent work in historical geography has guided the sub-discipline towards increased emphasis on archival research and asking searching questions of the source material, which is 'consonant with an interpretive turn in social science more generally, which has given credence to historiography and discourse as truths of a kind'.[13] To conduct a proper study of how societies grow, change, decline, or reconstruct themselves, it is acknowledged that

---

11 P. Routledge, 'A spatiality of resistances' (1997), 70. **12** M.L. Pratt, *Imperial eyes: travel writing and transculturation* (1992), 7. **13** G. Henderson, 'Landscape is dead, long live landscape' (1998), 94.

a full mastery of the relevant documents is essential, [as is also] a much deeper understanding of how the old society functioned and how the new settlers inserted themselves into, and attempted to reconstruct the society. We need to have a much greater appraisal of the 'terrain' (not just physical but infra-structural and cultural) in which people in these societies worked and made a living … before we can provide a fuller picture of Irish society and its transformation.[14]

In attempting to recover the geographies of the colonized world of early modern South Tipperary, lack of evidence constitutes a recurring problem, especially in the pre-1641 period, for 'it is often the case that simply not enough is known about colonized groups given the asymmetries in the historical record for anyone approaching the colonial period'.[15] Consequently, my approach to all sources consulted in connection with this research has especially involved the interrogation of documents at an interpretative level, stressing their qualitative significance, and guided by the aim of examining issues of 'contestation' in the sources. In doing so, I make extensive use of GIS-generated maps to aid the mining of data, for 'historical GIS has the capacity to let researchers investigate what had long been too massive, too slow, too complicated'.[16]

Throughout this work, I hope to demonstrate that the examination of the dialectic between Protestant and Roman Catholic communities is not only a valid avenue of enquiry, but one that allows the adoption of a multi-disciplinary methodological framework; while paying due attention to structure and agency, this involves a detailed descriptive analysis of quantifiable data, through the medium of mapping the spatial distribution and diffusion of relevant phenomena. This exploration has led to the creation of maps detailing various aspects of the changing distribution and territorial organization of the Protestant and Roman Catholic communities in South Tipperary. The mapping of sites of rule and resistance at the micro-scale has proved an integral component of my interpretive analysis of their changing geographical inter-relationship both with each other and with the colonial administration.

With regard to my chosen period of study, 1570 provides a convenient starting point at a time when dividing loyalties and religious differences first became apparent, following the excommunication in 1569 of Queen Elizabeth by the pope and contemporary with the reassertion of New English colonial control over Ireland. The year 1841, which saw the final great push by Anglicans of the Established Church to retain political influence and arrest the continuing decline in their hegemony, constitutes the end-point of the narrative. The intervening 270 years with which this study concerns itself constitutes a hugely significant period in the carving out of spaces of power and identity, in the consolidation of territorial control and in the contestation of hegemonic decline of early modern English colonialism in Ireland.

14 W.J. Smyth, 'Making the documents of conquest speak' (1992). 15 Yeoh, 'Historical geographies of the colonised world', 149. 16 D.W. Holdsworth, 'Historical geography: the ancients and the moderns' (2002), 672; A.K. Knowles (ed.), 'Historical GIS: the spatial turn in social science history' (2000).

The Reformation and sixteenth-century identity formation

The condition of the Irish Church in the early sixteenth century was such that reformation was long overdue, for both clergy and laity were implicated in abuses in this period of religious decadence. Christianity in Ireland has its earliest roots in the monastic system and this system still had a lot of influence over religion in sixteenth-century Ireland, not least because of the material power and distribution of the various religious orders. A considerable number of religious foundations had failed in Ireland during the two centuries prior to the Reformation: in South Tipperary at Ardfinnan (Franciscan Third Order); Clonoulty (Knights Hosp.); and Kilcommon, near Cahir (Benedictine), while numbers in the remaining religious houses were often quite low.[1]

In Gaelic Ireland, prior to the twelfth-century reform of the Church and the enforcement of clerical celibacy, hereditary succession to ecclesiastical offices and clerical marriage were extremely common. These practices produced ecclesiastical families (although forbidden by canon law), as a result of tactical papal tolerance of clerical marriage. The Church with which the religious reformers came into contact in Gaelic dioceses beyond the Pale was thus distinctive in character.[2] Research of papal registers has revealed a host of dispensations were granted for sons of clerics to hold benefices, many in direct succession to their fathers.[3] The straitened circumstances of clergy were such that some were forced to supplement their stipends by engaging in commerce; in 1490, Matthew Mulryan, abbot of the Cistercian abbey of Holy Cross, on the northern fringe of South Tipperary, was accused by the head of his Order of engaging in the wine trade and of being one of his own best customers.[4]

The spiritual dynamism of the older religious orders in the Church had long been eroded by the secular trends at work among the diocesan clergy. The submission made in 1498 by Abbot Troy of Mellifont is a case in point: many of the Irish abbeys of his Cistercian Order were headed by non-clerics, the habit of the Order was not worn in foundations beyond the Pale, and there was a general trend towards control of the monasteries and their vast properties by great lay families. Simony and pluralism characterized abbatial appointments, an example of simony being the transfer by Abbot William O'Dwyer of his abbey of Holy Cross to a layman in 1534.[5] Many important churches were in ruins at this time, including

1 B. Bradshaw, *The dissolution of the religious orders in Ireland under Henry VIII* (1974). 2 K.W. Nicholls, 'Rectory, vicarage and parish in the western Irish dioceses' (1971). 3 C. Mooney, 'The Church in Gaelic Ireland' (1969), 14–17. 4 C. Lennon, *Seventeenth century Ireland* (1994), 128–9. 5 Ibid.

the cathedral churches of both Ardagh and Clonmacnoise.[6] The earl of Kildare, though not impartial, probably spoke truly when declaring that the churches in Cos. Tipperary and Kilkenny were generally in ruins through the system of papal provisions 'so as and if the king's grace do not see for the hasty remedy of the same, there is like to be no more Christianity there, than in the midst of Turkey'.[7]

By the Reformation, the mendicant orders – unlike the older monastic orders – had succeeded in rejuvenating themselves through the Observant reform, a movement that commenced on the Continent during the fifteenth century in an attempt to return monastic communities to early Christian ideals.[8] By the 1470s, urban friary communities, though comprising a mixture of Old English and Gaelic Irish members, were in their preaching attuned to the needs of urban congregations through their libraries and were also in contact with rural dwellers of their respective hinterlands through alms-seeking missions.[9] The Observant friars exhibited a religious vigour lacking elsewhere in the Irish Church, for as an unknown government official noted in the state papers of 1515,

> Ther[e] is no archebysshop ne bysshop, abbot ne prior, parson ne vycar, ne any other person of ye Churche, highe or lowe, greate or smalle, Englyshe ne Iryshe, that useyth to preche the worde of Godde, saveing the poore fryers beggars.[10]

This potential threat to the success of the Reformation in Ireland was recognized as early as the mid-1530s by George Brown, newly-appointed Protestant archbishop of Dublin, who attempted to influence the Irish Observants to amalgamate with the Conventuals, a campaign which failed as Observant houses outnumbered Conventual foundations in Ireland by this time.[11] The movement had reinvigorated many foundations – particularly Franciscan and Dominican friaries and to a lesser extent those of the Augustinians and Carmelites – and although only a handful of new Observant foundations in fifteenth-century Ireland were situated in dioceses of Anglo-Ireland, several long-established communities in the towns became Observant, as occurred in 1536 at the Franciscan friary of Clonmel.

Monastic and secular worlds became very closely involved with each other in the later fifteenth century, especially in colonial frontier areas such as Co. Tipperary, where local families supplied the leading members of religious houses. The property-rich monasteries were heavily involved in lease-holding and landholding, and in addition to their interaction with religious orders through land- and office-holding the lay gentry were commonly retained by them as stewards and land agents. Lack of central supervision within dioceses and congregations meant that local monastic houses could and did pursue commercial ends in alliance with local families of importance. Headships of monastic communities were sought after by local

6 R. Bagwell, *Ireland under the Tudors*, i (1885), 296. 7 'State of Ireland and plan for its reformation in 1515', *Cal. SP, Henry VIII (Ireland), 1534*, ii, 1–31, also ibid., 297. 8 P. Conlan, *Franciscan Ireland* (1978), 20; 24. 9 Lennon, *Seventeenth century Ireland*, 120. 10 *Cal. SP, Henry VIII (Ireland), 1534*, ii, 15; C. Maxwell, *Irish history from contemporary sources, 1509–1610* (1923). 11 *Cal. SP (Ireland), 1534*, 25.

nobility and gentry: in Tipperary and Kilkenny, where the premier family was the Ormond Butlers, branches of the family held the abbatial positions at Athassel and Inishlounaght, near Clonmel, for decades prior to the 1540 dissolution; the former through the archbishop of Cashel, illegitimate brother of the earl of Ormond; the latter through James Butler, son of the earl. At Cahir, the prior, Edmund Lonergan, was under the tutelage of Sir Thomas Butler, baron of Caher.

The pre-eminence of the Butler family in monastic office in South Tipperary commenced when the Cistercian abbey at Inishlounaght came under the control of the Cahir branch of the family. Walter Butler was abbot between 1503 and 1509 and was succeeded in 1510 by James Butler, the last pre-Reformation abbot. Inishlounaght had become totally Irish in its practices, with the abbot transformed into a chief and the tenants into clansmen. In a lease of December 1519, the abbot, 'with the consent of his convent', granted to Thomas Butler, his kinsman, a lease of portion of the monastic estate for sixty years. In 1537, this abbot, also dean of Lismore, was represented by the citizens of Waterford and of Clonmel as 'a man of odious life, who taketh yearly and daily men's wifes and burgesses' daughters and [who] keepeth no divine service but spendeth the goods of his church in voluptuosity'.[12] An extract of the state papers describes the jury at Clonmel charging 'several of the regular priests in that part with keeping lemans or harlots and having wives and children', while similar irregularities were identified at the Athassel foundation of Augustinian canons regular, and the Carmelite prior of Lady abbey, near Ardfinnan, 'keepeth a mistress and provideth no divine service in his buildings, which are useth as the parish church since time immemorial'.[13] Divine service was also lacking at the Augustinian priory of Cahir, where the 'prior doth not celebrate the liturgy'; at the Carmelite priory of Clonmel, where 'the prior useth to have his harlot and no divine service'; and at Inishlounaght, where 'the liturgy is not celebrated except a few masses by verba and the monks each have a concubine and household'.[14]

On reading the evidence of monastic abuses in Co. Tipperary, one has to doubt the total impartiality of the jurors. The absence of serious charges in the case of most religious houses other than neglect of divine office points to the possibility of reports being exaggerated to help reach a predetermined outcome. When a motive was sought for the suppression of the monasteries of England, various charges of evil living were brought against the monks and a commission of inquiry was set up to inquire into the moral state of the religious houses. In Ireland such proceedings were dispensed with and, with one or two exceptions, no such charges were brought. Normally, Irish monks were charged only with neglecting divine service and with the practice of concubinage, and these allegations were often not without foundation. A visitation of Holy Cross abbey in 1536 reveals that even then – four decades after the reform of the Cistercian Order in Ireland had been urged by its senior prelate, Abbot Troy of Mellifont – the state of monastic observance was by no means perfect.[15]

---

12 Bagwell, *Ireland under the Tudors*, 298. **13** C. Ó Conbhuidhe, *Studies in Irish Cistercian history* (1998), 51; *Cal. SP Henry VIII (Ireland)*, ii, 312, 315; *Letters and papers, Henry VIII, 1864–1932*, iii, 510. **14** *Cal. SP Henry VIII (Ireland)*, ii, 300; Bradshaw, *Dissolution of the religious orders*, 29. **15** Ó Conbhuidhe, *Cistercian*, 50.

Various reasons have been given by historians for the dissolution of the monasteries in Ireland and England during the reign of Henry VIII. One of the principal
motives, as far as the Irish monasteries were concerned, was undoubtedly the king's
well-grounded fear that all those concerned with religious houses would always, at
heart, remain allies of the pope. For this reason, he made no distinction between
the wealthy monasteries and the poorer mendicant houses. The commission for
the suppression of the monasteries issued by the king's authority is remarkable in
that the only real accusation brought against the monks and nuns of Ireland is that
of being addicted to 'the pestiferous doctrines of the Roman pontiff'.[16] Indeed, the
commission is remarkable not so much for what it says as for what it does not say.
Had the monks, friars and nuns been for the most part men and women of evil
lives, it is certain that the state papers would not have been silent on that point, for
it would have been a good argument in favour of the king's proceedings. Reform
had been ongoing within the mendicant orders for over a century and the monastic orders also entered into this improvement from the last decade of the fifteenth
century, so that while the indiscretions of some houses played into the hands of the
king, the situation on the eve of suppression was arguably far better than it had
been for decades. Although recorded instances of 'evil living' survive, both
Protestant and Roman Catholic ecclesiastical historians are in general agreement
in favour of the religious. Galway, Clonmel and Waterford all supplied instances
of 'evil life' in certain monasteries and, while other notices of immorality among
the friars existed, no charge of this kind was entered against them at the dissolution. The natural deduction from this silence seems to be that the orders were generally staffed with men of respectable lives.[17]

The impending closure of the monasteries was apparent four years before it took
place, with the declaration in 1536 by the Irish parliament that Henry VIII was
supreme head of the whole Church in Ireland. The reaction of the religious communities was to give long leases of the abbey lands to selected individuals, Gaelic Irish
and Old English alike. At Suir abbey, Inishlounaght, the abbot leased most of the convent lands to Lady Joan Fitzgerald, wife of the treasurer of Ireland, Sir James Butler
(subsequently 9th earl of Ormond) and to their son, Edmund. In a lease dated June
1539, he granted them all the abbey lands lying between Kilmanahan and Clonmel
in the county of Waterford, an area amounting to more than 2,900 statute acres.

The earliest reformation of the Irish Church commenced late in 1538, when
the Irish privy council held a visitation of Carlow, Kilkenny, Ross, Wexford,
Waterford and Clonmel that was partly ecclesiastical in remit, during which 'the
kinge's supremycia [was preached] togeder with the plucking downe of ydolles and
the extinguishing of the busshop of Rome's auctoritie' and several of those opposing the new religious philosophy were put to death at each location.[18] In Waterford,
among those executed was 'a frier whom we commanded be hanged in his habite
and so to remayne upon the gallowes for a mirror to all other his bredren to live
trulie'.[19] The very language of this account of the first post-Reformation clerical

---

16 Ibid., 52. **17** Ibid.; W.A. Phillips (ed.), *History of the Church of Ireland*, ii (1933), 231. **18** *Cal. SP
Henry VIII (Ireland)*, viii, 47 cited in W.P. Burke, *History of Clonmel* (1907), 34. **19** Ibid.

martyrdom in Ireland is imbued with superiority, proclaiming notions of English reformed 'truth' over the 'errors' of the Church of Rome. Granted the effectiveness of the Observant movement among friars in the fifteenth and early sixteenth centuries, this treatment of a friar much beloved for being of the people must have caused outrage, with long-term consequences centred on his immediate achievement of the symbolic space of martyrdom.

From Waterford, the Privy Council proceeded to Clonmel, where arguably the most important event in the history of Protestantism in sixteenth-century Ireland took place: the gathering of the Irish hierarchy at St Mary's church, Clonmel, to swear to the supremacy of the king and against that of the pope.

> At Clonmell [18 January 1539] was with us twoo archebysshops and eight busshops in whose presence my lord of Dublin [George Browne, Protestant archbishop] preached in advauncying the kinges supremacy and the extinguishment of [that of] the busshop of Rome. And his sermon fynyshed, all the said busshops in all thoppen audience took the [oath] mencioned in th[e] acts of parliament, bothe touching the kinges succession and supremacy, befor[e] me, the kinges chaunceller and divers others ther[e] present ded the lieke ...[20]

On sifting the inferential evidence, the presence beyond doubt of the archbishops of Cashel and Tuam and the bishops of Limerick, of Cork and Cloyne and of Waterford and Lismore can be established.[21] This take-over of the dioceses by the Anglican Church in turn brought increasing New English hegemony to local parochial structures throughout Ireland. This involved the effective transfer of parish church livings and the collection of tithes to the Established Church, which thereby inherited long-established income and territorial organizational deficiencies.[22] A central feature of this early extension of English Protestantism – in addition to utilization of the now dissolved monasteries as key foci in the re-conquest – is the use made of extensive monastic lands to reward some Old English lords, but more particularly the New English officials and soldiers who colonized the edge of this centralizing state's expanding world.[23] These early thrusts should not be underestimated, for these confiscated lands became the first anchors of New English settlement and colonization on the island of Ireland, while the 1570s and 1580s saw the completion of the absorption of the former Church lands and the opening up of large tracts of Munster to formal state plantation, following the crushing of the Desmond rebellion.[24] The Old English were for the first time treated the same as the Gaelic Irish, and New English colonial policy – which for some time shifted between strategies of assimilation and coercion – hardened in favour of the latter approach.[25]

No real attempt was made to impose the statutes of the reformed religion in Ireland beyond the Pale until the 1570s, after an interval of over thirty years. The

20 *Cal. SP (Ireland), Henry VIII*, 117. 21 Bagwell, *Ireland under the Tudors*, 296. 22 H.F. Kearney, *Strafford in Ireland, 1633–41* (1959), 107. 23 R. Loeber, *The geography and practice of English colonization in Ireland, 1534–1609* (1991), 11–22; also Bradshaw, *Dissolution of the religious orders.* 24 W.J. Smyth, 'Ireland, a colony' (2000), 159. 25 Ibid., 160; N.P. Canny, 'Early modern Ireland, *c.*1500–1700' (1992).

commitment of bishops of the Established Church to the Reformation in the second half of the sixteenth century was vital if it was to take hold in the rural dioceses of Ireland, but outside of a few walled urban centres, efforts were questionable. The great deficiency of the Anglican Church in Ireland was its failure to assimilate and control the population of the Pale region and the older walled towns.[26] This may be attributed to the fact that most of the bishops of the Established Church were conformed Irishmen, and their initiative to spread the Protestant faith was not as strong as that of English bishops. However, there was no territorial reform of the Established Church until the last decade of the sixteenth century, when some parochial rationalization took place and a serious attempt was made to lay the basis for a Protestant ministry at a parochial level in Ireland.[27] This delay had far-reaching consequences, leading ultimately to the failure of the English government to convert the local population to Protestantism.

There is no record in the state papers of lords deputy or other government dignitaries raising questions of religious allegiance in South Tipperary during the thirty years following the dissolution of the monasteries. This inertia applied to some extent over most of Ireland, but particularly to the Ormond palatinate of Tipperary, centred on its seat at Clonmel. It would seem that the declaration in 1539 of the loyalty of the townspeople to the crown was deemed satisfactory and the townspeople's gratification at the dissolution of some of the religious houses of the area, particularly that of Inishlounaght, was also noted with approval.[28] However, the entire population of town and palatinate remained Roman Catholic, with the town council appointing the parish priest.

In April 1570, the bull *Regnans in excelsis* issued by Pope Pius V excommunicated Elizabeth, 'the pretended queen of England' who 'dared to eject bishops, rectors of churches and other Catholic priests from their churches and benefices [and] to bestow these and other things ecclesiastical upon heretics' and declared her crown forfeit and her subjects to be 'forever absolved from any sworn oath to her and from any duty arising from lordship, fealty and obedience'.[29] This action transformed the political and religious landscape overnight and played into the power struggle between the Ormond Butler and Desmond Fitzgerald dynasties. New English officials now questioned the loyalty of Roman Catholic subjects and religion was increasingly the essential 'ethnic' marker, sharply distinguishing the New English Protestant elite in Ireland from their Roman Catholic neighbours. The position of priests was particularly difficult: due to their attendance at various universities on the Continent, following the destruction of the monastic schools in Ireland and the perceived tainting of Oxford and Cambridge by the 'heretics', Roman Catholic priests came to be regarded as 'traitors' and 'rebels' in the pay of Spain and a government spy network watched ports and principal towns from this date. The creation of the provincial presidencies of Munster and Connaught in 1566, which integrated the administration of these regions into central state policy,

---

26 Smyth, 'Ireland, a colony', 171.   **27** A. Ford, *The Protestant Reformation in Ireland, 1590–1641* (1997), 23.   **28** Burke, *Clonmel*, 36.   **29** Given at St Peter's, Rome, 27 April 1570: see L.E. Eakins, 'Papal bull of Pius V against Elizabeth' (1995–2002).

further facilitated this surveillance. Sir William Drury, on appointment as lord president of Munster, reported Irish clerical students returning from training in Louvain in the Spanish Netherlands to be

> the merest traitors and breeders of treachery that live. Whereof there are in these parts about Waterford and Clonmel four principal prelates. John White is worshipped like a God between Kilkenny and Waterford and Clonmel. He subordinates all the dwellers of those parts to detest the true religion established by her Majesty.[30]

By the 1590s, the effects of a constant supply of Counter-Reformation preaching in South Tipperary and its hinterland can be discerned, which was ironic given that the Protestant Reformation was itself so little in evidence. Government surveillance was much in evidence, however, with official correspondence replete with reports sent from spies set to watch the priests.

> Ther[e] is one Sir Teage O'Swyllyvan, an earnest precher of popery still preching from howse to howse in Waterford, Clonmell and Fidreth ... [and] in his sermons cursinge all people that exercise authoritie in her Majesties name ... Sir William Ocherohy, a semynary lately come from Roome and now dwelling att Clonmell, Cassell and ffiddert ... Sir William Trehie (come from Spaine and borne in Cashell) most commonly sojourning at Clonmell ... Sir Piers Kely order'd by Dr Crahe [bishop of Cork and Cloyne] and still sojourning between Waterford, Clonmell and Cashell ... Sir Garrett Rollea, a man in very great compte in Clonmell ... Sir Walter, a priest of T[h]omond now residing at Clonmell.[31]

This circuit method of preaching employed by the Roman Catholic Church enabled it to spread its clergy further territorially, particularly in the hinterland between towns, and so lessen the chances of detection by government officials. It contrasts sharply with the lack of Anglican preaching. 'Sir' before the name of a priest indicated he had not graduated in a university, but, graduate or not, there can be no question as to the adequate supply of Roman Catholic priests and preaching in late sixteenth-century South Tipperary, particularly in the populous hinterlands of Clonmel, Cashel and Fethard. The urban focus of these reports is remarkable, evidencing a realization on both sides that the battle for religious supremacy would be won or lost in and around the towns.

In Ireland a large number of people, mostly clerics, were recognized as martyrs in period from *c.*1560 to *c.*1655, of which seventeen were subsequently beatified as representative Roman Catholic martyrs. This was the culmination of a process commenced in the nineteenth century as a result of the 'devotional revolution'. The vast majority of its causes were dropped along the way – a 1918 list includes

---

30 *Cal. SP (Ireland), Henry VIII*, cited in Burke, *Clonmel*, 37; W.H. Rennison, *Succession list* ([1921]), 17. **31** *Cal. SP (Ireland)*, cited in Burke, *Clonmel*, 37; 305.

the names of 258 prospective candidates whose deaths occurred, or allegedly occurred, between the mid-sixteenth and the early eighteenth centuries, with most (243) dating to prior to 1655. Several of these had native or clerical links with South Tipperary.[32] Many were publicly hanged for treason, which was punished as a civil crime, while religious crimes could be punished by burning. In Ireland, the meaning of certain executions had long been contested: the imposition of martial law on large stretches of the country for long periods, especially in the later sixteenth century, meant that state-sanctioned executions, or executions allegedly sanctioned by the state, might not necessarily gain acceptance as the will of the people.[33] For the ritual of execution to be effective, all concerned – state representatives, victim and audience – were required to play the parts set out by the nature of that ritual. Control over the meaning of the ritual could easily slip from the hands of state and be removed or, more dangerously, inverted.[34] The problem that faced the New English colonial administration in Ireland was that of retaining the loyalty of those elements of society who were disposed to give it, while at the same time discouraging the religious forces which allied the Gaelic Irish and Old English with the Roman Catholic powers of Spain and France, as well as the pope.

The executions of some of the most prominent and able Roman Catholic missionaries in Ireland were designed to rid the community of those fomenters of disorder who sought to divide or remove the people's loyalty – as the New English administration perceived it – and to provide example to others who might be tempted to do the same. The laws against Roman Catholic seminaries in Ireland forced those who could afford it to send their offspring to the European continent for education. Some went with the express intention of ecclesiastical careers, while others formed belated vocations. An interesting third way was the watchful manner in which both Irish clerics overseas and Vatican officials watched constantly for promising Irish students at continental universities who might prove to be of ecclesiastical material. Dermot O'Hurley, born near Emly and a law student and professor at Louvain for some fifteen years, was such an individual. His professorship at Louvain was followed by four years at Reims, after which he departed for Rome.[35] In 1581, while still a layman, he was asked to become archbishop of Cashel. He accepted and after advancement to the four minor and three major orders in sixteen days, left for Ireland, landing at Skerries, north of Dublin. He was recognized while staying with the baron of Slane and left for his southern ecclesiastical province, staying with the loyal Protestant, Thomas Butler, earl of Ormond, at his castle at Carrick-on-Suir. At the request of the baron, who was under duress from the New English administration, he returned to Dublin, where he was imprisoned in Dublin Castle, tortured at length and eventually hanged on the eve of Ormond's return from England.[36] The holding of his execution in Dublin and not in the provinces – the site of his alleged misde-

32 D. Forristal, *Seventeen martyrs* (1990); D. Murphy, *Our martyrs* (1896); M.V. Ronan, *The Irish martyrs* (1935), 198–213.   **33** D. Edwards, 'Beyond reform: martial law and Tudor Ireland' (1997), 1–5.
34 C.J. Tait, 'Adored for saints: Catholic martyrdom in Ireland, *c.*1560–1655' (2001); also 'Harnessing corpses: death, burial, disinterment and commemoration in Ireland, *c.*1550–1655' (PhD, UCC, 1999).
35 J.J. Meagher, 'The beatified martyrs of Ireland (3): Dermot O'Hurley, archbishop of Cashel' (1999).
36 Forristal, *Seventeen martyrs*, 2: entry for Dermot O'Hurley, deceased 20 June 1584.

meanours – established a new trend: the New English administration increasingly dealt with troublesome Roman Catholic clergy in the larger urban centres with their English garrisons, rather than overload the loyalties of provincial Roman Catholics by holding them in the rural districts.[37]

Executions were often decided upon in an arbitrary manner, usually in response to immediate circumstances and were similarly inadequate as a response. The problem was compounded by the fact that, unlike in England where the execution of Roman Catholic 'traitors' occurred before audiences of mixed sympathies, audiences at Irish executions were far more homogeneously Roman Catholic. In this way, Irish executions – while undoubtedly inspired by their counterparts in England – became watered down and more unstable and ineffective (in terms of the state's attempt to impose its own meaning on the proceedings) than originally intended.[38]

The first step in the road to martyrdom was the capture and imprisonment of the individual concerned. One of the earliest cases in Ireland occurred in August 1579 and concerned two Franciscan friars, Patrick O'Healy and Cornelius O'Rourke. They were arrested by spies at Dingle and, after fruitless attempts to convert them, were hanged at Kilmallock by order of Sir William Drury, lord president of Munster: the former had been ordained in Spain and in 1576 was created bishop of Mayo, since united to Tuam; the latter was the eldest son of the prince of Breffny.[39] They were buried under the high altar at Clonmel Franciscan friary, their position in the chancel indicative of the symbolism of their martyrdom. This first killing of a Roman Catholic prelate since Henry VIII broke with Rome shocked many and, combined with the address of the condemned to the crowd shortly before their execution and copious subsequent writings by their Franciscan brethren – both Irish and non-Irish – ensured they swiftly attained *fama martyrii*, the fame of martyrdom.[40] The impact of these killings for politico-religious purposes was to create heroic martyrs, which helped to harden the resolve of the Roman Catholics of Munster against the Established Church.

The suffering of the martyr and his endurance of suffering was central to these narratives. The authorities rarely resorted to torture, except in the famous case of Dermot O'Hurley, archbishop of Cashel, whose encounter with the 'torture of the boots' was extensively described by hagiographers.[41] A particularly 'symbolic' martyrdom was that of Maurice MacKenraghty, chaplain to the earl of Desmond, captured in West Cork by Viscount Fermoy and conveyed to Thomas Butler, 10th earl of Ormond, who had him imprisoned in the gaol of Clonmel, seat of his county palatinate. Here, as in other southern towns, Counter-Reformation Roman Catholicism was beginning to make a real impact and the citizens of the town were encountering difficulties combining loyalty to the pope with loyalty to the queen.[42]

---

37 Argument presented by Dr David Edwards, department of History, UCC, in his paper 'Making martyrs: martial law and the Roman Catholic clergy in Elizabethan Ireland' to the conference *Age of massacres: violent death in Ireland, c.1547–1650*, held at Collins Barrack, Dublin, 20 April 2002. 38 Tait, 'Adored for saints'. 39 Forristal, *Seventeen martyrs*, 1–2: they deceased 13 August 1579. 40 B. Millett, 'The beatified martyrs of Ireland (1): Bishop Patrick O'Healy, OFM and Con O'Rourke, OFM' (1999). 41 P.F. Moran (ed.), *The Analecta of David Rothe, bishop of Ossory* (1884), 17–29. 42 J. Coombes, 'The beatified martyrs of Ireland (5): Maurice MacKenraghty' (2000), 57–64.

Outside of the planted areas, Roman Catholics were still propertied and mass was frequently said in the houses of the merchants and gentry, who in many cases also maintained the priest.[43] MacKenraghty officiated at the first documented instance of a house mass in sixteenth-century South Tipperary on Easter eve, 11 April 1585, when Victor White – a prominent Roman Catholic of the Clonmel mayoral dynasty, whose family had still used the parish church in 1577 – obtained permission from the governor of the town gaol for the priest to spend the night at his house. The governor in turn secretly informed Sir John Norris, lord president of Munster, then in Clonmel, as to this valuable opportunity of catching the principal inhabitants in the very act of hearing mass. Soldiers rushed the house early next morning and arrested the owner, the congregation having escaped through the back windows and doors. As mass had been about to commence, the soldiers found the chalice and other requisites. The priest was not discovered under the heap of straw that was his hiding place and the owner was consequently sentenced to death. He was saved on the voluntary surrender of the priest, who although he was offered his life in return for renouncing the Roman Catholic faith and acknowledging the queen as head of the Church, he refused to do so, or to give the names of any of his congregation.[44] Sentence of death, when eventually passed, was accepted with stoicism by those condemned. They often expressed joy and resignation to death on their way to the scaffold and through this non-resistance of his fate, the martyr could undermine the meaning of the proceedings from the start.[45]

In this age of print culture, Roman Catholic writers sought to compete with New English Protestant literature through the serial retelling of the stories of the martyrs. Rochford (1586), Howlin (1599), Rothe (1617) and others perpetuated the memory of the martyrdom of MacKenraghty through the publication of lengthy biographies, which gave account of his highly symbolic execution at Clonmel, during which the power of the New English colonial administration and its military supremacy was displayed.

> He was long kept [18 months] in prison [at Clonmel] where with much patience he confirmed Catholics in the faith ... and gave to all an example of the true Catholic religion ... While he was brought to execution he spoke with such piety and wisdom that many were moved to tears ... At the place itself, having asked the prayers of the people and given them his blessing, he was hanged. While half alive he was beheaded and the whole night the soldiers kept watch upon the quartered body lest it should be taken away by the Catholics. The following day the four quarters [of his body] were set upon the market cross in the centre of the town, the head on a loftier eminence to be seen by all.[46]

43 P.J. Corish, *The Catholic community in the seventeenth and eighteenth centuries* (1981), 33. **44** Letter from the Irish college of St Anthony, 20 March 1586, cited in Burke, *Clonmel*, 38–9; also Forristal, *Seventeen martyrs*, 3: entry for Maurice [Kenrechtin] McKenraghty, deceased 20 April 1585. **45** Nicholls, 'The theatre of martyrdom', 72. **46** P.F. Moran (ed.), *Spicilegium Ossoriense*, i (1874–84), 89–91; idem., *Analecta*, 17–29.

This gruesome public episode constituted the first clerical killing of the Reformation on the soil of South Tipperary. Those who witnessed it were undoubtedly almost instantly aware they had witnessed the martyrdom of a priest for his faith. This *fama martyrii* persisted in Clonmel and its environs and was commemorated locally through the naming of the area off Gladstone Street where MacKenraghty was captured as 'Martyr Lane' down to the Cromwellian period, indicative of the impact of the execution on the local population.[47] The regard with which the townspeople held MacKenraghty was very probably responsible for the extraordinary growth of vocations to the priesthood in Clonmel and its vicinity, particularly to the religious orders: recruits to the Jesuit Order included Andrew Mulrony, Nicholas Leynagh, Thomas Shine and Thomas White.

The laws against Roman Catholic seminaries in Ireland forced those who could afford it to send their offspring abroad for education, where they gravitated toward established centres of learning in Spain, France, Italy and the Spanish Netherlands, and where many trained in religion.[48] The remains of MacKenraghty were interred in the Franciscan friary at Clonmel, in the vicinity of the high altar, adjoining the two Franciscan martyrs brought there in 1579. Further evidence of the lasting memory of these events remains in the exhumation of these three clerical martyrs from their unmarked graves during the Confederation of Kilkenny in 1647 and their re-burial in Askeaton abbey in Co. Limerick amid immense symbolic ceremony and re-edification following decades of perceived contamination by the 'heretics'.[49]

Wondrous or miraculous signs are crucial to the attribution of sanctity to a 'martyr'. Stories were widely reported of bodies or body parts of the martyrs remaining incorrupt, or of their exhibiting signs of life such as bleeding and perspiration. The head of Maurice MacKenraghty, who was martyred in 1585, which was placed on the market cross in Clonmel, was alleged to have become red and perspired each day at 10 a.m., a marvel attributed by the townspeople to the fact that he had been accustomed to say mass at that time every day.[50] Such miracles of incorruption had a powerful effect on contemporary and subsequent Roman Catholic attitudes, since they provided further evidence that the martyr was alive in heaven, which further reinforced religious devotion. The influence of the martyr was such that his body became the primary focus of his power. In allowing the burial of the corpse of any martyr to slip from their hands, the New English government effectively admitted that there was a point at which their power to coerce ended. The decent burial of the body of the martyr saved it from exposure until it disintegrated and it could therefore be effectively mobilized as a religious and political resource, a site of pilgrimage and devotion. These events served to turn the majority of the population ever more against the New English and their Church.

---

47 Inquisition of 20 March 1622, at Clonmel, cited in Burke, *Clonmel*, 57. **48** E. Hogan, *Distinguished Irishmen* (1894), 48–51; 107–8; 353; others followed as diocesan priests. **49** Burke, *Clonmel*, 57. **50** Murphy, *Our martyrs*, 162–3; M. O'Reilly (ed.), *Memorials of those who suffered for the Catholic faith in Ireland* (1868), 123–5; Moran, *Analecta*, 482.

2

Rejuvenation and reform:
the re-organization of Roman Catholicism

Prior to the dissolution of the monasteries and their academies, many Irish priests were educated at one or more of the monastic schools in Ireland, while the more promising travelled to Oxford, Cambridge, Paris, or one of the principal universities of France, Italy or Iberia. After the dissolution, all potential Roman Catholic priests had to be educated overseas, which in the wake of deteriorating political relations between England and the Continent led to their being regarded from the mid-1550s by the English government in Ireland as spies, traitors and rebels in the pay of Spain, for 'Counter-Reformation Catholic countries still operated a supernational, multi-linguistic network of religious personnel and exchanges'.[1] The wider religious geography of Western Europe furthered the potential for mistrust and conflict between the religion of the colonizers and this vernacular religion.

The foundation of colleges on the European Continent by Roman Catholics from the last quarter of the sixteenth century was a consequence of the decree passed in the 23rd session of the Council of Trent (1563), which required each diocese to establish a course of training for aspirants to the priesthood in a house specially chosen by the bishop.[2] In these islands, the decree was inoperative because of the prohibition on Roman Catholic schools and seminaries from early in the reign of Elizabeth. The only way for Irish, English and Scots Roman Catholics to fulfil the requirements of the Council of Trent was to set up seminaries abroad, which came to be known as the Irish, English and Scots colleges respectively. Some Irish clerics and scholars had enrolled in the universities of Paris, Bologna, Salamanca, Alcalá de Henares, Valladolid and Cologne prior to the Reformation, so that established networks of contact already existed before the mid-sixteenth century.[3] However, the creation of distant new Irish seminaries devoted to the education of Roman Catholic clerics is itself a striking movement. From the mid-sixteenth century, therefore, small groups of Irish students began to attend some of the universities of Spain, France and the Spanish Netherlands. Louvain had Irish students during the second quarter of the sixteenth century, as had Salamanca from the 1570s, almost two decades before its Irish college was founded. Already, in 1577, the English government in Ireland was concerned at this turn of events, when Sir Henry Sidney, lord deputy in Ireland, informed Queen Elizabeth that 'there be some principal gentlemen [of

---

1 Smyth, 'Ireland, a colony', 158–86. 2 T.J. Walsh, *The Irish continental colleges movement* (1973), 10–13.
3 Ibid., 35–6; J.J. Silke, 'The Irish abroad, 1534–1691' (1976).

Ireland] that have sons in Louvain, Douai, Rome and other places where your Majesty is hated [rather] than honoured'.[4]

Early groups of clerical students resided in rented accommodation at each city before achieving sufficient funds to establish a college, usually through the donation or bequest of a generous nobleman. The Irish college in Paris may be dated to 1578, when John Lee, a Dublin priest, and six clerical students arrived there to attend the College de Montaigu and styled themselves 'the community of the Irish students in Paris'.[5] However, it was twenty years before they were fortunate enough to receive a considerable financial endowment from the president of the high court of Paris, which enabled them to take up residence in a purpose-built dwelling by the turn of the seventeenth century. Similar situations led to the formation of other Irish colleges both for secular and regular clergy across Europe, concentrated heavily in the territories of the arch-enemies of England, namely France and Spain. Some 44 were established in all, the majority between 1590 and 1620: nine had a fleeting existence, surviving less than a decade, but the remainder endured for a century on average, from their date of foundation.[6] A dozen colleges were commenced after 1640, the last in 1697, with the majority enjoying considerable success in attracting students from various parts of Ireland on the understanding of their subsequent return to the Irish mission. No country that had separated from Rome at the Reformation would tolerate a Roman Catholic seminary, so no college was established in any of the north German or Scandinavian states. It is surprising, however, that none was established in staunchly Roman Catholic Bavaria and Lorraine, or in any of the Italian states outside of those under papal control.

The majority of the Irish colleges founded abroad – particularily those in the crucial late sixteenth and early seventeenth century – were manned initially by members of Old English dynasties, particularly townsmen and merchant families who possessed established trading links with the Continent.[7] David Kearney, archbishop of Cashel 1603–24 and scion of a prominent Cashel family, supported, even possibly inspired the securing of the Iberian colleges for the Jesuits. In this he had the compliance of official court circles in Spain, who agreed that control by the Jesuits would ensure stability, eliminate unhealthy contests for control of constituent colleges, and aid equal representation of the provinces within them.[8] The Spanish Netherlands were deemed particularly suitable to the foundation of Irish colleges, even more so than the Iberian Peninsula, due to their proximity to Ireland, the regular presence of an Irish regiment, and the presence of an atmosphere conducive to their establishment. In the early eighteenth century, however, France began to replace the Spanish territories as the principal support of the Irish colleges.

The critical decade of rejection of the Reformation in Ireland may have been the 1580s, as from this time Irish colleges were being established in Spain and the Spanish Netherlands, a treacherous action in the eyes of the English government,

---

4 T. Ó Fiaich, *The Irish colleges in France* (1990), 8; L. Swords, *Soldiers, scholars, priests* (1985). **5** Ó Fiaich, *Irish colleges*, 8–9. **6** See app. III for details of burses open to South Tipperary students in the Irish colleges. **7** M. Percival-Maxwell, *The outbreak of the Irish rebellion of 1641* (1994), 13; Corish, *The Catholic community*, 21. **8** Silke, 'The Irish abroad, 1534–1691', 619.

particularly after their defeat of the Spanish Armada in 1588. Already by 1607, one-third of all Irish colleges abroad had been established and almost three-quarters of them were founded before 1630. The Pale and the wealthier towns of the south-east had become emphatically Roman Catholic in ethos by the 1580s and contained the principal centres of what came to be termed 'the recusant church'.[9] This development was critical to the geography of religion and settlement in Ireland.

South Tipperary formed an important part of the south-eastern core area of recusancy and through the recruitment of above-average numbers of her native sons to the Irish colleges on the Continent, contributed heavily to strategies of New English resistance. The most noteworthy came from the White family, a wealthy Old English mercantile dynasty of Clonmel, which controlled the town politically between 1400 and 1650 and supplied all candidates for sovereign (subsequently mayor) in that period. Two brothers, Thomas and Stephen White and a nephew, Peter, were prominent Jesuits, while an elder brother, James, was vicar apostolic of their native Waterford and Lismore diocese. His brother, John, was deposed as sovereign of Clonmel in 1606 for recusancy, while near kinsmen Patrick and Nicholas White were heavily fined for refusing to accompany Sir Henry Brounker, lord president of Munster, to a Protestant service in St Mary's church.[10] The White family were of key importance in Clonmel and its South Tipperary and Waterford hinterlands, because of their obstinate adherence to the Roman Catholic faith and resistance to the encroachment of Anglicanism in their town. Besides the mayor, the two bailiffs and eight out of seventeen burgesses in Clonmel Corporation during the first half of the seventeenth century bore the surname of White.[11]

Thomas White, like many others of his period, sought his theological training abroad at the University of Valladolid, where he was in attendance by 1582. On observing the condition of many fellow seminarians, he resolved to use his allowance and influence to relieve their destitution. A contemporary account noted the

> great charity of Father Thomas White, natural of Clonmell, seeing so many poor scholars of his nation in great misery at Valladolid, having no means to continue their study nor language [other than] to beg, having given over his private commodity, did recollect and reduce them to one place which he maintained by his industry and begging, until, by his petition to Philip the Second … a college of Irish students was founded.[12]

The success in obtaining royal support for the community was a consequence of two visits by White to the residence of Philip II and an audience with the monarch while in Valladolid. A large donation was given to them and a house endowed at Salamanca styled 'The Royal College of St Patrick for Irish Nobles', which was entrusted to the Jesuits on its foundation in 1592. White abandoned his fledgling seminary at Valladolid and brought its nine students to Salamanca.[13] Philip II per-

---

9 See further in Smyth, 'Ireland, a colony'. 10 Burke, *Clonmel*, 49–50. 11 Watson, *A dinner of herbs*, 61. 12 John Coppinger, *Mnemosyniam to the Catholics of Ireland* (1608), 268, cited in Hogan, *Distinguished Irishmen*, 49; Burke, *Clonmel*, 466. 13 P. O'Connell, *The Irish college at Alcalá de Henares, 1649–1785* (1997), 11–13; idem, *The Irish college at Lisbon, 1590–1834* (2001), 15–16.

Fig. 1: Fr Thomas White SJ [14]

sonally wrote the following letter from Valladolid to the University of Salamanca encouraging good treatment of the Irish seminarians.

> To the rector, chancellor and cloister of the University of Salamanca: as the Irish youths who have been living in this city have resolved to go to yours to avail of the opportunities it affords for advancement in literature and languages, a house having been prepared for them, in which they intend to live under the direction of the Fathers of the Society of Jesus, I will allow them a good annual stipend and I desire to give them this letter to charge you, as I hereby do, to regard them as highly recommended and not allow them to

14 White was born at Clonmel in 1556; his portrait, painted *c*.1607 (see fig. 1), is inscribed 'The Venerable Fr Thomas White of the Society of Jesus, a native of Clonmel in Ireland, missionary apostolic and first Jesuit of the Irish seminarians in Spain, who died at his Santiago de Galicia college, 27 May 1622': see Burke, *Clonmel*, 469.

be ill-treated in any way, but to favour and aid them as far as you can; in order that, as they have left their own country and all they possessed in it for the service of God Our Lord and for the preservation of the Catholic faith and as they make profession of returning to preach in that country and to suffer martyrdom, if necessary, they may get in that university the reception they have reason to expect. I am certain you will do this and become benefactors to them; so that with your subscription and that of the city, to the authorities of which I am also writing, they may be able to pursue their studies with content and freedom and thereby attain the end which they have in view. I, the King, given at Valladolid, the 3rd August 1592.[15]

White entered the Society of Jesus on 11 June 1593, thus retaining, as vice-rector, practical control of the college of which he was also spiritual director.[16] Upon the death in 1594 of the founder of the new Irish college at Lisbon, White was appointed as rector there. In 1605, he was involved in founding a new Irish college at Santiago and, by 1612, another at Seville. He continued to undertake an active role in the financing of these colleges through preaching tours until his death in 1622. The significance of the colleges founded by White can be seen from the outset, in that key clerics of the Counter-Reformation in Ireland obtained their priestly training there, such as the famous Geoffrey Keating, creator of the *Foras Feasta ar Éirinn* origin legend, who attended Salamanca for a time.

By the late sixteenth century, a substantial Irish mercantile community were finding conditions at home less attractive, set up as merchants in the ports of their trading partners in France, Spain, Portugal and the Spanish Netherlands.[17] As early as 1596, Thomas White was able to collect money for his college at Salamanca from the Irish merchants of Bayona, in Galicia and in 1598 successfully continued his fundraising or questing tour among the Irish merchants of Bilbao, besides also the nobility and ecclesiastics of note in Spain, Portugal and Italy.[18] These merchants were from the strongly recusant southern and eastern districts of Ireland and predominantly settled in the French ports of Nantes, St Malo, Rennes, Le Havre, Calais and Bordeaux; the Spanish ports of Bilbao, Santiago, Bayona, Cádiz, Jérez and San Lucar and the Portuguese capital of Lisbon, as well as Rotterdam and Antwerp in the Netherlands.[19] The Roman Catholic gentry, townspeople and merchants cooperated in conveying young men to France, Flanders, Spain and Italy with remarkable success. The Irish college at Salamanca had remarkable success in attracting seminarians from the south-east of Ireland and particularly from the united diocese of Waterford and Lismore, the home region of its founder. Just over 200 students were enrolled between 1592 and 1611; an average of 11 per year, while in the eight years from 1602 to 1610, some 23 arrived from Waterford and Lismore

15 Philip II, king of Spain, to the rector, chancellor and cloister of the university of Salamanca; translation from the Spanish original in Hogan, *Distinguished Irishmen*, 53–4; R. Whelan-Richardson, 'The Salamanca archives' (1995), 117–8. **16** D.J. O'Doherty, 'Fr Thomas White, founder of the Irish college, Salamanca' (1922). **17** Canny, *Making Ireland British*, 418–31. **18** O'Doherty, 'Fr Thomas White', 587. **19** Silke, 'The Irish abroad', 613.

alone.[20] The tradition of several members of a family joining is evident, with 4 Waddings, 3 Whites, 3 Walshes and 2 Comerfords listed. Of these merchant families, 3 Waddings became Jesuits, while one Walsh did likewise and his brother subsequently became an archbishop. Increasingly, scions of Gaelic Irish, as well as Old English dynasties, made their way to Irish colleges on the Continent for clerical training, indicative of the successful spread of *fama martyrii* and subsequent efforts by Keating and others to assist in overcoming of conflicting regional identities in the common pursuit of Roman Catholic Church revival.

Following the suppression of the monasteries and the transfer of parish churches to the establishment, the Roman Catholic religious ideal was kept alive in Ireland by the mendicant orders, in particular by the Franciscan Observant friars, who by living near their ruined friaries in the rural context, or as servants in the households of principal parishioners in the urban context, carried on the traditional role of their Order. In South Tipperary, particular concentrations occurred in urban areas, where Franciscans, Dominicans, Augustinians and Cistercians kept up a discreet presence, so that all population centres of any size were served by at least one religious order. A continuous presence was maintained at Tipperary and Fethard by Augustinians; at Clonmel, Carrickbeg and Galbally by Franciscans; at Cashel by both Franciscans and Dominicans; and at Holy Cross by Cistericans. The mechanisms used by these religious communities to survive is often not now fully known, though at Holy Cross abbey the Cistercian community survived by initially conforming to the Reformation of Henry VIII in the period 1540 to 1553 and subsequently through connivance with the new proprietor of their monastic estate, Thomas Butler, 10th earl of Ormond. Ormond and the monastic community appear to have adopted an ingenious system, whereby leases of the abbey estate were made out to members of the actual monastic community. In this way, leases were made out in 1571–2 to John Riane, who had succeeded as abbot in 1564 and again in 1581 under the guise of John Monk, meaning John, monk of Holy Cross. The Cistercians were thus enabled to continue their community at the abbey until the arrival of Cromwellian forces in 1649.[21]

The continuation of the monastic community at Holy Cross is verified by a number of independent sources, which show that the monks provided an important psychological boost to the Irish side in the war against English occupation. Hugh O'Neill visited the abbey with his army in 1600 and presented gifts to the monks following veneration of their relic of the true cross; Red Hugh O'Donnell visited the abbey in 1601 and 'asked the prayers and blessings of the monks', for which he 'presented the community with oblations, offerings and alms'.[22] The survival of the monastic community was not a simple matter. The monks lived as countrymen in various houses of the parish and in times of intense persecution were forced to leave the area for short periods.

20 O'Doherty, 'Fr Thomas White', 583; the Salamanca papers are held at St Patrick's college, Maynooth since the closure of the Irish college, Salamanca, in 1951; P. Power, *Waterford and Lismore* (1937), 367. **21** C. Ó Conbhuidhe, *The Cistercian abbeys of Tipperary* (1999), 227–33.   **22** Fr Malachy Hartry, 'Triumphalia chronologica monasterii sanctae crucis in Hibernica', translates 'Triumphant chronology of the monastery of Holy Cross in Ireland': the original manuscript in the library of St Patrick's college, Thurles, was edited in 1895 by D. Murphy of Dublin; Ó Conbhuidhe, *Cistercian abbeys*, 230–3.

By the early seventeenth century, the province of Munster was well served by priests in proportion to its total population and there was a presence of some religious in all of its counties. A government document dated November 1613 and entitled 'the names of sundry priests and friars', records that Kerry had 8 regular and 13 secular clergy; Limerick had 18 secular clergy, 4 Friars Minor and 3 Dominicans; Clare had 8 seculars and 6 Franciscan friars 'verie old'; in Cork there were 21 seculars and 9 Friars Minor, while Waterford had 14 seculars, 3 Jesuits, 5 Friars Minor, one Augustinian and 3 monks of St Bernard (Cistercian); a vicar general administered each diocese in the absence of a consecrated bishop. Co. Tipperary was well organized under David Kearney, resident archbishop of Cashel, with 19 seculars and 5 Jesuits.[23]

The healthy condition of the Franciscan Order in Munster in the early decades of the seventeenth century is apparent through its reorganization at provincial chapters held at Roscrea (1609), Waterford (1615), Cashel (1621) and Limerick (1629).[24] These involved considerable risk, as evidenced by the chapter of 1621, held at Cashel, when those attending had to flee before a troop of the lord president's horse.[25] The Cashel residence was confiscated and the chapter dispersed, but the community soon returned. In 1627, Fr John Gould, guardian of Cashel, copied the lives of 33 saints from a manuscript belonging to Saints Island, Lough Ree, while *c.*1629, Brother Michael O'Clerigh copied the life of St Declan and St Ciaran of Saigir from a manuscript held at Cashel Convent.[26] Similar re-organizational activities were in progress in Dominican circles, as evidenced by the provincial synods held at Limerick (1629) and Fethard (1632).[27]

The singular importance of the religious orders during the Counter-Reformation was acknowledged in 1623, when the archbishop of Dublin wrote of the existence of some 200 Franciscans at that time in Ireland 'who are especially to be commended, because they never suffered themselves to become extinct in the kingdom and were the only religious who maintained the fight in some districts'.[28] To solve training difficulties and aid renewal, Franciscan candidates were trained in a network of Irish colleges run by the Order on the Continent. Accordingly, in 1606, the Franciscan college of St Anthony at Louvain in the Spanish Netherlands was opened; St Isidore's in 1625 at Rome and the college of the Immaculate Conception in 1631 at Prague. Irish Franciscans also had the use of a Polish friary at Wielun for some years and a temporary residence in Paris.[29] As with the secular colleges, each Franciscan college had a particular recruitment focus during this period of transition from regional to national identity: Leinstermen went to Prague, Ulstermen and Connaughtmen to Louvain, while Munstermen were attracted to Rome. On average, 10 newly trained Franciscan friars returned to Ireland each year: Prague, with a capacity of 100 students, provided 5 or 6; Louvain and Rome, with a capacity of 40 students, provided 2 or 3 annually.[30]

The Jesuits established their influence in Munster, particularly at Clonmel and Cashel, through their 'zeal as missionaries, their authority as papal emissaries, their

23 TCD MS 566. 24 W.D. O'Connell, 'Franciscan re-organization in Munster during the sixteenth century' (1939). 25 Ibid., 41. 26 Ibid., 42. 27 T.S. Flynn, *The Irish Dominicans, 1536–1641* (1993), 243. 28 Conlan, *Franciscan Ireland*, 32. 29 Unsuccessful foundations were attempted at Jablonow (Poland) and Namslaw (Silesia). 30 Conlan, *Franciscan Ireland*, 33.

provision of educational opportunities and their practical encouragement of anti-English rebellion'.[31] Their political subversion provoked suppression by the Protestant authorities, which in turn provided religious justification for continuing their activities.[32] A conference of the Society of Jesus was held in 1604 at Clonmel, attended by all five Jesuits on the island at that date, of which three were noted as preachers in the vicinity in a contemporary spy document: Andrew Mulrony SJ and Nicholas Leynagh SJ in Clonmel and Walter Wall SJ in Carrick-on-Suir.[33] All three were native sons of their preaching district, which was just as well as the risk to their lives was considerable, the head of a Jesuit in the province of Munster being valued by the New English colonial administration at £40.[34] The successful staging of this meeting was crucial in providing the impetus for the extension of the Society of Jesus throughout Ireland and the first formal Jesuit foundation in the province of Munster was made at Clonmel in 1606.[35] A crucial reason for the Jesuit success is revealed by a report of attorney general Sir John Davies, who on visiting Clonmel in 1606, noted it as

> being in the liberty [of the county palatinate of Tipperary and consequently] is more haunted with Jesuits and priests than any other town or city within this province, which is the cause we found the burgesses more obstinate here than elsewhere ... the Jesuits and priests of name that have lately frequented the town are Nicholas Leynagh Jesuit, Andrew Mulrony Jesuit, Richard White priest, Gerrard Miagh priest, William Crokin priest. Among these Nicholas Leynagh hath special credit and authority ...[36]

The palatinate of Tipperary, under the authority of the earl of Ormond, enjoyed virtual self-government from its seat of administration at Clonmel. Though a Protestant, Ormond remained sympathetic to Roman Catholicism, mindful of the profession of his fellow landed relatives. His control of Cos. Tipperary and Kilkenny, as lord palatine in the former and principal landowner in both, provided an excellent base for a Counter-Reformation Roman Catholic revival and also shielded the area for quite a time against New English immigration. The dominant population in virtually all of the towns in Munster was Roman Catholic, ruled by burgesses sympathetic to the needs of their priests, so that concealment from the New English authorities in urban areas was relatively easy. This was certainly the case in the three corporate towns of the Tipperary palatinate: Clonmel, Cashel and Fethard. Here, however, as throughout Munster, the surveillance of the provincial government was such that clerics needed to disguise themselves as grooms, surgeons, servants, esquires with sword and lance and even as fools and strolling players. Clonmel Jesuit, Nicholas Leynagh, wrote in 1607 that the members of his Order were 'dispersed and like night robbers we long for darkness, [as] no place is safe for us on account of the number

---

31 L. McRedmond, *To the greater glory: a history of the Irish Jesuits* (1991), 38. **32** Watson, *A dinner of herbs*, 59. **33** McRedmond, *To the greater glory*, 38; *Cal. SP (Ireland), 1604–6*, 380; Burke, *Clonmel*, 47; 305–6; Power, *South Tipperary*, 60. **34** For contemporary examples, see *Cal. SP (Ireland), 1604– 6*; 190; Burke, *Clonmel*, 47. **35** P. Power, *Placenames of Decies* (1952), 150. **36** *Cal. SP (Ireland), 1611–14*, 165; 474–6; *Carew MSS 1603–25*, 136.

of our pursuers. A[ndrew Mulrony] and W[alter Wall] are well and selling their wares.'[37] The Jesuits continued in their Counter-Reformation advance regardless, for later that year the lord president of Munster, the earl of Thomond, found the province 'swarming with priests' and ordered the placing of cavalry and competent officers in Co. Tipperary 'where most of these devilish priests and seminaries are relieved [especially] in Clonmell [and] Cashell' in the hope of taking some of them, those towns being their chief resort. It was reportedly 'impossible for any officer to lay hands upon them; for they are so befriended that the officers are no sooner known to come into the country but the priests are presently conveyed away.'[38]

Clonmel and Cashel were principal centres of the recusancy core in south-eastern Ireland. Innumerable reports and accounts from government and Jesuit sources record the stoutness with which the townspeople resisted the Established Church, particularly in the early seventeenth century. In 1606, John White *fitz*Geoffrey, brother of Thomas White SJ, was deprived of the sovereignty of Clonmel for recusancy and was one of twelve citizens of Clonmel and Cashel sent to Cork gaol. Over a year later, of fourteen burgesses of Munster still in gaol, 'eight are of Clonmel, four of Cork and two of Kinsale, who are still restrained because they obstinately refuse to enter into that bond [to come to church]'.[39] At every assize held in Clonmel, fines and imprisonment were dispensed by the New English administration and the names of recusants who refused to attend Protestant service every Sunday and holyday published by the Protestant minister, as required by the law. In the second decade of the seventeenth century, the grand jurors of Clonmel, being all Roman Catholics, refused to proceed with the persecution of their co-religionists and were themselves subjected to penalties.[40] A large number of these were from Old English gentry families.

There is wholesale evidence of a close relationship between the Jesuits and the Vatican and their joint involvement in Irish affairs during this period of state surveillance and suspicion was further aided by the information and influence of an expanding overseas Irish regular and secular clerical network. Aware of these developments, the New English administration in Ireland made considerable efforts to counteract them through a government spy network. A report of 1615 noted of South Tipperary,

> In ye diocese of Lismore, Fr Richard White priest, general vicar … Fr Thomas Sheyne a Jesuit and a preacher now residing in Edward White's house in Clonmell. Fr Andrew Mulronie, a Jesuit. Fr Nicholas Leynagh, a Jesuit residing in his brother's house. Thomas Magrath had a father a friar [residing in his house, who is] authorized by the pope to discharge ye faculties of a bishop.[41]

The religious orders were to the fore in the encouragement of Irish Roman Catholicism. In 1619, a bull of Pope Paul V granted an indulgence to the titular abbot of Inishlounaght concerning pilgrims visiting St Patrick's church, a dependency of the abbey.

37 *Cal. SP (Ireland), 1606–8*, 258; Burke, *Clonmel*, 48.   38 *Cal. SP (Ireland), 1606–8*, 99; 207.   39 E. Hogan (ed.), *Hibernia Ignatiana* (1880); Burke, *Clonmel*, 50.   40 Burke, *Clonmel*, 51–2.   41 BL Add. MSS 19,836, cited in ibid., 48.

Paul the fifth, to every one of Christ's faithful who shall see the present letter, greeting and apostolic benediction. For the increase of religion and the good of souls, we grant through our pious charity out of the heavenly treasures of the Church, mercifully in the Lord, full indulgence and remission of the temporal punishment of sin to all the faithful of either sex, who, truly penitent, having gone to confession and holy communion, visit the church of St Patrick belonging to the Cistercian Order in the diocese of Lismore, Ireland. Such visit to be devoutly made on the feast of Pentecost or on the feast of St Patrick, any time from first vespers to sunset on the feast day, the person so visiting to pray for peace among Christian rulers, for the uprooting of heresies and the exaltation of the holy mother church. The present grant is to be valid for thirty years. We will also that the present grant be null and void in the case of persons to whom a plenary or partial indulgence has been granted for visiting the said church. Given at Rome in the church of St Mary Major under the ring of the Fisherman the sixth day of March in the year one thousand six hundred and nineteen, being the fourteenth of our pontificate.[42]

This may be interpreted as a prelude to the revival of the abbey affected in 1641 and terminated by the arrival of Cromwell in 1649. The second and third decades of the seventeenth century witnessed great revival and increasing openness in Roman Catholic worship. A constant feature of Jesuit reports to Rome concerning the south-east of Ireland is accounts of crowds flocking for their counsel. At Carrick-on-Suir, the Jesuits recorded 'the crowds who come to mass and to hear the sermons swarm about the door and the windows, as there is not room in the chapel …'[43] The thriving condition of the Roman Catholic Church in the all-important province of Cashel in the first three decades of the seventeenth century is described in a letter of 1632 from the archbishop to the Vatican, wherein he notes his ecclesiastical province had 'a great number' of regular and diocesan clergy.[44] Bishop Comerford reported in 1630 that he had 40 secular clergy and 30 regulars in his diocese of Waterford and Lismore.[45]

The boldness of the Jesuits did not, however, make for good relations with the other religious Orders, as evidenced by their encounter with the Franciscans at Clonmel. Here, in setting up a permanent Jesuit residence, they attempted to take over the vacant Franciscan friary and its church, as well as exhorting the townspeople to refuse the Franciscans entry to the town, alleging a papal grant for Jesuit use of the friary. The superior of the Irish Franciscans visited Clonmel and reported their aggression to the Vatican.[46] The Roman Catholics of Clonmel and district benefited from this power struggle, as thereafter the Franciscans maintained an uninterrupted succession at Clonmel for fear of being usurped by the Jesuits. There was also much rivalry between the regulars and seculars over interpretations, approaches and territory.[47] In South Tipperary, competition from Jesuits had resulted in the

42 Ó Conbhuidhe, *Cistercian abbeys*, 146. 43 McRedmond, *Jesuits*, 42. 44 Flynn, *Irish Dominicans*, 273. 45 Kearney, *Strafford in Ireland*, 110. 46 Power, *Placenames of Decies*, 160. 47 Flynn, *Irish*

revival of the dormant Franciscan friary at Clonmel in 1616, while a potentially similar situation led to the revival of their friary at Cashel in 1618.

The urban centres continued as the primary battleground for the Counter-Reformation. In 1630, the concentration of Roman Catholic clergy within the urban centres of the south-east was so great, the bishop of Waterford and Lismore complained his clergy 'kept to the towns'.[48] This had much to do with the position of these centres as primary recruiting grounds for both secular and regular clergy, in that the towns had direct trading links to the Continent and it was comparatively easy for the younger sons of gentry and merchants to make their way to seminaries abroad. A measure of the religious and political linkage between Ireland and the Continent may be seen in 1648, when Fr Francis O'Sullivan, Franciscan guardian of Clonmel and provincial of Ireland, was successful in obtaining financial aid from Spain to help the Confederate cause.[49] The friars in the continental colleges actively supported the Confederacy of Kilkenny, with Fr James Fitzsimons as their secret agent in London and Fr Luke Wadding posted as Irish agent in Rome.

The eight years in the 1640s during which the Confederacy operated as de facto government of Ireland heralded the open revival and rebuilding of not only those religious houses which had maintained a discreet presence in the vicinity of their monastic foundations, but also several of those which had been extinct since the suppression of 1540. The Franciscan foundations at Carrickbeg and Galbally were revived in 1644–9 and the groundwork laid in these five years allowed their permanent revival in 1658. The Cistercians also re-established themselves in this period, in 1622 removing their novitiate at Kilkenny to nearby Kilcooley abbey, under the jurisdiction of Holy Cross abbey. Suir abbey at Inishlounaght, near Clonmel, was also revived in 1644–9, while at Holy Cross the abbey buildings were so ruined that another dwelling was built to house the monks. The abbot resolved to 'cover in the whole church, which through the inclemency of the seasons and the cruelty of the heretics has remained without a roof'.[50] The religious orders gave their wholehearted support to the Confederate administration at Kilkenny, as its very existence allowed considerable renovation and reinstatement of their foundations and some re-structuring of their provincial territorial organizations.[51]

Old English families in the south-east of Ireland were central to the supply of novices to all the religious orders and constituted a key aspect of the Counter-Reformation. Whole families gave of themselves, particularly the White merchant dynasty at Clonmel, whose endeavours as Jesuit founders and rectors of Irish colleges in Spain have already been noted. Similarly, several members of the prominent Tirry, Kearney and Hackett mercantile dynasties at Cashel and Fethard became members of the Dominican and Augustinian orders, through the influence and example of these orders, who maintained a continuous presence in these parishes. Whole branches of families were recruited into the Orders at their home base and usually spent a considerable time abroad as students. John Baptist Hackett of Fethard

Dominicans, 273. **48** Bishop Comerford, cited in Kearney, *Strafford in Ireland*, 110. **49** O'Connell, 'Franciscan re-organization in Munster', 44. **50** Ó Conbhuidhe, *Cistercian abbeys*, 241–3; see further in app. I. **51** P. Linehan, *Confederate Catholics at war, 1641–49* (2001).

joined the Cashel Dominicans in 1622, studied in the Irish colleges in Spain and later lectured at Milan, Naples and Rome. His two cousins, Patrick Kearney and Pádraigín Haicéad, both of Cashel, joined the Dominican Order in the town in the late 1620s.[52] Both studied abroad, the former returning as prior of the Cashel Dominican convent from 1638 until 1651, while the latter was a famous Irish poet who strongly supported the Confederate cause in his writings, most notably in 'rouse your courage, Banbha', a political poem written in response to the Ormond peace treaty of 1646 and which forcefully recommended loyalty to the papal position.[53] Their ancestry was steadfastly Roman Catholic: Haicéad's maternal family were the Kearneys, related to the Butlers of Dunboyne and his uncles included Bishop Patrick Comerford of Waterford and Lismore and Philip Kearney, clerk of the Confederation of Kilkenny.[54] Similarly, the faithful perseverance of the Jesuits at Clonmel and Cashel, the Cistercians at Holy Cross, and the Franciscans throughout the whole district, inspired many recruits from the Old English merchant classes.

The increasing boldness of the Roman Catholic laity, led by their clergy, was not without consequence in the volatile 1640s. The replacement of the papal envoy with a papal nuncio, Cardinal Rinuccini, was welcomed as the re-establishment of the status quo, but his urging of the combination of politics with religion, as seen in his excommunication of those Gaelic Irish and Old English supporting the Ormond peace treaty of 1646, split the Irish clergy, secular and regular, into pro- and anti-nuncio factions. It directly affected Roman Catholicism in South Tipperary, leading to the overrun of the Rock of Cashel on 13 September 1647 by the troops of Lord Inchiquin. The massacre of the congregation barricaded within the cathedral – among whom were seven priests, viz. Theobald Stapleton, Edward Stapleton, Thomas Morrissey (seculars); Richard Barry (Dominican); Richard Butler, James Saul (Franciscan) and William Boyton (Jesuit) – and the loss of the Jesuit residence at Cashel regained just a few years earlier, had far reaching repercussions.[55] This act was seen as retribution by the New English administration for the massacre of Protestants at Cashel on 1 January 1642 by members of the local Gaelic Irish gentry, disillusioned with the undermining of their status by the New English. Certainly the rising of 1641, which initially encompassed most Gaelic Irish dynasties but only a minority of the Old English, had revealed to the Protestants the extent of their precarious position *vis-à-vis* the Roman Catholic majority population. During 1642 all principal places of settlement in South Tipperary fell into Confederate hands and the Roman Catholic clergy were restored to the parishes. The clergy trained in the network of Irish colleges on the Continent had developed overseas contacts and linguistic skills during their clerical training in exile and these were put to use during the Confederacy. A small armada of fourteen armed ships was organized from the three French ports of St Malo, Nantes and Rochelle. These cities all had sizeable Irish merchant communities and which were also home to communities of Irish clerical students.[56] The Old English by tradition and blood

52 Flynn, *Irish Dominicans*, 118–9; 123. **53** M. O'Riordan, 'Political poems in the mid-seventeenth century crisis' (1995), 115–16. The poem was written in Irish under the title 'Músgail do mhisneach, a Bhanbha'. **54** Ibid. **55** McRedmond, *Jesuits*, 68; 70–1; Tait, 'Adored for saints'. **56** Ó Fiaich, *Irish*

relation were allied to England and sought security, political equality and religious tolerance; the Gaelic Irish who acknowledged no allegiance to the crown, sought the undoing of the plantations and were hostile in principle to the New English and their Protestant religion.[57]

In a succinct contemporary account of the coming together of the Gaelic Irish and Old English, an anonymous pamphleteer noted with alarm how, 'until of late', it had been 'evident'

> the Old English race [in all] parts of the kingdom, despised the mere Irish, accounting them to be a barbarous people, void of civility and religion; and other of them held the other as an hereditary enemy; and so it would have continued for many years yet to come, had not this latter times produced a change. First, their frequent marriages one with another, which in former ages were rarely seen. Secondly, the mere Irish (by their travel abroad) are civilized, grown to be disciplined soldiers, scholars, politicians and further instructed in points of religion than accustomed, whereby the ancient dislike and contempt is laid aside. Lastly, the late plantation of New English and Scottish in all parts of the kingdom whom (with an unanimous consent) the natives repute as a common enemy; but this last is the first and principal cause of their union.[58]

The missionary activities of priests from Old English backgrounds in Gaelic areas of Ireland, and the influence they are likely to have exerted over the political attitudes of the Gaelic lords under whose patronage they operated, was also a significant reason.[59] Religion, therefore, through the influence of the Roman Catholic Church, proved the most decisive factor in uniting the Gaelic Irish and Old English communities. Full advantage was taken of contemporary martyrdoms and hagiographies, for 'the principle of unity and cohesion was provided by a variety of Catholicism which conveniently erased the regional variations of the past'.[60]

In south-eastern Ireland generally and in South Tipperary particularly, the success of the Counter-Reformation depended to a great extent on the religious orders, with their international connections and stewardship of Irish colleges on the European continent. Franciscans, Dominicans and Augustinians adapted to secularization, moving virtually unhindered throughout extensive areas like a religious commando unit in secular dress and were subsequently joined in the last quarter of the sixteenth century by the Jesuits. Tipperary was equated with the threat of Jesuit intrigue and militant Counter-Reformation activities from the early seventeenth century and by the early 1630s was perceived by the New English administration as 'a receptacle, den and common thoroughfare for all leaud and ill-affected persons flying from every [province] to infect our other loving subjects'.[61]

---

colleges in France.   **57** Canny, *Making Ireland British*, 402–60.   **58** 'A discourse of the present state of Ireland, 1614', cited in ibid., 411–12.   **59** Ibid.   **60** A. Clarke, 'Colonial identity in early seventeenth-century Ireland' (1978), 57; 71.   **61** *Cal. SP (Ireland), 1647–60: addenda*, 160.

3

Incompetence and inertia:
the visitations of the Established Church

In terms of spatial implications, one of the most far-reaching consequences of the New English colonial intrusion into Ireland in the sixteenth century was the appropriation by the Established Church for its own purposes, of the entire system of diocesan and parochial frameworks and their associated settlements. Because the Established Church was the inheritor of the territorial infrastructure of the pre-Reformation Church, Roman Catholic worship was extruded from old diocesan centres such as Cashel, Emly and Lismore and these sites ceased to have any meaning in the religious lives of the majority of the population. In the early eighteenth century, the united Cashel and Emly archdiocesan centre was moved from the substantially Protestant archiepiscopal cathedral city of Cashel to the more populous Roman Catholic town of Thurles and similarly, the episcopal seat of Waterford and Lismore diocese was moved from Waterford to Carrick-on-Suir and later to Clonmel, before its eventual return to Waterford at the end of the eighteenth century.

The geographical impact of the Reformation was felt most keenly in the transitional areas between eastern and western Ireland, where two peoples and two cultures struggled for supremacy. It may be for this reason that 'deserted or aborted villages' are most prevalent in a county such as Tipperary, where the Anglican Church had comparatively few adherents.[1] The impact of the New English minority religious group, with its civil and military backing and adoption of the existing parish network on the old church-centred village, was that

> the bonding role of the pre-Reformation parish church was stripped away when the old medieval parish centres were taken over by the new minority state church [and] unless revitalized by [New] English immigrants, selected by the new landlord as the anchor point of his new estate village or managing to survive in areas of great assimilitative power as in much of Co. Limerick and in parts of Co. Tipperary and Co. Kilkenny, the old parish settlement centres fossilized and died.[2]

A major hindrance to the state church was its inheritance of the pre-Reformation ecclesiastical system, whereby Ireland was divided into 32 dioceses at national level. The network of civil parishes originated in the twelfth century ecclesiastical reform, as modified by the Norman invasion. In areas of Norman influence small compact

---

1 T. Jones-Hughes, 'Historical geography of Ireland from c.1700' (1984), 163. 2 W.J. Smyth, 'The dynamic quality of Irish "village" life: a reassessment' (1988), 110.

parishes developed, often corresponding with feudal tenures. In South Tipperary, the fertile lowlands of the central plain contained a whole series of minute parishes, while the upland parishes on the southern, north-western and north-eastern extremities were characteristically large. This system, which 'at its best had been untidy', was equally unsuited to contemporary needs.[3] England, although a larger, wealthier and more populous country had only 17 dioceses, while Wales had just 4 dioceses. It followed that clerical talent was likely to be spread even more thinly in Ireland than Wales, since better qualified clergy would tend to aim only for the uppermost positions, or else leave for (or remain in) England. The 'valor' manuscript has highlighted Westmeath, Wicklow, south Kildare, Carlow, north Wexford, Waterford (excluding the city) and most of Tipperary, as frontier zones with 'English' Ireland, containing parish livings that were very poor. The situation in the diocese of Cashel was one of 'wretched poverty' and just two dioceses – Dublin and Meath – had the financial resources that were in any way adequate to mount the sort of reform campaign contemplated in England.[4]

Overall, the impact of the Reformation on clerical wealth in 'English' Ireland was to reduce drastically the number of livings that were financially attractive to the better-educated clergy. Many of the parish livings were impropriate to a lay proprietor and had more of this wealth been appropriated to the endowment of secular colleges, schools and a university, the reform campaign in Ireland could have succeeded. Instead, far too few preachers were available for the intended campaign of conversion. It would be over-simplistic to argue, however, that these economic shortcomings were the sole cause of the outcome of the Reformation in Ireland. As in parts of England and Wales, this would have merely slowed the process, without affecting the eventual outcome.

There are two major reasons for the serious decline in the condition of pre-Reformation church buildings from the second half of the sixteenth century and therefore of the parochial organization, of the Established Church in South Tipperary and beyond. Through a lack of Protestant ministers and parishioners on the one hand and a determined 'collapsing' of the old ecclesiastical territorial organization including the management of tithe incomes by recusant Roman Catholics on the other, many church buildings fell into terminal decline. A situation developed in which the local population no longer felt any responsibility for the upkeep of the local parish church, with the result that the great majority of churches were in a state of ruin, or at least great disrepair, while the houses of the local Roman Catholic gentry (and of the merchants in the towns) became the new 'hidden' centres of worship for members of this denomination. This development actually benefited both local Roman Catholic and Protestant landowners, with tithes and church lands farmed out to gentry of both persuasions.[5] A further blow to the territorial hegemony of the Established Church came in the Cromwellian period, when government and settler support were no longer specifically Anglican and the Protestant interests were divided. After the Restoration of 1660, Protestantism remained

3 Corish, *The Catholic community*, 21–2.   4 S.G. Ellis, 'Economic problems of the Church' (1990), 251; G. Williams, *The Welsh Church* (1976).   5 Kearney, *Strafford in Ireland*, 107.

Map 2: The civil parishes of South Tipperary

divided, with locally important urban and rural Protestant families continuing their adherence to Quaker, Baptist, Independent and Presbyterian dissenting traditions, thus diverting important support away from the Established Church.

It is extremely difficult, in view of the scanty amount of original source documentation surviving, to ascertain how the existing clergy of the mid-sixteenth century Irish Church received the Reformation and what proportion of them were actually reformed by it. Some clergy certainly conformed, as several incumbents who had originally been appointed by the pope were re-appointed by Edward VI. However, conformity to the state church and conversion to the principles of the Protestant Reformation were two very different things, the key difference being that the former was a passive action and the latter an active form of religious identification. Conformity contains an implication of obedience to the state rather than religious conviction, for 'if conviction does not follow conformity rapidly dissipates'.[6] There were also those clergy who refused to conform at all, even in a nominal sense and they were consequently removed from office. Such clergy and laity, constituted the vast bulk of the population. This had far-reaching consequences in distancing the majority population from the Established Church and, even at this early stage, there was some rationalization of the territorial organization. In 1568, the diocese of Emly was united to the diocese of Cashel, although the Roman Catholic Church kept up a nominal and intermittent episcopal succession at Emly until amalgamation with Cashel in 1695.[7] Territorial rationalization also took place at a parochial level, commencing in the period between 1588 and 1610 in the southeast and south-west of South Tipperary, and with further progress in the 1620s and 1630s in the east around Fethard, so that on thirteen occasions, one civil parish was grouped with another to form a parochial union.[8] However, the majority of territorial rationalization took place in the two decades after the Restoration.

In an episcopal church, the welfare of the whole organization is closely connected with the calibre of the episcopate, with any suggestion of disrepute sure to generate disrespect. One of the principal reasons for the failure of the Reformation in the archdiocese of Cashel and Emly and subsequently in the diocese of Waterford and Lismore was the episcopal appointment of Miler Magrath to these sees. A former Franciscan friar and son of a Gaelic Irish chieftain of Ulster, Magrath arrived from Rome early in 1566 as papal appointee to the vacant see of Down and Connor. After he had conformed and taken the oath of supremacy, Queen Elizabeth appointed him in September 1570 to the vacant see of Clogher. In 1571, he was raised to the archbishopric of Cashel and Emly, a see he systematically pillaged in favour of his Roman Catholic family throughout his half-century tenure. During this time, the archdiocese reached the lowest financial and administrative depths of its entire history, with disastrous consequences for clergy and laity. On the expul-

---

6 N.P. Canny, 'Why the Reformation failed in Ireland' (1979).   7 S.J.D. Seymour, *Cashel and Emly* (1908), 11.   8 *1588*: Rochestown to Tubrid, Kilgrant to Killaloan; *1605–6*: Temple-etnay to Killaloan, Modeshill to Kilvemnon, Ballyclerihan to Cashel; *1615*: Aghacrew and Kilmiclon to Toem; *1620*: Crohane to Lismalin; *1622*: Templetenny to Shanrahan, Donoughmore to Kiltegan; *1634*: Clonbullogue to Tipperary; *1637*: Corroge to Tipperary; *1639*: Neddans to Ardfinnan: Seymour, *Cashel and Emly*; Rennison, *Succession list*.

sion of the Welshman, Marmaduke Middleton (1579–82), from the see of Waterford and Lismore, royal officials sought to appoint someone with the diplomacy, tact and sensitivity of an Irish background. Apparently they failed, for Magrath was appointed to that see also as a 'temporary' compromise measure, which lasted seven years, until 1589.

In 1584, the canons of St Patrick's cathedral, Dublin made a report on the deficiencies endured by parishes throughout Ireland, as a result of being wholly or partly impropriate to laymen. This report had particular significance to the united dioceses of Cashel, Emly, Waterford and Lismore, covering the whole of South Tipperary, where almost every parish was in one or other category, or at least subject to a diversion of funds to the Magrath family. It was found that due to the greediness of these laymen, no preachers and only a few reading ministers were to be found in these parishes 'but rather a company of Irish rogues and Romish priests'.[9] Vicars were hired at such a menial stipend that in order to earn enough to subsist, they 'travelleth like a lackey to three or four churches in a morning … and there once a week readeth them [the congregation] only a gospel in Latin and so away … and so the poor people are deluded'.[10]

The Jesuits were given a free hand in their Counter-Reformation mission in the province of Munster generally because Magrath, in his archiepiscopal city of Cashel, was well removed from much of his province and diocese. His practice of keeping all livings (parishes) in his united dioceses vacant and diverting their annual income to his sons and extended family meant that most parish churches became ruinous. Initially, he appeared to favour a stringent anti-Roman Catholic policy, as shortly after his arrival in 1571, he arrested a number of openly non-conformist friars for preaching against the queen; but he rapidly released them when James *fitz*Maurice Fitzgerald wrote to him, threatening to burn his property. In 1582, a letter of Magrath's from London was intercepted and found to contain warnings to certain Roman Catholic bishops and priests of their imminent arrest, so that inconsistencies regarding his loyalties were already in evidence by that date.[11] With Magrath's active co-operation, his wife, an unreformed Roman Catholic, subsequently warned many priests of intended raids. His role became that of the two-way agent, aiding whichever side he thought would better advance his own interests.

In 1588, Magrath was instructed by the New English administration to present a survey of his united dioceses of Waterford and Lismore. This was done, but the surviving manuscript at Trinity College, Dublin neglects to mention any church land or other income, the archbishop having confined it to a listing of churches and clergy.[12] Most parish churches were listed as 'ruinous' and without officiating clergymen. Some of the few clergymen recorded were actual 'papists'. That several of the South Tipperary clergy were of the Roman Catholic persuasion is beyond doubt, such as Thomas Geoffrey, vicar of Kilcash, whose chalice bearing his name and title 'presbyter', dated 1599, is still in use in the Franciscan friary of Clonmel. The said Geoffrey was suspended in 1591, presumably for non-con-

9 Seymour, *The diocese of Emly* (1913), 191. 10 Ibid. 11 Conlan, *Franciscan Ireland*, 26. 12 TCD MS 566: visitation of Waterford and Lismore dioceses, November 1588.

formity, but officially 'for manifest contumacy and notorious irregularity'.[13] The visitation of 1588 is written in Latin and one of the terms most frequently used is '*vacatus*', the Latin for 'vacant'. The date of the visitation gives it an added value, for it was at a time of extreme confusion in Established Church affairs. The state clergy were neither in numbers or qualifications equal to the work assigned them. However, the visitors did identify and preserve for researchers the problems the Reformation was encountering in Ireland at this crucial period, particularly in finding competent clergymen to fill vacant posts. The lay propriators of the tithes of many parishes could not be induced to provide sufficient stipends for the existing clergy and often withheld the revenues for their own use, styling themselves rector or vicar of the parish.

The visitation makes clear the failure of the Established Church to gain control over the parish structures of the strongly recusant south-east. The presence of Irish Roman Catholic names in such a high proportion among the clergy is testament to the fact that many were unreformed Roman Catholic priests, who held onto their cures through favour of local patrons and through the tolerance of the archbishop, to whom personally it was a matter of little concern what rites they practised or what doctrines they held. The diocese of Waterford and Lismore suffered much from the influence of lay proprietorship and the neglect and non-residence of its diocesan. An average of 51 per cent of clerical offices in both the individual and combined dioceses of Waterford and Lismore were vacant, appropriated by the Magrath family or controlled by laymen. The problem was worse in that portion of the diocese of Lismore lying within South Tipperary, where in the rural deaneries of Ardfinnan and Kilsheelan, over two-thirds of posts were thus affected. Map 3 further illustrates the problems caused by Magrath in the provision of rectors and vicars for the parish churches. The civil parishes of the diocese of Lismore within the bounds of South Tipperary numbered 34, of which 15 were filled by ostensibly Protestant ministers, while of the reminder, 17 were kept vacant and a further 2 cures – those of Outeragh and Kilcash – were in the hands of openly Roman Catholic clerics. The greatest concentration of resident clerics was in parishes adjoining the valley of the river Suir, where two-thirds were located.

Magrath was replaced as bishop of Waterford and Lismore within months of this visitation, the intermittent seven-year search for a successor having been spurred on by this evidence of his inefficiency and corruption. Thomas Weatherhead (1588–92), the short-lived successor to Magrath, is illustrative of the continuation of wholesale corruption and inert leadership in the state church in this period. Weatherhead proved as infamous as Magrath, for in 1589 the lord deputy wrote of his 'insufferable wickedness', claiming that while warden of the collegiate school at Youghal, he had lobbied for the position, had 'sold off all his sources of income and suffered his honest wife and poor children to wander up and down [the town], begging and ready to famish'.[14] In 1591, Weatherhead and Magrath illegally left the country, leaving both dioceses leaderless for over a year. While nothing further is

---

13 Power, *Waterford and Lismore*, 351.   14 D. Cowman, 'The Reformation bishops of the diocese of Waterford and Lismore' (1984), 34.

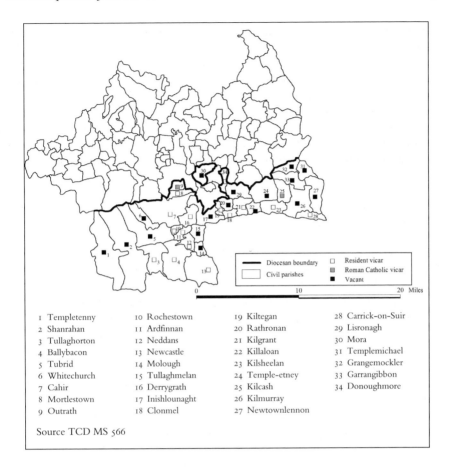

Map 3: The episcopal visitation of Lismore diocese, 1588

known of Weatherhead, who presumably remained overseas, Magrath returned the following year, had charges of negligence against him dropped and regained control of not only Cashel and Emly – which he held until his death – but also of Waterford and Lismore, which he held a further sixteen years until 1608.[15] This continuing sequence of corruption and careless indifference served only to confirm the people, both Gaelic Irish and Old English, in their opposition to both the Reformation and the Established Church.

The central core in the reclamation of the country for Rome was not so much Dublin or Cork, but rather the urban settlements of the south-east, particularly Waterford and Clonmel. This area, because of its established links with the European Continent, led the field in the rejection of the reformed faith and therein, the New English establishment. From the evidence, the missionary efforts of the Society of Jesus were central to this development. A contemporary observer noted that 'per-

15 P. Ryan, 'Miler Magrath, 1522–1622: archbishop of Cashel' (MA, UCD, 1962).

verse recusants come out of England for the most part to Waterford, the sink of all filthy superstitions and idolatry …'[16] In 1596, it was stated that until quite recently, the citizens of Waterford 'came very orderly to church, but first their women grew tired of it and that being unpunished their men left it and they being unpunished, the mayors, sovereigns and port-reeves for the most part have left it'.[17] Barnaby Rich, in describing the religious condition of Dublin, Drogheda and Waterford in 1589, observed

> the word of God hath been for many years most plentifully preached but to such an obstinate people that wilfully resisting the truth [they] can rend no other reason the most of them, but that they will do as their fathers have done before them and that their uncles, their aunts, their cousins and their kindred do thus believe.[18]

Generally urban areas were better served with Protestant vicars, but their inhabitants remained obstinately recusant. However, despite increasing references to private houses being used for the celebration of the mass, it is true that many of the laity, particularly those in the upper echelons of society in the Pale and other areas of dominant English influence, continued to attend service and sermons, but not receive communion in the Established Church. In this way, they can be more accurately classified as adherents rather than members of the state religion, also known as 'crypto-Catholics' or 'church papists'. It is also probably true to say that some of these people continued to attend the parish church because it was the traditional place of worship of previous generations and they did not at this point see fit to relinquish it for a secret chapel of an inferior nature. The extent to which religion was in a state of flux in South Tipperary may be illustrated by the example of the Whites of Clonmel, who, as late as 1577, continued to attend at the parish church and be buried in their ancestral vault within its walls. The liturgy was sufficiently Catholic for this to continue, yet it was sufficiently Protestant by 1588 for the vicar, William Prendergast, to be confirmed as vicar of St Mary's parish and treasurer of Lismore cathedral by the visitation of that year. Yet even this conformity was filled with uncertainty. In a most unwelcome piece of negative publicity for the Established Church, Prendergast reverted to Roman Catholicism on his deathbed in 1605 'and having done public penance, he received the holy *viaticum* and passed out of this life to the great edification of everyone'.[19]

In South Tipperary, many rural parishes remained without a pastor and their churches slowly deteriorated or were subjected to random vandalism by displaced Roman Catholics. The ways of Magrath certainly weakened the resolve of several of his clergy for the reformed faith, doubtless encouraged either directly or indirectly by Jesuit missionary efforts, as passive recusancy began to change to outright rebellion. In 1601, Magrath was actually attacked while visiting Lismore, with the result that when in 1605 he was required to proclaim the king's decree against recu-

---

16 Ibid., 34.   17 Watson, *A dinner of herbs*, 60.   18 Barnaby Rich, cited in Canny, 'Why the Reformation failed in Ireland', 433.   19 Watson, *A dinner of herbs*, 58; 60.

sants, Jesuits, seminarians and priests in Clonmel and district; he was escorted by a troop of horse. This proclamation had no affect whatsoever, as at Cashel the following year, the attorney general, Sir John Davies,

> found only one inhabitant that came to church, for even the archbishop's own sons and sons-in-law dwelling there are obstinate recusants. We indicted more than 100 in this poor town. [At] Clonmel, a well built and well kept town, my lord president [of Munster] did justly offer to the principal inhabitants that he would spare to proceed against them if they would yield to conference [with the Protestant vicar] for a time and became bound in the meantime not to receive any Jesuit or priest into their houses; they peremptorily refused both, where upon the chief of them were bound to appear at Cork before the lord president and council presently after Easter there to be censured with good round fines and imprisonment.[20]

The assertion about recusancy in the immediate Magrath family was not unprecedented, for apparently it was quite common among families of the native clergy who continued to serve the Established Church in the early seventeenth century. Magrath's ambiguous and pivotal role was also the subject of discussion in the Vatican, for in 1612, the cardinal secretary of state in Rome wrote that 'his conversion would be glorious for the Church and would greatly comfort the Catholics of Ireland and England and strengthen many who are wavering in the faith'.[21]

Magrath's misconduct gave rise to a further visitation, without which analysis of the territorial condition of the Established Church in this period would not be possible. The royal visitation of 1607 was initiated by the lord deputy and undertaken by the archbishop of Dublin and the bishops of Kildare and Ferns on behalf of the government. It focused exclusively on the four dioceses of Cashel, Emly, Waterford and Lismore,[22] and on the 'many and very foul disorders and abuses [allegedly] committed by that Archbishop Magrath in the government of those dioceses'.[23] The report highlights the utter neglect by Magrath of his pastoral charge and 'his participation in simony and leasing over of the livings to his sons and allies to the havoc of the church'.[24] A thorough investigation was made in the four dioceses concerned and the abuses uncovered were enormous. Much of the information was gleaned from six inquisitors chosen from Magrath's closest confidents among the clergy, who testified under oath, viz. Daniel Hurley, a civilian; John O'Shea, chancellor of Cashel; Donal O'Hogan, archdeacon of Cashel; Theodore O'Brien, archdeacon of Emly; Donald McTeig, a vicar from Emly; and Richard Daniell, archdeacon of Waterford and diocesan registrar; the result of their cross-examination is shown in map 4.[25]

In Cashel and Emly, it was discovered that not more than six parish churches were in good repair in the united diocese. The condition of the majority of parish

20 E. Hogan, *The description of Ireland and the state thereof as it is at this present in anno. 1598* (1878), 209–10; *Cal. SP (Ireland), 1606–8*, 475–6; Ford, *The Protestant Reformation*, 45. 21 Watson, *A dinner of herbs*, 58. 22 *Cal. SP (Ireland), 1606–8*, 235. 23 *Cal. SP (Ireland), 1603–6*, 474–5. 24 P.B. Phair, 'Seventeenth century regal visitations' (1978), 81. 25 Ibid., 237.

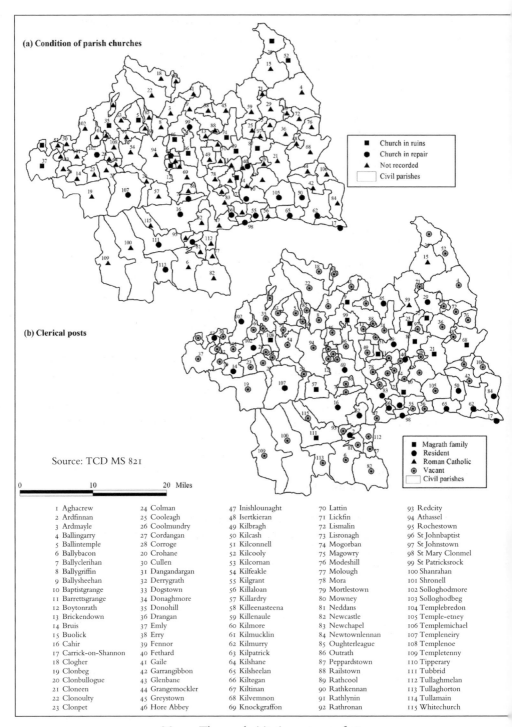

(a) Condition of parish churches

Church in ruins
Church in repair
Not recorded
Civil parishes

(b) Clerical posts

Source: TCD MS 821

0   10   20 Miles

Magrath family
Resident
Roman Catholic
Vacant
Civil parishes

1 Aghacrew	24 Colman	47 Inishlounaght	70 Lattin	93 Redcity
2 Ardfinnan	25 Cooleagh	48 Isertkieran	71 Lickfin	94 Athassel
3 Ardmayle	26 Coolmundry	49 Kilbragh	72 Lismalin	95 Rochestown
4 Ballingarry	27 Cordangan	50 Kilcash	73 Lisronagh	96 St Johnbaptist
5 Ballintemple	28 Corroge	51 Kilconnell	74 Mogorban	97 St Johnstown
6 Ballybacon	29 Crohane	52 Kilcooly	75 Magowry	98 St Mary Clonmel
7 Ballyclerihan	30 Cullen	53 Kilcornan	76 Modeshill	99 St Patricksrock
8 Ballygriffin	31 Dangandargan	54 Kilfeakle	77 Molough	100 Shanrahan
9 Ballysheehan	32 Derrygrath	55 Kilgrant	78 Mora	101 Shronell
10 Baptistgrange	33 Dogstown	56 Killaloan	79 Mortlestown	102 Solloghodmore
11 Barrettsgrange	34 Donaghmore	57 Killardry	80 Mowney	103 Solloghodbeg
12 Boytonrath	35 Donohill	58 Killeenasteena	81 Neddans	104 Templebredon
13 Brickendown	36 Drangan	59 Killenaule	82 Newcastle	105 Temple-etney
14 Bruis	37 Emly	60 Kilmore	83 Newchapel	106 Templemichael
15 Buolick	38 Erry	61 Kilmucklin	84 Newtownlennan	107 Templeneiry
16 Cahir	39 Fennor	62 Kilmurry	85 Oughterleague	108 Templenoe
17 Carrick-on-Shannon	40 Fethard	63 Kilpatrick	86 Outrath	109 Templetenny
18 Clogher	41 Gaile	64 Kilshane	87 Peppardstown	110 Tipperary
19 Clonbeg	42 Garrangibbon	65 Kilsheelan	88 Railstown	111 Tubbrid
20 Clonbullogue	43 Glenbane	66 Kiltegan	89 Rathcool	112 Tullaghmelan
21 Cloneen	44 Grangemockler	67 Kiltinan	90 Rathkennan	113 Tullaghorton
22 Clonoulty	45 Greystown	68 Kilvemnon	91 Rathlynin	114 Tullamain
23 Clonpet	46 Hore Abbey	69 Knockgraffon	92 Rathronan	115 Whitechurch

Map 4: The royal visitation returns of 1607

churches was not recorded, but of eighteen churches roofed – many of which were in indifferent repair – the majority lay in the south-east and south-west of the county within the well-populated hinterlands of the nucleated settlements of Clonmel, Carrick-on-Suir and Cahir. North of Cahir parish, only four churches were in some repair: the decaying cathedral at Cashel, along with the parish churches of the towns of Tipperary and Fethard and of the village of Bansha. The cathedral church of Emly was ruinous, as was the parish church of the walled town of Cashel, and there is sufficient evidence to indicate the majority of parish churches in the hinterlands of Cashel and Fethard were also in ruins.

The general disrepair of the churches had much to do with the leasing of their annual profits by the archbishop and many of the church offices were also distributed to his favourites, most notably the chantership and archdeaconry to his sons James and Marcus respectively, and the chancellorship to his kinsman, Redmond Magrath. In addition to the misappropriation of these three prominent offices, 12 parishes of South Tipperary were in the hands of members of the Magrath family; just 24 had a resident cleric, predominantly clustered in the south-east and west, of which 2 were Roman Catholic. Some 26 livings were distributed between relatives and friends of the archbishop and only 2 of these were supplied with preaching by a curate.[26] A massive 79 parishes, constituting almost 70 per cent of the total number in South Tipperary, were vacant upon visitation.

As had been found two decades earlier in 1588, most of the livings were being deliberately kept vacant by the archbishop, so as to enable the diversion of their revenues for the use of his household. In Lismore, the visitors found 'seven or eight un-beneficed English preachers, which are lately come over with the undertakers [of the Munster plantation] and are not otherwise provided for' and appointed them to some of the many vacant livings in that diocese.[27] Several vicarages had been granted by Magrath to schoolboys, which 'carry a pretence to be granted *studii gratia*, yet it is affirmed that there is not a schoolmaster in either of those dioceses authorized by the archbishop to teach scholars'.[28] Of the cathedral parish the visitors reported the worst abuses, for the seat of the diocese was

> in decay, its profits leased by this archbishop, for how much we could not learn. There is an organist, but the vicar's choral are but half in number, on half pay and are almost disbanded by the archbishop. There is a dean's manse. The parish church is much ruined. The chancellor is a late household servant of the archbishop; the latter has the fruits of the treasurership and his son, that of two-thirds of the archdeaconry, the archdeacon having just one-third. There is no schoolmaster in the diocese of Cashel and Emly. Emly cathedral is utterly decayed and fallen; the dean is eighty years old and unable to travel.[29]

Such was the inferior condition of the Established Church in 1607, when compared to the resurgent Roman Catholic Church, that the authorities began to

26 M.A. Murphy (ed.), 'Royal visitation of Cashel and Emly, 1615' (1912). **27** Ford, *The Protestant Reformation in Ireland*, 88. **28** *Cal. SP (Ireland), 1606–8*; 241; Seymour, *Cashel and Emly*, 11. **29** Ibid.

despair, wishing their 'bishops and others that have cure of souls were but half as diligent in their several charges as these Jesuits are in the places where they haunt, [and] the people would not receive and nourish them as now they do'.[30] There were instances where Roman Catholic priests were actually appointed to a vicarage or curacy. The archbishop himself held three chapter stalls and nine parishes, received the yearly income there from, but took no steps to see that divine service was performed. In still more parishes, there was but a nominal incumbent who received as little as one-third or one-quarter of his rightful stipend, the remainder being paid to a relative or friend of the archbishop. It would seem there was much justification in the conclusion of the visitation committee that many of the incumbents 'have little learning and sufficiency and are indeed better fitted to keep hogs than serve in the Church'.[31] In the words of the archbishop of Dublin, these conditions were 'sufficient motive to induce the people in these two dioceses of Cashel and Emly (containing 40 miles in length as he is credibly informed) to conceive and think that among them [the Protestants] there is no religion'.[32] The commissioners deprived all the various clerics whose livings were leased, who were tainted by simony or minority, or whose fruits had been taken by lay persons and had their fruits sequestered and reserved to the next incumbents.

The situation in Waterford and Lismore was not so serious as in Cashel and Emly, but still a cause for concern to the colonial administration. The deanery of Lismore, with certain glebe lands, was leased by the dean and chapter to the archbishop's use, who in turn sold the lease to a merchant in Waterford, leaving the deanery with scanty means of support. Other benefices were similarly leased, with the fruits of two vacant livings received by the archbishop's daughter, who was a widow.[33] Government officials saw Magrath as the most scandalous of all the clergy of the Established Church in Ireland. In the words of the attorney general 'his exemplary punishment will add credit to religion', but Sir John Davies added the wish 'that they who find great beams in his eyes would also pull the mottes out of their own'.[34] As a direct result of the royal visitation, Magrath was forced to resign Waterford and Lismore the following year but was granted Killala and Achonry as compensation, which he actually used to support kinsmen and retainers expelled from Cashel and Emly archdiocese by the visitors.

The colonial administration found it expedient to allow Magrath to continue as archbishop of Cashel and Emly, but he ceased to have any interest in them, leaving their administration to one of his sons, a recusant. On account of his great age and the fact he was seldom resident in his see 'but [rather] absent in the north [of Ireland] upon his own temporal lands', a royal warrant was issued in September 1610 for the appointment of William Knight as his coadjutor. Knight was to have all the profits arising from the jurisdiction of the archbishop's son, with the promise of the archbishopric upon the death of Magrath.[35] This closer scrutiny and accountability led Magrath to fear his own imminent deposition and the removal of his family from

30 Burke, *Clonmel*, 49; *Cal. SP (Ireland), 1606–8*, 475–6. 31 *Cal. SP (Ireland), 1606–8*, 242; Seymour, *Diocese of Emly*, 193. 32 Ibid., 236. 33 Ibid., 23–8. 34 Ibid., 194. 35 *Cal. SP (Ireland), 1608–10*, 501.

Table 1: The royal visitation of 1615 in South Tipperary

	Churches in repair	Churches in decay and churches in ruins	Chancel in decay, nave in repair	Chancel in repair, nave in decay	Recusant vicar
Lismore	11	14 + 10 = 24	4	3	1
Cashel	27	05 + 48 = 53	3	3	4

their holdings. Accordingly, he sent for the provincial of his former Franciscan order, then dwelling at Cashel and expressed his desire to return to the Roman Catholic Church and 'to recant in the presence of the heretical church', if the pope so commended him, though this should expose him to certain death. The pope assured Magrath, for his part, of a 'loving reception' if he returned.[36] This undertaking was merely a politically astute manoeuvre on the part of the archbishop, which had the desired effect upon the English administration in Ireland, for as lord deputy Chichester noted, 'the archbishop is stout and wilful … it were better not to discontent that heady archbishop and leave him at liberty, for he is a powerful man among the Irish of Ulster and able to do much hurt by underhand practices, in which he is well experienced'.[37] The colonial administration thus remained apprehensive about Magrath's extensive landed and family connections in the province of Ulster, where he seems to have succeeded his father as chieftain of the Magrath clan and they consequently left him undisturbed in his career of alienation and appropriation, giving the Roman Catholic Church freedom for activity in most parts of Munster.

Between 1607 and the rebellion in 1641, further visitations were held which better demonstrate the overall condition of the Established Church, in terms of finance, manpower and the condition of church fabric. The royal visitation of 1615 is far more comprehensive than that of 1607, for instead of merely noting a parish vacancy, or the name of the incumbent, it contains additional comments regarding deficiencies in existing church fabric and the distribution of clergymen. The information required by the commissioners included all titles of ecclesiastical promotions and benefices, names of incumbents, the yearly value of every living, the impropriations and the proprietors; parishes which might be united or divided were to be listed and, likewise, locations where parish churches might be erected. The bishops were required to give notice of all persons 'who exercise any jurisdiction derived from the bishop of Rome'; bonds were to be taken out for the sure performance of repairs to the churches or chancels and it was to be made known generally that the king commanded that the money collected in fines from recusants 'be converted for the relief of the poor of the parish [as] workmen and labourers [who] shall be set to work to amend the churches and adorn them'.[38] In this way, further details on the final years of the chaotic Magrath episcopate are available. As table 1 indicates, very serious deficiencies remained in 1615, ranging from the recusancy of several of the vicars to chronic dilapidation in the fabric of the parish churches.

36 Phillips (ed.), *The Church of Ireland*, ii, 552.   **37** *Cal. SP (Ireland), 1611–14*, 241.   **38** Phair, 'Seventeenth century regal visitations', 82.

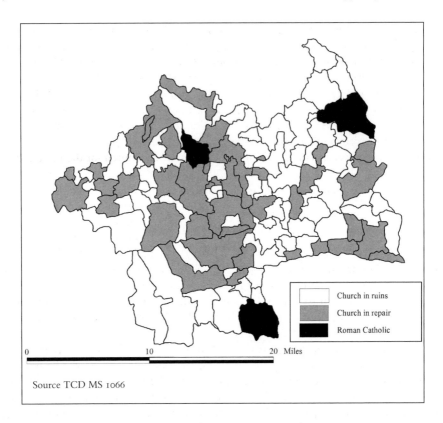

Map 5: The royal visitation returns of 1615

Map 5 further illustrates the condition of the parish churches of South Tipperary in 1615. Two vast corridors of ruinous churches, one bisecting the county and occupying much of the eastern half, the other comprising the large upland parishes to the south and south-west, can readily be seen. Conversely, areas of active Anglican ministry can also be identified, particularly that comprising the central zone, radiating outward from the fertile hinterland of the ecclesiastical city of Cashel northwards to Donohill and Clogher, southwards to Tubrid, as far west as Tipperary and Emly and east towards Fethard; further detached zones comprising the parishes and hinterlands of Clonmel and Carrick-on-Suir adjoining the river Suir, occupied the south-eastern corner. Of 34 parish churches in that part of South Tipperary within the diocese of Lismore, only 11 were in repair; while in the Cashel and Emly portion, 27 of 81 parish churches were usable, also one-third of the total number available. Of those churches in repair (as table 1 indicates), 7 had a chancel in decay, 6 had a nave in decay and 5 more were actually staffed by recusant vicars for Roman Catholic congregations. No less than 44 clerical posts lay vacant in the Cashel and Emly portion of South Tipperary. In several parishes, although in possession of the services of a cleric, divine service had been only twice or three times provided in the previous year.

The zones of weakness for the Established Church, particularly in terms of decayed church fabric and absentee clergy, were conversely the regions of greatest Counter-Reformation resistance and Roman Catholic reconstruction. The Roman Catholic nature of the parishes of Ballingarry, Ballygriffin, Oughterleague and Killenaule is openly admitted in their classification 'no service of God'. This had continued unchecked since the royal visitation of 1607, with the problem extending to Newcastle, whose rector is stated as being recusant. Of the repair of churches, it is stated that 'throughout the dioceses, the parson and vicar are bound to repair or build the chancel and the parishioners the body of the church for the most part'.[39] Certainly, the church fabric had suffered much thanks to the recusancy of the majority of the parishioners, for several of the churches then in repair were still continually threatened with ruin. In addition, rebellion threatened church fabric, for once the Roman Catholics perceived their former parish church to have been 'desecrated' or 'tainted' by the Protestants, they did not hesitate to embark upon deliberate strategies to bring about its ruin. The decay of so many parish churches noticed in the royal visitation of 1615 is a powerful demonstration of the territorial failure of the Anglican Church in Ireland by the early seventeenth century. The effect of the late sixteenth century rebellions is mentioned in connection with four parish churches: at Newcastle and at Cahir, where 'the church is decayed in the roof by rebellion'; at Outeragh, where 'the roof is burnt by rebels' and at Tullaghorton, where the 'church decayed in the rebellion time [and] the parishioners are all absent'.[40] This loss of the allegiance of local parishioners is noticed everywhere, particularly in the county town of Clonmel, where the visitors noted 'the most part of the fruits, consisting of the offerings, now are lost through the recusancy of the parishioners. [There is] a schoolmaster by name of John Wade, by whose license we know not and [who] comes not to church'.[41] This resistance to supporting the local church pivoted on the power of surviving gentry families and on the withholding of tithe income by the proprietors of church livings.[42] However, in areas where a considerable body of New English Protestants had recently arrived, as in several rural parishes like Cullen, on the border with Limerick, the services of a reading minister were provided and 'the lord president [of Munster] promiseth to see this church [re]bylded in a short time, [as] so he doth upon all his lands'.[43]

The royal visitations demonstrate with abundant clarity the shortcomings of the parochial clergy, many of whom were promoted far too quickly, often spending a number of years in office before being ordained to the diaconate or priesthood. The rector of Cahirconlish, Co. Limerick, bordering South Tipperary, was described as 'a most unworthy man [who] hath been minister eight years, but doth confess that he never yet celebrated baptism or communion'.[44] In addition, several incumbents were described as 'students in the college', which signified attendance at Trinity College, the income of their livings being applied to pay their educational expenses. Some of these teenage schoolboys even had Roman Catholic priests as curates in their absence. Such irregularities were not to be found in the more impor-

39 TCD MS 1066: royal visitation of 1615. 40 Ibid. 41 Ibid. 42 Smyth, 'Ireland, a colony', 173.
43 TCD MS 1066. 44 Seymour, *Diocese of Emly*, 193.

tant urban parishes, but rather exclusively in rural areas. Many rural benefices were subsequently deemed surplus to the needs of the Established Church and were permanently united to a nearby parish, which usually had a town, village or estate at its core. Seven parishes which had a church in repair in South Tipperary in 1615–34 were not used subsequent to the restoration of the Established Church in 1660.

It is too easy to lay the entire blame for the ruinous condition of the parish churches of the four dioceses of Cashel, Emly, Waterford and Lismore on Archbishop Miler Magrath, though as diocesan he was responsible for it to a very large degree of it. The royal visitation of 1615 shows that several of the churches and church offices had been abandoned or neglected for decades, even centuries, by the pre-Reformation Roman Catholic Church. Indeed, the clergy succession lists compiled by Seymour and Rennison for their respective united dioceses of Cashel and Emly and of Waterford and Lismore, show that many prebends and offices were already deemed to be 'extinct' in the period between 1200 and 1500.[45] Some benefices had such obscure sub-divisions that the very sites of some chapels were unknown in the time of these early seventeenth century visitations. Also, in view of the small Protestant population, it is very likely that the handful of parish churches sufficiently in repair in 1615 – covering as they did the principal urban centres and their hinterlands – were adequate to supply their spiritual needs. Even after the influx of New English Protestants associated with the Munster plantation from the 1610s, as later confirmed by the distribution of deponents in 1641–2, few rural parishes had any Protestant parishioners. In 1622, the parish church of Aghacrew in the north-west of South Tipperary was typical in its 'decay, having neither parishioners nor other means'.[46]

In Cashel, Emly, Waterford and Lismore, a total of 20 royal presentations were made to benefices within six years of the visitation of 1615, about three-quarters of which were made within a fourteen-month period.[47] It is worth noting that the greater part of the new appointments was of English rather than Irishmen, so that few ministers could speak the Irish tongue. This is in marked contrast with the 1607 returns, which reveal a surprising prevalence of names of Gaelic Irish and Old English origin.[48] The reign of James I brought approximately 70 appointments to the 4 dioceses in question, of which only 13 bore names of Gaelic Irish or Old English background, while only another 8 were appointed during the reign of Charles I.[49] From the early seventeenth century, the state can thus be seen to have

45 Seymour, *Cashel and Emly*, 6–7; also Rennison, *Succession list.* **46** Report of the commission of 1622, in ibid., 93. **47** *Fiants of James I*, 567–631; I am grateful to Mr Kenneth Nicholls of the department of History, UCC for pointing me in the direction of this source. **48** Murphy (ed.), 'Royal visitation', 296–311; Ford, *The Protestant Reformation*, 34–5, 88–9, 98–9. **49 James I (1603–25)** *1612*: Donat O'Hogan, rector of Toem, Ballintemple, Rathleynin and curate of Kilvemnon; *1615*: Peter Butler, rector of Fethard; Randolph Hurley, precentor of Emly; Peter Flanagan, rector of Solloghodmore and Toughcluggin; *1616*: Edmund Donnellan MA BD, archdeacon of Cashel, prebend of Crohane, rector of Crohane, Ballysheehan, Killenaule and Ballingarry; *1617*: Roger Fahy, rector of Templeneiry (prebend of Killardry from 1623); Nicholas Fleming Jnr., rector of Tullamain, Brickendown, Buolick and curate of Kilcooley; Gerald Fitzgerald, archdeacon of Emly (rector of Bruis from 1631); *1620*: William Ingoldsby, rector of Kilconnell; Patrick Kelly, rector of Crohane (curate of Lismalin from 1634); *1621*: Owen O'Harran, prebend of Killardry; Thady O'Grady BA, chancellor of

moved powerfully to reinforce the Established Church in Ireland with Englishmen as bishops and parochial clergy. This served further to anglicize the Church and reinforce the link with British colonization, thereby increasing its associations with what the majority of the Irish population perceived as an alien culture.[50]

In the two decades after 1615 significant territorial advancement was achieved.[51] This progress was aided by the death of Magrath in 1622 and the fact the dioceses of Waterford and Lismore and of Cashel and Emly had been given 26 years and 12 years respectively to recover from his atrocious mismanagement. Although this development was far too late to influence the conversion of the local population, the Protestant parishioners subsequently enjoyed a more ample complement of beneficed clergy – the majority of whom were resident – and, also the assistance of a number of curates, by virtue of numerous royal presentations. The increase in the New English Protestant population of South Tipperary, which commenced in the 1610s, aided the attraction of increasing numbers of university-educated clergy from England, the closest links being with western districts of Cheshire, Wales, Devon and Cornwall.[52] The growth in the supply of university educated clergy in late sixteenth and early seventeenth-century England transformed Ireland into a career opportunity for many clergy. Ireland provided a ready source of parishes and experience for graduate ministers, particularly the less qualified reading ministers, who, faced with increasing competition from university graduates, found preferment difficult in England.[53] The extended families of the Irish clergy also benefited, as in the case of John Bayae, who having 'spent three years in the service of his uncle [Malcolm Hamilton] the archbishop of Cashel', now 'hopes to go to France to learn the use of arms and the French tongue'.[54]

The contribution of Trinity College, Dublin was initially on a small scale, having suffered severely in the Nine Years War (1594–1603), losing rents from its outlying estates. Even by 1615, only 23 graduates were serving in the 24 dioceses of Ireland covered by the royal visitation.[55] However, the potential which the college had for supplying future needs was indicated by the number of students – usually untrained but intended for the ministry – who were supported at Trinity by benefices without cure in their native dioceses. This provided a means by which a bishop could educate a new generation of native Protestant clergy.[56] Together with the influx of English clergy, this had the effect that by the 1630s, vicars and rectors increasingly held a university degree. While many clerics continued to hold more than one benefice, the likelihood of their being conveniently situated in an adjoin-

Emly and rector of Toem; *1624*: Richard Butler, rector of Kilronan; **Charles I (1625–49)** *1625*: John Fitzgerald, treasurer of Cashel; *1629*: William Stapleton, rector of Kilvemnon; *1634*: Murtagh Byrne, curate of Donaghmore, Kiltegan and St John Baptist Grange; Robert Browne MA, rector of Mealiffe, curate of Athassel and Kilfeakle; Henry Kelly, curate of Gaile; Farrol Kelly, curate of Ballingarry and Killenaule; *1637*: Andrew Hayes MA, rector of Tipperary: see Seymour, *Cashel and Emly*; Rennison, *Succession list*. **50** Percival-Maxwell, *The Irish rebellion of 1641*, 23; Ford, *The Protestant Reformation*, 116–7, 148–9. **51** Phair, 'Seventeenth century regal visitations', 82–3; Ford, *The Protestant Reformation*, 100. **52** Ford, *The Protestant Reformation*, 100. **53** Ibid., 73–4. **54** Letter from [David] Watson to Sir John Maxwell, 10 January 1635, T-PM/113/252: Maxwell of Pollok papers, Strathclyde Regional Archives, Glasgow, in B. Donovan and D. Edwards: *British sources for Irish history, 1485–1641* (1997), 316. **55** TCD MS 1066. **56** Ford, *The Protestant Reformation*, 77–8.

ing parish was extremely high. These unions of parishes were often necessitated by their relative poverty, as in 1616, when the parishes of Clonmel, Cahir and Grangemockler were united under John Alden for this reason.[57] Even in the 1630s this practice continued, with Hugh Gore installed as vicar of the adjoining parishes of Inishlounaght, Neddans and Ballybacon in 1635 and subsequently made vicar of Inishlounaght, Cahir and Clonmel in 1638.[58]

The royal visitations were conducted in an effort to ascertain church property, order the activities of the higher and lower clergy, and thereby strengthen the Established Church. They operated at uneven intervals and did not always command the full support and co-operation of secular officials. However, they do point to a far greater tightening of the organization of the Established Church, under royal direction, as part of central government policy. The visitations of 1607 and 1615 differ from that of 1588 and from those conducted post-1660, in that they were made by commissioners appointed by the king to enquire into the state of particular dioceses. Those of 1588 and post-1660 were episcopal visitations by bishops of their particular dioceses and obviously had a far smaller coverage than did the royal visitations. In the complete absence of other records, this series of early seventeenth-century royal visitations provides valuable information on the clergy and organization of the Established Church. They reveal, for instance, that prior to the disturbances of 1641, political circumstances operated adversely for its office holders, limiting their effectiveness in enforcing uniformity, and that the state was gradually obliged to countenance the existence of officials of the Roman Catholic Church, wherever it was possible to establish their independence of papal activities in secular affairs. The depositions and examinations taken after the 1641 rebellion provide further evidence of this.

The doctrinal and ideological unity of the early seventeenth-century Established Church played an important role in fostering a distinct Protestant 'self-image'. Archbishop James Ussher, whose *Discourse* was of singular importance in the construction of a suitable origin legend, with others, sought a distinct identity for Irish Protestants, which recognized their minority status and gave rise to a sense of communal solidarity. The means used by preachers was biblical analogy, where England and Ireland were equated to Judah and Samaria and some clergy identified the New English in Ireland with the Israelites, God's chosen people. The Irish could be castigated as worshippers of false Gods, like the nations that the Israelites encountered in the chosen land and since the New English in Ireland dwelt among a Roman Catholic majority population, their position could be further equated to the Israelites living among the heathens.[59] The history of the Israelites afforded Archbishop Malcolm Hamilton of Cashel with abundant proof of the danger of tolerating 'popish idolatry', when he railed against the tendency of Charles I to move towards tolerance of Roman Catholicism in Ireland, exhorting his Majesty

57 Burke, *Clonmel*, 285.   **58** Rennison, *Succession list*, 114; 121; 122; 130; 154; 157. After the Restoration, Gore became successively treasurer of Lismore (1662–4); dean of Lismore (1664–6) and bishop of Waterford and Lismore (1666–91).   **59** Ford, *The Protestant Reformation*, 191–2.

to have a special care of the suppression of idolatry in all your kingdoms, but in special in Ireland where it reigns as a sin that rent the kingdom of David in sunder [and] where all the realm is full of altars not to the worship of God but to Baal. [Although] the whole realm swarms with priests, yet at last I doubt not but that a number will come to our church; and when they have tasted of the sweetness of the word of truth one shall draw another as Philip did Nathaniel.[60]

The situation of the Church as a 'chosen people' by leading members of its hierarchy helped solidify its position *vis-à-vis* Roman Catholicism in the battle for hegemonic supremacy in the hearts and minds of the whole population on the island of Ireland. Its prospects had been seriously harmed by Counter-Reformation preaching, the transfer of allegiance of many of its Gaelic Irish and Old English clergy to Roman Catholicism and its increasing association with the New English colonial project in Ireland. Its unwieldy territorial structures and the abuses of clergy such as Miler Magrath served both to disable the reformed church financially and to make it visibly unattractive to the ordinary people. Yet while the Church failed as a missionary church in this period, its major achievement lay in the creation of a Protestant church and a Protestant community with a clearly defined sense of identity. In addition, elements of reform and improved territorial distribution were becoming apparent by the 1630s as it emerged from the doldrums, stronger in membership as a result of the ongoing plantation of Munster.

---

60 TCD MS 1188, cited in Ford, *The Protestant Reformation*, 211.

4

Conquest and reaction: the plantation of Munster and the 1641 rebellion

When the Desmond rebellion of 1579–83 ended with the killing of the earl of Desmond, the English administration believed it to be the end of unrest in the province of Munster and therefore a prime moment for the establishment of a super-imposed plantation settlement of loyal English subjects. The extension of the plan-tation system through large parts of Ireland was seen as 'the only ordinary means to reduce the people to civility and religion … [they] tend to bring law and order, to banish Irish customs [and] to disappoint foreign expectations.'[1] By 1584, the province of Munster was subdued, leaderless and much depopulated.[2] The vast acreage of the rebel leaders, most notably the earl of Desmond, was divided among individuals known as undertakers, in lots consisting of 4,000 to 12,000 acres. Over half a million acres of Desmond lands were available and it was against this back-ground that the earliest phases of the plantation of Munster were implemented.

Planters in Munster were prohibited from retaining Gaelic Irish occupiers on their estates, because it was thought that intermixture of the existing population with the New English would endanger the future of the colony. Intending settlers were required to take up residence in nucleated communities 'without interrup-tion or intermixture of others'; land was to be leased only to those 'born of English parents'; heirs female were permitted to marry only 'those born of English parents or children of patentees'; the employment of Irish servants was forbidden and it was specifically decreed that 'none of the mere Irish … shall be maintained or per-mitted in any family there'.[3] A completely separate society was thus envisaged for Munster, an apartheid system with the settlers informed from the outset of oppo-sition 'by the savage people of the country, being stronger than the inhabitant English, [so that] the enterprise may be easily quailed'.[4] In almost every plantation in Ireland, however, these regulations set out in theory were disregarded in prac-tice: some inter-marriage occurred and the Gaelic Irish were extensively used as tenants, a situation unavoidable given the shortfall of New English immigrants from the numbers originally expected.

Many of the Old English and Gaelic Irish gentry of Munster remained loyal throughout the Desmond rebellion of the 1580s and were thereby exempt from confiscation of lands. Some families conformed to the Established Church and inter-

---

1 R. Dunlop, 'The plantation of Munster, 1584–89' (1888), 250. 2 C. Lennon, *Seventeenth century Ireland* (1994). 3 Grant of the queen to the undertakers, 27 June 1586; Act for Planting of Habitations in Munster, 21 December 1585, cited in N.P. Canny, 'Dominant minorities: English settlers in Ireland and Virginia, 1550–1650' (1978), 53. 4 Ibid.

married with English planter families which, combined with the capabilities of the court of wards as an instrument of conversion, ensured that some old land-owning families had, by the mid-seventeenth century, become virtually indistinguishable from the New English in outlook and behaviour. The most notable conquest of the court of wards – whose dual purpose involved the winning of Roman Catholic heirs to Anglicanism as well as providing suitable husbands for the daughters of Protestants – was James Butler, who succeeded as 12th earl of Ormond in 1633. Some other families conformed independently, an outstanding example of assimilation being the core O'Brien of Thomond dynasty, which by the early decades of the seventeenth century identified so completely with the Protestant cause as to permit their younger sons enlist in the United Provinces army against Spain.[5] These were the 'in between' people, among a minority of Protestants with a Gaelic Irish heritage, as were also the Ormond Butlers from the Old English perspective. The Thomond family in particular were ardent supporters of the plantation of New English Protestants, undertaking to establish settlers on their vast estates, a portion of which lay within the western extremity of South Tipperary, centred on Cullen.[6] These and other dynasties, while keeping some of the old ways (which in the case of Thomond included the patronage of Gaelic bards) increasingly associated with the Protestant landed families that had arrived in Munster with the plantations and increasingly assumed significant roles in the New English-led administration of Ireland, at both local and national level.

The surveying of lands for the plantation of Munster commenced in 1584 and between 1587 and 1595, 35 undertakers were successful in taking out letters patent for estates. Little initial progress was made, which undermined the settlement from the outset and allowed many former occupants to re-establish themselves, usually as tenants of the head-landlord in the immediate vicinity of their own former estate.[7] The New English settlers in Munster found not a wilderness, but rather a populated waste land and although the existing inhabitants could be and were enlisted as subtenants, their presence, counter-claims and resentment made for confusion, which would soon promote strife.[8] The only barony of South Tipperary to come within the Munster plantation was that of Clanwilliam – in consequence of having been part of the forfeited Desmond estates – so that it was very much on the periphery of the overall plantation, constituting one entire seignory and a portion of a second. The seignory of Swiffin,[9] in the parish of Kilshane, near Tipperary, comprised some 3,000 acres allocated to the earl of Ormond as undertaker. It was a minor seignory, less attractive to Protestant settlement than the 11,000 acres of Sir Edward Fitton of Cheshire, centred on Knockaney, Co. Limerick, 4 ploughlands of which lay within South Tipperary, around the castle and lands of Cullen.[10] Fitton was also granted the castles and lands of Ballynecourty,

5 Canny, 'Why the Reformation failed in Ireland', 441. 6 Idem, *Making Ireland British*, 94; 99–100; 430. 7 See D.J. Butler, 'Butler of Rouskagh, Co. Tipperary' (2003); idem, 'House of Rouskagh' (2003). 8 Dunlop, 'The plantation of Munster', 250–69. 9 The seignory of Swyfien (Swiffin), alias Mounte Ormonde, was granted to Thomas, earl of Ormond and Ossory, on 26 April 1586: see *Chancery Inquisition 67–72, James I*, no. 13, cited in GO (Blake-Butler) MS 12,025. 10 M. MacCarthy-Morrogh, *The Munster plantation* (1986), 258.

Clonbeg and Dungrud in the Glen of Aherlow, one ploughland.[11] In the secondary plantation scheme of 1594–7, a George Sherlock was granted a moiety of
Cleghile and Corroge, near Tipperary town, while the newly founded Trinity
College, Dublin was granted one carucate of land in Aherlow, in addition to lands
near Knockaney.[12]

The extent of New English settlement in South Tipperary during the late 1590s
is unknown, but is certain to have been scattered by the failed Desmond rebellion
of 1598–9 under James *fitz*Thomas, the Sugaun earl, under whom the Fitzgeralds
and their retainers made one final effort to regain their lands. Sir Edward Fitton,
undertaker of Knockaney and Cullen, fled to England with many of his settlers.
Many minor Old English and Gaelic Irish landed families were guilty of involvement, but were given a general pardon in the fiants of Elizabeth in order to reduce
the impossible financial burden of maintaining order in Ireland. The unrest of the
late 1590s was, however, also responsible for the introduction of some Protestant
dynasties to South Tipperary, as in the case of Thomas Baker, who had come to
Ireland with the Sussex expedition of 1599. In 1603, he settled at Knockordan
Castle, west of Tipperary town, leasing 324 acres from a son of Archbishop Magrath
at Ardavullane.[13]

Order was fully restored in Ireland during the course of 1603, in the wake of
which the gradual tightening of New English control in the provinces became
increasingly apparent. The town has generally been regarded as a significant agent
of colonization: in Ireland, towns bear the imprint of a succession of colonists from
the counties of Britain. The many charters issued in the first quarter of the seventeenth century in particular ensured the creation of parliamentary boroughs in
areas of considerable New English settlement, while efforts were intensified to
return Protestant members for the more established walled settlements. From the
first decade of the century, patents were also granted for the establishment of fairs
and weekly markets, often linked to landed estates, for which reason Ireland is rich
in planned towns and villages.[14] Some sixteen fairs were patented in South
Tipperary between 1607 and 1640, the majority of which were founded by Old
English and Gaelic Irish landowners. From 1615, however, New English Protestants
founded virtually all fairs, with the earliest patents taken out in south-western Iffa
and Offa barony. In that year, Sir Patrick Murry and his wife, Elizabeth, took out
a fair patent for their lands at Ballyboy, near Clogheen; in 1619, Sir William Fenton
of Mitchelstown took out a patent for the holding of a fair at Drohid, or 'the
bridge' over the river Owentar at Shanrahan, between modern-day Clogheen and
Ballyporeen.

By the 1610s, the hinterland of Tipperary also contained a considerable body
of New English Protestant farmers, tradesmen and labourers, particularly at Cullen,
Corroge, Aherlow and Toem. In December 1608, the freehold of Cullen Castle
and estate, formerly part of the Fitton seignory, was granted by James I to the earl

11 Seymour, *Diocese of Emly*, 188.   12 Ibid.   13 See *A history of a Tipperary parish: Lattin-Cullen*.   14
Jones-Hughes, 'A historical geography of Ireland, *c*.1700', 157. A full post-1600 listing is provided in
app. II.

of Thomond at an annual rental of £9. In 1611 this was increased to £12, which combined with the desire of Thomond to settle his estates with Protestants, led to Cullen being leased to William Warter. As head-tenant, Warter resided at Cullen Castle and leased some 5,500 acres at Cullen and Emly. Another tenant, Thomas Baker of Knockorden Castle, leased 1,000 acres at Solloghodbeg.[15] The accompanying economic growth is indicated by the foundation of two fairs in this western corner of South Tipperary: in 1627 at Toem and in 1634 at Cullen.

The Ormond seignory of Swiffin was among a minority of lands consistently omitted from population estimates of the Munster plantation, perhaps as a result of its peripheral status,[16] the exception being the military service 'muster roll of 1611', in which ten men are returned as fit for duty, indicative of the presence of perhaps ten New English households on that estate.[17] Swiffin remained in the hands of its original grantee, 'that gleaming product of the court of wards' transforming abilities – the loyal and Protestant 12th earl of Ormond'.[18] In an indication of the completeness of his conversion, Ormond later observed that his

> father and mother lived and died papists and bred their children so and only I, by God's merciful providence, was educated in the true Protestant religion, from which I never swerved towards either extreme, not when it was most dangerous to profess it and most advantageous to quit it.[19]

Ormond and his English-born countess were categorized by ethnicity in the 'civil survey' itself. In the index, however, Ormond was classed as 'Irish papist', though a Protestant, while his wife was correctly seen as 'English Protestant'. The need felt by Ormond to state his absolute faith in Protestantism came not only from his 'papist' ancestry, but also from the fact he was seen as 'a malignant in the eyes of the state'.[20]

The evidence of the 'civil survey' allows an examination of the extent and location of Protestant landownership in South Tipperary in 1640 on the eve of the rising of 1641–2, providing as it does the names of landowners, the extent of their holding and its annual valuation. The distribution of Protestant lands in South Tipperary on the eve of rebellion is illustrated in map 6.

Some 57,000 acres lay in Protestant hands by 1640, divided among 21 estates, with particular concentrations of acreage at Emly, in the extreme west; at Shanrahan and Templetenny, in the south-west; and at Kilcooley, in the north-east of the

---

15 *History of a Tipperary parish: Lattin-Cullen*; Baker's descendants hold the distinction of longest known continuous New English residency in South Tipperary (since 1599), having purchased their present residence at Lismacue, Bansha in 1703. **16** Population enquiries of 1589 and 1592 and commissions of 1611 and 1622, in MacCarthy-Morrogh, *Munster plantation*, 293–6. **17** *Cal. Carew MSS, 1603–24*, cited in ibid., 295–6. **18** MacCarthy-Morrogh, *Munster plantation*, 244; R.B. MacCarthy, *A short history of the Church of Ireland* (1995), 39. This was a specific mechanism whereby one skilfully acquired possession of property by procuring the grant of legal guardian (or wardship) to heirs to estates who were in their minority. **19** Ormond, cited in MacCarthy, *Church of Ireland*, 39. **20** Argument presented by K.W. Nicholls in his paper 'The other massacre: English killing of Irish, 1641–8' to the conference *Age of massacres*, 20 April 2002.

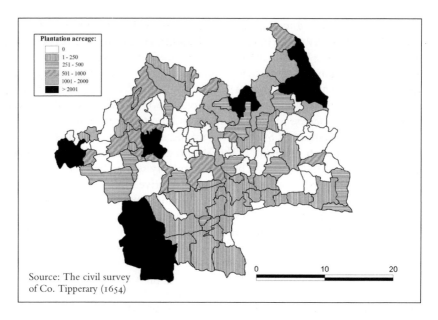

Plantation acreage:
0
1 - 250
251 - 500
501 - 1000
1001 - 2000
> 2001

0   10   20

Source: The civil survey
of Co. Tipperary (1654)

Map 6: New English land ownership, 1640

county. This acreage was distributed among the five baronies of South Tipperary
as follows: 2,500 acres in Kilnamanagh, 15,000 acres in Slieveardagh, 8,000 acres in
Iffa and Offa, 9,000 acres in Middlethird and a massive 22,000 acres in the western
barony of Clanwilliam. Much of these lands were held by the non-resident earl and
countess of Ormond, who personally owned more than half of the Protestant lands
of South Tipperary, so that three-quarters of these lands were held *in absentia*.

Leases of lands of the Established Church contributed significantly to Protestant
estates and this post-Reformation takeover of the parochial glebe lands was responsible for the earliest scattering of new immigrants into the county, most especially
in northern Tipperary.[21] As deposition analysis later reveals, there was a deliberate
introduction of New English tenants by both old and new landowners in the pre-
1641 period. Some 2,800 acres lay directly in the hands of members of the
Established Church hierarchy and parochial clergy, while a further 3,400 acres were
sub-let to New English Protestant tenants. Leases were also successfully competed
for by Roman Catholics, with a significant 2,400 acres distributed between a few
Old English and Gaelic Irish dynasties still maintaining a special relationship with
the Established Church. The largest single holding, comprising 1,000 acres at
Killaldriff in the parish of Killardry, was leased to Edward Butler of Ballydrehid,
while another Roman Catholic, Magrath of Glean, a direct descendant of
Archbishop Miler Magrath, leased 700 acres from the diocesan chapter at Emly.
The other Roman Catholic landholders were spread around Cashel district, viz.
Edward Stapleton: 301 acres; James Sall: 176 acres; Richard Haly: 176 acres; Pierce

21 Smyth, 'Property, patronage and population', 133.

Butler of Shanballyduff: 37 acres; and Cahir, viz. Sir Robert Walsh, John Sherlock esq. and Pierce Sherlock: 30 acres.[22] The Established Church estates were pre-dominantly located in the hinterland of Cashel, where the largest New English leaseholder, Sir William Fenton, held 345 acres at Knockgraffon, with significant lettings assigned to William Kingsmill (341 acres) and William Young at Cashel (176 acres), to Robert Powell near Fethard (294 acres) and to the earl of Cork, whose 150 acres were distributed throughout South Tipperary.[23]

A highly significant portion of New English lands came from leases and mort-gages given by Gaelic Irish chiefs and also by some Old English dynasties in need of ready funds, for

> the extension of the common law system of property rights to Ireland turned land into a marketable commodity, powerfully standardized land-measures and landholding arrangements island-wide and made central the concept of private property. As an integral part of the new estate system, the leasing contract became a powerful instrument for regularizing and reordering life and land use in the townlands.[24]

New law thus became a central component of colonization and state expansion, with wholesale undermining of legal titles to land held by the old elites resulting in the augmentation of the new estates of many ruthless and enterprising colonists. The situation in South Tipperary is best clarified through baronial analysis.

In Clanwilliam barony, Thomas Baker of Knockorden held over 1,000 acres in the parishes of Lattin and Solloghodbeg from the Heffernan and Magrath clans of those respective parishes. Other leaseholders included Gamaliel Warter, who leased 800 acres from Ryan of Solloghodbeg and Sir Hardress Waller of Kilmallock, who held 180 acres by mortgage from Burke of Shanballymore, in addition to extensive holdings from the Ormond estate.[25] Clanwilliam had, of course, been partially included in the Munster plantation and, therefore, was subject to the estab-lishment of New English landowners from the late sixteenth century. As a result of this, it subsequently contained half of all Protestant lands in South Tipperary, across 11 estates.[26] New English inhabitants of the town of Cashel, in the adjoin-ing Middlethird barony, were also establishing greater influence in Clanwilliam in the pre-1641 period. James Hamilton, son of the Anglican archbishop of Cashel, had procured leases of the tithes and affiliated religious lands of Donohill by 1640, while George Conway had similarly acquired those of Ballintemple, Kilpatrick, Moyaliff and Oughterleague.[27]

In Iffa and Offa barony, most Protestant lands were held on lease from the bishop of Waterford and Lismore, with two significant exceptions: Thomas and John Grove of Rochestown held 464 acres at Derrygrath and Rochestown from Wyse of Waterford and 200 acres at Kilsheelan from Shea of Kilkenny, both Roman Catholic

22 'Civil survey', ii, 363–8; 376–84. **23** Ibid., 376–84; 403–12. **24** Smyth, 'Ireland, a colony', 164; L.M. Cullen, *The emergence of modern Ireland* (1981), 109–39. **25** 'Civil survey', ii, 13, 48–52, 55, 59–60, 65. **26** Ibid., ii, 6, 8–10, 13–14, 17, 19–20, 22, 24–8, 38–9, 42, 48–9, 51–2, 55–6, 59–61, 363–4. **27** Ibid., 82, 86–7, 90, 105.

merchants; Robert Cox of Bruff, an absentee landowner, held 346 acres on mortgage from Keating of Moorstown at Inishlounaght, Derrygrath and Cahir.[28]

In the barony of Middlethird, William Kingsmill held over 570 acres at
Ballysheehan and Erry on mortgage from Sall of Cashel. The head of the Hackett
clan mortgaged some 700 acres at Ballysheehan and Kilconnell to Sir Philip Percival,
who also held over 2,000 acres between leases at Rathlennon, in Clanwilliam
barony, from the earl of Thomond and Richard Butler of Kilcash and at Clogher
and Clonoulty, in Kilnamanagh barony, from O'Dwyer of Ballagh.[29] In addition,
the Percival lands at Killenaule and Lismortagh, comprising some 500 acres, were
leased from the crown following forfeiture by their original Gaelic-Irish owner,
William Brett of Lismortagh, for an act of war on his neighbour, which was turned
to the advantage of the New English administration. The 'civil survey' noted his
trial 'at an assize held at Clonmell about the year 1634 for treason in burning the
dwelling house of Patrick Kearney of Knockanglass and [he] was condemned and
executed for the same'.[30] Percival was well positioned to build up an extensive network of such properties throughout Ireland, particularly in Cork, Tipperary and
Waterford, via the remunerative and influential positions he held in the New
English administration. His father, Richard, was appointed as the initial clerk of
the Irish court of wards in 1616, having been an official in the English court of
wards prior to that. He himself was clerk and registrar of the court of wards in
Ireland, clerk of the crown and keeper of the public accounts from 1628.[31] In
Tipperary, he purchased, leased and acquired the mortgages and wardships of exten-
sive lands throughout the county.[32]

The acquisition of ancestral lands by advantageous lease and mortgage from economically vulnerable Gaelic Irish clans was thus a significant territorial strategy,
responsible for the settling of the majority of New English from the 1610s in South
Tipperary. From the late sixteenth century, it had been argued that New English
interests in Munster would be most readily strengthened by the advancement of
the newcomers 'into the Irish areas by way of mortgages, "for those Irish lords are
in great poverty and want" and the settlers, by that policy, win still upon them
without force'.[33] The expansion of the court of wards from 1622 saw a further deterioration in the position of the Old English and Gaelic Irish in the unplanted counties of Ireland, including Tipperary. Wardships were increasingly granted to officials of the court of wards, at the cost of many Old English families.[34] The Irish
custom of mortgages thus proved advantageous to the 'moneyed newcomers' and
by the late 1630s, the rate of this type of land acquisition was clearly accelerating,
which played a part in the build-up of animosities prior to the outbreak of rebellion in 1641. This is typified by Greenvil Halls, who in 1638 obtained an 80-year
lease of almost 900 acres from the O'Dwyers in the south of Clonoulty parish, on
payment of a fine of £200. This he later assigned to another New English

28 Ibid., i, 273, 320 (Grove); 311, 318, 361 (Cox). 29 Ibid., ii, 13, 95, 101–2. 30 Ibid., 384, 399.
31 H.F. Kearney, 'The court of wards and liveries in Ireland, 1622–41' (1955–6); idem, *Strafford in
Ireland*, 18; 44. 32 'Civil survey', ii, 8, 13–14, 95, 101–2, 359, 384, 399. 33 MacCarthy-Morrogh,
Munster plantation, 81. 34 Kearney, *Strafford in Ireland*, 18–19; Canny, *Making Ireland British*, 430–1.
35 'Civil survey', ii, 94–5; ibid., 81–2.

landowner, Anthony Shercliffe of Cork, who subsequently rented out the lands to the inhabitants for a specified annual rent.[35]

The increasing economic exclusion of the Gaelic Irish and Old English by a New English immigrant ascendancy aggressively exploiting the newly-established free market in land, together with expanding New English influence at local and national level in the early seventeenth century, laid the groundwork for unrest and renewed rebellion in 1641.[36] The Elizabethan military conquest and reinforcement of English authority in Ireland, complete by 1603, accommodated the more exclusivist form of colonial government that was to emerge in the early seventeenth century. In this period, 'a narrower definition of 'Englishness' emerged, from which the [Roman] Catholic Old English [and Gaelic Irish] were clearly excluded'.[37] In the aftermath of the Elizabethan conquest, the gradual growth in a market economy and the volume of trade along with the development of a more significant urban network were the principal indices in the pattern of reform, improvement and expansion of English settlement in the early decades of the seventeenth century.[38]

A collective identity was constructed between the Gaelic Irish and Old English, particularly in the early decades of the seventeenth century, which was further facilitated by a sense of shared history, geographical contiguity and intermarriage.[39] Many Old English landed families intermarried significantly with Gaelic Irish dynasties and by the seventeenth century, the two were influencing each other in many aspects of political, economic and social life, in what has been termed 'a mature stage of Anglo-Norman accommodation to Gaelic social norms'.[40] Origins and history became a political tool utilized by contemporary historians in the construction of identity, most notably by Geoffrey Keating in his influential and widely read *Foras Feasa ar Éirinn*, completed *c*.1633, which constructed an explicitly Irish Roman Catholic identity. Keating successfully integrated the Old English into the Irish national myth and identity and his interpretation of the past gave an honoured antiquity to contemporary reforms in the Roman Catholic Church, while demonstrating to the Old English that they had more in common with the Gaelic Irish than with the New English. The former had been the dominant English interest in Ireland at the start of the seventeenth century, but were increasingly sidelined by New English interests from the 1610s; Keating was crucial to their contesting, jointly with the Gaelic Irish, the growing New English hegemony. The work of Keating – a secular priest trained in the Irish colleges on the Continent and based in South Tipperary during the first half of the seventeenth century – enjoyed 'unrivalled popularity among all elements of the Catholic community in Ireland'.[41] Combined with the activities of Counter-Reformation clergy in the province, this renewal of identity by the Roman Catholics 'indirectly fostered a sentiment of

36 Argument presented by M. Ó Siochrú and J. Morrill, during their joint paper 'The Cromwellian massacres: the English and Irish experience' to the conference *Age of massacres*, 20 April 2002. **37** S.G. Ellis, *Tudor Ireland* (1985), 319. **38** Cullen, *Modern Ireland*, 26. **39** See Butler, 'House of Rouskagh', for a case-study of this inter-marriage between the ethnic groups. **40** M. Caball, 'Faith, culture and sovereignty' (1998), 130. **41** B. Cunningham, 'Seventeenth century interpretations of the past: the case of Geoffrey Keating' (1986), 126; eadem, *World of Geoffrey Keating* (2000); Caball, 'Faith, culture and sovereignty', 137.

opposition to New English Protestantism, in so far as their Catholicism laid open the Gaelic Irish and Old English to discrimination on religious grounds'.[42] The significance of the emerging sense of integrated identity being diffused by Keating and others, with its inherent nationalism and Counter-Reformation influences, was that it increasingly served to distinguish and differentiate the Gaelic Irish and Old English 'papists' from the New English community and administration. By 1618, Co. Tipperary was already feared by the New English administration as 'the usual rendezvous of priests and Jesuits and other ill-affected persons'.[43]

By the beginning of the seventeenth century 'the stage was set [in Ireland] for new endeavours as colonization became big business, involving large investments of capital, goods, people, livestock and ideas'.[44] The scale and power of the immigrant thrusts was such that it is entirely possible that, by the late 1630s, the increasing number of New English settlers in Ireland had forced the marginalization of both the Irish elites and the country people to a critical new threshold.[45] Religious conflict was raging across Europe at this time, a period when identities locally in Ireland were being forged around either a New English Protestant colonial or a Counter-Reformation Irish Roman Catholic ethos. The situation pertaining to Ireland can be compared only to Bohemia, where 'a land-owning class of one religion was substituted for another and thorough religious change occurred', for the New English who oversaw and inhabited Ireland regarded events there as 'another act in the same drama which had already been played in Central Europe with such dire results'.[46] Roman Catholics and Protestants in Ireland were both profoundly influenced by the radical changes of European history, in its seventeenth-century configurations and subsequently, by the clashing dynastic and political systems as well as intellectual and confessional confrontations, for the 'climate [was one] where all issues of the day were tinged with religion, [which they in turn] themselves touched and modified'.[47] The bitterness of 1641 and its aftermath arose, at least partially, from these deep structural tensions.

Closely related to this increasingly tense situation was the government initiated 'commission for the remedy of defective titles', established by James I in 1606,

> which on pain of fine or forfeiture, required all Irish landowners to prove their title to their land … The failure of many to do so resulted in the wholesale redistribution of lands in Wexford, Leitrim, Longford and other areas of the midlands between 1610 and 1620, while after 1635 this was extended to Clare, Connaught and the lordship of Ormond with a view to planting these areas with [New] English colonists.[48]

Such plantation strategies subsequently had a dramatic impact on the actions of established Gaelic Irish and Old English landowners through the early decades of the sev-

42 Cunningham, 'Native culture and political change in Ireland, 1580–1640' (1986), 170.   43 *Cal. SP (Ireland), 1615–25*, 217.   44 W.J. Smyth, 'The western isle of Ireland' (1978), 5.   45 Smyth, 'Ireland, a colony', 163.   46 T. Barnard, 'Crises of identity among Irish Protestants, 1641–85' (1990), 44.   47 R.J.W. Evans, *The making of the Habsburg monarchy* (1979), 69–70, 196–7.   48 J.H. Ohlmeyer, '"Civilizing of those rude partes"' (1998), 139.

enteenth century. The 'tremendous gap' between Munster of the late sixteenth century – as described by members of the first plantation begun in the 1580s – and the
province thirty years later – which was 'favourably and optimistically described' in
contemporary traveller accounts has been commented upon.[49] There was much settlement of Ireland by English immigrants during this period, without official state
direction, and the number of British settlers migrating to Ireland during the first half
of the seventeenth century 'is likely to have been greater than that of the total movement to North America over the same period'.[50] The quest for ownership of land led
to a revolution in Gaelic Irish strategies *vis-à-vis* the New English administration, as
'in order to survive and succeed in a "civilizing" English world and to be considered
"worthy subjects", they had no alternative but to exploit the economic advantages of
the English system of landlord-tenant relations and of a commercial economy'.[51]

   Prior to the plantation of Munster, the representatives of English local and
national government in Ireland had predominantly been Old English country gentlemen and burghers. They comprised virtually all the elected representatives in
the corporations and parliaments of Elizabeth, acquiesced in the dissolution of the
monasteries and generally fought on the side of the government. Throughout,
they remained Roman Catholics and were allowed freedom of worship for the
most part prior to the death of the queen in 1603. The advent of the new settlers
in the plantations changed the political situation, in that a body of Anglo-Irish
landholders was now available whose religion was a guarantee against continental
intrigue and whose very existence depended on maintaining and extending the
New English Protestant interest.[52] Accordingly, power progressively passed to the
New English colonists, who manned the executive, dominated parliament and
filled high offices to the virtual exclusion of the hereditary ruling class. The vice-
president of Munster, in a letter of 1611 to the lord deputy that is particularly illustrative of the growing efforts to ensure the ascendancy of the New English
Protestants, observed that while there was 'hope that one conformable man at the
least will be chosen for the three towns of Youghal, Dungarvan and Dingle' by
their burgesses,

> all the rest are desperate. [In] Tipperary and Cross Tipperary [there is] no
> hope of any Protestant [member. Among the] burgesses for the cities [of]
> Limerick, Waterford, Cork [there is] no hope of any Protestant. [Among
> the] burgesses for the five ancient boroughs [of] Kinsale, Kilmallock,
> Clonmell, Cashel, Fethard [there is] no hope of any conformable [person
> being returned. Among the] burgesses for the new boroughs to be erected,
> viz., Tallow, Mallow, Baltimore, Lismore, Tralee, Ennis and Askeaton, all
> Protestant [members are] expected [and] by this computation, the Protestants
> will be in a majority of six votes …[53]

49 M. MacCarthy-Morrogh, 'The English presence in early seventeenth century Munster' (1986), 173.
50 N.P. Canny, 'Migration and opportunity: Britain, Ireland and the New World' (1985), 30.   51
Ohlmeyer, 'Civilizing of those rude partes', 141.   52 Ford, *The Protestant Reformation*, 225–6.   53 *Cal.
SP (Ireland), 1611–14*, 165; *Cal. Carew MSS, 1603–24*; 136.

The principal consequence of the failure of the Reformation in Tipperary and else-where pre-1641 was that the growing political and administrative hegemony of the New English colonial administration was not underpinned by the consolidation of its intrinsic Protestant ideology in the localities. As early as 1600, the potentially explosive nature of this deficiency was recognized by Sir George Carew, lord pres-ident of Munster, when he resolved to 'handle the matter of religion as nicely as I may … [for] if it do appear in the least that any part of their [the Irish] punishment proceeds for the matter of religion, it will kindle a great fire in this kingdom'.[54] Religion thus became the basic benchmark for determining notions of difference and exclusiveness, from this time forward transcending all other economic, ethnic, or class divisions.[55] It was a conveniently employed distinction between 'colonizer' and 'colonized', or 'the perfect litmus'.[56]

Ireland did not, however, conform to any conventional colonial model. The exclu-sivity of the New English regime – as legitimized on religious grounds – was a con-tinuous, dynamic feature of early modern Irish society, transcending all levels. Notions of English racial and religious superiority were propagated by English officials in a manner that depicted Roman Catholicism as the hated and feared embodiment of 'oth-erness'. Its association with Continental intrigue and interference in internal affairs was continued in discourse by such officials as Davies and Carew, the latter using the exam-ples of Cos. Kilkenny and Tipperary, claiming that the missionary activities of the Jesuits masked a broader design to 'raise up the spirits of the ill-affected to revolt' and to 'assure the coming of Spanish aids'.[57] All of this served to consolidate the perceived relation-ship between Roman Catholicism and treason as the 1641 rebellion approached.[58]

The deteriorating conditions in Munster throughout late 1641 as the popular rebellion spread were documented by Carte, who details the great difficulties encountered by the leading Old English and Gaelic Irish landowners to secure con-trol of their tenants and retainers, noting that

> the gentry of Tipperary, [given the] aptness of the vulgar sort to plunder their English neighbours, laboured all they could within their respective dis-tricts and neighbourhoods to correct their insolence. But notwithstanding all their care, the common sort were so addicted to plunder, that about the 6th of December, they assembled 500 of them together and marched in a body towards Cashel, in order to take the city and pillage the English, but several gentlemen of quality in the county and some of the Roman Catholic clergy of Cashel, hearing of their resolutions, met them in their march and by fair words and sermons, diverted them from that wicked attempt and pre-vailed with them to return, without offering violence to any body.[59]

The gentry sought and obtained an audience with Sir William St Leger, lord president of Munster, where they made determined efforts to present themselves as loyal subjects and

---

54 *Cal. Carew MSS, 1589–1600*, 469–70. 55 D. Cairns and S. Richards, *Writing Ireland* (1988), 19–21.
56 MacCarthy-Morrogh, *Munster plantation*, 282. 57 *Cal. SP (Ireland), 1600–1*, 425. 58 See, for exam-ple, ibid. 59 T. Carte, *The life of James, duke of Ormond*, ii (1851), 266.

told him that they waited upon his lordship to be informed how affairs stood and that they coveted nothing more than to serve his Majesty and preserve the peace; and desired that he would be pleased to qualify them for it with authority and arms, in which case they would not fail to suppress the rabble and secure the peace of the county.[60]

The response of St Leger appeared to reflect the firm exclusiveness of contemporary New English colonial administration in Ireland, for he 'did not receive their representation and offer in the manner they expected; but in a hasty furious manner answered them that they were all rebels and he would not trust one soul of them, but thought it more prudent to hang the best of them'.[61] The severe actions of St Leger, in seeking to maintain order in Tipperary during late-1641, was a factor of central significance in the intensification of the distrust of the New English administration which transcended all levels of society and stimulated outright rebellion. His remarks underline the extent to which the New English distrusted the arming of the Roman Catholic elite and resisted their incorporation into provincial administration, so that by 1641 those professing Roman Catholicism were seen as traitors and rebels. They further served to guarantee the alienation of the Roman Catholic gentry of Munster, who were now assured of their permanent exclusion from provincial government. In many ways, 'after 1641 there was no going back'.[62]

Carte observed that governors in Ireland, such as St Leger, were 'the likeliest persons in it to get by the troubles of the kingdom and to raise their own fortunes by the ruin of those of private gentlemen'. He submits, furthermore, that the Roman Catholics had thereafter every reason to believe that

> the lord justices really wished the rebellion to spread and more gentlemen of estates be involved in it, [so] that the forfeitures might be greater and a general plantation be carried on by a new set of English Protestants all over the kingdom, to the ruin and expulsion of all the Old English and natives that were Roman Catholics.[63]

Due to a lack of evidence, it is difficult to assess further the extent to which such fears reflected a design of the New English administration in Munster to instigate rebellion or general discontent to their own ends. It is, however, possible to analyse the distribution and nature of the outrages perpetrated during the armed revolt that commenced in the province of Ulster on 23rd October and which was in progress in South Tipperary within weeks. The primary record of occurrences during the rebellion is contained in 33 manuscript volumes of depositions and examinations from those affected by the rebellion, predominantly New English Protestants, collected over a period of 12 years from 1642. The volume pertaining to Co. Tipperary contains over 200 depositions and examinations, two-thirds of which were gathered during the 1640s and the remainder in 1652–4 under the Cromwellian admin-

---

60 Carte, *Ormond*, 265–6. **61** Ibid., 266. **62** Conversation with Prof. W.J. Smyth, department of Geography, UCC. **63** Carte, *Ormond*, 263.

istration. Of 133 depositions sworn during the 1640s, 94 were by former residents of South Tipperary and 39 by former residents of the north of the county.[64] Some 80 additional examinations were sworn in 1652–4, so as to obtain additional material from Protestant survivors to secure the guilt of the offenders, while also gaining some Roman Catholic perspective on the events. The depositions themselves are a series of imperfect documents; a catalogue of grievances of the wronged, often unconfirmed and possibly exaggerated claims and allegations of material losses and massacres.[65] It is likely that the sworn depositions contained some errors, owing to bias, defective memory and the lapse of time, but the combined depositions of Protestant clergymen, tenant farmers, respectable tradesmen and members of their households cannot be put aside as intrinsically worthless.

The depositions are eminently useful in research of the distribution of New English settlement in the pre-1641 period and indicate the deliberate introduction of considerable numbers of New English Protestant tenants by both old and new landowners. The modernising Old English families of the Everards in south-west Tipperary, the Ormond Butlers at Swiffin in Clanwilliam and the Ikerrin Butlers in Slieveardagh, as well as a number of New English – such as Fenton at Templetenny, Percival at Ballintemple and Clonoulty, Kingsmill and St Leger at Ballysheehan and Cashel, Warter at Cullen, Waller at Greenane, Esmond at Clonoulty and Baker at Solloghodbeg – had all been responsible for the introduction of new tenants and the initiation of new settlements.[66] Details of the exact period and method of introduction of tenants are sketchy. The July 1642 deposition of William Blake, a miller on the Warter estate at Cullen, reveals him to have been 'an inhabitant of Cullin [sic] the space of 22 years', indicating that he had commenced his mill in about 1620.[67] As a mill was a key economic component of any settlement initiative, it is probable that this date marked the commencement of the colonial development of Cullen by its leaseholder since 1611, William Warter – a settlement that was sufficiently advanced by 1634 to secure the grant of a fair patent.[68] In the barony of Iffa and Offa, Sir Richard Everard had 'before the rebellion planted most of his estate with English tenants',[69] while the granting of fair patents at Ballyboy in 1615 and Drohid in 1619 may be taken as indicative of similar economic development in this area. Depositions were sworn by the representatives of some 28 New English Protestant households associated with the adjoining Everard and Fenton estates around Clogheen and Ballyporeen/Templetenny in south-western Tipperary so that, combined, they equalled in scale the primary centre of pre-1641 Protestant settlement in South Tipperary, at Cullen. The scale of pre-1641 New English immigration into South Tipperary, a predominantly

64 See TCD MS 821: A total of 1414 depositions were sworn by Munster Protestants during the 1640s, of which number, Cork, at 904, contained the largest number from a single Irish county; South Tipperary contained just under one-tenth of the total number: see Canny, *Making Ireland British*, 336. 65 T. Barnard, '1641: a bibliographical essay' (1993), 173–86. 66 See 'civil survey'; also Smyth, 'Property and patronage'. 67 TCD MS 821, fo. 274. 68 See app. II for fair patents; app. IV and V for the ranking and distribution of Protestant landholders. 69 'An account of the rebellion of 1641, written for the duke of Ormond in 1680', cited in T.P. Power, *Land, politics and society in eighteenth-century Tipperary* (1993), 67.

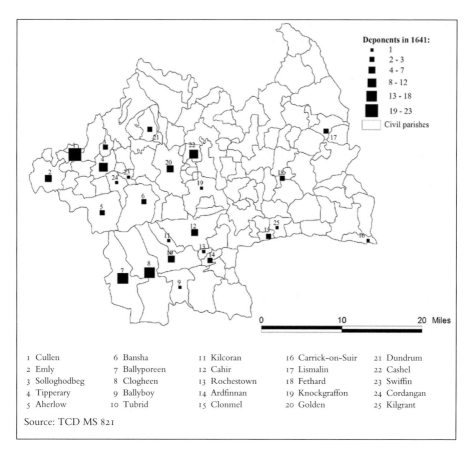

Deponents in 1641:
- 1
- 2 - 3
- 4 - 7
- 8 - 12
- 13 - 18
- 19 - 23
- Civil parishes

1 Cullen	6 Bansha	11 Kilcoran	16 Carrick-on-Suir	21 Dundrum	
2 Emly	7 Ballyporeen	12 Cahir	17 Lismalin	22 Cashel	
3 Solloghodbeg	8 Clogheen	13 Rochestown	18 Fethard	23 Swiffin	
4 Tipperary	9 Ballyboy	14 Ardfinnan	19 Knockgraffon	24 Cordangan	
5 Aherlow	10 Tubrid	15 Clonmel	20 Golden	25 Kilgrant	

Source: TCD MS 821

Map 7: The distribution of Protestant deponents in 1641–2

unplanted area, is indeed striking; and the key elements of an immigrant settler community can be seen to have been established by that time.

The depositions are useful in ascertaining the location of concentrations of Protestants in pre-1641 South Tipperary and also their material possessions and economic attainments. As map 7 illustrates, there is a heavy emphasis on the western half of the county, with some 85 per cent of deponents residing west of centre. East of centre, only a handful of depositions are recorded: the important urban settlements of Clonmel, Carrick-on-Suir and Fethard are between them represented by only six depositions and the total of nine deponents for this eastern half of South Tipperary amounted to just 5 per cent of the depositions registered. The western and south-western districts, in contrast, contained 95 per cent of deponents, centred around a number of foci namely Cullen-Emly, Tipperary-Aherlow and Cashel-Golden in the upper western half; Clogheen-Ballyporeen and Cahir-Tubrid in the lower western half. The most significant result of this analysis of the spatial distribution of deponents is not so much the western prominence, which was not unexpected given the inclusion of Cullen and Tipperary districts as outliers of the

Munster plantation, but rather the equal importance of Clogheen-Ballyporeen to Cullen-Emly, indicative of the extent of New English penetration of unplanted areas at the instigation of their improving landowners.

Many Roman Catholics were extremely well disposed towards their Protestant neighbours and it was with the greatest reluctance that they took up arms against them, even displaying occasional help and compassion during the actual insurrection. The deposition of Lady Barbara Browne, wife of Sir John Browne of Hospital, Co. Limerick, records that she was conveyed to Cork by a convoy under Patrick Purcell, 'with wonderful civility, telling her he had been twice excommunicated before he would take up arms and that he would rather suffer for his religion than act as he did, if he did not think there was the king's authority for it'.[70] Many deponents recorded acts of kindness and mercy by the Roman Catholics, the deposition of Jane Cooper of Cullen noting the kindness of Derby Ryan, who had protected 'the poor innocents' from the orders of Lord Roche to strip and kill them and who 'said he would lose his own blood before one drop of the poor innocents blood should be spilt'.[71] The majority of South Tipperary deponents complained of the illegal removal of cattle and other valuables from deponents, with lengthy accounts of stolen goods and commodities given alongside estimates of their value. The murders that took place were confined to Cullen, Golden and Cashel, all places of strength in the barony of Clanwilliam where Protestant settlers of the surrounding hinterlands had sought shelter. In total, some 70 Protestants were killed in South Tipperary, which victims, in common with most in the south of Ireland, were tenants of Irish landlords who had counted on the protection of overlords and had left it too late to flee to safety.[72]

In Clanwilliam barony, considerable disturbances occurred in the hinterland west of Tipperary, stretching as far as Cullen and Emly, which affected merchants, clergy, tenant farmers and gentry. The Revd Andrew Hayes, rector of Tipperary, Shronell and Cordangan, deposed he was robbed of goods to the value of almost £300, as well as his church livings.[73] Mrs Ann Baker of Knockordan Castle, who was widowed during the disturbances, deposed on behalf of herself and her six children that her husband died after defending their castle against siege for sixteen weeks and that on surrendering the following week, she was robbed of goods amounting to over £7,000 and the family stripped of their clothes.[74]

However, it was in connection with the castle of Cullen that some of the most stirring series of incidents in South Tipperary occurred. At the outbreak of rebellion, Gamaliel Warter was in possession of Cullen Castle, having succeeded to his father's estate some months previously. In the immediate hinterland of Cullen, there was by this time a considerable body of affluent Protestants, comprising retainers of the Warter household and independent farmers and tradesmen who were tenants on the estate. When the disturbances commenced, the settlers acted on the advice of Turlough MacBrien, one of the insurgents, that it would be advisable for

70 Seymour, *Diocese of Emly*, 206. **71** TCD MS 821, fo. 202–3. **72** Argument presented by K.W. Nicholls in his conference paper 'The other massacre', 20 April 2002. **73** TCD MS 821, fo. 33. **74** TCD MS 821, fo. 169–70.

them to take shelter in the castle of Cullen. Accordingly, men, women and children began to flock in from Cullen district, no doubt including adjoining townlands in Co. Limerick, until there were 'about eleven score men, women and children' within the castle and bawn.[75] Cullen was the sixth largest English plantation settlement in a hierarchy of twelve across the Limerick district and seems to have contained an early Protestant dissenting congregation, in that the Revd John Cooper – mentioned posthumously in the deposition of his wife, Jane – cannot be found in Anglican clerical succession lists. His designation as 'minister of the gospel' is further evidence of his dissenting outlook, a term approved of by the Cromwellians.[76] It was noted as early as 1598 of the Munster plantation that there was no control over the religious outlook of the planters, which had resulted in 'English papists, puritans, brownists [and] atheists' settling in the province, thus increasing the likelihood of an Independent congregation at Cullen, the only recorded pre-Cromwellian Protestant dissenting congregation in north Munster.[77]

The village of Cullen, which the 'civil survey' describes as 'a castle in good repair and a mill with several thatched houses inhabited', was scene of arguably the worst atrocities against Protestants in South Tipperary, due mostly to the large number of affluent settlers dwelling in its vicinity. The persons named in connection with the siege of Cullen Castle give some idea of the social strata of the settlement, which comprised

> The Revd John Cooper and his wife, Jane; old Mr Thomas Whitby and his two daughters; William Blake, miller, and his wife, now both at Clonmel; John and Katherine Jones; Richard Ely, merchant, now at Clonmel; William Hibbard; Josias Browne, a blacksmith; Margaret Dixon, thatcher's wife; John Parker and his wife, now at Clonmel; John Coate, a husbandman; Richard Pullin, a sawyer; and divers other Englishmen, women and children.[78]

In the early days of the unrest, not all the settlers barricaded themselves in Cullen Castle and some had remained in nearby houses. In this way, two Englishmen and two Irishmen in charge of Warter's horses were captured – the English were hanged and the Irish let go free.[79] Other cruel acts included the murder of a 7-year-old boy, sent out by the Cullen garrison to obtain tobacco, while carrying a white paper in a cleft stick. Although his safe passage had been guaranteed, the child was seized and on refusing to 'turn to mass', was hanged.[80] The siege would have ended quickly if the attackers had the use of artillery weapons, but their absence led to it lasting some six months. Towards the end, in late July 1642, the attackers withdrew some distance, owing to the tediousness of the siege, thus enabling those within the castle to harvest some of their ripening corn. Emboldened by their success, a party of between 50 and 60 persons went out two days later, but were unex-

75 Ibid., fo. 272.   **76** Ibid., fo. 202; fo. 204: 'an account of the siege of Cullen Castle, written by the late Revd John Cooper, minister of the Gospel and preserved by his wife'.   **77** MacCarthy-Morrogh, *Munster plantation*, 198; 258.   **78** TCD MS 821, fo. 272.   **79** Ibid.; also Seymour, *Diocese of Emly*, 213. **80** Ibid.

pectedly ambushed by the Irish. They managed to kill two rebels, before being forced to flee to the castle, but many English were killed or left for dead during the flight. The total number killed is variously estimated at from 31 to 35 persons, the confusion arising from the 'sixteen or seventeen left for dead', many of whom crawled back to the castle under cover of darkness. Some subsequently died of their wounds, one person having 35 cuts on her. A few days later with supplies exhausted, the garrison surrendered and was conveyed under escort to the English at Cork. The economic losses of the settlers were estimated to be in excess of £14,000, which explains the sustained nature of the siege.[81]

At Goldenbridge, as at Cullen, a large number of English from its hinterland sheltered in and around its castle. In the storming of the castle, after a siege lasting eleven weeks, at least nine of the English were killed, including a child, a heavily pregnant woman and another bedridden with sickness. According to a Roman Catholic account in the Carte manuscripts, some of the English were thrown into a deep hole or pit where they were buried alive and an infant was thrown over the bridge into the river Suir, where it drowned.[82] The community in Golden district was as diverse as at Cullen and the deceased included a shoemaker from Wales, a Scotsman, a dyer, a manservant, a tanner and a lady's maid. At Golden, as elsewhere, intimidation from the Roman Catholic majority won its converts, with the revelation by the Revd Kilby that 'Thomas Phillips, having turned papist, is making powder for the rebels'.[83] Kilby further testified to the statement of 'Fr Thomas Gregory O'Donine', a Dominican of Cashel, who presumably from his knowledge of Continental affairs, on being asked by the rebels as to what should be done with the besieged English, replied 'why to kill them all, for they will never be rid of them in this kingdom, till they take that course, for which we have an example in France in the like, for until the great massacre there, they could never be freed of the heretics'.[84]

Cashel was scene of the third great atrocity against Protestants in South Tipperary. This centrally located walled city in the barony of Middlethird had attracted vulnerable rural Protestants not only from its own hinterland, but also from the western portion of the county as far distant as Cullen, as testified by Gilbert Johnston, who swore that he 'and divers other English Protestants betook themselves for their safeguard into the city of Cashel'.[85] In November 1641, on hearing of the success of the rebellion in other parts of Ireland, insurgents drove cattle and sheep off the lands of New English settlers in the counties of Cork, Waterford and Tipperary. Among those settlers affected was Kingsmill of Ballyowen, north of Cashel and his brother-in-law, St Leger, president of Munster.[86] In retaliation for this act, St Leger had a total of 15 or 16 locals killed without trial between that area and nearby Goldenbridge. On 1 January 1642, by way of revenge, the Irish insurgents massacred some 26 English inhabitants of Cashel. Their number included four officials of the Anglican Church, viz. the Revd Mr John Lowe, rector of Cloneen;

81 TCD MS 821, fos. 265–82; Seymour, Diocese of Emly, 212–14. 82 Ibid., fos. 42–3; 58, 59; see M. Hickson, Ireland in the seventeenth century (1884: 2 vols), ii, 41; 252, for full transcripts. 83 TCD MS 821, fo. 154. 84 Ibid. 85 Hickson, Ireland in the seventeenth century, ii, 40; TCD MS 821, fos. 42–3. 86 TCD MS 821, fos. 229–33.

the Revd Mr John Lindsey, rector of Ballintemple; the Revd Mr Bannister, a cleric
of Cashel; and Mr Carr, schoolmaster of Cashel. The professions of some others
are also given and include those of innkeeper, brewer, cooper, tapster, tyler and
glazier, valuable indicators of the diverse economic composition of the New English
Protestant community in this period.[87]

About 300 New English refugees were sheltering in Cashel, in addition to its
usual number, and most were saved through the mercy of Roman Catholic inhabitants and clergy of the town, who requested safe passage for them to Cork, an
English stronghold. According to the examination of Simon Sall, taken at Clonmel
court in 1652, one Irish man was hanged for the murders of several English at
Cashel, under order of the Irish leaders.[88] In addition, a number of submissions by
the Roman Catholic inhabitants of the Cashel district to his Grace, the duke of
Ormond, survive in the Carte manuscripts.[89] While a slightly different version of
events is offered on occasion, the recollection of both sides largely concur. Most
interesting is the assistance and protection given considerable numbers of the English
by the Jesuit and Franciscan fathers of Cashel. This is attested by a Protestant depon-
ent of Cashel; and one of the Roman Catholic deponents alleged that Fr Redmond
English, a Franciscan, was so zealous in saving the English, he hid some of them
under the altar. This was proved at English's trial during the Cromwellian period;
his life was spared and he was allowed to stay in the district.[90]

Outside of Clanwilliam and Middlethird, the English settlers suffered considerable loss of property through robbery and confiscation, most notably in the barony
of Iffa and Offa. The English tenants of Sir Richard Everard of Clogheen, numbering as many as 88 households, were subjected to economic reduction and intimidation and conveyed to nearby Mitchelstown.[91] Intimidation was widespread in
this barony, with several examples of symbolic battle, most notably in the successful conversion of the Revd Richard Butler, vicar of Kilronan, who 'turned papist'
and Thomas Graves of Tubrid, near Cahir, who had 'gone to mass [and] lives with
the rebels in Rochestown Castle'.[92] At Rochestown there was also a lengthy siege,
although not one that ended in bloodshed. The deposition of Thomas Grove, late
lessee of the castle and lands of Rochestown, located midway between Cahir and
Ardfinnan, is especially revealing of the extent of the uprising of Old English landed
families, in alliance with local Gaelic Irish clans, against the New English Protestant
interest. Grove was a wealthy target, having taken long leases of lands in Cork and
Waterford and at Golden and Rochestown in South Tipperary, while residing constantly at Rochestown Castle. He deposed losses of 60 cows, besides horses and
sheep, money, plate and corn, to an array of local Old English landowners, who
during a five-week siege, 'with divers others to the number of 400',

> deprived the besieged of their water, […] it was above two furlongs [from]
> the house [to the river] and so [the occupants] rebuilt [their supply] by saving

87 Ibid., fos. 223–61. **88** Ibid., fo. 253. **89** See Hickson, *Ireland in the seventeenth century*, ii, 240–56,
for extensive transcripts of Roman Catholic accounts of the events. **90** Ibid., 244; 253. **91** TCD MS
821, fo. 183: deposition of George Tarry; fo. 184: deposition of Christian Jones. **92** Ibid., fo. 67: deposition of Revd Mr Simon Lightfoot; fo. 69: deposition of Revd Mr Charles Prince.

the rain that fell upon the leaden [roof]. [In the] meantime they [the rebels] brought a sow[93] to the bawn wall and having broken it down they approached the castle wall, but those of the castle broke the sow, first with stones, [at] which those that were in it ran away, which afterwards they [the besieged] cut in pieces and burnt [it, …] and recovered the benefit of the water for the first time in this siege […] After a little rest, they were besieged a further five weeks, during which time they sent for respite to the lord president [of Munster] and other garrisons […] and not receiving any aid, being debarred again of their water, were at length forced to yield up the castle of Rochestown upon quarter and were brought to the lord of Cahir's house.[94]

Besides the Grove family, there was a garrison of 9 English men in Rochestown Castle and some 40 women and children, of which 30 were English refugees from the parish of Tubrid. Here, as in the walled towns of Clonmel and Carrick-on-Suir, there was no bloodshed and the rebels conveyed many Protestants to the Cork district, a Protestant stronghold. The majority of those New English remaining came together in Carrick-on-Suir, where 80 were housed in the manor house by the countess of Ormond, herself an English Protestant. From Carrick-on-Suir they were brought in several boats on the river Suir to Waterford, from whence they returned to England.[95]

The depositions reveal an underlying religious and sectarian discourse, which informs research of the nature of the conflict and the rationalization of its excesses. It is significant that in analysis of the depositions at national level, it is the Roman Catholic clergy who are presented as masters in the art of refusal to bury Protestants and participating in, indeed leading, disinterments.[96] Rites of desecration such as refusal of burial to Protestants, the disposal of their corpses, their burial facing downwards and their ejection from consecrated ground, were tactics that derived their effect from the exploitation of core religious beliefs and attitudes. In South Tipperary, no written evidence of these practices exists in the depositions and examinations, though at Clonmel, as in many other corporate towns in the hands of Roman Catholics, it is alleged that Protestants buried in both church and churchyard were exhumed during the 1640s and their remains burnt or thrown into ditches.[97] The inference was that Protestants were to be removed from the company of the righteous, for they had no hope of resurrection. Removal from church and churchyard constituted exclusion from the community and to be excluded from the community was, in effect, to cease to exist. There may be truth in the allegation, for in this decade the bodies of three clerical martyrs were exhumed at the Clonmel Franciscan friary and re-interred at Askeaton, Co. Limerick, in a ceremony indicative of the Roman Catholics determination to cleanse them from contamination by the 'heretics'.

The rising of 1641–2 had considerable implications for the mindset of New English colonists in Ireland. Religious distinction served to heighten political and

---

93 A framework of wood, covered with hides to protect the attackers from overhead assault, used in undermining a wall. **94** TCD MS 821, fo. 56. **95** Power, *South Tipperary*, 67. **96** C.P. Meehan, *The rise and fall of the Irish Franciscan monasteries* (1872), 352. **97** T. Fitzpatrick, *Waterford during the Civil War, 1641–53*, 25.

social tensions, which became re-constituted as a polarized struggle between the basic groups of 'Irish papist' and 'English Protestant', as later delineated, for example, in the 'civil survey'. Such terms were in use at the time of the rebellion, as in a letter of Sir William St Leger to Sir Philip Percival, rebuking those responsible for 'putting the king's arms into the papists' hands' while also assuring him that his castles were 'safe in the hands of honest Englishmen'.[98] Much of the formation of this exclusive identity can be observed from contemporary works, particularly that of Temple, who viewed the 1641 revolt as a sign that the Irish were irredeemable and would always pose a deadly threat to England and its people. The reading public in England were frequently supplied with pamphlets in the early months of the rebellion in 1641–2, which promised 'the latest news from Ireland' and relied upon a small number of particularly gruesome events. These were much recycled with slightly altered titles in order to provide their own perspective.[99] Temple's work on the atrocities committed by the rebels and Irish population at large in the massacre of New English Protestants provided a great deal of new information not contained in the pamphlets of 1641–3 and although the section on atrocities comprises less than a quarter of his partisan book, it largely accounted for the enduring popularity of the work.[1]

The arrival and numerical increase of the New English Protestant community in South Tipperary district, their aim of economic and political ascendancy in assuming the privileges of the ruling landed elite and their increasing exclusiveness and differentiation from the Old English and Gaelic Irish in the three decades prior to 1641, provided the background for the rising of that year. By a variety of ingenious methods – from government commissions into land titles and the securing of guardianship of minors through the court of wards, to well-connected individuals purchasing lands or obtaining mortgages and leases from economically vulnerable landed dynasties – the New English dramatically increased their share of South Tipperary lands between 1620 and 1640. In addition, an increasing number of progressive landholders encouraged the settlement of New English tenants on their estates, so that by 1641, the population and wealth of the New English had reached its greatest level to date.

The all-consuming drive by the New English to govern provincial Ireland and monopolize power through the towns and fortifications, alongside efforts to increase Protestant representation in the ruling administration, placed them as perceived bulwarks of colonial authority and hegemony in the mindset of the Gaelic Irish and Old English and consequently prime targets for attack in the rebellion of 1641.[2] The

98 *Egmont Manuscripts*, i:1, 148; I am grateful to Mr K.W. Nicholls, department of History, UCC for this reference. **99** Examples include, *The last news from Ireland, being a relation of the hostile and bloody proceedings of the rebellious papists there at present*; *A brief declaration of the barbarous and inhumane dealings of the northern Irish rebels* (London, 1641); *A continuation of the Irish rebels proceedings with our victories over them*; *A most exact relation of a great victory obtained by the poor Protestants in Ireland*; *The truest intelligence from the province of Munster* (London, 1642); *The English and Scottish Protestants happy triumph over the rebels in Ireland*; *Joyful and happy news from Ireland* (London, 1643). **1** *The British library general catalogue of printed books* mentions editions of 1646, 1648, 1679, 1713, 1716, 1724, 1746, 1751, 1766, 1776, 1812; Barnard lists further editions of 1674 and 1698, see 'Crises of identity', 55; K.M. Noonan, '"The cruell pressure of an enraged, barbarous people"' (1998), 159. **2** See, for example, TCD MS 821, fos. 7; 234; 255.

increasing economic, social, political and religious exclusion of these two groups is obvious from many of the depositions analysed. This, combined with the heavy-handed reaction of the lord president of Munster to robberies by base elements on his lands in South Tipperary, led the Gaelic Irish and Old English gentry to abandon their strategies of accommodation and facilitation of the New English and unite under the common platform of Roman Catholicism. The murder of Protestants, together with the robbery and expulsion of many others from the county – as detailed by the depositions – was as a result of a partial loss of control by the gentry over their tenants and retainers and the welding together of religion and politics. By 1641, particularly in the wake of the extensive reporting of atrocities perpetrated during the rebellion, Irish 'papist' barbarity was placed as polar opposite to the vaunted 'civility' of Anglican Protestantism, the very essence of Englishness.

5

New English settlement strategies and state-sponsored garrisons

Property in land was the key element of control in the Irish landscape. In 1641, the majority of the land of South Tipperary was in the hands of Roman Catholics, of both Old English and Gaelic Irish ethnicity. The former were particularly concentrated in the fertile central, eastern and southern areas of the county, where high land values and an established tradition of urban settlement and commercial activity prevailed.[1] Protestant landownership in the pre-1641 period was limited, with 21 estates recorded by 1640, the majority of them owned by absentees. New English settlement was consequently sparse and scattered, with a primary concentration in the western half of South Tipperary. This comprised of a few outlying settlements of the Munster plantation, predominantly located between Cullen on the Co. Limerick border and the city of Cashel in the central plain and also a portion of the Everard estate around Clogheen. However, the introduction and promotion of new improving English tenants was not confined to New English landowners, as some Old English Roman Catholic landowners were also involved. The impact of this settlement in the three decades prior to 1640 was disrupted by the 1641 rebellion, which caused a general dispersal of Protestant households. There was, however, considerable continuity from pre-1641, particularly in the rural communities, which received Cromwellian military augmentation during the 1650s.[2]

The Cromwellian settlement had a far greater impact than its predecessors on the landowning class and distribution of Protestants; in large measure, the origins of the eighteenth- and nineteenth-century Protestant landowning class can be traced to the arrival of Cromwellian soldiers, adventurers and entrepreneurs from 1650. The towns and castle garrisons were the foci of this settlement, not only in South Tipperary, but also throughout Ireland. These were perceived bastions of Roman Catholic ideology, central to the control and domination of the majority population and for this reason, they were the primary targets of Cromwell. The early obtaining of the surrender of the walled towns of Cashel and Fethard and the castles of Ardfinnan and Cahir, besides numerous smaller ones, was fundamental to the establishment of the Cromwellian Puritan regime in the South Tipperary district.

Only a handful of Irish walled towns were capable of contesting the Cromwellian military advance, of which the county town of Clonmel was one, withstanding siege for twelve weeks despite a chronic shortage of both men and

1 Smyth, 'Property, patronage and population', 109–14. 2 See P.S. Robinson, *The plantation of Ulster* (1984) for evidence of continuity of pre-1641 settlement in that province, in the aftermath of the rebellion.

ammunition. The 'army muster roll' of January 1650, published by Gilbert, shows about 1,400 men in Clonmel garrison, of which 150 were in out-garrisons at Kilcash, Ballydine and Castle Coonagh. O'Neill had the use of 1,600 men during the siege, of whom one-quarter were armed only with pikes and 200 had no arms whatsoever; the Cromwellians numbered 9,000 men, all well armed and supplied. Both sides comprised seasoned soldiers: the Cromwellian Puritans outside the walls, filled with religious and political fanaticism, had heard for much of the previous decade of the massacre of their fellow Protestants in the rising of 1641–2 and set out to avenge this wrong; the Roman Catholic garrison within Clonmel were Ulstermen especially selected for their willingness to fight for the survival of their religion and way of life.

A variety of tactics were utilized by the Cromwellians to take Clonmel: bribery, terror and force. Firstly, Cromwell's success at bribing Captain Fennell of the Clonmel garrison, a native of the area, was by chance discovered by O'Neill. The plan was to open one of the gates to the Cromwellians, but on finding a completely local garrison on one gate, in spite of his requirement that all be garrisoned in a two-thirds Ulster, one-third local proportion, O'Neill became suspicious and uncovered the plot.[3] Secondly, in an approach designed to terrorize the inhabitants, Nicholas Mulcahy, parish priest of Ardfinnan, was brought before the walls of Clonmel, where he was publicly beheaded for refusing to influence the garrison to surrender.[4] Cromwell finally resorted to military force, turning his arsenal on the town walls. Following five weeks of cannonade, O'Neill had a false cul-de-sac constructed inside the most damaged stretch of walls, within which almost 2,500 Cromwellians were killed upon storming the newly opened breach. However, as ammunition was wanting, O'Neill left the town under cover of darkness, while the mayor negotiated with Cromwell for good conditions for the town, the latter then oblivious to the retreat of O'Neill. On learning of the clever mechanism employed, Cromwell honoured the terms of surrender and there was no massacre to go down in popular martyrology.[5] This was in direct contrast to the town of Drogheda, where Cromwell had made an example of its citizens, in order to ensure compliance elsewhere on the island.

The hard-won Clonmel became the headquarters of a Cromwellian precinct responsible for the administration of the whole of Co. Tipperary. Colonel Jerome Sankey – a former curate of the Church of England, graduate of Cambridge University and ardent evangelical – was installed as county governor, aged 29 years; he founded Clonmel Baptist Church in 1652. Under his direction, priest hunting and sanctions against Roman Catholicism recommenced. The parish priest of Clonmel, Thomas White, was successfully concealed as a servant in the Irishtown house of his kinsman, James Brennock.[6] Others were caught in the year 1650–1; three priests, Miles McGrath, O'Higgins and William O'Connor, were subjected to a public execution at Clonmel, being either beheaded or hanged, the last being stripped naked at his execution.[7] There were also a number of high-profile lay mar-

3 Burke, *Clonmel*, 72. 4 Ibid., 74. 5 Ibid., 65–79. 6 See 'Poll Money Return', in ibid., 252. 7 Ibid., 81.

tyrs. Geoffrey Baron of Clonmel, a leading merchant, when his execution had been decided upon, asked to be allowed return to his house in the town, 'and finding there a new suit of white taffitie, with all the addresses suitable as if to be presently married, adorning himself therewith, rode gallantly ... towards the place of execution'.[8] When asked why he dressed so well for the scaffold, Baron allegedly replied

> that if to marry a creature he did no less and now that he was of belief that his soul departed at this instant from this body, did straight enjoy the pleasures of heaven, in the consummation of the eternal nuptial felicity and to bestow this last livery upon the relict companion of the soul, was the least of his duty.[9]

The speech made from the gallows was central to the system of English execution as an opportunity for the condemned to confess his or her crimes and to display the repentance that might still save their souls, thereby legitimizing both the punishment and the 'whole structure of secular and religious authority'.[10] In Ireland it was inverted by the condemned to exhort the faithful to remain true to the Roman Catholic faith. Possibly the only surviving document which professes to be an accurate version of such a speech in the Irish context records that made by the Dominican, Terence Albert O'Brien, bishop of Emly, in October 1651, before his death in Limerick and which was published as part of a pamphlet a few weeks later. It contains a statement of the reasons for this death in a profoundly political sense and is also a very personal argument for his being considered a martyr. He argued that he 'was born and baptized in the bosom of the church of Rome (the ancient and true Church) and in that profession I have ever since lived and in the same I now die', rather than 'forsake the temple and truth of God' and although acknowledging his charge of treason, repeatedly declared that he had taken arms 'for thine honour, the king's happiness and the Church's preservation'.[11] It is unfortunate that the backwardness of the Irish printing industry meant that we are not furnished with other such accounts. It was undoubtedly the case that O'Brien was not speaking in a vacuum: the last dying speech of the martyr was a long-established genre, though many would have been much less eloquent in their statement of beliefs.

The execution of martyrs, aided by last speeches from the gallows, had a profound effect on the psyche of the Roman Catholic population of South Tipperary and was aided enormously by the propagation of miraculous events through the oral tradition. In 1652, for example, the funeral procession of Cashel Franciscan martyr, John Kearney, while en route from his place of execution at Clonmel to his place of interment at Cashel, met his 'spiritual child', Maria Grey, on the road who, kissing the corpse's hand, 'commended herself to his prayers very devoutly [whereupon] the dead man, in the sight of several persons worthy of credit, pressed

8 Meehan, *Irish Franciscan monasteries*, 232.   9 P.F. Moran, *Historical sketch of the persecutions suffered by the Catholics of Ireland* (1907), 161–2. This execution also took place in 1651.   10 J.A. Sharpe, '"Last dying speeches"' (1985), 163.   11 H. Fenning, 'The last speech and prayer of Blessed Terence Albert O'Brien, bishop of Emly, 1651' (1996), 52–8; see especially, Tait, 'Adorned for saints'.

her hand in his as if he was still alive'.[12] The Roman Catholics who saw it believed the martyr heard the prayers of this woman and such reported incidents were central to the oral transmission of *fama martyrii*, the fame of a martyr.[13] Similarly, the period immediately after an execution could lead to crowd disturbances. Following the execution in 1654 of the Augustinian, William Tirry, 'he was cast out and presently bleedeth out of his nostrils abundantly, so that every one ran apace to gather his blood with their handkerchiefs and to get some piece of clothes or other things'.[14] A blind woman was reputedly cured after touching his habit.[15]

Sites on the landscape became points where the power of the martyr could be more easily accessed and places where martyrs were executed or buried attained a certain degree of notoriety and cult following. Indeed it has been argued, 'the power of the martyr is stronger in the immediate vicinity of his martyrdom'.[16] At Fethard, in acknowledgment of Tirry's three-year ministry in the town and district, the Roman Catholic mayor had his body buried in the Augustinian abbey there.[17] The location of the grave of the Dominican Richard Barry, martyred in 1647 at Cashel during the burning of the cathedral on the Rock by Lord Inchiquin, remained in the local psyche into the late nineteenth century, when it was pointed out to a visiting church historian as being under a linden tree in the grounds of the ruined Dominican convent of that town.[18] These acts were almost contemporary with the 'civil survey', the colonial survey document in which the Cromwellians further enhanced the construction of difference between 'English Protestant' and 'Irish papist'. These actions, together with the writings and poetry of such Counter-Reformation clerics as Geoffrey Keating and Pádraigín Haicéad, aided and justified the welding together of the various aspects of pre-1641 Roman Catholicism in Ireland into a single political entity.

In the two years after the siege of Clonmel, a guerrilla war was commenced against the Cromwellians of South Tipperary from strategic upland areas of the district. These guerrillas were predominantly displaced Gaelic Irish landowners and included a minority of Old English. They comprised of a portion of five regiments and were under the general command of Colonel Edmund O'Dwyer of Dundrum. Their strategies of resistance involving incursions against the walled towns caused many innocent Roman Catholics of all backgrounds to be slaughtered by the Cromwellians, more out of frustration than retaliation, for in two years Sankey lost only one officer and five men. In an attempt to subdue the guerrillas, Sankey summoned all the inhabitants of a parish near Fethard where one of his men had been killed, chose five of them by throwing dice and had them hanged in reprisal.[19]

Following the signing of a truce at Cahir Castle in 1652,[20] the Cromwellians concentrated on the symbolic avenging of the massacre of local Protestants recorded

12 Murphy, *Our martyrs*, 343.   **13** B. Millett, 'The beatified martyrs of Ireland (11): John Kearney OFM (priest)' (2001), 239–48.   **14** J. O'Connor, *A priest on the run: William Tirry OSA, 1608–54* (1992), 27.   **15** Moran, *Analecta*, 115.   **16** M. Roberts, *Poetry and the cult of the martyrs* (1993), 112.   **17** O'Connor, *A priest on the run*, 27–8.   **18** R. Walsh, 'Some of our martyrs' (1894), 312–13.   **19** Power, *South Tipperary*, 72.   **20** Articles of a truce signed 23 March 1652, at Cahir Castle, by Colonels Edmund O'Dwyer, Donough O'Dwyer and Walter Butler on the one part and Colonels Jerome Sankey, Solomon Richards and Adjutant Allen on the other, cited in Burke, *Clonmel*, 81–3.

in the depositions of 1641–2 and a high commission was opened at Clonmel to try those guilty living within the county. Sankey adopted an ingenious position for the disposal of many of the Roman Catholic gentry, whereby if any tenant or retainer of a particular family was found to have been present at these massacres, it was sufficient evidence for the head of that family to be charged with treason. In this way Captain James Butler of Boytonrath, Captain Pierce Butler *fitz*Thomas of Shanballyduff and his eldest son Thomas Oge, Thomas Butler *fitz*John of Derryclooney, Richard Burke of Ballywade, Patrick Keane, Thomas Kent of Lough Kent, James Butler of Ruscoe, Colonel Teige O'Meagher, Colonel Donough O'Dwyer, Theobald Butler, Hugh Ryan, Ullick Burke of Lismacue, Bryan Kearney of Ballybeg, James Burke of Scartfield and several others, were committed to jail at Clonmel. Upon examination, Butler of Derryclooney and Burke were found innocent and the others were hanged at Clonmel on 10 May 1653 for the murders at Cashel and Golden Castle in 1641–2.[21] The soldiers that fought under these gentry leaders were either transported to foreign service or left voluntarily, so that within four years, a large number of fighting men had left the county for the service of Spain and the military capability of the local population was drastically reduced.

By the start of 1654, schemes were in train for the transplantation of the remaining Roman Catholics of the district, leaving only those in the employ of Protestants, those whose trade was deemed necessary to the continuation of the New English settlement and those landholders who were judged innocent or incapable of involvement in the recent wars. The confiscated lands were handed either to Adventurers (persons who had advanced money under the Adventurers Act 1642, to the English government to wage war in Ireland), or to soldiers in the Cromwellian army who were due wages; both were remunerated with Irish land. In order to discover the amount and quality of the land to be planted, surveys were carried out. This was the commencement of the mapping, surveying and itemising of seventeenth century Ireland, producing what has been termed the 'documents of conquest'. These documents, particularly the 'civil survey' and also the 'down survey', allow an evaluation of the nature and distribution of social and settlement transformations and also provide original and geographically comprehensive views of social and settlement hierarchies prior to the Cromwellian settlement.

The 'civil survey' (1654) used local knowledge to determine baronial boundaries, the estimated value of the various townlands and their owners and occupiers in 1640 prior to the outbreak of rebellion, together with the conditions of title.[22] New English landownership in 1640 was quite limited, being largely confined to the western half of the county. From 1654, however, Cromwellian soldiers were granted large estates in the baronies of Slieveardagh and Kilnamanagh, while all available lands in the remaining baronies of South Tipperary – Clanwilliam, Middlethird, and Iffa and Offa – were assigned to the Adventurers. This ownership and control of land was the fulcrum of economic and political power in seventeenth-century Ireland.[23] The Cromwellian plantation that commenced in 1654

21 Blake-Butler NLI MSS 12,025–30. **22** R. Simington, *The civil survey of Co. Tipperary, 1654–6* (2 vols: 1931). **23** Smyth, 'Property, patronage and population', 104.

Table 2: The religious and ethnic composition of South Tipperary in 1659–60*

Barony	Barony total		New English percentile	New English tituladoes			Other tituladoes
	Gaelic Irish/ Old English	New English		Gent	Esquire	Total	
Slieveardagh	2,101	307	12.74	10	3	13	10
Iffa and Offa	4,729	223	4.50	14	3	17	25
Middlethird	3,778	134	3.42	14	4	18	16
Clanwilliam	2,713	180	6.34	16	6	22	15
Kilnamanagh	1,749	92	4.68	3	2	5	1
Total*	15,070	930	6.33	57	18	75	62

* A multiplier of 3.0 is required to obtain total population.
Source: S. Pender (ed.), *A census of Ireland, c.1659* (1939), 295–329.

revolutionized landownership, but not land-occupancy; for, although there were sufficient Cromwellian landowners, there were insufficient Protestant tenants, so that extensive use had to be made of the Irish who had escaped transplantation to Connaught.

The survey of the walled town of Clonmel in 1654 is illustrative of the numbers of Cromwellians actually involved in urban districts and the new political order is nowhere better epitomized in the study area than at Clonmel.[24] Not a single Gaelic Irish surname remained, for all had been banished to the Irishtown without the walls. Some 87 individuals held the 95 property allocations within the walls, including 18 army officers, 4 gentlemen and 8 females, presumably army widows. A few residents with rural estates moved to their lands before the end of the decade, renovating existing tower-houses for fortified habitation, as evidenced by the poll taxes of the mid-1660s. The poll tax of 1659–60,[25] conducted in the last year of the Cromwellian protectorate, allows a glimpse of English settlement prior to the Restoration, at both an urban and rural level.

Table 2 gives the population distribution of Gaelic Irish/Old English and New English households in each of the baronies of South Tipperary, excluding the towns of Clonmel and Carrick-on-Suir (Iffa and Offa) and Cashel and Fethard (Middlethird). In this way, it may be seen that with the exception of the barony of Slieveardagh, which had been allotted to the military, the English averaged less than 5 per cent throughout the rural districts of South Tipperary. Even with the addition of Slieveardagh, the New English comprised only 6.3 per cent of the South Tipperary population. Map 8 shows the distribution of their settlement by benefice (i.e. parish union) in 1659–60 and uses a multiplier of 3.0 for each adult returned as paying the poll money ordinance, so as to obtain a working estimate of total

24 See Burke, *Clonmel*.   25 Pender, *A census of Ireland, c.1659*.

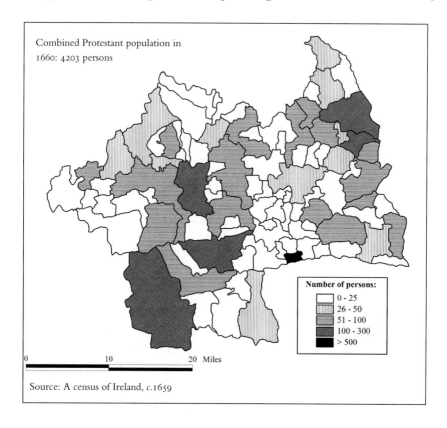

Map 8: New English settlement distribution, *c.*1660

population for each household. It highlights the spread of New English Protestants (compared with 1640–1), based on the distribution of deponents. In 1641, there was proven Protestant settlement in only four parish unions east of a median line drawn north-south across the study area, namely in the towns of Clonmel, Carrick-on-Suir and Fethard and the estate village of Viscount Ikerrin at Lismalin. New English settlement lay primarily west of this median line, concentrated in the estate settlements of Cullen, Shanrahan and Templetenny, the walled city of Cashel and to a lesser extent in the villages of Golden, Tipperary, Cahir, Tubrid and Emly. Map 8 reveals a far more even distribution in 1659–60, with Protestant communities in excess of 25 persons in many districts, although just five parish unions had a community exceeding 100 persons, viz. Cahir, Shanrahan, Athassel, Lismalin and Ballingarry, while a further 17 contained between 50 and 100 persons. There is continuity from before 1641 in the endurance of considerable rural New English communities in the vicinity of areas returning considerable numbers of depositions. By 1659–60, additional rural concentrations had formed at Killaghy, Modeshill and Castle John along the eastern boundary, Castlegrace in the south-west and Greenane Castle in the west, centred on their respective state garrisons. These are investigated later in this chapter.

Table 3: The religious and ethnic composition of Clonmel in 1661

Town District	Gaelic Irish/ Old English	Catholic percentile	New English	Protestant percentile	Total persons*
Walled area	94 (282)	24	300 (900)	76	394 (1,182)
Northern suburbs	211 (633)	98.5	3 (9)	1.5	214 (642)
Southern suburbs	102 (306)	92	9 (27)	8	111 (333)
Eastern suburbs	84 (252)	98	2 (6)	2	86 (258)
Western suburbs	67 (201)	88	9 (27)	12	76 (228)
Total population	488 (1464)	63	323 (969)	37	881 (2,643)

* Total population in brackets; source: 'pole money book [1661]', in Burke, *Clonmel*, 247–55.

At the other end of the scale, benefices in several districts of the county, particularly the entire Clonmel hinterland and much of that surrounding the towns of Cashel, Fethard and Tipperary, contained less than 25 Protestants each. Clonmel, the county assize town, was the key stronghold of South Tipperary Protestantism and its 'pole money book [1661]'[26] reveals the presence of some 394 adults within the walled town. Outside the walls were 476 persons, of whom 214 were in Irishtown, 111 in the north suburbs, 86 in the east and 76 beyond the bridge. Of those within the walls, 270 can be definitely categorized as New English through surname analysis, which with the addition of 30 persons in consideration of a missing half-page[27] totals some 300 New English Protestant adults resident within the walls. In addition, an occasional settler of the lower class is found in the suburbs outside the walls, numbering 9 persons in the west suburbs, 3 in the north suburbs, 2 in the east suburbs and 9 in the south suburbs, a total of 23 adults in 13 households. There was usually a reason for their residence in these areas with almost one-half involved in the corn or woollen milling and related industries, or placed there by the corporation as law enforcement constables. The ethnic population distribution of Clonmel is set out in table 3, where the recommended multiplier of 3.0 has been applied,[28] so that the figure within brackets represents total population, including children. Examination of this document through surname analysis, suggests that the estimates of its editor,

26 'Poll money book of Clonmel [1661]', in Burke, *Clonmel*, 247–55. 27 Burke estimates this half-leaf to have contained 44 names, which on observing the section where the omission occurred would have been at least three-fourths New English, requiring an addition of 30 Protestants and 14 Roman Catholics to the total. 28 W.J. Smyth, 'Society and settlement' (1988), 55–83.

Table 4: The hearth money returns for 1665 and 1666–7*

Barony	Total households		Total New English households		New English households as a percentage of total		
	1665	1666–7	1665	1666–7	1665	1666–7	Average
Middlethird	702	1655	140	235	19.94	14.19	17.06
Iffa and Offa	1,562	1,785	320	173	20.48	9.69	15.08
Slieveardagh	397	974	64	126	16.12	12.93	14.52
Clanwilliam	690	1,511	106	134	15.36	8.86	12.11
Kilnamanagh	338	971	44	55	13.01	5.66	9.33

* A multiplier of 5.0 may be used to obtain total population; 6.0 for urban centres.[29]
Source: T. Laffan, *Tipperary's families* (Dublin, 1911).

Burke (1907) and also more recently Power (1993) are inaccurate, the former regarding the ethnicity of the residents, the latter regarding their total number.

The New English within the walls comprised all classes, ranging from gentry families, comprising 23 persons, to the 40 Protestant servants and labourers in their employ. There were also a considerable number of widows, 20, almost all the wives of soldiers. Burke estimated the immigrant population to constitute not quite one-fifth of the town's population,[30] but an analysis of surnames has revealed the New English had a 3:1 numerical ascendancy over the combined Old English and Gaelic Irish within the walled town area and while their share in the various suburbs was by comparison minute, their overall combined percentile was comfortably in excess of one-third of the total population.

Further analysis of the spatial distribution and ethnic composition of the population of South Tipperary is possible through the survival of transcripts of hearth money rolls for the years 1665 and 1666–7. The return for 1666–7 is more complete, though the returns for the urban settlements would appear to be better in 1665. The distribution of New English households in South Tipperary, as a percentage of total households, is given by barony in table 4. The gross underestimation of total population in 1665, as compared with 1666–7, may be clearly seen on examining the first column and this greatly affected all baronies save Iffa and Offa, which contained the two primary urban settlements of Clonmel and Carrick-on-Suir.

Population estimates for the four walled towns are lacking in 1659–60, but the 'poll money book' for Clonmel – the primary New English settlement of South Tipperary – assists in building a more accurate representation of total settler population dispersal from the walled towns in the period from 1660 to 1665. The total number of New English at Clonmel increased from *c.*969 persons in 1661 to *c.*1,140

29 B. Gurrin, *Pre-census sources for Irish demography* (2002), 73; for levels of evasion, see S.T. Carleton, *Heads and hearths: the hearth money rolls and poll tax returns for Co. Antrim, 1660–9: appendices* (1991). **30** Burke, *Clonmel*, 90.

persons by 1665, an increase of almost 20 per cent. This increase was largely due to the economic opportunities offered by Clonmel, as county assize town and a growing concentration of settlers in its fertile hinterland engaging in trade and aspects of supply with the urban walled settlements of Clonmel, Carrick-on-Suir and others adjacent to the river Suir. The walled settlements of Cashel, Carrick-on-Suir and Fethard are likely to have also experienced population increase. On the evidence of the hearth money rolls (1665), some 60 households at Cashel – 45 per cent of the population of the walled city – carried New English surnames; at Carrick-on-Suir, 43 households comprising one-third of the total population and at Fethard, 12 households comprising one-eighth of the total population. These figures display not only the importance of the towns to the English, but also the relative position of each constituent town commercially.[31] Based on the situation at Clonmel, these urban settlements are likely to have increased their proportion of New English households by as much as one-fifth (see table 5), as part of the post-Restoration redistribution of population, so that a reduction of this nature is required to estimate their 1659–60 population:

Table 5: An estimate of New English urban households, 1659–60

Town	1665	1666–7	Average	-1/5	1659–60
Cashel	62	55	59	12	47
Fethard	13	11	12	2	10
Carrick-on-Suir	43	–	43	9	34

Source: Pender, *A census of Ireland*; Laffan, *Tipperary's families*

Following the application of the appropriate multiplier, substantial growth in the Protestant population in the baronies of Middlethird and Clanwilliam of 60% and 30% respectively is apparent. A modest 3 per cent increase for Iffa and Offa barony indicates an underlying decline of rural population, offset only by population increase in or transfer to the walled towns of Clonmel and Carrick-on-Suir. The small northern barony of Kilnamanagh registered virtually no change, but the eastern barony of Slieveardagh, containing several upland areas, recorded a significant decline by almost one-third. This last was likely due to its being allotted to soldiers and military personnel, many of whom sold their estates to those of their officers and comrades willing to remain in Ireland after the restoration of the monarchy in 1660.

The chief importance and relevance of the hearth money rolls and the surveys of conquest, despite omissions and imperfections, is their demonstration of New English settler distribution throughout South Tipperary at all levels, urban and rural. The survival of the old gentry areas in the south-east and south-west of Iffa and Offa barony, in the east of Middlethird barony and in pockets elsewhere, is much in evidence, demonstrating the half-conquered nature of South Tipperary. In the

---

31 Laffan, *Tipperary's families*: entries for Cashel city; ville de Carrick; ville de Fethard.

mid-1660s, the descendants of the Gaelic Irish represented about 70 per cent of the county population and still retained 40 per cent of the more substantial two-hearth houses; the descendants of the Old English, comprising 25 per cent of population, controlled 48 per cent of the better houses, an impressive figure under the circumstances; the New English, while representing only 5 per cent of the population, had come to occupy 12 per cent of the total number of houses with more than one hearth, but 70 per cent of the houses with five or more hearths.[32]

By 1665, Clonmel still maintained the highest actual and relative numbers of New English of any South Tipperary town. Their share of the population within its walls stood at 54 per cent – which figure had decreased significantly from the 76 per cent recorded five years earlier – but their economic, social and cultural hegemony was undiminished. By 1665, New English Protestants comprised 78 per cent of the wealthier inhabitants of Clonmel – as measured by the number of hearths per household – and the importance of the town as a facilitator for settler progression from merchant to landed status continued. While initial New English infiltration into Clonmel was in the administrative, legal, military-political and ecclesiastical spheres, it was, by the mid-1660s, a classic example of the merchant-dominated urban settlement phenomenon.[33] The leaders of the new economic order swiftly amassed considerable mercantile wealth, allowing the purchase of extensive country estates in the Clonmel hinterland and beyond by the close of the seventeenth century. The nature and speed of the consolidation of territorial control by the New English colonial ruling minority of necessity required the continued provision of state-sponsored and private garrisons to maintain hegemony.

Many New English households remained within the walled towns, rather than risk encountering the dispossessed 'Tories' or 'Raparees' – as Irish guerrillas were termed – by occupying rural castles or tower-houses. This ensured a continuation of the settler emphasis on urban habitation. The provision of state-sponsored garrisons in South Tipperary commenced during the Cromwellian protectorate with temporary provisions made for the Protestant settlers remaining at Cullen and Golden, which besides defending against marauding Irish guerrillas, brought in additional New English households. The rebuilding or repair of existing tower-houses or castles at Castlegrace, Cahir, Greenane, Kiltinan, Poulkerry, Blenaleen, Lismalin, Killaghy and their garrisoning at the expense of the Commonwealth, as well as the provision of the purpose-built Fort Ireton at Longford Pass, had a twin objective: the extension of Protestant settlement into a few key rural areas, centred on a fortification, around which agriculture and industry could safely operate; and the eradication of remaining pockets of resistance that continued their campaign of harassment from bases in upland, forested and marginal areas. The distribution of these garrisons is shown in map 9. Three locations, Greenane, Killaghy and Castlegrace, were utilized so as to protect Protestant industrial and agricultural proto-colonies. At Castlegrace, near Clogheen, a stone house, castle and turrets within a bawn had been repaired, within which stood 'some thatched houses, cabins and a grist mill, which mill was lately built by Captain Thornehill and the best part

32 Smyth, 'Property, population and patronage', 132; Laffan, *Tipperary's families*, 137. **33** Ibid., 132.

of the houses and cabins by his tenants upon the said lands'.[34] At Longford Pass, a compact earthwork defence was constructed in 1653–4 named Fort Ireton, to protect the key artery of communication between Dublin and Cork from guerrilla interference.[35] In addition, there were Cromwellian garrisons in the walled towns of Cashel,[36] Clonmel,[37] Carrick-on-Suir,[38] Fethard,[39] and in Cahir Castle,[40] for the protection of the inhabitants of these principal settlements. State and other garrisons headed by Cromwellian officers were also maintained in pockets of resistance, particularly at the castles of Killaghy,[41] Greenane,[42] Dundrum and Ballagh – the last two strongholds of the O'Dwyers of Kilnamanagh in the north-west – and also at the castles of Kiltinan and Golden, which had also shown considerable opposition to the Cromwellian campaign. There were also a number of privately sponsored garrisons, mainly in areas of significant pre-1641 New English settlement, as at Cullen, Rehill, Dundrum, Swiffin and Golden; or where a grantee was perceived as particularly vulnerable, as at Castle John in the barony of Slieveardagh, near Carrick-on-Suir, where the towerhouse of Captain Shepherd was garrisoned by 27 English soldiers at his own expense.[43]

The presence of these garrisons at strategic locations throughout the county allowed the consolidation and extension of Cromwellian settlement in surrounding areas and would doubtless have continued but for the premature ending of the Cromwellian protectorate after just one decade. The restoration of the monarchy under Charles II in 1660 created uncertainty among Cromwellians as to whether lands granted to or purchased by them would be forcibly returned to their original owners and this temporarily halted the progress in settlement by Protestants. In their tower-houses and other fortified dwellings across South Tipperary, sturdy Cromwellians prepared to maintain by force what they had obtained by force, or other means. Consequently, Protestant royalists raised a volunteer foot regiment at Clonmel, in case fanatical elements of the disbanded Cromwellian military should rise against the new government. In the event, the success of the king's declaration on the settlement of Ireland in placating both Cromwellian and Gaelic Irish with promises that could not be fulfilled rendered this unnecessary. The Cromwellian land grants were largely left undisturbed and with the exception of adjustments allowing estate restoration to Protestant royalists and some of their Old English Roman Catholic relatives, there was no restoration of the Gaelic Irish to their estates.

---

34 'Civil survey', i, 371. **35** Ibid., 49. **36** In 1659, 'Cashel citadel', built by Colonel Le Hunte, at a cost of £1,000, was listed as a recommended garrison, with a force of 30 men: *Cal. SP (Ireland), 1647–60*, 675; 687–8. **37** Clonmel citadel was commenced in 1652: see R. Loeber, 'Irish country houses and castles of the late Caroline period' (1973), 3. In 1659, a garrison of 60 men is listed for Clonmel: *Cal. SP (Ireland), 1647–60*, 687–8. **38** The 'down survey' map for Iffa and Offa barony depicts 'Carricke' as a defensible enclosure, with the word 'fort' on the north side of the bridge over the river Suir. **39** Fethard is not listed as a recommended garrison, but was a completely walled and defensible town. **40** Cahir Castle was a recommended garrison in 1659: *Cal. SP (Ireland), 1647–60*, 687–8. **41** 'Civil survey', i, 142: 'Upon the said lands stands a castle lately repaired at ye states charge with a bawn, two thatched houses within the same and twelve houses and cabins abroad … there is ten acres of timber wood upon this land, eight miles from Carrick'. **42** Ibid., ii, 42: 'On said land stands a castle, garrisoned and thirty thatched houses and cabins'. **43** 'Civil survey'; Pender, *A census of Ireland*.

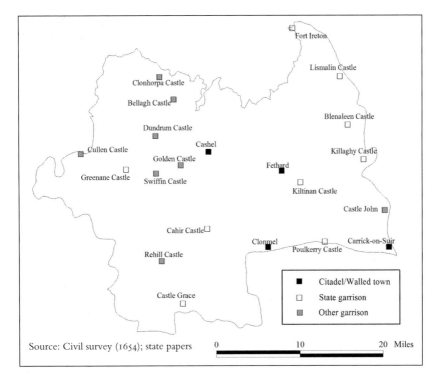

Map 9: The Cromwellian garrisons, *c*.1650–60

Only the hardier element among the Cromwellians actually took up residence on their country estates during the Cromwellian protectorate, as did the staunch Presbyterian, Captain Matthew Jacob, in 1654, in his hilltop castle fortress of Knockkelly. Most of the early outward movement from the walled town of Clonmel was by well-connected army officers. A considerable number of settlers, believing the risks of rural dwelling too high, continued to remain within the towns in this period and lived off a combination of mercantile interests and estate rental. Even in the first two decades after the restoration of the monarchy, many continued in this habit, as with Charles Alcocke, the grantee of Powerstown, near Clonmel; John Staples of Kiltinan, near Fethard; Edward Hutchinson of Knocklofty, near Clonmel; and Richard Moore proprietor of sundry Tipperary estates and of Kilworth, Co. Cork, who all lived and died in Clonmel. Every effort was made to capture and exterminate 'Tories', those Irish who persisted in guerrilla warfare, with rewards offered and proclamations made at the assizes and encouragement given to loyal subjects to shoot them on sight. Some were apprehended and executed at the ensuing assize trial, as on 25 July 1666 at Clonmel, when it was reported 'James Ryan, James Kennedy, two Tories and John Shea, a harbourer of them, were hanged. To-morrow Edmund Tobin, a Tory, [and] old Thomas Shea, a harbourer are to die.'[44]

---

44 Kearney to Ormond, 25 July 1666, cited in Burke, *Clonmel*, 439.

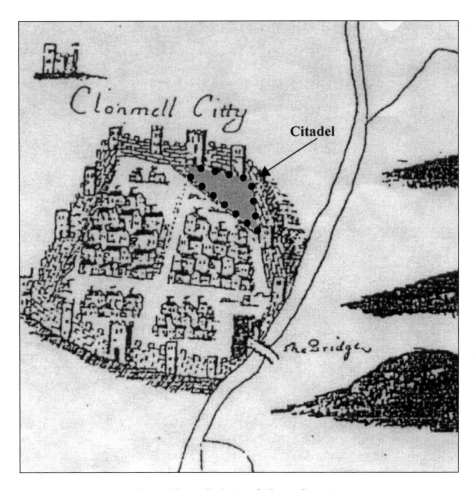

Fig. 2: The walled city of Clonmell, *c.*1665

The fort or citadel of Clonmel, constructed in 1652–3, is depicted as a triangular area within the walled town in the 'down survey' (see fig. 2). It had not been maintained in the immediate post-Restoration period and during the French invasion scare of 1666 the earl of Orrery complained 'Clonmell has but one company [of soldiers] in the town and citadel, [and] no guns [are] mounted nor any scaffolds [from which] to fire over the walls of the citadel'.[45] In 1673, when Ormond's chancellor in the Palatinate spoke of dismantling the citadel, the Cromwellian inhabitants, fearful of the Irish seizing the town in a repeat of 1641, strongly protested to Ormond, by letter sent from the mayor and corporation. In the event, their protest was unavailing, for in the negotiations for the establishment of the Huguenot-operated woollen industry at Clonmel, the duke of Ormond's surveyors determined upon using the

---

45 Orrery to Ormond, dated at Charleville, 25 May 1666, in T. Morrice, *A collection of the state papers of the Right Hon. Roger Boyle, first earl of Orrery,* i (1743), 282; ibid., 111.

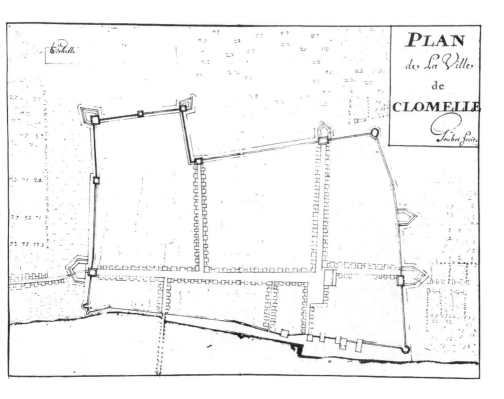

Fig. 3: The fortifications of Clonmel, *c.*1690

fort as its centre of manufacture. The citadel was demolished in 1673, for 'we cannot find any place so convenient as your Grace's fort, which is walled in …'[46]

The Tories continued their guerrilla activity for over half a century after 1660, with the support of the wider population, and so kept settler insecurities active. Their memory and actions lived on in the ballads sung at country firesides, such as 'Séan O'Dhuibhir a' Ghleanna' and 'Eamonn an Chnoic'.[47] There was a particular fear among Protestants of the unknown, almost invisible, activities and gatherings of the dispossessed 'papists', as demonstrated by an official of state who in May 1667 noted that in Tipperary

> Irish papists (and several [of them] are enlisted [in] both horse and foot [regiments]), are buying arms and fixing old ones. Since the enlisting, the priests have had great meetings, one at Knockgraffon of about 800 men, whereof many [were] armed: their pretence was for consecrating a priest. Another great meeting [was held] in [the barony of] Clanwilliam on the edge of Kilnamanagh, under the pretext of a match at hurling.[48]

46 9 August 1673, Alcocke to Mathew; 22 December 1674, Nelthorp to Ormond, cited in ibid., 493–4.
47 'John O'Dwyer of the Glen' and 'Ned of the Hills': see *Poets and poetry of Munster*, 1st series. **48** Letter to Dublin Castle of 9 May 1667, cited in L.P. O'Caithnia, *Scéal na hIománs: ó thosagh ama go*

Often their leadership incorporated elements of the dispossessed Old English landowning classes, even kinsmen of the duke of Ormond, as well as Gaelic Irish proprietors.

The war of 1690–1 added several new contingents to the Tories, who plagued the Cromwellian and Williamite occupiers to a very considerable extent. It highlighted the premature nature of the decision to demolish the citadel at Clonmel and allow that at Cashel to become ruinous. In the winter of 1690, the Williamite engineer Romer – who was engaged in strengthening the fortifications of Cork and Thurles – augmented the redoubt at Longford Pass as it was central to controlling the mail-coach road from Dublin to Cork.[49] Two regiments of the Danish army of William III wintered in 1690 at Cashel, where the fortifications were strengthened late that year (see fig. 3),[50] while Clonmel, being regarded 'a very considerable pass', crucial to the success of the campaign, had its fortifications strengthened by the Danish regiments housed there, under the direction of Brigadier Elnberger. The plans for the strengthening of Clonmel had much to do with the difficulty the Cromwellians had experienced in taking the town in 1650. A letter of 1679 from the rector, Dr Samuel Ladyman, to the duke of Ormond, which mentions the 'strengthening of the fortifications and the building of new dwellings at Clonmel', indicates some provision was being made at that time.[51] Goubet's plan of 1690 for the strengthening of the walled town reveals the construction by that date of six ravelins,[52] with a counterscarp.[53]

Following the Williamite campaign, the Tories or Raparees resumed their harassment of the settlers and by 1694, it was remarked of Tipperary that

> the Tories are in several parties, sometimes ten, twenty, thirty or more in a company and not only rob houses and travellers but strip, beat or kill the people. They also surround the fairs and set upon persons going to or coming from them, so that trade or commerce in this country is almost totally damped.[54]

This interruption of economic development in the north-central districts of South Tipperary led the corporation at Cashel to draw up elaborate plans for the repulsion of Raparees in 1694.[55] By the summer of 1696, a vigorous campaign of suppression was in operation throughout the region, further assisted by an Act of Parliament (1697), which enacted that all losses caused and damage done by Tories, Raparees and other rebels, should be charged on the inhabitants of the barony in

1884 (1980), 4. **49** P.M. Kerrigan, *Castles and fortifications in Ireland, 1485–1945* (1995), 133. **50** PRONI: T689/1, 47, 49. **51** Ladyman to Ormond, 12 September 1679, *Ormond*, v, 203, cited in R. Loeber, 'Irish country houses', 14. Danish troops were also housed at Carrick-on-Suir and Cahir. **52** A solid triangular fortification, comprising a detached outwork, with or without flanks, usually raised in front of the curtain where it is too long to be defended by adjacent bastions, or to protect an exceptionally weak stretch of curtain, such as a bastion tower or gateway to the walled town. **53** Goubet Plan: NLI MS 2742; K. Danaher and J.G. Simms, *The Danish force in Ireland* (1962), 90. A counterscarp is the side of the ditch opposite the rampart; a curtain is the stretch of wall between bastions. **54** Moore papers, cited in Connolly, *Religion, law and power*, 204. **55** Finn, *Cashel*, 21.

which they were committed, according to the religious denomination of the offenders.[56] In addition, the posting of soldiers at newly constructed redoubts and outpost barracks in the years immediately after 1700 largely eliminated the problem.

Following the ending of hostilities in Ireland in 1691 and on the European continent in 1697, the army of William III comprised 90,000 men, of which 20,000 were stationed in Great Britain and 8,400 in Ireland. The English parliament, having paid for the war, was resolutely opposed to such numbers in peacetime and wished to reduce the British number to the 7,000 maintained at the end of the reign of Charles II in 1685. After a standoff between monarch and parliament, it was resolved that surplus men and pensioners be sent to Ireland, so that the number in Britain was maintained at the level desired and that in Ireland increased to 12,000, to be maintained at the sole charge of the Irish exchequer. This English resolution was passed while the Irish Parliament was in recess, but no objections were forthcoming from the Protestant settlers, as it aided the protection of their small numbers; 12,000 was to remain the number maintained on the Irish army establishment until 1769. The army was entirely composed of British Protestants from this time on, with Irish regiments annually sending officers to recruit in Great Britain. Significantly, even Irish Protestants were rejected for army service during the first half of the eighteenth century. Already, due to processes of assimilation, it was difficult to distinguish their lower classes in manner and dress from Irish Roman Catholics.[57]

The Irish garrison was the first in Europe to be exclusively housed in barracks. The contemporary practice in England and on the Continent was for soldiers to make their own arrangements with innkeepers. Such an arrangement in Ireland was impracticable, since there was both a scarcity of inns and an army of exceptional size and the crown was obliged to employ its unpopular right to billet soldiers on the population. The early development of a barrack network can be traced to events in the 1690s, when Protestant householders in walled towns displayed increasing exasperation with these arrangements. They were glad of protection, but an invasion of personal household space by their protectors was abhorred. A strong garrison was maintained at Clonmel throughout the post-Restoration period – in 1662, there was a troop of horse with 91 men under Lord Shannon, a foot company of 93 under Captain Sir Francis Foulke and a foot company of 97 under Captain Charles Blount: a total of 284 men – but as there was no barrack, the soldiers, save a few quartered in the fort or the turrets on the walls, were billeted on the inhabitants. This caused considerable unrest among the inhabitants, particularly as soldiers were in debt to many of them. At length, after unsuccessful petitioning of the government for reimbursement, several of the Cromwellian mercantile class at Clonmel, led by Protestant dissenters, resolved to convey their complaint to the lord lieutenant, the 2nd duke of Ormond.

> May it please your Grace, Richard Hammerton, Edward Batty, Anthony Lawrence, George Collett and William Vaughan, able inhabitants of the said

56 7 William III, c. 21, cited in Burke, *Clonmel*, 440. **57** K.P. Ferguson, 'The army in Ireland from the Restoration to the Act of Union' (PhD, TCD, 1980), 70–1.

town [of Clonmel], refuse to quarter or pay the allowances for quartering [the soldiers] contracted for as formerly, [and] by their examples and instigation have caused the several other persons under named to do the like and obstinately persist therein …[58]

A scheme for the building of barracks was inaugurated in the parliamentary session of 1697–8. Sir William Robinson, in one of his last acts as engineer, surveyor and director general of forts in Ireland, chose the sites and regiments were split up and generally quartered in single troops or companies. In the four years following 1698, about £100,000 was spent by the Irish House of Commons on the accommodation of some 270 cavalry troops and foot companies in stone barracks in over 100 locations across the island. These were built 'for the ease of our subjects of Ireland from the burden of quartering our army there and for securing the dangerous passes from Tories and Raparees'.[59]

Ground was allotted for the construction of barracks within the walled towns, as at Clonmel in 1699, where the first barrack of South Tipperary was completed in 1700.[60] Barracks were usually constructed in or adjacent to a considerable settlement, but those smaller barracks erected at strategic sites, whose primary aim was the eradication of rebel hideaways and the maintenance of arteries of communication through upland districts, were designated redoubts. Redoubts were smaller barracks offering accommodation for only half-a-company and their situation was often a clear indication of their purpose.[61] Some 35 were constructed in Ireland: 14 in Munster, 13 in Ulster, 6 in Connaught and 2 in Leinster. Tipperary contained 6 redoubts – more than any other county, 5 of which lay within South Tipperary – so that combined with adjoining districts of Limerick and Waterford, it constituted the largest concentration of redoubts in the kingdom. South Tipperary, as a key strategic location between the major port cities of the south and possessing several upland areas notorious for rebel activities, was given an above average allocation of strategically located redoubts: those of Galbally, Nine-Mile-House, Killenaule, Four-Mile-Water and Ballinamult were all constructed in response to the presence of banditry which followed the Jacobite war. Longford Pass redoubt, located on a slight eminence overlooking the Dublin-Cork mail-coach road, was a rebuild of the Cromwellian Fort Ireton, erected in 1653–4. The redoubt constructed there was a small two-storey stone building inside man-high earthen ramparts. A permanent military redoubt was provided in 1700 at the estate village of Cullen, to protect the remnant Protestant colony there. Figure 4 reproduces a contemporary depiction of this crossroads settlement – comprising a church, forty predominantly Protestant inhabited dwellings and the castellated mansion of the Warter head-tenant family, with the Roman Catholic mass-house at a distance.

58 A list of 48 persons is annexed to this document: *Ormond Papers*, x:5, 55–6.   **59** Resolution of the Barrack Board (1700), cited in Ferguson, 'The army in Ireland', 78–9.   **60** Power, *Land, politics and society*, 20; D.J. Butler, 'Defence from the dispossessed' (2004).   **61** A small square fort on a rampart, sometimes constructed of stone, with or without flanks, or bastions.

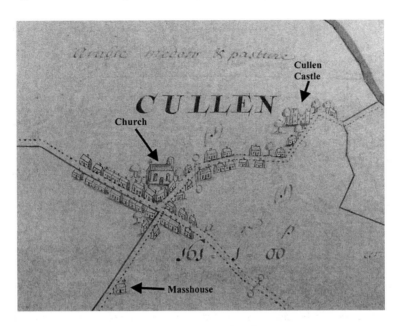

Fig. 4: The estate village of Cullen (1703)

The distribution of barracks symbolized the consolidation of spatial order, in the regulation of space contested between the new settler elite and the old landowners, turned Raparees. The military garrison was an important prop of the Ascendancy in Ireland from the mid-seventeenth century and the maintenance of a standing army suited both the colonial administration and the Irish ruling class. Besides unrest from various regional and national disturbances, there was the threat of a French invasion in an age of continuing Anglo-French hostility. Consequently, Ireland, seen as the weakest link from a British Isles point of view, was much better provided with barrack buildings than England. This network of barracks was built with the active support of the Ascendancy, but without any coherent plan, for it was observed

> the greatest part of the barracks in Ireland have been placed in various parts
> of the kingdom at the solicitation or by the interest of gentlemen whose
> estates were to be benefited by soldiers being resident upon them. Some of
> these barracks were originally built by country gentlemen and others have
> been situated at the discretion of a barracks board, most of them without
> regard to a military arrangement of the troops.[62]

The purposes for which the army existed were 'the security of the kingdom from foreign and internal enemies, the support of the civil magistrates, the aiding [of] the collection of revenue and the having an eye to the popish interest'.[63]

---

62 J.L. McCracken, 'The political structure, 1714–60' (1986), 82–3. **63** Ibid.

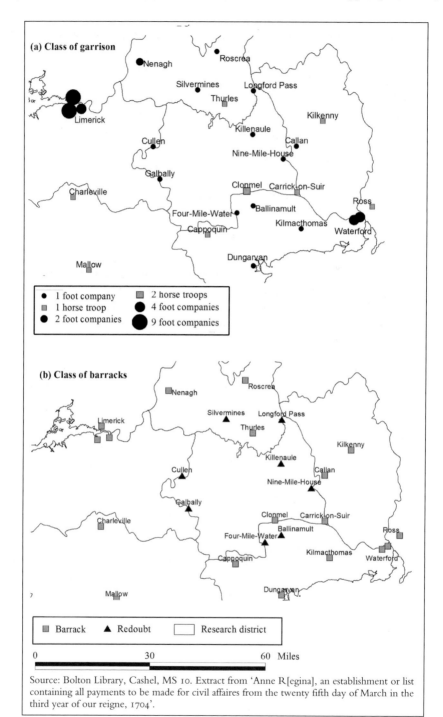

(a) Class of garrison

Nenagh   Roscrea
Silvermines   Longford Pass
Thurles
Limerick   Kilkenny
Cullen   Killenaule
Callan
Nine-Mile-House
Galbally
Charleville   Clonmel   Carrick-on-Suir
Four-Mile-Water   Ballinamult   Ross
Cappoquin   Kilmacthomas   Waterford
Mallow   Dungarvan

Legend	
● 1 foot company	▪ 2 horse troops
▪ 1 horse troop	● 4 foot companies
● 2 foot companies	● 9 foot companies

(b) Class of barracks

Nenagh   Roscrea
Silvermines   Longford Pass
Thurles
Limerick   Kilkenny
Killenaule
Cullen   Callan
Nine-Mile-House
Galbally
Charleville   Clonmel   Carrick-on-Suir
Ballinamult
Four-Mile-Water   Ross
Cappoquin   Kilmacthomas   Waterford
Mallow   Dungarvan

Legend	
▪ Barrack ▲ Redoubt	☐ Research district

0   30   60 Miles

Source: Bolton Library, Cashel, MS 10. Extract from 'Anne R[egina], an establishment or list containing all payments to be made for civil affaires from the twenty fifth day of March in the third year of our reigne, 1704'.

Map 10: The distribution of garrison stations in the district, *c.*1704

As an examination of early eighteenth-century military documentation reveals and map 10 further illustrates, South Tipperary played a key role in the military strategy of the south of Ireland, because of its central location between the port cities of Limerick, Cork and Waterford, where large numbers of foot soldiers were stationed.[64] The two most noteworthy elements of the distribution of barracks around South Tipperary was the eradication by the military establishment of upland Tory strongholds, as at Galbally, Cappoquin, Ballinamult, Nine-Mile-House and Four-Mile-Water; and the protection of rural Protestant communities, as at Cullen (agricultural) and the Silvermines (industrial). The detail of the 'army establishment report' (1704) is remarkable, particularly as another survey of comparable detail is absent before 1811. In the intervening period, reports were intermittent in both coverage and frequency, but from surviving eighteenth-century returns of principal barracks, it is apparent that the majority suffered from neglect, deficient construction or design, under-investment, or a combination of all three.[65]

It is clear from both military and civilian correspondence, however, that Protestants continued to encourage the settlement of military detachments among their own populations for security and protection. A prime example is a letter from the mayor of Clonmel to Dublin Castle, wherein he combined a declaration of loyalty with a request for reinforcements to bolster the Protestant interest, believing

> the town may conveniently quarter two companies and upon an emergency as many more and at their request I desire you will acquaint their Excellencies that the Protestant inhabitants of Clonmel are pleased with every opportunity of showing their zeal for his Majesty's service and that they will upon all occasions give the utmost proofs of their steady loyalty for his sacred person and government.[66]

Urban commerce and land continued to be the main sources of New English power, as they had been of the Old English and Gaelic Irish communities before them. The provision of both urban and rural garrisons was vital to the protection and encouragement of urban entrepreneurial dynasties and their consequent gradual diffusion from the walled urban centres of Clonmel, Carrick-on-Suir, Cashel and Fethard to landed estates in their rural hinterlands. There was considerable symbiosis between urban trade and country estates, which functioned as joint anchors of settler hegemony.

64 Bolton library, Cashel, MS 10, extract from 'Anne R[egina], an establishment or list containing all payments to be made for civil affaires from the twenty fifth day of March in the third year of our reigne, 1704'; R. Wyse-Jackson, 'Queen Anne's Irish army establishment in 1704' (1949), 133–5. **65** See comments of a visiting inspector of barracks in H.P.E. Pereira, 'A detail of the several regiments of dragoons and horse reviewed by Major-General Honywood in Ireland, 1729' (1949), 142–3; idem, 'Quarters of the army in Ireland, 1769' (1954–6), 230–1. **66** George Cole, mayor of Clonmel to Dublin Castle, 20 September 1746, cited in W.P. Burke, *Irish priests in the penal times* (1914), 349.

6

The landed estate and corporate towns: anchors of settler hegemony

The extension of the English common law system of property rights to Ireland turned land into a marketable commodity and made central the concept of private property. The leasing contract became a powerful instrument for regulating and reordering life and land use in townlands across Ireland. New law had thus become a central component of colonization and state expansion, just as the undermining of the legal titles of land held by the old elite saw new estates vastly augmented by enterprising and ruthless colonists. Effectively, law was up to the settler parliament to create. Under this system, the sons of English gentry came to Ireland prior to 1641 as planters and after 1650, as adventurers and soldiers. They generally dominated the property and economic scene. Their Englishness convinced them of their superiority over the Irish and of their right to rule Ireland and they were determined to advance, civilize and improve the economy and the landscape through advanced methods, by coercion where necessary.

The Cromwellian military settlers were notable for landowning, though not all received an automatic grant of land for military or financial services. In South Tipperary, a considerable number were lowly, enterprising Englishmen who made their fortune by entering the entrepreneurial and merchant classes. Their key to success was urban influence. Sir William Petty, in summarizing the consequences of the Cromwellian settlement, estimated that by 1672, British Protestants controlled three-quarters of all the lands, five-sixths of the best houses and, crucially, almost all of the houses in the walled towns and places of strength, most coastal locations and at least two-thirds of all foreign trade.[1] Urban dominance by the Protestant settlers, particularly at Clonmel and Cashel, led to success in the various categories of merchant and as bankers and agents for landed estates, which in turn enabled a relatively swift progression to the ranks of the landed gentry within one or two generations.

Clonmel was especially noteworthy in the raising of entrepreneurial dynasties to landed gentry and even aristocratic standing, and families such as Carleton, Hamerton, Kellett, Perry and Moore progressed to ownership of landed estates in the period from the last quarter of the seventeenth century to the turn of the eighteenth century. Richard Carleton from Cambridge began as a wine merchant in High Street, from which he retired in 1676 to a country estate named Darlinghill in the Clonmel hinterland. His descendants entered the peerage. Richard Hamerton,

---

[1] Smyth, 'Ireland, a colony', 168.

who dealt in timber, moved from a grand townhouse famous for its proclamation 'Welcome all to Hamerton Hall' written over the entrance, to a country estate at Ballyneale; Richard Kellett, through successful trading, founded the Kellett estate at Clonacody, on the Fethard Road, in 1703; Richard Perry was leasing large areas of land at Knocklofty by the 1690s and founded the Perry estate at Woodrooffe in the 1740s. The most successful of all was Richard Moore, who was at Clonmel by 1655 and who through land broking and agency, died in 1690 in possession of estates in Kilworth, Co. Cork, besides extensive Tipperary estates at Barne, Hore abbey and elsewhere.[2]

South Tipperary was particularly successful in retaining merchant gentry within its bounds, owing to its centrality at the crossroads of the south midlands, between the ports of Cork, Limerick, Waterford and Youghal. In addition, the presence of the river Suir, navigable inland as far as Carrick-on-Suir and Clonmel, and its connection to the network of primary mail-coach routes linking the four major Irish cities – Dublin with Cork and Limerick with Waterford – were key attractions. Conditions were, as elsewhere in rural Ireland, quite rudimentary in this late seventeenth century period, though in the towns there had been some progress since the Restoration. In 1689 a diarist mentions

> Clogheen ... a little town that has some good houses ... [and] Clonmel ... one of the prettiest towns I have seen, though small. It is walled ... the principal streets are in the form of a cross with a handsome town house much about the centre of it, the streets [are] clean and the houses well built, [with] a navigable river running by the side of it next which are the ruins of a large old convent, then in possession of the Franciscan friars.[3]

These were but isolated instances of modernity and confined to certain urban areas. Dean Swift, subsequent to a visit to rural Tipperary, expressed his overall impressions of the district to the dean of Emly, observing it to be

> like the rest of the whole kingdom – a bare face of nature, without houses or plantations, filthy cabins, miserable, tattered, half-starved creatures, scarce in human shape; one insolent, ignorant, oppressive squire to be found in twenty miles riding; a parish church to be found in a summer day's journey, in comparison of which an English farmer's barn is a cathedral ...[4]

This quotation is particularly illustrative of the unimproved late seventeenth and early eighteenth century Tipperary landscape. The evidence is that little building of consequence took place prior to 1730 and that the network of churches of the establishment was exceedingly sparse. At Kilcooley, for example, the residence of

Fig. 5: Killaghy Castle, Mullinahone

the landlord was the old tower-house of Buolick, while his agents, the Cooke family, lived in the ruinous Clonamiclon Castle.[5] This was the lot of the majority of landed gentry, who partly due to their inherent insecurity and partly due to a lack of funds for improvement, were consigned to live in the dark, dank rooms of tower-houses, abbeys and other ruins on their country estates, which they repaired to serve as their seat. A few families grafted a new wing onto the side of their towerhouse in the period *c*.1670 to 1730. In South Tipperary, the only Protestant family to do so during this period was the Cromwellian Despard dynasty, building a five-bay, two-storey wing onto Killaghy Castle, near Mullinahone.

In general, the insecurity of Protestant settlers was such that they quickly appropriated ancient Celtic and ecclesiastical heritage for their own uses, in a statement of their power and presence: not only that they had arrived, but that they would remain. At Kiltinan churchyard, the Jacob dynasty built a prominent vault, while at Ballinure churchyard, on the estate of the Taylors of Noan House, the family tomb was centrally positioned against the inside gable, where the altar had formerly stood. On the Woodrooffe estate in the mid-eighteenth century, the early Christian church of 'teampeall na cille', had its entrance and windows closed off with iron gates and grilles to serve as a vault for the Perry family. Throughout the countryside, in a symbolic statement of their power and specific identity, New English settlers chose prime locations within pre-Reformation churches and churchyards in which to place their vaults.

One of the earliest country houses in Ireland was the Elizabethan manor-house, dating from *c*.1568, at Carrick-on-Suir, grafted onto Ormond Castle by Thomas

5 Neely, 'The Protestant community', 136.

Butler, 10th earl of Ormond. The existence of this house owed much to the special relationship that developed between Queen Elizabeth and the earl, the fact he was a Protestant, and the premier position of the Butler dynasty of which he was head nationally, and locally in their hereditary county palatinate. The supremacy of this family is demonstrated by the construction of a large mansion house on a portion of the Friary lands within the walled palatinate town of Clonmel in the immediate post-Restoration period. However, even this was partially defensible, being located within the walls, close to the citadel.

All other prominent examples of house building in this period came from the various Butler dynasties – all relatives and in-laws of James Butler, duke of Ormond and lord lieutenant. Many of these families were enabled to remain propertied Roman Catholics in this period through their special relationship with this Protestant head of the family, and in South Tipperary there included the baron of Cahir and Butler of Kilcash. The Butlers of Cahir Castle lived at Rehill Castle from the 1640s – which was succeeded by Rehill House in the late seventeenth century – at the rural heart of their 10,000-acre estate. The Butlers of Kilcash renovated their towerhouse after the Restoration, so that by 1677 it was referred to as the 'mansion house of Kilcash'.[6] The duke of Liria, while on a visit to Kilcash in October 1720, wrote of the quality of the estate there for hunting purposes, for 'in winter, there is a great quantity of woodcock and I often went out for a couple of hours before dinner to a wood below Kilcash and I always came back with a dozen, or a dozen-and-a-half birds'.[7]

The earliest non-defensible country house of South Tipperary was built *c*.1670 at Thomastown, Golden, between Cashel and Tipperary, as the seat of George Mathew, a member of the small New English Roman Catholic community in Ireland. Mathew could avail of a relationship to the Butler dynasty, being half-brother to the lord lieutenant, the duke of Ormond. Subsequent extensive improvements in the 1710s at Thomastown estate were achieved by frugality, which reportedly involved the family living on the Continent for seven years on £600 annually, so as to devote the greater part of the £8,000 annual rental to the laying out of a 1,500 acre demesne and fitting out the house with 40 guest rooms. It is also probable this lengthy overseas sojourn had to do with the attainder of the duke of Ormond in 1715 for supporting the Stuart cause, the opportunity to provide a continental Roman Catholic education for the family, and the allowing of the more severe period of penal law enforcement to pass.[8]

In contrast to the extended Butler dynasty, New English Protestants were generally much slower to improve their towerhouse seats. The critical privatization of the Irish landscape, both socially and economically, only began with the construction by the settlers of large-scale mansions, so that 'the Big House, with its own

---

6 NLI MS D 4957, dated 3 December 1677. **7** Flood, *Kilcash*, 64–6. The duke of Liria, James *fitz*James Stuart, was son of Thomas Butler's former commander, the duke of Berwick and his sister-in-law, Honora Burke, daughter of the earl of Clanrickard. Butler's wife was Margaret Burke, who married firstly in 1689 Viscount Iveagh, of Co. Down and on being widowed in 1696, married Thomas Butler of Kilcash later that year, keeping her title. **8** Power, *Land, politics and society*, 97.

complex of elaborate interior spaces with highly differentiated functions' became a 'powerful expression of individualism, privacy and high social status [that] further required a distancing and a shielding of the Big House from the mundane world of commerce and agriculture outside the gates and the widespread poverty beyond'.[9] This process commenced late in South Tipperary, as only a handful of country estates saw the building of a seat in the fifty years preceding 1730. The house of wealthy merchant Stephen Moore at Barne, near Clonmel – still extant with some Jacobean windows to the rear – was built *c.*1700 and later remodelled as a French chateau. Shanbally – the O'Callaghan seat near Clogheen – was completed *c.*1723 by this convert family who, following a successful legal career, had purchased the estate of the Old English Roman Catholic Everard family.[10] Marlow – seat of the Pennefathers at Clonoulty and named after their place of origin in England – also dates to this period. Dundrum, seat of the Maude dynasty, was completed about 1730 to designs of the architect of the parliament house in Dublin, Sir Edward Lovett Pearce; while the hub of the local Church establishment, the archbishop's palace at Cashel, was built in 1730–2 to the design of the same architect.[11] The use of this architect is itself evidence of the close connection of the South Tipperary provincial landed gentry with the core of Ascendancy Ireland, via Dublin townhouse residences and the participation of several dynasties in central and local government. There were doubtless other houses that have long since disappeared, for in a diary entry of 1773, Dorothea Herbert, daughter of the rector of Carrick-on-Suir, mentions her childhood home – a villa on the outskirts of town built in the 1670s and leased by the parish as the rectory – in which William of Orange reputedly slept after the battle of the Boyne.[12]

In the turbulent 1690s and the cash-starved early decades of the eighteenth century, many landlords sought to stabilize their rentals by attracting resident, improving Protestant head-tenants, who could guarantee cash payments and were, through lease covenants, held responsible for the development of their holdings. The concept of improvement had evolved from the seventeenth century assumption that British colonization was synonymous with agricultural transformation and that New English tenants would establish a new order of agriculture, technically superior to indigenous systems. The assumption that persons of recent English origin, or simply Protestants, would be more inclined to divide, plant and improve lands and build solid stone farmhouses, remained in the mentality of the gentry into the later eighteenth century.[13]

The 'improvements' of these tenants or middlemen had a symbolic as well as a utilitarian purpose, for they provided visible signs in the landscape of a stable and civilizing Protestant society. In particular, they were a self-conscious assertion of superior values to those of the indigenous population, reflected in formal building styles and the use of slate, brick and stone, as opposed to the more casual vernac-

---

9 W.J. Smyth (unpublished paper), 41.   **10** W.J. Smyth, 'Estate records and the making of the Irish landscape: an example from Co. Tipperary' (1976), 39–49. It was superseded in 1812 by the Nash designed Shanbally Castle.   **11** See A.P.W. Malcomson, *Archbishop Charles Agar* (2002), 334–83 for a comprehensive study of the building and history of the Cashel palace.   **12** D. Herbert, *Retrospections, 1770–1806* (1988), 20.   **13** D. Dickson, *New foundations: Ireland 1660–1800* (1987), 118–19.

ular use of thatch and mud or stone. While many Anglo-Irish landowning families preferred to obtain Protestant tenants where possible, documentary evidence of such bias is difficult to obtain. A rare example, which analyzes the entire situation, comes from the papers of a gentleman resident in the Cashel hinterland, writing in 1737, who declared that he

> and every other gentleman wou[l]d have good substantial Protestant tenants if we cou[l]d get them, but as they are not to be had we must take the best we can get, or have our land wast[e] w[hi]ch is next to having no estate.[14]

The area between Cashel and the border with Limerick contained a number of estates with a Protestant-dominated tenantry. Many Protestant families, with surnames such as Damer, Southcote and Pennefather, already held leases from the Ormond estate in the later seventeenth century. The disposal of large areas of this estate to retrieve the solvency of the Ormond family – particularly in the baronies of Clanwilliam and Middlethird during the 1690s – combined with the sale of the confiscated estates of the duke of York, greatly aided this wholesale introduction of new Protestant dynasties into South Tipperary. Some existing tenant farmers, such as Southcote of Greenane near Tipperary, ancestor of Mansergh, were able to buy out their leases and greatly extend their lands.

In addition, these estate sales attracted new Protestant merchant dynasties from elsewhere in Ireland to settle in the area, so that many of the estates in the western half of South Tipperary were created from this decay in the fortunes of the Butlers of Ormond and the House of Stuart.[15] In Clanwilliam, the principal purchaser was Sir John Meade of Ballintubber, Co. Cork, who obtained almost 5,000 acres in the mid-1690s. It was the policy of this family to lease to Protestant head-tenants, with the result that the landscape of the whole western bank of the river Suir was developed into small estates during the eighteenth century and by 1800, there was a marked concentration of gentry-style houses in the eastern portion of Clanwilliam barony.[16] Andrew Roe, a Dublin merchant and Protestant dissenter, purchased lands totalling 2,000 acres between Clanwilliam and Middlethird and established the family seat at Roesborough, near Tipperary, in the 1690s. Matthew Bunbury of Carlow was the purchaser of Kilfeakle. These new estates, besides many longer established ones, were, to some degree, sub-let to Protestant head-tenants in what has been termed 'the initiation phase' of landlordism.[17] The Dublin dissenter and money-lender, Joseph Damer, purchased an extensive estate at Shronell, near Tipperary town, in the 1690s, which was characterized by the granting of leases to 13 Protestant head-tenants in the 1708–50 period, while the neighbouring Smith–Barry estate had 10 such tenants in the same period.[18] Both of these developments had a positive impact on local Protestantism, strengthening rural congregations and their sense of community. This increase in number

---

14 Letter of 17 March 1737 (Cooke papers), cited in Power, *Land, politics and society*, 148.   **15** Marnane, *Land and violence*, 14–15.   **16** D.G. Marnane, 'Land ownership in South Tipperary, 1849–1903' (PhD, UCC, 1991).   **17** Smyth, 'Estate records', 35–9.   **18** Marnane, 'Land ownership', 15.

Fig. 6: Clonbrogan House, Mogorban

was directly responsible for the rebuilding of several parish churches in the period from *c*.1730 to 1750.

In the baronies of Iffa and Offa, Middlethird and Slieveardagh, those who bought Ormond lands were predominantly existing landowners of Cromwellian back-ground and Cromwellian merchant families based in Clonmel, who sought to invest their profits in country estates. Here also, landowning families made perpetuity leases to Protestant families, as with Solomon Watson, a Quaker from Carlow, who took a long lease of former Ormond lands at Clonbrogan, Mogorban *c*.1720 and whose substantial stone-built farmhouse (fig. 6), survives virtually unaltered. The subsequent further obtaining of leases by the Watson dynasty and their in-laws the Boles', established a concentration of improving dissenter head-tenant farmers at Mogorban, midway between Cashel and Fethard, where the landscape was trans-formed through the building of gentry-style farmhouses, the planting of trees, the licensing of Woodhouse – the private house of the Boles family – for meetings of the Society of Friends and the enclosure of a plot of ground as their burial ground.

Few large houses were built prior to 1730 in South Tipperary; when landown-ers did leave their stone fortifications, they tended to build the solid three and four bay Georgian houses of medium size, which still exist in large quantity in every district. The general lack of interest by Irish landowners in building and landscape improvement prior to 1730 led to the foundation of the Dublin Society in that year, by a minority who argued that

> building on our estates makes our residence there convenient and agree-able, will greatly influence our successors to continue on them and pre-serve the seat of the family and not only repair, but improve it; and where

Fig. 7: The house of Anthony Chearnley at Burncourt, built *c*.1740.

this is wanting, an estate suffers as much by the absence of the landlord, as a ship does by the want of a captain, when the crew is left to themselves. This is a great and necessary circumstance to the well-being of Ireland, especially where often in great estates of several thousand acres you will not meet with two houses of stone and lime, fit (I will not say for a gentleman, but even) for a farmer to live in.[19]

The creation of still relatively small demesnes in this period and their new geometric landscapes of avenues, lawns, plantations, walls, estate cottages and model home farms began an anglicization and reordering of the landscape, which trend developed and intensified throughout the eighteenth century. This progression is well illustrated in the view of the house and grounds of Anthony Chearnley of Burncourt, near Clogheen – a head-tenant on the O'Callaghan of Shanbally estate – shown in fig. 7. The zeal of some settlers in beautifying, ordering and planting the landscape of their estates is demonstrated in a marriage of 1734, where the wife brought as her dowry, not a sum of money but rather a satchel of acorns.[20] The planting of trees was given impetus after 1740 when the Dublin Society began to offer premiums and medals for the greatest number planted annually, in this way setting about changing a pattern of behaviour that was not generally perceived as appropriate to developing ideas of managing land.

The sale of the Ormond and York estates in the later 1690s and early 1700s to wealthy tenants and Dublin merchants increased the number of resident landed gentry and developed landed society in a way that a large landowner such as the duke of Ormond could not. The sales were directly responsible for the introduction of some 20 Protestant landowning dynasties to the baronies of Clanwilliam

19 Memoir of Revd Dr Samuel Madden, published in 1738, cited in A. Crookshank, 'The visual arts, 1603–1740' (1986), 414. **20** *Irish Times* 19 August 1986, cited in Watson, *A dinner of herbs*, 92.

and Iffa and Offa alone and allowed merchants and existing landowners – with and without local holdings – to enter or expand into the network of landed estates. These sales also increased the religious diversification of the landed English, as wealthy Protestant dissenting merchants from urban areas of Ireland bought into South Tipperary estates. In this way, John Pyke of Woodenstown and John Perry of Woodrooffe established estates surrounding these townlands in the Clonmel hinterland and were principal supporters of the Clonmel congregation.[21]

Andrew Roe – a Dublin merchant who had been attached to New Row Independent congregation in that city and who purchased several townlands in Clanwilliam in the 1690s – established a seat near Tipperary town called Roesborough and proved the mainstay of the recently united Independent – Presbyterian congregation of that town.[22] His role in supporting the fledgling congregation is revealed in the diary of the Revd John Cooke, who through meeting Roe in 1698 at Tipperary, 'a gentleman whom providence has very generously dealt to of the things of this world', was persuaded by Roe and his neighbours to supply them with preaching, which he performed for six years from May 1700.

> My work is to preach to a small congregation and to enjoy the advantages of retirement for the advantage of my studies. I am accommodated very comfortably in Mr Roe's house, my income being £50 to £60 per annum, as well as the convenience of Mr Roe's house.[23]

The call to Cooke reflected the recent unification of Independent and Presbyterian congregations in 1696; as Presbyterians were more willing and able to provide preaching supplies than Independents, these congregation remnants – as also at Clonmel and Tipperary – invariably became Presbyterian in outlook. The Protestant dissenters of the district surrounding Tipperary town, though a small community, included some gentry families of considerable wealth, particularly Damer of Shronell, with whom the Roe family intermarried. The progression of their Unitarian-Presbyterian cause, through obtaining the services of a resident minister, attracted quite a number of like-minded northern families to the area, who settled on the Damer estate at Shronell. This augmentation of the congregation involved the settlement of a colony of up to 60 linen-weaving households from Co. Londonderry, utilizing facilities provided by Damer. The influx likely commenced before the famine of 1741, as on 6 December 1730, Cork Presbyterian congregation noted the visit and admission to communion of 'Daniel White, weaver, son of Daniel White, a communicant with the dissenting congregation of Tipperary', while on 1 October 1738, 'Nicholas (bro. of Daniel) White [was] recommended by the Revd Mr Benjamin Smyth of Tipperary, in a certificate dated at Shronell, 7 August 1738'.[24]

Landlord goals centred on the concept of 'improvement'. Their main instruments in achieving these aims were resident head-tenants, or those holding long

---

21 Marnane, 'Land ownership', 15.   22 See R.L. Greaves, *God's other children* (1997).   23 Diary of Revd John Cooke, Presbyterian Church House, Belfast.   24 CAI, U87–1, minutes of vestry and other meetings of Cork Presbyterian meeting-house, Princes Street, 1717–1830; J. Hueston, 'The weavers of Shronell' (2002), 102; Marnane, *Land and violence*, 25.

leases of a considerable area of an estate. In the case of estates owned by most New English and also some Old English landlords, these tenants were desired – often required – to be Protestant. Such persons were required to reorganize their own farms, build stone houses with slated roofs, plant orchards and enclose their fields.[25] There were several instances of improving landlords in South Tipperary during this period, though the majority did not fully succeed in their stated aims. At Kilcooley, Sir William Barker in 1725 had proposed to build 'as fine and elegant a private gentleman's seat as any in Europe, as pretty an inland market [town] as ye country could afford, instead of botching it now about old abbey walls not proper or adapted to be anything to be justly called polite'.[26] His plans were still pending in 1736 and the scheme did not get much beyond initiating a modest plantation. Due to a weakness for lawsuits and extravagant living in England, his son continued to reside in the semi-ruinous abbey of Kilcooley which, with its narrow staircases and small rooms, would have been considered a miserable residence by any gentleman of the time.

South Tipperary, centrally located within the Cork-Limerick-Waterford triangle of dynamic port-cities and with coastal access via the river Suir, was ideally placed for estate-based industrial development in the post-Restoration period. This natural route, navigable for smaller boats, contained two inland ports – Carrick-on-Suir and Clonmel – with ancillary quay facilities. The French Protestants, or Huguenots, were remarkable for their specialized skills and as such were highly sought after to encourage industrial estate enterprise in Britain and Ireland, following their forced ejection from France in the sixteenth and particularly the seventeenth century. Under Cromwell, their cause prospered, through his employing some French settlers from England in his army and rewarding them with land grants in Ireland, besides having Huguenot clerics as preachers. Paul Amiraut, a Frenchman who migrated to England in the 1640s, became a vicar in Norfolk and took the Puritan side in the civil war; he was appointed Independent minister in Carrick-on-Suir under Henry Cromwell.[27] In 1656, a precedent was set in the proclamation 'that for the encouragement of foreign nations to come into Ireland to purchase or take to farm houses and lands there, letters patents of denization [should] be granted under the great seal of Ireland to all persons of what nation so ever professing the Protestant religion'.[28] Little came of this proclamation, due to changing circumstances for the Cromwellians, but in the immediate post-Restoration period – as early as 1662 – the duke of Ormond introduced into the Irish parliament 'An Act for encouraging Protestant strangers and others to inhabit Ireland'. Under its terms, all Protestants born outside the English dominions – having taken the oaths of allegiance and supremacy – could become naturalized subjects and upon payment of a fine of 20s. be admitted freemen of any incorporated town and to membership of any fellowship or trade guild. In England, no such Act could be passed, owing to the jealousy felt towards the refugees and the fact that the population there was already predominantly Protestant. Under the different circumstances pre-

---

25 Dickson, *New foundations*, 118–19.   **26** Sir William Barker to William Barker Jnr., dated 25 July 1736, cited in Neely, *Kilcooley*, 48.   **27** Also spelt Amyrault or Emerott: see G.L. Lee, *The Huguenot settlements in Ireland* (1936), 121.   **28** R. Dunlop (ed.), *Ireland under the Commonwealth*, ii (1913), 583.

vailing in Ireland, however, it was re-enacted by William and Mary, by Anne and by George I, as part of a concerted campaign to redress the religious imbalance.[29]

The evidence suggests that in an attempt to industrialize the country and improve his estates, the duke of Ormond – as lord lieutenant – appears to have determined to lead by example in his Tipperary county palatinate. In 1674, a leading economist set forth the advantages of the manufacture of worsted and coarse woollens for employment and improvement on the Ormond estate. Ormond entered into agreement with a Norwich manufacturer, Edward Nelthorp and also employed one Humphrey Hill as resident manager at Clonmel and an agent called Captain Grant to entice expert Walloon refugee weavers from their settlement at Canterbury. Captain Grant brought over 500 families of Walloons and French from Canterbury and distributed them among the Ormond estate towns. In this way, Huguenot linen weavers were established in Chapelizod, near Dublin, as were Walloon and Huguenot woollen manufacturers, weavers and combers in Clonmel and Carrick-on-Suir in South Tipperary and in Co. Kilkenny at Callan and Kilkenny city, where at each place houses were assigned them for 21 years 'without paying any rent save one piece of fine serge yearly'.[30] In proposing the establishment of a serge and cloth manufactory on the Clonmel estate in late 1674, Nelthorp settled principally on the old citadel or fortress of the walled town for it was

> so convenient [and] walled in, with the little house and other conveniences therein, for which your Grace receives but £10 per ann[um] with the addition of ten acres of land [and] as much other land as Mr Hill desires to it, for as long a time as your Grace usually lets leases, for it's probable I may improve it by erecting some buildings.[31]

A capital stock of over £20,000 was made available and £500 was laid out in tools. A surviving schedule of 1676 shows that there was then in stock 1,000 stones of wool, 5,400 pounds of other wool, 550 pieces of serge, 8,000 pounds of yarn, 48 kerseys, 22 broad cloths, 10,000 pounds of dyeing stuffs and 100 weavers' looms.[32] Clonmel was considered more central and accessible than the other centres in Ireland to which the manufacturers had been invited. A Monsieur de Fountisne seems to have come with the Clonmel Huguenot settlers as minister, but information on the settlers themselves is scant, other than suggested surnames – based on those most common in Canterbury – from where the South Tipperary colony was drawn. Guerin and St Clair are the only French surnames with proven association at Clonmel: the former remained into the nineteenth century, though as Roman Catholics; the latter was noted 'a Frenchman' in 1703.[33] The factory at

29 4 William and Mary, c.2; 2 Anne, c.14; 4 George I, c.9. **30** Nelthorp to George Matthew, agent of the Ormond estates, 22 June 1675 in Canon William P Burke collection, Mount Melleray abbey, fo. 24; also Burke, *Clonmel*, 104; S.J. Knox, *Ireland's debt to the Huguenots* (1959), 117. **31** Nelthorpe to Ormond, 22 December 1674, in Burke MSS, fo. 24; see also Burke, *Clonmel*, 494. **32** Power, *Land, politics and society*, 15; NLI MS 2360, fos. 95, 99, 125. **33** T. Gimlette, *The history of the Huguenot settlers in Ireland* (1888); Lee, *Huguenot settlements*, 118; 120; D.P. Savory, 'The Huguenot and Palatine settlements in the counties of Limerick, Kerry and Tipperary' (1947); T.P. Power, 'A minister's money

Clonmel flourished for 15 years preceding the outbreak of the Williamite war, despite considerable opposition from the corporation and the threat that 'other little manufactories may be set up on purpose to destroy ours'.[34]

At Clonmel itself, the colony enjoyed a monopoly of cloth manufacture and it is likely the majority of the woollen manufacturers settled there were Huguenot.[35] The residence of the majority of weaver households seems to have been around the north-western extremity of the walled town, in the vicinity of modern-day Bolton Street, which was so renamed in the eighteenth century from its original title of 'Weavers Row'.[36] Flemish (Walloon) woollen manufacturers were settled at Carrick-on-Suir, where half of the dwellings within the walled town were put at their disposal – together with 500 acres adjoining the walls, for 3 lives or 31 years – at a 'pepper corn' rent at first, afterwards increased to two-thirds of the old rental. It was also suggested that a company of Dutch brewers be brought to the town, underlining the under-developed nature of South Tipperary in the aftermath of the Cromwellian wars. Some foreigners of substance were involved, such as the Dutch merchant and woollen draper, Vastardus Graenix, who settled in Carrick-on-Suir in 1680. He actually brought his own house with him from Holland, which was rebuilt on part of the lands provided for the industrial settlement.[37]

The wool trade at Clonmel, Carrick-on-Suir and elsewhere was interrupted by the war of 1688–91, as an economic survey of the Ormond estate in 1692 reveals. Most of Carrick-on-Suir was then re-let to Protestant tenants and plans were under-way to encourage an enterprise there, which suggests the war had all but obliter-ated the earlier settlement.[38] The Dutch connection at Carrick-on-Suir persisted in the person of Graenix and also in that of John Newport, granted a renewal of a lease on his premises in 1697.[39] Similarly, a remnant of the Huguenot settlement at Clonmel was still in evidence in 1703, when the 'minister's money account' of that year recorded one remaining emigrant surname: that of St Clair, noted as 'a Frenchman'.[40] The passing of the 'Irish Woollen Export Prohibition Act' in 1699, as a safeguard to English industry, caused a downscaling of the industry in Ireland after 1700. It was now concentrated at Carrick-on-Suir, was focused solely on the domestic market and used local apprentices who had been trained by the Huguenot and Walloon weavers.[41]

The Ormond industrial enterprise was a primary one during this period and the best documented, but it was not the sole estate-sponsored attempt to import Protestant workmen into South Tipperary. A smaller-scale enterprise was tried at

account for Clonmel, 1703' (1987). **34** Edward Nelthorp to George Matthew, dated 22 June 1675, in Burke MSS fo. 24. **35** Carte, *Life of Ormond*, vi, 342; Lee, *Huguenot settlements*, 118; Gimlette, *History of the Huguenot settlers*. **36** P. Lyons, 'Norman antiquities of Clonmel burgh' (1936), 293. It is referred to as 'Weavers Lane' in E.A. Shee and S.J. Watson, *Clonmel: an architectural guide* (1975). **37** R. Loeber, 'English and Irish sources for the history of Dutch economic activity in Ireland, 1600–89' (1981), 72; 80–1: app. I and II, also NLI MS 2394, 163. **38** Power, *Land, politics and society*, 39, also NLI MS 2561, fos. 20–5; 34–7; BL Add. MSS 28877. **39** Newport, was also spelt Nieuport: see Loeber, 'English and Irish sources', 80–1; NLI MS D5287. **40** See Power, 'Minister's money account'. **41** See further in D.J. Butler, 'Beyond Roman Catholicism: other aspects of Christianity in Carrick-on-Suir' (2002): section on Huguenot/Walloon weavers.

The Commons coalmines in the Slieveardagh Hills, where coal had been mined since medieval times and which had been granted to the Langley family of Ballynonty, a member of which had been an officer in the Cromwellian army. In the decade after the Restoration, the family invited miners from established coal-mining areas of England – such as Lancashire – to work on their estate, as with Thomas Webster of Wigan, who came in 1670.[42] In addition, iron deposits were worked at nearby Grange and Killenaule, which doubtless involved similar families, though no records survive. This demonstrates early strategies devised by the Protestant ruling minority to further their economic hegemony in the context of the landed estate, the anchor of settler power. The introduction of Protestant workers and tenants to promote economic improvement was subsequently developed by the Anglican establishment as a strategy to obtain a monopoly on political power, backed by this landed status.

Following the Restoration, religion became the boundary marker between those who ruled and those who were to be subjected. It was employed by the Anglican establishment as an effective means of excluding Roman Catholics, in particular, from municipal and related offices and from landholding. As the Act of Settlement (1662) aptly summarizes 'the corporations of Ireland are now planted with English who have considerably improved at their own charges and [have] brought trade and manufacture into our kingdom, the disturbing or removing of which English would in many respects be very prejudicial'.[43] The Act of Explanation (1665) forbade the sale of houses within the towns to 'papists or popish recusants' and even those English who intermarried with the Irish fell under this ban. Under the Cromwellians and their descendants, the Protestants not only had a monopoly of the national parliament, but also of all forms of local governance, which was of equal if not greater importance. Regarding county government, their dominant position followed automatically from their wholesale acquisition of land. County administration was in the hands of the grand jury, appointed by the county sheriff from among the landlords of the county, the great majority of whom were Protestants. Similarly, almost all magistrates were drawn from the same landed class. The cities and towns were governed by municipal corporations – elected by tiny, highly selective, self-perpetuating voting bodies, often under the control of a patron dynasty – with power at all levels restricted to Protestants and, increasingly, Anglicans.

The county towns became powerhouses of the Protestant establishment, housing the garrison, assize courts and local administration generally, as well as the county gaol, session houses and churches of all denominations. Cromwellian policy with regard to urban settlement had three objectives: strategic, political and economic. The aim was not only to prevent Roman Catholic membership of civil government and grand juries, but also to expel the old merchant families from within the walls; in the political arena, this was developed to encourage the election of 'safe' mayors and aldermen; in the economic sense, governmental revenue depended heavily upon urban revenue. However, the counter-productive consequence was

---

42 Neely, *Kilcooley*, 41.   **43** Act of Settlement, section 15, cited in Burke, *Clonmel*, 97.

that, outside of Dublin and other selected urban centres, the expulsion of Roman Catholic merchants slowed economic recovery, due to a reduction in infrastructural wealth and in overseas trading contacts.[44] The most critical effects of Cromwellian rule were religious and economic, whereby the Protestant community was consolidated into a very powerful body, including many influential people of a non-conformist persuasion. In post-Restoration Clonmel a considerable number of hardy Cromwellian households refused to conform – subsequently members of the Presbyterian, Baptist and Independent dissenting congregations – and influential merchant landowners. The walled town area was stripped of its Roman Catholic majority and replaced by a population which was more than three-quarters New English Protestant. The strategy of the Cromwellians was continued and expanded under the post-Restoration establishment through borough control, whereby a stratigraphy of power was created by the local upper elite of Anglican families, who rotated the chief offices of the borough among themselves – at least initially – until a dominant family or patron emerged. A classic development of this policy was the creation of self-perpetuating voting bodies of burgesses, aldermen and freemen with the proviso that all must speak English and that their wives and children regularly attend the Established Church which – combined with the various oaths of allegiance – effectively excluded Roman Catholics and Protestant dissenters from the membership of corporations.[45]

The evidence from surviving corporation minutes of this period points to the establishment of an Anglican 'old boy's club' where leases were granted or renewed to favourites of the members. A minute of Cashel corporation in 1692 noted 'Thomas Prince is to have a renewal of his lease; he is to spend two guineas for a treat on the mayor and corporation'.[46] Corporate bodies also incurred considerable annual expenses in sectarian symbolism and annual commemoration, namely in proclaiming royal accessions, the births of royal children, the deliverance from the rebellion against Protestants in Ireland in 1641 and victory in battle over Roman Catholic countries, particularly France and Spain. In 1704, Clonmel corporation expended £3 10s. on the annual 12th of July celebrations, the ingredients being punch, beef, two quarters of mutton, two dozen chickens, besides minor expenses. A toast 'to the glorious, pious and immortal memory of William III, prince of Orange, who saved us all from popery, brass money and wooden shoes' was given, which covered the connection of Irish Roman Catholics with Rome – the centre of 'popery', with the dubious commerce and economy of the reign of James II and with the supposedly poor and ill-shod Roman Catholic subjects of Louis of France, harbinger of the Stuart household.[47]

Anglican corporate politics increasingly worked towards the total exclusion of the Protestant dissenters, who were seen as dangerous, potentially divisive and preventing the maintenance of a united Protestant front against Roman Catholicism.

44 Smyth, 'Ireland: a colony', 167. **45** M. Hennessy, 'Stratigraphies of power in early modern Ireland': paper presented at Conference of Irish Geographers, 5 May 2001, department of Geography, UCC. **46** Minute of Cashel corporation, dated 16 February 1692, cited in Finn, *Cashel*, 21–5. **47** Ibid., 5 June 1704, cited in Burke, *Clonmel*, 124.

At a local level, the dissenters were discriminated against and excluded at every opportunity. In 1703, the corporation of Cashel, alarmed at the expansionary tendencies of the Society of Friends recorded

> a report that the Quakers are building a meeting-house within the walls of this corporation, [and] ordered that Laurence Hickey esq., present mayor of this city, do consult [regarding] what course is fit to be taken in order to prevent their meetings within the said city.[48]

The Quakers had in fact maintained a discreet presence in the city of Cashel since 1657, through meeting for worship at the private house of George Baker, whose family in 1701 had converted an outhouse on his premises at Nicholas Street for use as a meeting-house.[49] In April 1704, a deed of trust was recorded for 'the house now built for use upon a religious account for meeting and assembling [of Friends] or otherwise', so that this solitary Protestant dissenting group in the archiepiscopal city was possessed of worship facilities of a similar calibre to the Roman Catholics, who worshipped from *c*.1700 in a thatched chapel in Chapel Lane, adjoining the former Dominican abbey. Both denominations prevailed, proving insuperable to the outright hostility of the corporation toward them in this period. In both cases, however, the only ground available to them to build meeting facilities was that already leased to a member of each respective denomination.[50]

Anglican domination of local political affairs had a far greater effect in compounding the inferior status of both Roman Catholics and Protestant dissenters throughout Ireland than had their exclusion from parliament. In the case of Presbyterians and other dissenting groups, the clause in the Sacramental Test Act (1704) requiring them to take communion annually in the Established Church had the effect of gradually driving them out of the municipal corporations.[51] In 1715, the resignation of Matthew Jacob Snr as a burgess of the corporation of Fethard, was brought about as 'he did not act as burgess since the Act of Parliament against the further growth of popery and has declared against acting and is willing to assign his place to Jacob Sankey [his son-in-law], who was elected'.[52] As Presbyterians, the Jacobs suffered some of the disabilities of the 'popery acts'. The progressive exclusion of Protestant dissenters was to prevent their undermining of the political weight of the Established Church in key corporate towns. Through the provision of the *Regium Donum* in the reign of Queen Anne, the government sought to curtail the establishment of new Presbyterian congregations and so limit the influence of the leading Protestant dissenting group. However, as the eighteenth century progressed, these restrictions were gradually eased as the ruling establishment realized the importance of the Protestant dissenting faction to the overall strength

48 Finn, *Cashel*, 22.   **49** J. Rutty, *The rise and progress of the people called Quakers in Ireland* (1818), 349–50. **50** FHL, deed box 17 F7, 'Assignment of premises at Nicholas Street, Cashel, 21 June 1703, bond for £200 sterling, deed of trust for Cashel meeting-house, 17 April 1704'.   **51** T. Bartlett, 'The origins and progress of the Catholic question' (1990), 3.   **52** W.G. Skehan, 'Extracts from the minutes of the corporation of Fethard, Co. Tipperary' (1969), 85.

of a Protestant interest holding a declining percentage of the overall population. The *Regium Donum* was consequently extended to cover the other dissenting denominations in the south of Ireland and the total annual grant to congregations was also increased on several occasions.

The exclusion of Roman Catholics from voting – a measure initiated in 1704 and completed by 1728 – meant that even in large county constituencies, electorates outside the province of Ulster were often small. While the absolute number of voters was small, it was the structure of Irish constituencies that predominantly supported Anglican supremacy. Of 300 parliamentary seats, 182 were for boroughs in which the franchise was restricted to members of the corporation and freemen. Each of the 32 counties returned 2 members of parliament, as did also the 8 county boroughs centred on large towns. There were also 'potwalloping' or manor boroughs where the voters were householders or freeholders within a limited geographical area, the majority of which had, by the second quarter of the eighteenth century, come under the control of a single patron family. The control of these patron dynasties was complete, so that they effectively nominated the members of parliament returned.

The process of particular political dynasties seeking dominance – which manifested itself in competition for seats in the House of Commons – did not become intense until parliament had started to meet regularly and frequently. There were five general elections between 1692 and 1714, compared with only two in the half-century that followed. However, several of the parliamentary candidates and the sheriffs who returned them in the Co. Tipperary elections were Roman Catholics – nominal converts to the Established Church – and it is possible the situation in Tipperary was directly responsible for the passing of an Act in 1728, which explicitly deprived Roman Catholics of the parliamentary franchise.[53] The problem of nominal conversion was endemic, with propertied converts swiftly made justices of the peace to the dismay of Protestants. The lord chancellor was not impressed, contending

> that encouragement should be given to new converts … but for a man of 40 years who has all his life lived [as] a violent Roman Catholic on his coming over to the Church of Ireland to be put into the commission of the peace, is a piece of policy beyond my understanding. Can he immediately forget all his friends and relations? Can he be so deaf to the ties of relationship as to give up a priest, his cousin or perhaps his brother, to be prosecuted?[54]

The reality was, of course, that such people had not forgotten their ancestry and connived at the protection of clergy and people from the penal laws. In addition, as the eighteenth century progressed, a considerable number of the Protestant gentry

53 J.G. Simms, 'Irish Catholics and the parliamentary franchise, 1692–1728' (1960–1), 28–37; Power, *Land, politics and society*, 222 (1 George II, c.9). 54 Lord Chancellor Phipps to the magistrates of the Dublin bench, cited in Burke, *Irish Priests*, 194.

were increasingly impressed by the devotion and self-sacrifice of the parish priests of their districts and often gave a decent site on which to build a mass-house.

As well as sending two members to parliament for the county, Tipperary contained three freeman parliamentary boroughs: Clonmel, Cashel and Fethard, where the electorate was confined to the mayor or sovereign, burgesses or aldermen and the freemen. Each of the three towns developed dominant family interests or 'patrons' during the early part of the eighteenth century. At Clonmel, the Moore family ruthlessly corrupted the freemen from before 1700, turning the town into a family pocket borough, though not without sustained opposition, particularly from the Bagwell family and their allies. The Moore family held one of the two Clonmel seats from 1692 until 1727, when efforts to win the second seat backfired and the return was declared invalid. This occurred when Stephen Moore, mayor in 1724–5, created his own roll of freemen voters to aid the victory of the Moore party.[55] Although the Moores were subsequently excluded from representing the town between 1733 and 1755, they continued to dominate the corporation until temporarily overthrown by the opposing Bagwell interest in 1748–50. The Moore family gained total control during the 1750s, with two members of the family representing the town continuously from 1761 until 1799, when ironically, the patronage was sold to John Bagwell, a descendant of the opposing interest of the 1750s.[56] Their interest was at its most effective in the securing of the vicarage of Clonmel for their offspring, through the vesting of power of presentation to that parish in the corporation, so that the three vicars of the period 1717 to 1810 were installed through the patronage of the Moores.[57]

Fethard became a pocket borough from about 1713, when Everard and O'Callaghan – both converts – were elected members for the borough by the Roman Catholic interest. The dominant interest to emerge was O'Callaghan: through association with Everard, a fortuitous marriage to a local Cromwellian heiress, a career in the legal profession and the possession of large quantities of available cash, later used to provide loans to Everard and to purchase his estates in the 1720s. O'Callaghan's initial return for Fethard in 1713 was a political favour from Everard, in part-repayment of a loan for debts. In 1721, O'Callaghan – whose grandson was later ennobled as Viscount Lismore – paid £11,500 for Everard's estate in Iffa and Offa, centred on Clogheen, which purchase, combined with political marriages, formed the basis for the family's subsequent rise in the landed class.[58]

Cashel also suffered the fate of becoming a family pocket borough, at the hands of William Palliser, archbishop of Cashel, 1694–1727, Theophilus Bolton, archbishop, 1730–44 and the Pennefather family of New Park, near Cashel. At the outset of the Palliser episcopate, the controlling interest in Cashel borough was most likely a confused form of power-sharing between the archbishop and a number

55 Burke, *Clonmel*, 115–6.   56 See Power, *Land, politics and society*, 226.   57 Revd Richard Moore AM, March 1717–October 1729; Revd Dr Joseph Moore, April 1730–January 1795; Revd Thomas May, April 1795–August 1810: see Burke, *Clonmel*, 287–9.   58 Skehan, 'Extracts from the minutes of Fethard corporation', 85–7; Power, *Land, politics and society*, 84; 226–7. The O'Callaghan family also controlled the borough of Enniscorthy.

of local men with influence in the corporation, particularly the Buckworth family and later, the Pennefathers. Richard Buckworth sat in parliament for Cashel, 1715–39 and was succeeded by his son, William, who sat for Cashel, 1739–53. The Buckworths were related to Archbishop Bolton and received favourable leases and renewals of leases of the Cashel corporation lands.[59]

The other controlling family in the borough of Cashel, the Pennefathers, appear comparatively late in the common council books of Cashel, with Kingsmill Pennefather of New Park mentioned as being an alderman in 1696 and serving as mayor in 1708–9. They were prominent in the parliamentary representation of Cashel, however, where Kingsmill Pennefather sat for Cashel, 1703–14 and then for Co. Tipperary, from 1714 until his death in 1735; his younger brother, Captain Matthew Pennefather, was MP for Cashel from 1710 until his death in 1733.[60] Their control of Cashel corporation increased after the death of Archbishop Palliser in 1727, when the Pennefather political dynasty commenced a process of excluding the freemen of the borough from its common council at its annual meeting. Freemen could not be excluded from voting in parliamentary elections, as the charter of the borough entitled them to do so, but by excluding them from the common council, the Pennefather dynasty obtained control over the future intake to the freeman body, where they already commanded a majority. Municipal elections were ultimately decisive of parliamentary elections and when a parliamentary by-election became necessary following the death of Captain Matthew Pennefather late in 1733, the Pennefather influence in the common council was not yet reflected in the freeman body and in the parliamentary constituency. The challenge candidate of Archbishop Bolton – Stephen Moore of Barne, near Clonmel – was returned. The defeated Pennefather party petitioned the House of Commons against this outcome, during which proceedings Bolton was heavily censured for high-handed actions and

> most of the evidence heard by the House consisted of rigmaroles about secret admissions of freemen by both sides in irregular places at irregular hours and the usual charges and counter-charges about voters being 'papists' or being 'married to popish wives'.[61]

A parliamentary committee of 1734 declared Moore unduly elected and seated Richard Pennefather in his place. Total control of the Cashel borough was still outside the Pennefather dynasty, since William Buckworth Carr, Bolton's nominee, succeeded Richard Buckworth at the aforementioned by-election of 1739 and sat until his death in 1753. From 1753, however, the Pennefather family became the dominant interest at Cashel, with both seats filled by Pennefathers until 1799 and Richard Pennefather representing the borough without interruption or contest from 1734 until his death in 1777.[62] During these years, the family were successful in operating a strategy of reducing the number of freemen and bringing

---

59 Malcomson, *Archbishop Charles Agar*, 287. **60** Ibid., 288. **61** Ibid., 289–90. **62** E. Hewitt (ed.), *Lord Shannon's letters to his son* (1982), 29; Power, *Land, politics and society*, 223; ibid., 290–1.

them under the control of the common council. Cashel survived the Union without disenfranchisement, though reduced to a single-member constituency with a seat at Westminster. The Pennefather dynasty continued to control it until finally disenfranchised by the Municipal Reform Act of 1840, at which date all sixteen members of the common council were members or relations of that family and Pennefather control was more entrenched than ever.

7

Rationalization and renewal: the territorial organization of the Established Church

The Cromwellian settlers were of great importance to the restored Anglican establishment and those who conformed to its doctrinal practices – particularly in rural areas devoid of substantial Protestant settlement – swiftly became central to parochial life. As a result of their distribution and the paucity of Protestant numbers in general, former Puritans influenced the appointment of many of their former preachers as Anglican ministers in the decade after 1660. In this way, Dr Samuel Ladyman, preacher of Clonmel since 1652, was in 1666 appointed vicar of St Mary's.[1] Similarly, the Revd Devereaux Spratt was appointed rector of Tipperary in 1669, recording in his diary that the settlers 'unanimously gave their consent for my living as a pastor and teacher among them and so I got titles for that place'.[2]

In the post-Restoration period, the Anglican establishment found itself church deficient. In the diocese of Emly, for example, only 12 churches had been in repair in the visitation of 1615. Most of these were subsequently damaged in the unrest of the 1641 to 1660 period. The rationalization of territorial organization by way of the amalgamation of civil parishes into enlarged areas of ministry had already begun in a small way in the pre-1640 period, involving the grouping of civil parishes as 'unions' or 'benefices'. An earlier rationalization commenced in the period between 1588 and 1610 in the south-east and south-west of South Tipperary, with further progress in the 1620s and 1630s in the east around Fethard, so that on thirteen occasions, a civil parish was grouped with another to form a parochial union.

A provisional territorial strategy was devised during the 1660s, in order that every Protestant in South Tipperary might be able to attend divine service in the Established Church with relative ease. Under this scheme, the 115 civil parishes of South Tipperary were divided into 17 temporary parochial unions, each attached to a church in repair where a resident clergyman officiated. This temporary rationalization of territorial organization, pending renovation of parish churches, is dated c.1670 and shown in the first part of map 11. It was flawed in that large areas of the south-western and eastern study area remained outside the area of active ministry, being on the periphery of the large parochial unions or benefices. It is unlikely that the scheme was in operation in this format for more than a decade, if it was indeed ever fully carried into effect. Its principal significance lies in the evidence it provides for Anglican population distribution. The western and north-western extremity was well served with churches, so that the pre-1641 concentration of

1 Burke, *Clonmel*, 286. 2 H.D. Spratt (ed.), *The autobiography of the Revd Devereaux Spratt, who died at Mitchelstown, Co. Cork, 1688* (1886).

Protestantism in that district of Emly diocese straddling Cos. Tipperary and Limerick continued, with churches at Emly, Tipperary, Toem, Galbally and Cullen, owing to remnants of the Munster plantation combined with a considerable Cromwellian inflow.[3] This compared especially well with the diocese of Cashel, which though twice as large in extent had only six churches in repair at this time, occupying the north-central district and the north-eastern extremity; the portion of Lismore diocese within South Tipperary also contained six churches available for use, in the south-eastern parishes of the Suir valley.

Contemporaneous with this scheme of temporary facilitation was another of great actual rationalization, when in the three decades from 1661, 47 civil parishes were united under the rector of an adjoining parish, usually centred on a settlement of some size.[4] Three primary zones of amalgamation can be identified: the largest, centred on Fethard-Killenaule, involved 18 parishes; the second, centred on Tipperary, involved 15 parishes; the third, centred on Athassel-Knockgraffon, involved 4 parishes. These were presumably civil parishes surrounded by hinterlands with a particularly low Anglican population. This creation of unions, while reducing the number of parish incumbencies, augmented the financial position and increased the church population of each new union, sometimes resulting in improved ecclesiastical services through the provision of a curate. An enhanced income and enlarged field of work encouraged the residency of at least a curate and increased the number of areas covered by Anglican clergy, who through their provision of church and related services on a weekly basis helped consolidate Anglican communities and establishment identity in each locality. The greatest rationalization occurred during the 1680s, by which time the scheme of facilitation inaugurated *c*.1670 would have informed church authorities on which parochial unifications were most likely suitable to local conditions. During that decade, a total of 10 parishes were united in the north-eastern study area, while in the hinterland of Tipperary, 5 parishes were so joined.

Despite the superior financial position of the Established Church in this period, it is ironic that the best information on the condition of contemporary Anglican parishes survives in the letters of the proscribed Roman Catholic bishop, Dr John Brenan of Waterford and Lismore.[5] Brenan, though receiving income of just £30 per annum while his Protestant counterpart received £2,000, points out that in the diocese of Waterford and Lismore in 1672,

3 There were about 20 Protestant households at Cullen in 1690: see Seymour, *The diocese of Emly*, 232; see also the near-contemporary (1703) depiction of the village in fig. 4. **4** *1661*: Kilfeakle, Templenoe and Kilshane to Tipperary; Solloghodbeg and Shronell to Cullen; Peppardstown, Rathcool, Crompstown and Mogorban to Fethard; *1663–4*: Whitechurch to Tubrid; Newtownlennon and Kilmurry to Carrick; *1669–70*: Bruis to Lattin; Rathleynin, Oughterleague and Kilpatrick to Ballintemple; *1672*: Graystown to Killenaule; *1675*: Kilcash to Killaloan; *1677–8*: Cordangan and Clonpet to Lattin; Magowry to Killenaule; *1682*: Solloghodmore, Toughcluggin and Kilcornan to Cullen; *1684*: Mowney to Lismalin; Kilbragh, Cloneen, Kilconnell, Railstown, Coleman and Coolmundry to Fethard; Ballygriffin, Dangandargan and Brickendown to Athassel; Dogstown and Boytonrath to Knockgraffon; Rathkennan and Clogher to Holycross; Buolick to Kilcooley; Cooleagh, St Johnstown, Lickfin, Isertkieran and Drangan to Killenaule; *1686*: Ballybacon to Tubrid; Donohill to Toem; *1691*: Corroge to Lattin: see Seymour, *Cashel and Emly*; Rennison, *Succession list*. **5** P. Power (ed.), *A bishop of the penal times* (1932).

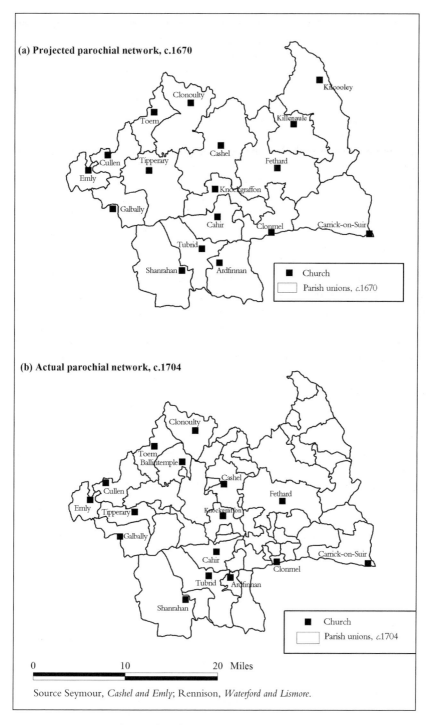

(a) Projected parochial network, c.1670

Kilcooley
Clonoulty
Toem
Killenaule
Cashel
Cullen
Tipperary
Fethard
Emly
Knockgraffon
Galbally
Cahir
Clonmel
Carrick-on-Suir
Tubrid
Shanrahan
Ardfinnan

■ Church
☐ Parish unions, c.1670

(b) Actual parochial network, c.1704

Clonoulty
Toem
Ballintemple
Cashel
Cullen
Fethard
Emly
Tipperary
Knockgraffon
Galbally
Cahir
Carrick-on-Suir
Clonmel
Tubrid
Ardfinnan
Shanrahan

■ Church
☐ Parish unions, c.1704

0   10   20 Miles

Source Seymour, *Cashel and Emly*; Rennison, *Waterford and Lismore.*

Map 11: Anglican Church territorial network, *c.*1670 and *c.*1704

the Protestant ministers with their large income have never built a single
new church and have not repaired the old ones that were built and endowed
by our Catholic forefathers ... [out of] two cathedral churches, 100 churches
and forty chapels, the cathedral of Waterford is kept in some repair, because
service is observed there, but the cathedral of Lismore is altogether ruinous
as are also the parochial churches, excepting twenty at most.[6]

Of the archdiocese of Cashel and Emly in 1687, Brenan reported that only 8 of the
60 medieval parish churches were roofed and repaired, although in possession of
Protestant ministers who held their 'revenues, tithes and other receipts'. The situation was the same in the city of Cashel, where the seat of the diocese was

quite a ruin, except one chapel, where, in summer time, the pseudo-archbishop officiates, together with his Protestant ministers, who have held possession of this see and enjoyed its revenues for many years. More than two
years ago the pseudo-archbishop died, but the church still remains in the
hands of the Protestant ministers, while the revenues of the archbishop are
collected by the government officials and paid into the royal treasury.[7]

The evidence of Brenan is backed by the episcopal visitations of the Anglican archbishop of Cashel and Emly dioceses in 1693 and 1694.[8] In these years, the diocese
of Emly returned just two churches in good repair: Duntrileague (Galbally), due
to the residency of the Cromwellian Massy family and Tipperary town; five others
were to be repaired, including Cullen and the cathedral at Emly, the chancel of
which had appeared in good repair in 1680 (see fig. 8).

Divine service was apparently performed in all seven churches, despite their condition. The reform of the wider diocese of Cashel and Emly gathered pace from the
late 1690s, though ironically two decades after similar reforms were instituted in its
proscribed Roman Catholic counterpart by Archbishop Brenan. At a visitation held
by Archbishop Palliser in 1698, his clergy of Cashel and Emly were ordered to procure communion plate for their parishes and most interestingly, 'to confer with ye
papists in order to reconcile them to ye church communion'.[9] Such visitations were
rare in both denominations: in the Roman Catholic due to state-imposed circumstances; and in the Established Church due to general incompetence.

In the absence of surviving sources, a fairly accurate picture of Anglican parochial
organization in South Tipperary *c.*1704 may be gathered from contemporary visitation extracts and transcriptions and examination of the date-marks of church plate.
The results reveal a settlement-based church distribution similar to that planned in
the *c.*1670 post-Restoration rationalization scheme. The complete absence of

---

6 Report to Propaganda from Waterford and Lismore diocese, dated October 1672, cited in Power,
A bishop of the penal times, 28–9.   7 Report to Propaganda from Cashel and Emly archdiocese, dated
6 November 1687, cited in ibid., 84–8.   8 These visitations, cited in Seymour, *The diocese of Emly*,
240–1, were incinerated in the Public Record Office fire (1922).   9 Visitation of 28 April 1698, held
at St John's parish church, Cashel, cited in ibid., 241–2. The cathedral church of St Patrick's Rock
was then out of repair and disused, but reopened in 1700.

Fig. 8: Emly cathedral, 1680

churches to the east and north-east of Fethard suggests that membership of the Established Church had plummeted in the barony of Slieveardagh, while the parish churches of Killenaule and Kilcooley had become disused. This confirms the decline in the New English population in Slieveardagh barony, identifiable as early as 1666–7. Elsewhere, the New English population seems to have been relatively stable, with parish churches renovated during the 1690s and estate churches provided at Ballintemple and Toem. Additional Anglican churches were provided from *c.*1730, not from the funds and influence of the Established Church, but rather from the private monies of resident gentry families.[10] The increased renovation of medieval churches and occasional provision of newly built ones owed much to private sponsorship, as at Shronell, through the influence and funding of Damer and also at Clonbeg (Dawson); Duntrileague (Massy), Tipperary (Smith-Barry); and Kilcooley (Barker). This development was indeed ironic, given that the proscribed Roman Catholic Church was utilizing a similar strategy, whereby leading gentry and head-tenant families helped to provide it with a network of mass-houses, backed by an equally impressive array of safe-houses for the clergy. However, in the contemporary Protestant establishment mindset, it was the differences not the similarities between the two churches that were emphasized, with a view to representing Roman Catholicism in an inferior light and emphasizing its connections with the political enemies of Britain in Europe.

The memory of the rebellion of 1641 and the various 'popish plots' – real and imagined – lived on in the hearts and minds of the New English settlers in Ireland for many decades after the actual events or scares took place. Throughout the decade of the Cromwellian protectorate, thanks for deliverance was channelled into the same anniversaries as were celebrated in England. It is significant that a proposal to commemorate the 5th of November gunpowder plot was defeated in the Irish Parliament

10 Emly diocesan visitation of 1744, cited in ibid., 243.

during the reign of James I, whom it had directly affected. Yet in 1655, the anniversary of the 5th of November was commemorated in Dublin 'with more solemnity than hath been usual these many years past', with prayers and sermons followed by 'the noise of great artillery and the blaze of bonfires before everyone's door, to the great content of the Protestants and the shame of the Roman Catholics'.[11]

Following the Restoration of 1660, the Protestant-dominated parliament at Dublin swiftly fashioned a quartet of thanksgiving festivals, with the primary acts of commemoration held on 23 October[12] and 5 November[13] and less sectarian commemorations held on 30 January[14] and 29 May.[15] The regular observance of these dates defined identity in the Protestant establishment, while the first two dates emphasized difference from and, inevitably, conflict with Roman Catholicism and Protestant dissent.[16] On such occasions, preachers drew upon Old Testament texts to make sense of the sufferings and triumphs they had experienced: their deliverance from the Roman Catholics of Ireland was likened to the liberation of the children of Israel from Egypt and interpreted as a providential blessing bestowed by the deity upon his favoured people. Anglo-Irish writers subsequently used a familiar set of polarized stereotypical images – freedom/slavery, reason/superstition, civility/barbarity, industry/idleness – to demonstrate that Roman Catholicism was the absolute inversion of truly reformed Christianity as they saw it.[17] This mentality continued in the eighteenth century, when several establishment-sponsored schemes were inaugurated, with the combined aims of the Anglicization, civilization and conversion of the Roman Catholic population.

Much information regarding the mindset of Protestants within South Tipperary in the post-Restoration period is available through the diary writings of an Anglican clergyman. Devereaux Spratt referred to the annual commemoration of 1641 as the 'solemn day of public thanksgiving for signal deliverance from the general intended massacre of the whole body of Protestants in Ireland' and as the church statutes commanded, in his sermons 'set out the horridness of the plot, the greatness of their [the Roman Catholics] sin in rebellion and God's great mercy in timely discovery'.[18] Just a few days later, the commemoration of the Gunpowder Plot was enacted, 'wherein the traitorous and bloody practices of the papists in this latter day were discovered'.[19] The action of the English colonial administration in the 1670s in banishing popish clergy and schoolmasters, restricting the carrying of arms by Roman Catholics and enacting other penal legislation was attributed to the fervent prayers of Protestant congregations at these commemorations.

---

11 T.C. Barnard, 'Crises of identity among Irish Protestants, 1641–85' (1990), 55–6; idem, Protestantism, ethnicity and Irish identities, 1660–1760' (1998); Carte, *Life of Ormond*, i, 22;   **12** 23 October 1641: the anniversary of the outbreak of rebellion against Irish Protestants.   **13** 5 November 1605: the discovery of the plot by an English Roman Catholic, Guy Fawkes, to blow up King James I and the English parliament; 5 November 1688: the landing of William III in England.   **14** 30 January 1649: the martyrdom of Charles I by the Cromwellians.   **15** 29 May 1660: the restoration of the British monarchy, under Charles II.   **16** Barnard, 'Crises of identity', 56.   **17** McBride, 'The common name of Irishman', 238–9.   **18** Spratt, *Autobiography of the Revd Devereaux Spratt*, 21–2. Spratt was referring to the *Form of divine service to be used October 23*, first included in the Irish prayer book in 1665 and published separately in 1708.   **19** Ibid.

Occasionally the subjugation and exclusion of Roman Catholics led to disturbances, as in 1672 at Clonmel when the mayor and corporation, returning from the
annual Gunpowder Plot commemoration service in St Mary's church, were 'set upon
by a mob, but no great harm [was] done'.[20] However, the incident was sufficiently
ominous for the lord lieutenant to order a return of the popish inhabitants of the corporate towns, so as to tabulate fully their religious composition *vis-à-vis* the Anglican
establishment.[21] In 1678, the so-called 'popish plot' made another appearance and in
a short time the English people were roused to a frenzy of anti-Catholicism. These
disturbances were mirrored in Ireland through a stream of 'narratives' and 'informa-
tions' consistent with the discoveries of Titus Oates. This led once more to the removal
of the Roman Catholic inhabitants of Clonmel to Irishtown outside the town walls,
save for a few necessary merchants and artisans, by proclamation of the lord lieutenant.[22] The distrust and insecurity displayed by the settlers, even prior to the accession of James II in 1685, is evident from a 1683 resolution of Cashel corporation,
where it was ordered that the night-watch consist of 'seven men [to] watch within
ye gate – four English and three Irish – to be commanded by an Englishman and that
six half pikes be forthwith made for the said guards'.[23]

It is certain that the events of 1688 had a dramatic psychological impact on the
Protestant community in Ireland, particularly those living in isolated rural communities and also in urban areas where they were in an overall minority. James II
made Kilkenny his campaign headquarters for the winter of 1689 and his proximity to South Tipperary caused wholesale panic and an exodus of Protestants from
a wide area of the surrounding district. Many of the principal Roman Catholic
families of the district were heavily involved in the Jacobite cause, particularly the
various Butler dynasties, as exemplified by Thomas Butler of Kilcash, who was
made a colonel in the Jacobite army and commanded a regiment which exceeded
400 soldiers, besides officers.[24] A glimpse of contemporary South Tipperary is possible through the diary of John Stevens, an officer in the Jacobite army, whose regiment passed through the area in 1689 and again in 1690. The flight of many rural
Protestants is demonstrated by the ability of the Jacobite regiment on arrival at the
Protestant colony of Cullen to 'hear mass, the church being then in the possession
of the Roman Catholics'.[25] Indeed it is recorded that the terror experienced by the
Protestants of Cullen was such that when the army of William prepared to leave
the area, they decided to march along with it, rather than risk their lives by remaining at Cullen.

Following the Williamite victory, the Protestant community was considerably
strengthened by the resulting estate confiscations from Jacobites. This brought many
new Protestant landowning families to the area and some Williamite army pensioners also became tenant farmers on Tipperary estates. It is impossible to map the
distribution of these tenant households, though French Huguenot households –

20 Watson, *A dinner of herbs*, 79–80. **21** Minute of Cashel corporation, dated 5 November 1673 and
17 February 1674, cited in Finn, *Cashel*, 11. **22** Burke, *Clonmel*, 107. **23** Minute of Cashel corporation, dated 2 August 1683, cited in Finn, *Cashel*, 15. **24** J.T. Gilbert (ed.), *A Jacobite narrative of the
war in Ireland, 1688–91* (1971), 206–7. **25** Murray, *Journal of John Stevens*, 137: entry for Cashel, 5 July
1690 and entry for Cullen, 6 July 1690.

with surnames such as Deeves, de Cantillon and de Mercier – were established as tenants on the Barker estate at Kilcooley in the early 1690s.[26] Their arrival may have set the scene for later experiments with Protestant estate colonies in South Tipperary. Moreover, Protestants identified an anchor point of power and security during this upheaval: the province of Ulster, where they held numerical ascendancy. The majority of those who fled the province of Munster went temporarily to the north, which avoided arduous sea crossings and made it relatively easy for them to return to their original holdings. It is significant that Munster Protestants should have identified with this bastion of Protestantism at this early stage. The Williamite victories of 1690–1 'confirmed the settler community's monopoly of power in Ireland, contributed new dates to the Protestant calendar, supplied the Protestant community with its totemic great deliverer in the shape of William III and reinforced the congruence between ethnicity, confession and political allegiance'.[27] The celebration of the victory over the Jacobites was often toasted in combination with other previously noted dates in the Protestant calendar. At the annual commemoration of the 1641 rebellion in Fethard, 100 men of the Co. Tipperary militia were put through military exercises before the sovereign of the town and a great number of spectators, which was followed by entertainment at a tavern afterwards,

> where they drank [the health of] the king, [the] royal family, the glorious and immortal memory of King William, the lord lieutenant and several other loyal toasts suitable to the occasion … the night concluded with bonfires, illuminations, [the] ringing of bells and other demonstrations of joy.[28]

The annual repetition of these events, at Fethard and all other corporate towns of Ireland, did much to establish the mentalities of Irish Protestants *vis-à-vis* Roman Catholics. Measures for the proscription of Roman Catholics had commenced even prior to the victory of William III, as evidenced by a minute of Cashel corporation, where in 1690, it was ordered that the 'many disaffected papists' then living in and around the city be required to give security for their good behaviour and those who could not afford to do so were to register their names with the town clerk. Following the victory of the Williamite forces in 1691, all Roman Catholics were promptly ousted from civic office in the city of Cashel and replaced by loyal Protestants. It was even 'ordered [that] John O'Mara, bellman, by reason of his incapacity as a papist, be discharged of his said office and that Henry Williams for the future serve as bellman'.[29]

In the aftermath of the Treaty of Limerick (1691) the blood relationship of certain Old English Roman Catholics – notably the Butlers – to the lord lieutenant, played a major part in their restoration to all or part of their estates; several were also pardoned for their role in the Jacobite cause. The classic example is Colonel Thomas

---

26 Neely, *Kilcooley*, 41.   27 J. Kelly, 'The glorious and immortal memory' (1994), 25–52.   28 *Pue's occurrences*, 29 October 1745.   29 Minutes of Cashel corporation, dated 19 February 1690 and 16 July 1691, cited in Finn, *Cashel*, 17–19.

Butler of Kilcash, who despite having been an officer in the Jacobite army, was restored in full to his estates. He was also one of the few Roman Catholics specially licensed under the penal laws to have in his possession a gun, a sword and a case of pistols – the mark of a gentleman. However, such licenses were occasionally revoked, as in August 1714 when he had to hand up his weapons to Richard Whitehead, justice of the peace and mayor of Clonmel and a Protestant.[30] Only 115 Roman Catholics on the whole of the island of Ireland were so licensed. Nine resided in Co. Tipperary, the highest number of any county, of whom five were relatives of the duke of Ormond.[31] Those pertaining to South Tipperary are set out in table 6.

Table 6: Roman Catholics licensed to keep arms (1704)

Name	Residence	Sword	Pistols	Gun
Colonel Thomas Butler	Kilcash	1	1	1
Colonel James Butler	Kilmoyler	1	–	–
Captain Thomas Dwyer	Bellacomisk	1	1	1
Thomas Travers	Burgess	–	–	1
Charles MacCarthy*	Rehill	1	–	–

* Guardian of Lady Cahir's son of Rehill, formerly at Carrignavar, Cork.
Source: *Archivium Hibernicum* 4.

The survival and immunity of these old landed families contributed greatly to the insecurity of local Protestants, as illustrated by the letter of a prominent Cashel inhabitant to Dublin Castle in 1708, who observed

the militia want arms and in my humble opinion it is very necessary they should be supplied speedily not only on account of the quality [but the] good estates of the papists who live among us. If their Excellencies please to order ammunition with the guns it will very much *encourage* our Protestant inhabitants.[32]

The key word here is 'encourage', for Cashel, with Clonmel, formed two key hubs of walled urban Protestantism in South Tipperary. Contemporary letters from provincial officials to the Dublin government make frequent demands for supplies of guns, powder and ammunition. In 1715, when the threat of Jacobite invasion loomed, Kingsmill Pennefather, although 'unable to find any arms worth speaking of in possession of the papists' at Cashel, still deemed it necessary to request Dublin to 'send powder and ammunition from Limerick or Waterford', as also in 1729, for 'the number of papists and other evil disposed persons is so great that it is hazardous for the civil power to put laws into execution'.[33]

30 Burke, *Clonmel*, 142–3; Power, *South Tipperary*, 84; Flood, *Kilcash*, 63.   **31** J. MacCaffrey, 'Irish Catholics licensed to keep arms (1704)' (1915).   **32** Kingsmill Pennefather to Dublin Castle, dated 29 March 1708, cited in Burke, *Irish priests*, 349.   **33** Ibid.

There can be no doubt that Protestants saw Roman Catholics in general as 'the other', whose many failings were negatively defined and highlighted at every opportunity. At the beginning of the eighteenth century, most Englishmen still saw Roman Catholicism as a powerful international force, which threatened their religion and liberties; and many also believed that 'popery' was gaining ground in Britain itself. There is substantial evidence that the great majority of the Roman Catholics in both Britain and Ireland gave their loyalty to the exiled Stuart dynasty for several decades after defeat in 1691 and continued to welcome with open enthusiasm the slightest prospect of an overthrow of the usurping Protestant government, as they saw it. In this situation, no Protestant could be accused of paranoia, for the fears repeatedly expressed regarding 'popish' conspiracy or insurrection were in fact very real and reflected the contemporary political situation.[34] The confidence of Protestants – like the hope of Roman Catholics – rose and fell in correspondence with a complex balance of political and strategic considerations. The Roman Catholics were seen, not only as third-class citizens coming far behind the establishment and Protestant dissenters, but also as something less than human. Writing about his responsibility for collecting the revenue in rural districts of South Tipperary, Samuel Bagwell, of Clonmel Unitarian stock, complained his work took in 'a very large walk in this county, [the] most part of it very wild and too well stocked with the vermin called papists who I fear will destroy me when I am among them upon my collection'.[35]

Fear of Roman Catholicism was intensified because it was the majority creed in countries on the European continent who were the political enemies of Britain, namely France and Spain. Significantly, Austria was not an object of fear, or mockery, because it was Britain's ally for most of the first half of the eighteenth century. The British media kept a close account of all continental activities that could be turned against the Roman Catholics of Britain or Ireland and the cruel treatment of European 'heretics' – as the Roman Church often referred to Protestants – played into their hands. Graphic accounts were carried in the British and Irish press of the ill treatment of European Protestants, for example, the massacre of Lutherans in 1724 in the ethnic German city of Thorn, within the Roman Catholic kingdom of Poland. Besides coverage of the event in journals and newspapers, a 32-page commemorative pamphlet was published in London the following year.[36]

In general, embarrassing cases involving Roman Catholic clergy and laity on the continent were seized upon by the Protestant press and reported gleefully and extensively. Roman Catholic rulers were depicted as proud and oppressive, ruling over a multitude of poor, ignorant peasants who wore wooden shoes, the symbol of their servitude.[37] This tied in neatly with the notion of the intelligent, liberated Protestants of northern Europe, versus the ignorant, subservient Roman Catholics of the southern countries. Ireland was seen as an anomaly, with the Thorn com-

34 Connolly, *Religion, law and power*, 249–50. 35 Samuel Bagwell to Dublin Castle, dated 14 March 1743, cited in Burke, *Irish priests*, 350. 36 *An alarm to Protestant princes and people, who are struck at in the popish cruelties at Thorn and other barbarous executions abroad* (1725); H. Fenning, 'Dublin imprints of Catholic interest, 1701–39' (1997–8), 131. 37 C. Haydon, *Anti-Catholicism in eighteenth-century England, c.1714–80* (1993), 38.

memorative pamphlet recommending transportation of every Irish Roman Catholic to Italy, France and Spain. Poverty and 'popery' were seen as interchangeable among the lower classes, while the continual participation of notable gentry families of Britain and Ireland in the Jacobite cause after 1691 created the opinion that all 'popish' landed families were traitors in thrall to Rome and a liability to the security of the state. Roman Catholicism, because it took its name and inspiration from Rome, was portrayed in eighteenth-century Britain and Ireland as 'outlandish', a territorially significant adjective.

The connection of Irish Roman Catholics with France was a particular fear of the Irish Protestant establishment, for it was in the Irish and English colleges of France that the majority of sons of merchants, gentry and aristocracy were educated. Even in England, though the majority were of reformed faiths, there remained strategically important Roman Catholic gentry in the north of the country, who the government presumed had intimate links with the continent and a considerable tenantry to support them in their disaffection. But this insecurity was much more prevalent in Ireland, where in 1717 it was stated that

> no popists stir except young men that go abroad to be trained in arms, with the intention of return[ing] with the Pretender. The papists being already five or six to one against us and a breeding people, you may imagine in what conditions we are like[ly] to be [in]. I may further observe that the papists being made incapable to purchase lands, have turned themselves to trade and [have] already engrossed almost all the trade of this kingdom.[38]

It is evident from this and other letters passing between the leading churchmen of Britain and Ireland that a palpable fear of the capabilities of Irish Roman Catholicism existed at the highest levels of the Protestant establishment. The rapidly evolving Roman Catholic Church organization and its development of a network of gentry safe-houses in Ireland, impenetrable to the Anglican establishment, demonstrates how this fear was well founded.

---

38 Archbishop William King to the archbishop of Canterbury, dated March 1717, cited in C.S. King (ed.), *A great archbishop of Dublin: William King D.D. 1650–1729* (1906), 208.

The Roman Catholic gentry safe-house network and the correspondence of Archbishop John Brenan *vis-à-vis* Church territorial organization

The Roman Catholic gentry and head-tenant households of South Tipperary and their kinsmen in adjoining areas of Kilkenny, Waterford and North Tipperary, were of the utmost importance to the endurance of Roman Catholicism in southeastern Ireland. Crucial in this regard were the many Old English landed families whom the New English had failed to reform to the Protestant religion. On the evidence of the 'civil survey', by 1654, only two Roman Catholic chapels in rural South Tipperary were still roofed and in use, viz. the estate chapel of Kilcash, home of Richard Butler of Kilcash, esq., where 'upon the said lands stands a castle and dwelling-house, the roof and lofts whereof are burnt and a bawn with divers thatched cabins and a little church roofed'; and of Ballyneale, home of Hugh Neale of Ballyneale esq., where there was 'a castle, being the said Neales mansion-house and many thatched cabins and a little church roofed'.[1] Little else had survived decades of uprising and rebellion, for the returns are full of castles variously described as 'unrepaired, ruinous, decayed, broken, derelict', which proportion approached 50 per cent of the tower-houses in Co. Tipperary and included the towerhouse at Kilcash.

The devotion of Old English families to the old faith is exemplified by the Butlers of Kilcash, whose matriarch, Lady Frances Butler, had a prayer book dedicated to her in 1654. The dedication is valuable for the glimpse it allows into a Roman Catholic gentry household of the period. Its author reflects

> on the piety and devotion, which in your ladyship I observed being at Kilcash … the great content which you took in speaking and conversing of spiritual matters … the orderly composition of your chapel, with those devout pictures of the altar, decent vestments, fine and clean altar clothes, the observance of the hours for prayer …[2]

Remarkably, the Kilcash family managed to maintain this house of prayer in the face of Cromwellian adversity and without the protection of their exiled kinsman, the duke of Ormond. With the restoration of the monarchy in England, the problems

---

1 'Civil survey', i, 267; 271. 2 J. and P. Flood, *Kilcash, 1190–1801* (1999), 46; 56; the author, Revd Paul of St Ubald, alias S.B., may have been a Butler.

of Old English dynasties became less acute and the various branches of the Butler family were promptly restored to their former estates under the lord lieutenancy of Ormond. Ormond had been raised a Protestant in England by the court of wards, following the death of his father while he was still a minor. This development – in combination with royal favour and the political heritage and landed wealth of the family – enabled his swift rise to head the Irish administration, with the result that many of his relatives were restored through political influence. In South Tipperary these included his brother, Richard of Kilcash, his half-brothers Toby and George Mathew of Annfield and Thomastown, his cousins the barons of Cahir and Dunboyne, and minor Butler houses at Ballycarron, Kilmoyler and elsewhere.[3]

The restoration of these families to their estates led to the availability of a network of safe-houses for the accommodation of Roman Catholic clerics in the most difficult years of oppression. As is clear from map 12, there were a considerable number of clergy bolt-holes in the South Tipperary district, comprising at least 16 properties, of which 9 were in Butler ownership or that of Butler kinsmen. These estates or head-tenant holdings occurred in two concentrations, with the larger area located to the south and west of the central district of South Tipperary – comprising 9 properties – 4 of gentry and 5 of head-tenant status; while the smaller area – located in the south-eastern corner and border districts with Waterford and Kilkenny – contained 6 properties, of which two-thirds were gentry households. Of the latter concentration, Kilcash was the primary safe-house, ranking among the most important and most frequented in Ireland. Its significance stemmed from its strategic rural location close to the upland area of Slievenamon and also its position adjoining several dioceses which, together with its chapel, made it suitable as a location for the ordination of priests. Dr James Phelan, bishop of Ossory, who had been chaplain to the household for eight years, held the earliest ordinations at Kilcash in 1670–1.[4] At nearby Garryricken, Co. Kilkenny – just two miles from the border with South Tipperary at Nine-Mile-House – a cadet branch of the Kilcash family set up residence in the late seventeenth century, and there are records of at least 10 ordinations at that house by the same bishop of Ossory in the 1675 to 1688 period.[5] The role of these two safe-houses in the ministry of Phelan is acknowledged in his last testament, where Colonel Walter Butler of Garryricken was appointed executor alongside the episcopal successor of Phelan, while the principal beneficiary was Butler, with a promise 'to pray God to bless him and all the family of Kilcash, to whom I was much obliged'.[6]

The centrality of the Roman Catholic gentry to the survival of their Church in this period is further testified by Bishop Brenan of Waterford and Lismore, who in a report to Rome in 1687, wrote

> the bishop is compelled to travel through his diocese visiting his friends among the gentry and is maintained by them for a great part of the year ... I may say confidently that there are no clergy on earth so badly off as to

---

3 'Hearth money roll for 1665', in Laffan, *Tipperary's families*, 30; Flood, *Kilcash*, 47; 57; 59. **4** Power, *South Tipperary*, 89. **5** W. Carrigan, *The history and antiquities of the diocese of Ossory*, iv (1905), 318. **6** Idem, 'Catholic episcopal wills (province of Dublin), 1683–1812' (1915), 85.

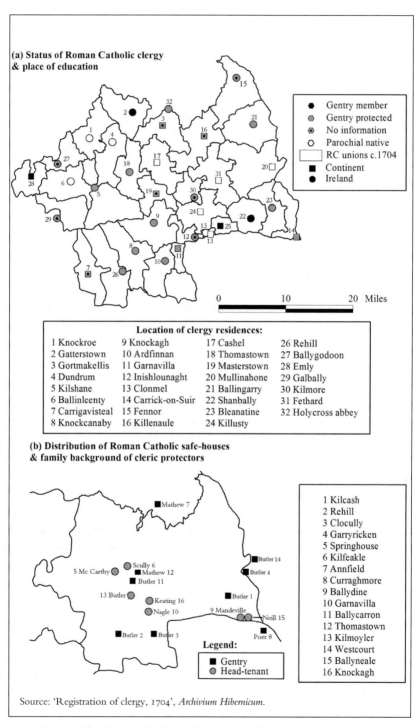

(a) **Status of Roman Catholic clergy & place of education**

● Gentry member
◐ Gentry protected
◉ No information
○ Parochial native
☐ RC unions c.1704
■ Continent
● Ireland

0   10   20 Miles

Location of clergy residences:

1 Knockroe	9 Knockagh	17 Cashel	26 Rehill
2 Gatterstown	10 Ardfinnan	18 Thomastown	27 Ballygodoon
3 Gortmakellis	11 Garnavilla	19 Masterstown	28 Emly
4 Dundrum	12 Inishlounaght	20 Mullinahone	29 Galbally
5 Kilshane	13 Clonmel	21 Ballingarry	30 Kilmore
6 Ballinleenty	14 Carrick-on-Suir	22 Shanbally	31 Fethard
7 Carrigavisteal	15 Fennor	23 Bleanatine	32 Holycross abbey
8 Knockcanaby	16 Killenaule	24 Killusty	

(b) **Distribution of Roman Catholic safe-houses & family background of cleric protectors**

Mathew 7

Butler 14

5 Mc Carthy   Scully 6
                   Mathew 12
                   Butler 11

Butler 4

13 Butler

Keating 16   Butler 1

Nagle 10   9 Mandeville

Neill 15

Butler 2   Butler 3   Poer 8

Legend:
■ Gentry
● Head-tenant

1 Kilcash
2 Rehill
3 Clocully
4 Garryricken
5 Springhouse
6 Kilfeakle
7 Annfield
8 Curraghmore
9 Ballydine
10 Garnavilla
11 Ballycarron
12 Thomastown
13 Kilmoyler
14 Westcourt
15 Ballyneale
16 Knockagh

Source: 'Registration of clergy, 1704', *Archivium Hibernicum.*

Map 12: The Roman Catholic clerical and safe-house network, *c.*1704

worldly comforts and were it not that they are entertained in the houses of the gentry, who may happen to be their parishioners, they would find it very hard to procure the means of living.[7]

Kilcash's situation in the diocese of Waterford and Lismore facilitated the shelter of Brenan, later also while archbishop of Cashel and Emly, and it was from the safety of the castle that he wrote many of his diocesan and provincial reports to Rome. In addition to sheltering the regional episcopacy, the Kilcash Butler dynasty supplied Christopher, a younger brother of Colonel Thomas Butler, who having studied at the Sorbonne in Paris, was consecrated archbishop of Cashel in 1712.[8] This appointment was as a result of the closeness of the family to the Jacobite court and the pope's continuing acceptance of the right of nomination to Irish bishoprics of James II, and latterly of James III, the Old Pretender. While this promotion was a proud honour for the family, political circumstances made Archbishop Christopher Butler's visits and safety a matter of great anxiety, an Act of William III having made it an act of treason for Roman Catholic bishops to return to Ireland.[9]

The selection of Butler as archbishop of Cashel and Emly and metropolitan of the southern province centred on his close relationship with the network of Old English landed families throughout the district who would shelter and provide for him. Professional priest-hunters abounded and in May 1713 it was reported to the authorities that the archbishop had been staying at Kilcash during the previous six months. The slow nature of communications in that period favoured the survival of clerics and a search of the castle and estate three weeks later failed to find any trace.[10] Bishop Richard Pierce of Waterford and Lismore also used Kilcash in this period, while other safe-houses available to Butler included nearby Garryricken and in his own archdiocese, Springhouse in the Glen of Aherlow – codenamed *Villa Domus Fontis* – where he consecrated two bishops, one for Cork and one for Killaloe in 1713. The subsequent public involvement in 1714–15 of his cousin, the 2nd duke of Ormond, with the Jacobite cause, made the archbishop all the more suspicious to the authorities, and it was even alleged that he was involved in a plot to help the Pretender to the throne.[11]

With the exception of the period during and immediately following the Cromwellian protectorate, popular notions of furtive eighteenth-century clergy presiding at mass-rocks are somewhat exaggerated. This is true of southern Ireland in general and the south-east (including South Tipperary) in particular. Recent research suggests that mass-rocks were more the result of a lack of resources on the part of an area rather than an indication of official persecution.[12] This suggestion is borne out by the resolution of Archbishop Brenan at a provincial synod in Thurles, held in October 1685, that priests in Munster should no longer celebrate mass in the open air and that exact registers of baptisms, marriages and deaths be kept. There

7 Report to Propaganda on the state of the diocese of Waterford and Lismore, dated 9 November 1687, cited in Power, *A bishop of the penal times*, 90–5. **8** T. Morris, 'The Butler archbishops of Cashel' (1955). **9** 9 William III, c. 16. **10** Spy report dated 6 May 1713, cited in Burke, *Irish priests*. **11** P.C. Power, 'Converts', 239; Wall, *Catholic Ireland*, 40–1. **12** S.J. Connolly (ed.), *The Oxford companion to Irish history* (1998), 352; Flood, *Kilcash*, 69.

are sufficient parish registers surviving from this period, particularly in the port cities, to indicate that the clergy adhered to this directive. The lack of registers in rural parishes prior to 1770 does not automatically point to excessive persecution, but more likely to a less organized method of keeping records on loose papers and a low survival rate of these documents. A few late-seventeenth-century registers survive from Dublin city and urban centres of the province of Leinster. The earliest register to survive in the province of Munster – from an urban parish in Cork city – dates from the beginning of the eighteenth century. In South Tipperary, the earliest Roman Catholic register in existence was started in the early 1740s in the rural parish of Killenaule, so that in certain areas, urban parishes were overtaken by the more organized rural ones. Certainly, Roman Catholic mass-houses had penetrated the Irish rural landscape to an astonishing degree by 1731 and the 'report on popery' of that year indicates a considerable supply of thatched mass-houses in South Tipperary built prior to the beginning of the reign of George I in 1714.

John Brenan, a lecturer of the Vatican Propaganda College and agent in Rome of the Irish clergy, was appointed to the vacant bishopric of Waterford and Lismore in May 1671. The Irish colleges in Europe were useful not only for the lecturing circuit they provided to their more promising students, but also for the opportunity they gave for interaction with Vatican officials. His appointment led to visitations, ordinations and the reformation of the parochial organization and of the rules of the united dioceses, through the holding of diocesan synods in the Roman continental style. Tolerance of Roman Catholicism was quite widespread in the three decades after the Restoration, during which period 1674–6 and 1679–85 were identified as years of persecution.[13] Brenan held annual synods when possible, as in 1672 and 1676 at Carrick-on-Suir and in 1677 at the Butler castle at Clocully, Ardfinnan.[14]

The power of the various Butler dynasties of South Tipperary and Kilkenny district was formidable in influencing the spiritual leadership of their Church. A petition was received in Rome in 1676 on behalf of Richard Butler of Kilcash, which was organized and signed by many branches of the wider Butler family, nominating John Brenan to the vacant archbishopric of Cashel. In 1677, he was elevated to this position and agreed to accept on condition that he be allowed to retain administration of Waterford and Lismore, with its superior income and more established network of gentry contacts and safe-houses.[15] Despite numerous attempts to discover him, his whereabouts remained unknown to the authorities from 1671, even until his death at Rehill in 1693. It is certain that among the safe-houses used by him were the Butler houses of Kilcash, Garryricken, Clocully and particularly Rehill – the last providing his most permanent shelter, through its central location close to the border between his two united dioceses and its heavily wooded terrain. This late seventeenth-century house is depicted in fig. 9. From the site of the mansion, a subterranean arched passage – its mouth now blocked

---

13 Power, *Waterford and Lismore*, 8–9; 28.   **14** C. Breathnach, 'Archbishop John Brenan (1625–93): his life and work' (1993).   **15** The income of Cashel archdiocese was £20 per annum, while Waterford had £30 per annum.

Fig. 9: Rehill House, near Cahir

by fallen masonry – leads towards a small stream and glen, 100 yards or so to the south-east. This passage, almost high enough for a man to stand upright in, was most likely constructed by the Butlers of Cahir to provide an effective method of escape and, if necessary, concealment.

Much documentary evidence regarding the post-Restoration territorial organization of both the Roman Catholic and Established Churches survives through the correspondence of Brenan with the Vatican, which comprises some 46 letters and reports written in the period 1672 to 1692.[16] The period of his tenure is of central importance, for it could be a period of considerable tolerance or intolerance of Roman Catholics, depending on political circumstances at the moment in time. In 1672, at his first diocesan synod – the first held for 40 years – Brenan reported having administered confirmation twice a day for the previous six weeks in the diocese of Waterford and Lismore, to a total of 15,000 persons, some as old as 60 years of age, during which he observed

> no alarm whatever. Although I proceeded with great caution, I was every-where recognized, even by the adversaries themselves, but I received no molestation whatever. During my visitation, some English Protestant gentlemen invited me to their houses and I went there, for the priests told me that those gentlemen showed them kindness during the time of persecution and to the great content of the clergy, I thanked the gentlemen for their benevolence. Such persons not only protected the priests in time of trouble but grant them land for building mass-houses and I considered our thanks were due to them.[17]

16 *A bishop of the penal times*, ed. Canon P. Power. **17** Ibid., 21–2.

This statement is particularly significant, as it proves the widespread existence of mass-houses as early as 1670 and makes clear their linkage to a safe-house support network of Roman Catholic gentry households. Yet in the atmosphere of suspicion and fear, a horde of state-sponsored spies and informers flourished and passions were continually inflamed by the publication of scores of pamphlets recording alleged treasons and crimes committed by Roman Catholic clergy. Many were prepared to bring charges for a financial reward and this phenomenon extended to Ireland, where two men from Waterford and Lismore diocese brought charges against Brenan and the primate, Oliver Plunkett. One such individual was Eustace Comyne, who was a resident of Carrick-on-Suir.[18] Circumstances could change drastically, as illustrated by this passage written in 1684 on the eve of the accession of James II to the throne, the high tide of Roman Catholic hopes, when Brenan noted that

> for six years, so violent has been the storm of persecution that I have not been able to hold even a private visitation. For the same reason during the past seven years, I have not held an ordination, but adopted the following course: to the aspirants I gave dismissorial letters that they might proceed to the Catholic countries to be instructed in literature and virtue and to be promoted to holy orders when by the examination they should be found worthy.[19]

The report continues by declaring that in most parts of the diocese, Roman Catholics held land – in fee or by lease – where oratories and mass-houses were erected, which were for the most part commodious and decorous. In a few unspecified upland parishes, due to a combination of poverty and the opposition of 'heretics' to giving mass-house sites on their estate, pastors celebrated mass on movable altars in the open air. Despite the deprivation of the period, the greater part of the clergy possessed silver chalices and decent vestments, as testified by the widespread survival of dated silverware. Brenan draws attention to the close link between the oratories and the surviving gentry families, who desired private masses in or near their own houses in order to avoid being associated with the open-air masses and other indignities.

The reform by Brenan of the diocese under his control allowed no tolerance for wayward clergy, as demonstrated in the matter of three Franciscan friars who apostatized in the diocese of Waterford and Lismore, one living with his wife and children, the other two in the house of the Protestant archbishop at Cashel, who protected and maintained them.[20] The close relationship between religion and politics is further revealed in the treatment by Brenan of the apostacy of Andrew Sall, a prominent Jesuit who had ministered at Clonmel and Cashel. Brenan was instrumental in arranging for the printing of two rejoinders to Sall in France and Flanders. These were widely circulated in Ireland, where they

18 Ibid., 17; one such was 'The information of Eustace Comyne' (London, 1680). 19 Report of Brenan to the Vatican, dated 13 July 1684, cited in Power, *A bishop of the penal times*, 74. 20 Report of Brenan to the Vatican, dated 24 April 1673, cited in ibid., 42.

SEAL OF ARCHBISHOP BRENAN.

Fig. 10: Archiepiscopal seal of John Brenan

made an impression, even among Protestants for their statements are sound and well arranged. This gave great joy to all the Catholics … to the great advancement of religion and the discredit of the apostate, who since the appearance of the books has been overwhelmed by confusion. His apostasy seemed to augur the Protestants that many Catholics would follow his example, but it is not known that, in almost two years, anyone followed him, excepting one artisan who was in his employment.[21]

In his visitation reports to the Vatican – given under his archiepiscopal seal shown in fig. 10 – Brenan noted that his united diocese of Waterford and Lismore had 30 parish priests in 1675, besides the services of 20 regulars, comprising 10 Franciscans, 2 Dominicans, 2 Augustinians, 5 Jesuits and one Capuchin, who with one exception were all graduates of Spain, Flanders or France. Waterford diocese had 5 parish priests, while the citizens of the city also had access to the services of a Dominican, 3 Franciscans and 3 Jesuits. The organization of the diocese of Lismore was particularly formidable by comparison to that of the Established Church, with the supervision of its 25 priests divided into 4 districts, each headed by a vicar forane, the Roman Catholic equivalent of a rural dean. In addition, there were 2 Franciscan residences: Clonmel had 3 priests, one brother and 4 novices in community at its diocesan novitiate, while Carrickbeg had 3 priests.[22]

The duke of Ormond, as lord lieutenant, accepted Roman Catholicism among his relatives and tenants in the post-Restoration period and was also central to allow-

---

21 Report dated 20 September 1675, cited in ibid., 48; the primary volume was 'The doleful fall of Andrew Sall' (1675) by N.F, exiled Roman Catholic bishop of Ferns.   **22** Report of Brenan to the Vatican, dated 20 September 1675, cited in ibid., 62–5.

ing the return of religious communities to the vicinity of their former convents, particularly in his county palatinate of Tipperary. This development did not go unnoticed among more evangelical elements of the New English administration, who were

> informed by the earl of Orrery that in the suburbs of Cashel there are [lately] erected two convents of friars and considering that the place is within the county palatine of Tipperary, we doubt not your lordship has power to suppress such buildings, which if not seasonably prevented may grow into great evils, but in case you have not power we upon notice shall supply that defect. It will be necessary that we be informed by whom and when those convents were erected and the names of the proprietors of the lands wherein they are erected.[23]

    The role of religious orders in Roman Catholic territorial reorganization was crucial and centred on their ministry as curates in urban centres and preachers in rural areas. Their threat to the progress of Protestantism lay in their insuperable ability to blend with the peasantry and was early recognized by the establishment. Combined, the Orders had a powerful influence on the reorganization of the Roman Catholic Church. By 1664, a mere four years after the end of the Cromwellian regime, the Jesuit mission in Ireland – which was particularly feared by the establishment – had revived ten residences, all in towns and cities where the Order had maintained a presence in the past and, therefore, had heritage and a sense of continuity. There was a heavy south-eastern emphasis, highlighting the close connection of the region with European ports. The Jesuits had houses at Kilkenny, Cashel, New Ross, Waterford and Clonmel; the remainder covered the important urban centres of Dublin, Cork, Limerick, Galway and Drogheda. The laity was integrated in the Jesuit mission, through the inauguration of a branch of the Sodality of the Blessed Virgin Mary at each Jesuit centre.[24] Jesuit schools were also inaugurated, through the willingness of local authorities to turn a blind eye. At Cashel, the Jesuits promised not to admit Protestants and to ensure their pupils paid fees to a local Protestant schoolmaster.[25] The Jesuit school at Cashel was founded about 1669 and continued until 1677, during which time

> its reputation spread through Tipperary and its neighbourhood. Several scholars came from a distance to it and were allowed to do so by the heretic schoolmaster on condition that none but Catholics should frequent the Jesuit school and they should pay the pension to him. Here, a roomy house was built for schoolrooms and for boarders. The first public result of the school was a notable drama, acted for the archbishop, Dr William Burgat, who had just come from Rome to the see of Cashel. It was witnessed with great favour by all, even by non-Catholics.[26]

23 Burke, *Irish priests*, 22–3. **24** McRedmond, *Jesuits*, 87. **25** H. Leonard, 'Irish Catholic education, 1669–85' (1969); McRedmond, *Jesuits*, 88–9. **26** Fr Stephen Rice to the Vatican, dated 15 July 1677, cited in Power, *A bishop of the penal times*, 84–8; Leonard, 'Irish Catholic education', 198.

Other religious orders were also resurgent in this period, with many re-establishing themselves in their old monastic foundations. Brenan reported 3 religious houses with public chapels in the city of Cashel: one was a Dominican residence containing 4 priests, another a Franciscan residence containing 19 friars. There was also a small Cistercian community consisting of an abbot and monk at Holycross and a monastery of Augustinians, 4 in community with a public chapel attached, at Fethard. In addition to these 31 regulars, there were about 30 seculars in Cashel and Emly diocese, each serving one or two chapels. Of 30 priests in the diocese, all except 2 had been educated abroad.[27]

The Cistercians regained a clandestine foothold in the vicinity of Holy Cross abbey by 1665, in obtaining the post of parish priest. In 1687, Brenan's diocesan report noted the existence of a Cistercian community in his archdiocese and though not named for security reasons, it was certainly Holy Cross. This is confirmed by the 'report on popery' of 1731, which recorded the parish priest of Holycross as 'Edmund Cormick, commonly called lord abbot of Holy Cross'.[28] The Franciscan friars maintained a continuous existence at Clonmel, where they vacated their friary in 1690, living among the people in Irishtown in secular clothing and acting as curates to the mass-house there. The friars returned to Carrickbeg in 1669, building a thatched house and later a thatched chapel in the grounds of the old friary, while under the protection of the Ormond family. At Cashel, they returned in 1658, living partly at nearby Derrynaflan and also at Thurles where they began mission work in the early eighteenth century, taking a lease from the Mathew family, in-laws of Ormond, in 1714. This eventually led to their total withdrawal from Cashel, with its resident Protestant hierarchy, to the predominantly Roman Catholic town of Thurles by 1740, where they were curate assistants at the 'big chapel' of the archbishop of Cashel and Emly. The friars at Moor abbey near Galbally also returned to their friary in 1658, where they remained until 1747, utilizing a second house at Killeenagallive – on the Limerick border, near Emly – in the period 1676–90.

Central to the survival of the religious orders was the Observant movement. Under its programme of rigour and austerity, each friar fended for himself in matters of income, food and drink through questing for alms in the surrounding countryside.[29] The monastic discipline was maintained through the holding of provincial visitations and chapters, such as the provincial chapter of the Dominican Order held in 1721 at Cashel.[30] Competition for space between religious orders was intense, however, with the various friaries each having their own hinterlands and questing boundaries. A complicated dispute with James Butler, vicar general of Cashel archdiocese, led to the withdrawal in 1747 of the Galbally Franciscans across the mountain to Mitchelstown, in the adjoining diocese of Cloyne, with the result that the questing territory of the Dominicans at Glanworth priory was encroached upon and by 1755 letters were being forwarded to Rome on the matter.[31] The

27 L. Howard, 'Irish Catholic education II, 1669–85' (1969), 313. **28** Ó Conbhuidhe, *Cistercian abbeys of Tipperary*, 256–7. The abbatical succession continued at Holycross until *c*.1750, when the Cistercian Order in Ireland became extinct. **29** Conlan, *Irish Franciscans*, 40; 45. **30** Fenning, *Dominicans*, 92; 622. **31** Conlan, *Irish Franciscans*, 80–4; letter dated 28 April 1755, cited in Fenning, *Dominicans*, 231.

Franciscans and Dominicans seem to have regularly been confrontational, as evidenced by surviving letters to Rome between 1668 and 1679, when the superior of the Clonmel Franciscans requested a decree against the pretensions of the Dominicans, then preparing to re-establish their long defunct convent in the town. The Dominicans made a second unsuccessful attempt at Clonmel in 1721.[32]

Following an act of the Irish parliament banishing all regulars with effect from 1698, conditions for those friars remaining in Ireland deteriorated substantially, with many arrests and deaths in gaol. Members of religious orders adapted to their new situation through undertaking duties as parish priests and curates, often in the vicinity of their old friaries. The enactment of the penal laws elicited sustained protest from the countries of Roman Catholic Europe, through their ambassadors to the English court, but to little avail, the most powerful monarch, Louis XIV of France, having excluded himself from influence through his treatment of the Huguenots. The exiled James II and his wife, Queen Mary, organized a collection across Europe for the support of the regulars now being expelled from Ireland, which amounted to 35,000 *livres*. By the end of 1699, the number of banished Irish clergy in Paris and its neighbourhood amounted to 383, comprising 118 Dominicans, 214 Franciscans, 26 Augustinians, 12 Capuchins, 5 Jesuits, 5 Canons Regular and 3 Carmelites.[33]

The organization of the Roman Catholic Church was much reduced by the banishing of bishops and those in authority, under the terms of the Banishment Act of 1697. The hope of the legislators was that the remaining clergy would conform, or at least that those holding out would have no successors to replace them, for want of anyone to ordain the successors. This last aim failed through the co-operation of merchants of Irish ethnicity – both in Ireland and the countries of Atlantic Europe – in shipping young Irishmen to and from the Irish colleges. Nonetheless, in an attempt to ensure there should be no successors to the existing clergy, all priests were located and enumerated by the Dublin Castle administration in the 'register of clergy' (1704).[34] The complete returns of this survey survive, ironically providing the earliest link in the clerical succession in most of the Roman Catholic parishes of Ireland. Although bishops and regulars were banned from Ireland, the Registration Act (1704) allowed Roman Catholic diocesan priests to remain in residence and practice in parishes throughout Ireland, provided they registered with the county sessions and provided security for their 'good behaviour'.[35] Already in the Treaty of Limerick, the defeated Jacobites had accepted a clause requiring them to take the oath of allegiance to William III and his successors, so registration and oath-administration posed no difficulty.

From the 'register of clergy' (1704), it is possible to illustrate and analyze the distribution of parish priests and the existing parishes in South Tipperary, giving the location of their residence, educational background and parochial accommodation (see map 12).[36] Of a total of 33 clerics, 4 came from local gentry families; 9

32 B. Millett, 'Four letters of Fr James White of Clonmel, 1668–79' (1976–7); Power, *Waterford and Lismore*, 161. **33** Burke, *Irish priests*, 132–3. **34** T. Ó Fiaich, 'The registration of the clergy in 1704' (1971). **35** Proudfoot, *Regionalism and localism*, 196; McCracken, 'The ecclesiastical structure, 1714–60', 96. **36** See further in app. VI.

ministered in their native district; 11 resided in the same townland as known local gentry households, presumably under their protection, and the background of the remaining nine remains unclear. It is highly significant that gentry or head-tenant families accommodated three-quarters of the clergy – in confirmation of the Brenan reports – and there is evidence of a clear strategy by Rome to rely on this key resource for the maintenance of both its clerical network and territorial organization. Some 40 per cent of these clerics were educated and ordained in one or other of the Irish Colleges on the European continent. The distribution of this elite is significant, in that they maintained an above average presence in key urban centres at Cashel, Clonmel, Carrick-on-Suir, Fethard and in ecclesiastical centres, as in the deaneries of Cashel and Emly. The 33 priests had charge of 31 parochial unions, which by 1731 contained a total of 48 mass-houses. A second priest resided in the important urban centre of Clonmel, while the parish priest of Newcastle and Inishlounaght – who resided alternatively at Glasha, Co. Waterford and Inishlounaght, Co. Tipperary – ministered to a contiguous union of parishes, a significant portion of which lay in Co. Waterford. These parochial boundaries were fashioned through the amalgamation of civil parishes into manageable areas, presumably during the Brenan episcopate in the second-half of the seventeenth century. They remained the anchor framework for Roman Catholic territorial organization throughout the eighteenth century, with only a few changes made at the beginning of the nineteenth century. Though the number of Roman Catholic houses of worship eventually increased from 48 mass-houses in 1731 to 55 chapels by 1830, this increase was largely in the provision of chapels-of-ease for the greater ease of attendance at worship of the majority of the population of each parochial union. Sometimes these chapels attracted settlement, or considerably augmented that which previously existed, so that the new chapels-of-ease swiftly became the main church of the union. In 1759 a chapel-of-ease to Donaskeigh was built at Knockavilla, while one for Knockgraffon was constructed at the new settlement of New Inn on the Dublin-Cork mail-coach route. By the time new churches were provided at each site in the first quarter of the nineteenth century, both had replaced the original chapel as parochial residence and head-church of their respective parish unions.[37]

The 'register of clergy' volunteers no information regarding the Roman Catholic chapels, a deficiency that can be addressed as a result of near contemporary reports sent by Brenan to Rome, in the last quarter of the seventeenth century, wherein he reported that the chapels of the country districts were built of mud and clay walls with straw thatched roof, the altar furniture 'for the most part, of a poor kind', but that 'this holds only of the country parts, for in the cities and towns, the chapels are befitting'. Most of the clergy lived in rural areas, supported by gentry households, for 'in the country, the gentry lives'. In the towns, Roman Catholics had built 'not churches, but public chapels ... [with] fixed altars, clean and decent vestments and silver chalices and crucifixes and other sacred images'.[38] Through the

---

37 W.G. Skehan, *Cashel and Emly heritage* (1993): entries for Knockavilla-Donaskeigh and New Inn-Knockgraffon.   38 Report to Propaganda from Cashel and Emly archdiocese, dated 6 November 1687, cited in Power, *A bishop of the penal times*, 86.

fortuitous survival of the Brenan correspondence, it may thus be seen that the Roman Catholic Church organization was unequalled in its ability to adapt to changing circumstances *vis-à-vis* its relationship with the Anglican establishment and proved largely impenetrable to the state authorities. Roman Catholics were not the only denominational grouping to experience exclusion, however, as the Protestant dissenters, who had themselves formed the religious establishment during the Cromwellian protectorate, were also forced to rely on the kinship network and financial support of their constituent merchant and gentry families in the crucial post-Restoration period.

9

———

'Careful of their breeding': strategies of the Protestant dissenters

With the settlement of property titles complete by the mid-1660s, religious differ-ences began to arise among the Protestant settlers themselves. Prior to 1650, there were no dissenting Protestants in southern Ireland outside of the largest port cities and isolated households in the Munster plantation. The re-establishment of the Anglican Church in 1660–2, removed Protestant dissenters from the central polit-ical influence they enjoyed under the Cromwellian protectorate, and their signif-icance was further neutralized by subdivision into Presbyterian, Independent, Baptist and Quaker groups. The implications of the proclamation in January 1661 against meetings of 'papists, Presbyterians, Independents, Anabaptists, Quakers and other fanatical persons' resonated for some time.[1]

The survival of dissenting congregations after the Restoration depended gen-erally on the numerical, but particularly on the financial, strength of each congre-gation, for in the absence of any central fund or organization, each congregation prevailed or failed on its own resources. Dissenting congregations suffered sub-stantial decline in the early 1660s, with many Cromwellian households withdraw-ing to England or America, selling their estates to those who chose to remain. This ultimately had dire consequences for dissenting congregations, particularly those in rural areas, though the distribution of meetings for worship remained constant, at least initially. Quite a number of dissenting congregations survived from the Commonwealth period and after 1660 they played an important role in the urban and rural economy in several parts of Ireland, as in South Tipperary and district.

The Established Church in Ireland dissociated itself from the dissenters to a large degree, for it saw them as a threat, divisive of the Protestant interest. While the estab-lishment referred to Roman Catholics derisively as 'papists', 'popists' or 'romanists', dissenters, particularly the smaller sects such as the Baptists, Quakers and Independents, were referred to as 'fanatics', 'schismatics' or 'Anabaptists'. The Roman Catholic Church also used these terms in describing the Protestant dissenters, for in 1673, Archbishop Oliver Plunkett reported that Bishop John Brenan of Waterford had taken refuge with him, 'because his city is full of fanatics and mad Presbyterians'.[2]

In the immediate post-Restoration period in South Tipperary, there were some disturbances, as the old Cromwellian religious regime battled for survival under royalist Episcopalians. In the county town of Clonmel, where the Cromwellians

---

1 J.C. Beckett, *The making of modern Ireland, 1603–1925* (1969), 124. 2 Power, *A bishop of the penal times*, 32.

felt themselves more secure numerically and financially than elsewhere in the district, religious disturbances occurred in 1660. On learning of the King's intention to erect a new episcopal hierarchy, some Cromwellian dissenters organized a petition praying that the 'godly ministers of the gospel who have so long laboured among us might be continued and countenanced'.³ In the upheaval surrounding the implementation of post-Reformation Anglicanism in 1660–2, wholesale arrests were made at this dissenter stronghold, where the conflict grew so intense that it was seriously proposed to remove 'the phanatiques' out of the walled town, as had been done with the Irish in the previous decade.⁴ When the bishop of the diocese was brought to preach at Clonmel in an appeal for unity, the dissenters, undaunted, held a meeting for worship in the house of Thomas Batty – who was then in gaol for non-conformity – at nearby Inishlounaght (Marlfield). Information was conveyed to the governor of the town, a company of soldiers was sent to Marlfield and the entire congregation marched to the town gaol, where

> Zephanii Smith, one of those arrested, was asked by a soldier why he was not at church then to hear the bishop preach and he replied that he did preach himself in church before now and hoped to preach there again in God's due time and if he had been at mass, or at an alehouse among a company of drunkards, swearers or heathens, he doth suppose he should not have been tormented.⁵

Smith was a known Independent and this meeting for worship was probably a combined one of Independent, Presbyterian and Baptist elements, called to present a united front. Protestant non-conformity – the threat from within the Protestant community – received far more attention from the provincial Protestant establishment in the immediate post-Restoration period than did Roman Catholicism, the perceived threat from without. One Clonmel dissenter was reported as saying that 'there must be another bout or blow for it and that very suddenly'.⁶ The fact that dissenting meetings for worship were held in secret in the houses of individuals served only to heighten establishment fears, although this was a natural consequence of the ban on public meeting-houses. Because of this ban, few meetinghouses were built in Ireland before the 1680s, which was not true of the provincial towns until the early eighteenth century.⁷

The relationship between the Established Church and the primary dissenting denomination, the Presbyterians, was tainted by the imposition of the Sacramental Test, whereby all dissenters pursuing public office and a variety of related careers were obliged to communicate at least once annually in a church of the establishment. Presbyterians in turn saw Anglicans as ridden with the ritual and superstition of the 'papists'. Protestant denominational inter-relations varied with the changing political environment and much depended on the attitude of the local Anglican

3 Burke, *Clonmel*, 99. **4** *Carte papers*, 32, 172; cited in ibid. **5** Richard Perrot, mayor of Clonmel to Ormond, dated 27 May 1660, cited in ibid.; Greaves, *God's other children*, 86. **6** Burke, *Clonmel*, 86. **7** D.J. Butler, 'The meeting-house of the Protestant dissenter' (1999), 119.

establishment, particularly clergymen. Cromwellian influences had remained strong among all New English settlers, including those who had conformed to the Established Church, and there was always a strong preference among Anglicans for low-church doctrine and practice, which many hoped might lead to a re-integration of the dissenting congregations. But some Anglican clergymen so despised their fellow Protestants who dissented from the Established Church, that they had preference for Roman Catholics. The most prominent example was Thomas Milles, bishop of Waterford and Lismore, who was of the English high-church persuasion. Milles' intolerance of dissenting Protestants extended to his forbidding his clergy to have any dealings with them and to requesting the city recorder that their new meeting-house be demolished. He thought it wrong that the Presbyterians 'should enjoy so handsome a place when poor Father John, the titular [i.e. Roman Catholic] dean of Waterford, has no better than a thatched cabin without gates'.[8]

Though their distribution was quite diffuse, the membership of dissenting congregations tended to be located in towns and their hinterlands. In South Tipperary, one-third of the congregations and three-quarters of the membership centred on Clonmel and its hinterland and included a number of wealthy landowners and merchants. Three-quarters of the remaining congregations were located in or near settlements; English Presbyterians and Independents were each represented at Clonmel and Tipperary (see map 13). These depended on loopholes for their survival, as with the Independent / Presbyterian congregation at Tipperary town, under the Revd James Wood, who had been Independent minister at Youghal from 1657 until the Restoration. He did not conform and was appointed schoolmaster of the Erasmus Smith grammar school in Tipperary, which was exempt from episcopal visitation during Smith's lifetime. Colonel Jerome Sankey, as governor of the Erasmus Smith schools trust from 1657 to 1684, allowed the survival of this fellow dissenter as minister-schoolmaster. During his time at Tipperary, Wood wrote *Shepardy spiritualized* (London, 1680), which he dedicated to his 'beloved friends, the sheep masters and shepherds in the county of Tipperary and Ireland'.[9] In the absence of a ministerial supply, the Presbyterians of both Clonmel and Tipperary seem to have availed of Wood's ministry in the decade after 1660.[10]

The centrality of Colonel Sankey (former military governor of Clonmel precinct during the Cromwellian protectorate) to the survival of Protestant dissent over a wide area of the province of Munster becomes apparent in the early 1670s, when it is recorded that he, with others, petitioned the presbytery of Antrim for resident ministers to be placed at centres of Protestant dissent in the south of Ireland. The willingness of Ulster Scots Presbyterians to work with English dissenting groups in the south, combined with the survival of wealthy landowners like Sankey, secured the future of these congregations. A resident Presbyterian ministry was inaugurated at Clonmel, Cork, Limerick, Waterford and other key Munster towns between 1673 and 1675; the Revd William Cocks was installed as Presbyterian minister of

8 Memorandum dated 8 September 1709, in 'Diary of the Revd John Cook', Presbyterian Historical Society, Belfast. **9** See Kilroy, *Protestant dissent*, 68; 135; Barnard, *Cromwellian Ireland*, 192. **10** Burke, *Clonmel*, 99; 294; D.J. Butler, 'Presbyterianism in Clonmel, 1650–1977' (2003).

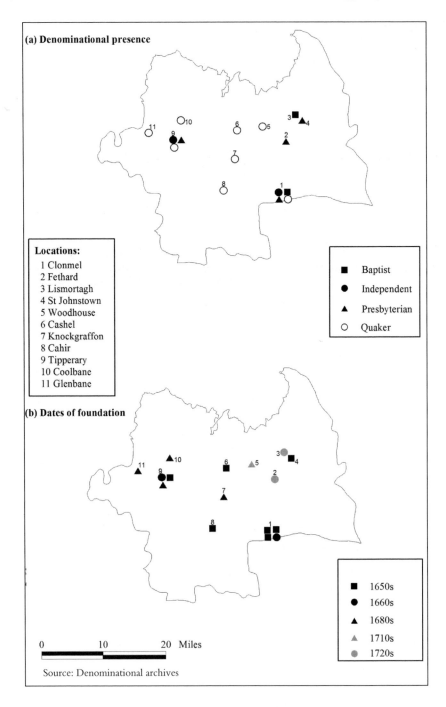

(a) Denominational presence

Locations:
1 Clonmel
2 Fethard
3 Lismortagh
4 St Johnstown
5 Woodhouse
6 Cashel
7 Knockgraffon
8 Cahir
9 Tipperary
10 Coolbane
11 Glenbane

■ Baptist

● Independent

▲ Presbyterian

○ Quaker

(b) Dates of foundation

0   10   20   Miles

Source: Denominational archives

■ 1650s

● 1660s

▲ 1680s

▲ 1710s

● 1720s

Map 13: The Protestant dissenting congregations, *c.*1650–*c.*1730

Fig. 11: The Erasmus Smith [Abbey] grammar school

Clonmel, with stated supply of Tipperary in 1673, while Wood continued as Independent minister of both towns.[11] This ambiguity was rectified in 1679 through the application by Cocks to have Wood ordained by presbytery as minister of the united Independent / Presbyterian congregation at Tipperary, in which role he continued until 1688, when he fled the disturbances. In 1696, the Presbyterians and Independents formalized this cooperation by forming the presbytery of Munster, where in each area the dominant congregation – usually Presbyterian – became the accepted denomination. In 1695, Independent congregations existed at Dublin, Limerick, Carlow, Cork, Wexford and Tipperary; in 1696, all but that of Dublin united with Presbyterian meetings.[12]

The Presbyterian Church, from its base in the province of Ulster, was the only dissenting denomination capable of providing a resident ministry in the south of Ireland in this period, which was far more desirable than a supply from elsewhere. South Tipperary membership and financial support was drawn from an array of Cromwellian families in the Clonmel hinterland, with satellite meetings at Tipperary and Fethard, prior to the appointment of resident ministers there in 1700 and 1728 respectively. It is unclear where the Clonmel dissenting congregation met initially, but it is likely they took over the former Franciscan friary *c.*1691, as congregation accounts show they re-slated the nave in 1704–5.[13] This act, coming shortly after the vacation by the friars of the last continuously occupied urban friary in Ireland, was a highly symbolic take-over of sacred space. A precedent had been set in the

11 *A history of congregations in the Presbyterian Church of Ireland*: entry for Clonmel congregation. **12** Greaves, *God's other children*, 378. **13** The Riall account book reveals an annual salary of £100 to the Revd John Shaw, minister in 1706, made up by a personal levy on the congregation: see Burke, *Clonmel*, 294.

building of the Main Guard palatinate courthouse in 1674 by the duke of Ormond, on the site of the friary infirmary, using stone from both the friary and additional sandstone brought from the Cistercian abbey at nearby Inishlounaght (Marlfield).[14] This gave added symbolism to the building later used for the trial of Fr Nicholas Sheehy in 1766. One other invasion of sacred space by the secular arm of the establishment took place in South Tipperary, through the building of the Erasmus Smith [Abbey] grammar school in 1680, on the site of and using stone from the Augustinian abbey of Tipperary town.[15] In 1820, this school was rebuilt on the same site (fig. 11), utilizing much of the earlier material, so that by this date, only the main entrance arch of the Augustinian friary remained.

The post-Restoration numerical weakness of the Baptists was due in large part to their failure to establish a significant membership base beyond the Cromwellian military establishment in the 1650s.[16] Their wealth at the Restoration can be seen through the Clonmel congregation, which in 1659 had installed Robert Carr as pastor, while the 'hearth money roll' (1665) lists his successor, a Pastor Hough, living in a substantial eight-hearth house which probably doubled as manse and meeting-house.[17] Much information on the ensuing geographical contraction of the Baptist denomination in Munster can be drawn from the Cork church book.[18] As I have argued elsewhere, heritage and origins were of the utmost importance to non-established or proscribed denominations in a state where there was an official religion.[19] The maintenance of a separate Baptist identity proved difficult, as demonstrated by the membership of the Cloghkeating Baptist Church, near Cloughjordan in North Tipperary, where by the early eighteenth century many had 'gon[e] off to a different profession and are now so blended, as scarce to be distinguished'.[20]

The Cork church book gives insight into the system of preaching supply from Cork to its mission station at Clonmel (subsequently Lismortagh) in South Tipperary. The Cork congregation had been rescued from extinction in 1704, at the expense of a few wealthy Cromwellian families, through the provision of a pastor, a graduate of the newly established education fund for the Baptist ministry.

> At the same time [in 1704] there was a small people at Clonmel, destitute of a pastor, who though incapable of supporting one, were willing to contribute according to their ability and most anxious for a [preaching] supply. In line, Mr Pettit was ordained at Clonmel as pastor of the church of Cork and of that place jointly and supplied both places during his lifetime.[21]

The selection of Clonmel for the joint ordination was a practical one, in that its congregation was still in possession of their chapel. This is significant, for persecu-

14 M. Quinlan, 'The Main Guard, Clonmel: the rediscovery of a seventeenth-century courthouse' (1994). 15 Marnane, *Land and violence*, 11. 16 C. Kirtland, *A history of the Baptist denomination in Ireland* (1868), 9; 14. 17 Laffan, *Tipperary's families*: ville de Clonmel. 18 Cork church book: a bound volume of folio MSS held at Cork Baptist Church. 19 D.J. Butler, 'An historical geography of the Irish Baptist churches, 1650–1870' (1998); idem, 'The meeting-house of the Protestant dissenter'; idem, 'Representing Christianity in Ireland' (2001). 20 Cork church book, fo. 17. 21 Ibid., fos. 22–4.

tion at Cork during the 1680s had required that congregation to give up their urban meeting place and to withdraw to the residence of the Riggs family, at Riggsdale, six miles from the city. Surviving documentation relating to the Baptist chapel at Clonmel is limited to an entry in the registry of deeds, when the house in High Street was leased to generate income, in order to meet the costs of the monthly preaching supply.[22]

The Baptist meeting at Clonmel seems to have predominantly comprised second-generation Cromwellian households. As a result of inter-marriage with members of the Established Church and the outward movement of urban merchant families to landed estates, the congregation dwindled to the point where no members remained at Clonmel. In 1723, the lease of the chapel premises was sold and the remnant of the congregation – concentrated in the Fethard-Killenaule hinterland, ten miles north of Clonmel – commenced meetings at Lismortagh in the house of a member.[23] This meeting continued to be important in the linkage with Cork, for the succeeding minister of the joint charge was ordained in 1729 at Lismortagh, in the presence of the four pastors remaining in Ireland.[24] Inter-denominational cooperation was essential for the survival of outlying mission stations dependant on preaching supplies. At Cork, the Presbyterian minister assisted the Baptist pastor by assuming his preaching responsibilities during the one weekend each month he attended Clonmel or Lismortagh.[25]

The last of the trio of dissenting denominations in South Tipperary, the Society of Friends, was not part of the Cromwellian regime, though almost contemporary with it. The Friends first appeared in Ireland in 1653 and two member families were holding house meetings in South Tipperary by the end of the decade: George Baker in Cashel, by 1657, and George Fennell, near Cahir, from 1659.[26] The Quakers were more a sect than a denomination in these years and were ostracized by the Anglican establishment for their refusal to pay tithes or acknowledge dignitaries. The years after 1660 saw considerable expansion of the sect in Munster and Leinster, through the conversion of some existing Cromwellian families, but predominantly through the arrival of increasing numbers of converts from England to settle Ireland, augmented by 'travelling Friends' as the Quaker lay ministry was referred to by its membership. Their expansion in South Tipperary from bases at Clonmel, Cashel and Cahir took place in the years from 1680 to 1720. As late as 1701, nearly half of the Quaker meetings in Ireland – 26 of 53 – gathered in private homes: in Munster, 5 of 11 did so.[27] House-meetings were established at Tipperary town and the nearby townlands of Coolbane and Glenbane, as well as at Knockgraffon and Woodhouse

22 RD 23/325/13741: registered 6 August 1719, 'a stone house slated, with a thatched house backwards in High Street', in a bond dated 23 August 1718, between Spencer and Johnson, business partners, Clonmel and Pettit, gent, Cork, the partners to pay Pettit £250 sterling and 8 per cent per annum interest. **23** RD 42/277/26200: registered 29 April 1724: lease dated 4 March 1723. **24** Cork church book, fo. 25; K. Herlihy, 'The early eighteenth-century Irish Baptists: two letters' (1992). In 1729, the Cork church had a membership of 47 adults, which probably included Lismortagh. **25** Pastor Pettit, Cork to Pastor Elisha Callender, America, dated 25 November 1725, cited in Herlihy, 'The early eighteenth-century Irish Baptists'. **26** FHL, Tipperary monthly meeting records. **27** Greaves, *God's other children*, 308.

(Mogorban) in the Cashel hinterland. This system saw continued expansion through the south, east and north of Ireland, targeting areas of considerable Protestant settlement and siphoning members from existing congregations. Many of these meetings were short-lived and of these five house meetings, only that at Tipperary town ever constructed a meeting-house. By 1750, only Woodhouse continued as a licensed house for worship.

Clonmel was one of a small minority of Irish provincial towns, which simultaneously sustained three Protestant dissenting congregations in the post-Restoration period, for in addition to the Baptists and the united Independent-Presbyterian congregation; there was also a meeting of Quakers from 1661, held at the house of George Collett in Westgate Street, present-day O'Connell Street.[28] The establishment vilified the un-baptized Quakers, who were consequently denied burial among baptized Christians in parish graveyards. From an early stage, effectively from their arrival in Ireland, Quakers were buried in the garden of one of their membership. The garden of John Fennell at Kilcommonbeg near Cahir was first used in 1661 for the burial of one of his own children and was subsequently used for the burial of some 30 Friends from a wide area of Co. Tipperary up to 1738, when replaced by a larger ground at Ballybrado on the Fennell estate. The meetings at Cashel and Clonmel provided similar grounds in the early eighteenth century: at Clonmel, in 1709; that at Mogorban – donated by the Boles family of Woodhouse – opened in 1726 and replaced that at Cashel.

The Society of Friends was typical of the Protestant dissenting denominations in being a tight-knit community that realized it could not afford many losses if it were to remain viable. In 1714, the Quakers of Cahir recorded their unwillingness 'to part with Thomas Coborne and family to the province of Pennsylvania, America. We dissuade them from such a long and hazardous journey, he being ancient, but they are insisting upon it and desiring a certificate from Friends'.[29] A certificate of good standing was essential to any transfer from one Quaker meeting to another, which means that each removal was fully documented. On the whole, few South Tipperary members were lost to emigration, for in over six decades after 1682, just 12 individuals arrived in Pennsylvania from Tipperary monthly meeting.[30] Protestant dissent generally feared community losses to the Established Church, to Roman Catholicism and to emigration.

At all times in the history of English colonial settlement in Ireland, even prior to the Reformation, the settler colony was in danger of assimilation into the Irish population through intermarriage and contact conversion. This phenomenon had occurred within many Old English dynasties by 1650 and numerous acts were consequently passed by the Cromwellians forbidding inter-marriage between the New English and the Old English/Gaelic Irish ethnic groups. Protestant heiresses, perceived as particularly vulnerable to Irishmen, were protected under an Act of 1698, which stated that no Protestant woman possessed of real estate to the value of £500

---

28 Burke, *Clonmel*, 296.   29 FHL, Grubb collection S1856, MS box 56, 'minute of Cashel monthly meeting, dated 11 February 1714'; births and burials register of the Tipperary monthly meeting.   30 A. Cook-Meyers, *Emigration of the Irish Quakers to Pennsylvania, 1682–1747* (1902), 82–3.

could marry any person without first obtaining a certificate of his known adherence to Protestantism from the minister of the parish, the bishop of the diocese or a neighbouring justice of the peace. Further legislation followed until every eventuality from the taking advantage of a minor, to the marriage of any person 'who hath been a Protestant at any time' with a 'papist' had been legislated for.[31]

Private individuals made similar stipulations in order to preserve the segregation of New English dynasties from Irish Roman Catholics of any ethnicity, Gaelic Irish or Old English, titled or untitled. These are to be found in the wills and last testaments of settlers, for it was through inheritance that the traditions of the previous generation were maintained. The desire to preserve English ethnicity and Protestant identity is implicit in the will of a Cromwellian soldier, Charles Blount, later collector of the revenue for Clonmel, who died in 1663. He bequeathed his estate to his wife 'in confidence that she would be a tender mother to his children and improve the estate for her own and their advantage, careful of their breeding.'[32] More explicitly, the will of Andrew Roe of Tipperary, a Presbyterian, required that 'my daughter Mary shall marry a Protestant who has been educated and bred up on the Protestant religion, either as a Protestant dissenter or according to the Established Church of this kingdom, for at least twenty years before such marriage'.[33] The last testament of Sir Jerome Alexander of Kilcooley abbey is another example. He left his extensive estates at Kilcooley, Co. Tipperary, and Kilmainham, Co. Dublin, to his only child, Elizabeth, who was to forfeit all if she

> at any time after my decease marry and take [for] a husband any lord of Ireland by what name or title so ever he bears, or the son of any such lord, or nobleman whatsoever, or the son of any archbishop, bishop, or prelate, or any knight, baronet, knight esquire, gentleman or any Irishman, or [anyone] that comes of an Irish extraction and descent, or that hath been borne or bred in the kingdom of Ireland … or any papist.[34]

In accordance with her father's wishes, Elizabeth Alexander married in 1676, Sir William Barker of Bocking Hall, Essex, an English baronet.

The consequence of intermarriage with Old English or Gaelic Irish Roman Catholic dynasties was exclusion from family and community. Several examples of disinheritance on intermarriage with a Roman Catholic, or on conversion to Roman Catholicism, survive from South Tipperary. A prime example was John Wright of Cloneen, near Fethard. Although of impeccable Cromwellian ancestry, he converted to Roman Catholicism, was disinherited and the estate settled on his sister Margaret, who married a Protestant as stipulated by her parents.[35] Similarly, the will of John Langley of Lisnamrock, Killenaule bequeathed his

31 Burke, *Irish Priests*, 187–8: these were 9 William III, c.28; 6 Anne, c.16; 8 Anne, c.3; 12 George I, c.3; 19 George II, c.13 **32** Will of Charles Blount, dated 18 April 1663, cited in Burke, *Clonmel*, 327; 91. **33** Will of Andrew Roe of Tipperary Town, dated 1713 (transcript), in Grubb (Carrick-on-Suir) collection, NAI, Dublin. **34** Will of Sir Jerome Alexander, proved 1670, cited in Neely, *Kilcooley*, 33–4; 40. **35** Burke, *Clonmel*, 335.

house, goods and farm of Blackkettle of 253 acres to my son commonly called
Stubborn Jack, to him and his heirs forever, provided he marries a Protestant,
but not [if he marries] Alice Kendrick, who called me 'Oliver's whelp'.[36]

Dissenters often left money to aid the continuance of the small congregations in
which they had been raised or had spent a considerable portion of their lives. Leading
families were expected to provide worship facilities and, in a non-inflationary period,
congregations depended solely upon the interest from bequests of money or property to fund a minister's salary, in a manner quite similar to the strategies employed
by Roman Catholics. Both of these aspects are illustrated in the will of Andrew Roe,
who besides bequeathing money from his estates to the Revd Nathaniel Card of
Clonmel and the Revd Richard Edge of Tipperary and their successors, bequeathed
in trust for Tipperary Presbyterian congregation 'the house near my dwelling house
in the town of Tipperary, commonly called the meeting-house, with the yard or passage leading from the [Main] street of Tipperary thereto, for the remainder of my
term of years therein.'[37] The Presbyterians were involved in urban trade as merchants
and bankers and were, by the turn of the eighteenth century, enabled to invest in
large areas of urban property and also to purchase country estates on which to retire.
Damer of Tipperary and Vaughan, Riall and Bagwell of Clonmel were all merchant
bankers by 1700 and displayed a close kinship network.[38]

Stipulations designed to ensure that heirs remained within the fold of Protestant
dissent occur with remarkable frequency, with the names of executors providing
a comprehensive account of kinship networks in the local dissenting communities.
The will of John Colsery – after naming as executors two prominent members of
the Clonmel Presbyterian congregation, John Perry and Phineas Riall – demonstrated his wish that his family continue their separate identity outside the Established
Church, in a codicil requiring that each of his sons should obtain

> a certificate of their good behaviour and civil deportment and demeanour
> from any four or more of the following – John Pyke esq. [of Woodenstown],
> Mathew Jacob esq. [of Fethard], Mr Andrew Roe of Tipperary, the Revd Mr
> John Shaw Senior of Clonmell, Charles Alcocke esq., Mr Philip Carleton,
> Mr John Damer [of Tipperary] and Mr John Bagwell of Ballyboy, or be cut
> off with five shillings, the rest of the moiety share to go to the other.[39]

Despite inter-communal bitterness and general apartheid, there were occasional
cross-community gestures, as demonstrated by Colonel John Booker, who in 1664
bequeathed 'to the poor English inhabitants in Clonmell £5 [and] to the poor Irish
inhabitants £10 10s.' Even this gesture was frustrated, as in his final will of 1665;
these provisions were omitted in favour of family provisions, probably at the insti-

---

36 Will of John Langley of Lisnamrock, dated 3 March 1674, cited in J. Hassett and R. Fitzgerald (eds),
The history and folklore of Killenaule-Moyglass (1990), 112–13.   **37** Will of Andrew Roe of Tipperary.
38 Burke, *Clonmel*, 175; Power, *Land, politics and society*, 60–1.   **39** Will of John Colsery, dated 7
December 1699 (proved 1709), cited in Burke, *Clonmel*, 329–30.

gation of members of the Protestant community.[40] More often than not, the provisions of wealthy Protestants were solely in favour of their own community, as with that of William Vaughan, who in 1699 resolved

> to give and bequeath to the poor English Protestants of the town of Clonmell the sum of £20 sterling to be put out at interest for them by my executors and the interest thereof yearly to be distributed and given every new years day to whom and to such English poor Protestants as my executors hereafter named shall think fit.[41]

These wills and others of the period are valuable for they highlight the presence of poor English inhabitants soon after the Cromwellian settlement, dispelling the myth that all New English settlers were wealthy merchants and landowners. They also display a strong desire on the part of gentry, merchants and clergy to ensure that the Protestant poor were maintained by those of their own particular religious persuasion, and thus protected from falling-in with the locals. Inheritance stipulation, combined with diverse and innovative territorial strategies, may thus be seen as fundamental in preserving the integrity of the Protestant community in general, and Protestant dissent in particular.

The ingenious inheritance stipulations and territorial strategies employed by the various Protestant dissenting congregations demonstrate flaws underlying the image of the overall consolidation of power and control by the establishment. These signs indicate the achievement of only partial political, social and economic hegemony by 1730, with signs of a growing realization of this situation evident in contemporary local government papers.

---

40 Wills of Colonel John Booker, dated 20 May 1664 and 3 July 1665, cited in ibid., 327–8. **41** Will of William Vaughan, proved 1699, cited in ibid., 340.

10

Strategies of consolidation:
the charter schools and estate colonies

> The report was that, if the outbreak took place, neither men, women, nor children were to be spared; now I believe they [the Irish rebels] have condescended to say that women and children will be permitted to live … it would be better if all the stablemen at Curraghmore were Protestants. In this establishment, the men and women both inside and out are Catholics; that is what makes one feel so insecure.[1]

This quotation, dating from 1848 and referring to the rising at Ballingarry in South Tipperary, could easily have been taken from the depositions and examinations relating to the insurrection of 1641, or from a Cromwellian massacre of the 1650s. Its date and tone are indicative of the thread of continuity running through the entire period covered by this study. Sectarian tension became particularly acute in the 1710s and 1720s and Protestant insecurities, combined with a growing realization on the part of the local and national authorities of the political significance of the continuance of religious orders, prompted the initiation of a sample survey of their territorial organization in Cos. Mayo and Galway and the city of Galway.[2] A thriving underground Roman Catholic denomination was revealed in the findings of the report. At Galway, the mayor duly reported that his sheriffs had searched the reputed Augustinian friary in Back Street, but could not find any friars. Revealingly, the Augustinians' accounts for 9 November 1731 note the expense of 'a bottle of wine for ye sheriffs [costing] 1s. 1d'.[3] The sheriffs described the house of the Dominican Order as

> the friary in the west suburbs, called the Dominican friary, wherein is a large chapel, with a gallery, some forms and an altarpiece, defaced; in which said reputed friary, there are ten chambers and eight beds, wherein, the friars belonging to the said friary usually lay, but [we] could find none of them. It is an old friary, but some repairs [are] lately made in it.

That the Dominican friars were also merely in temporary hiding and that officials of the establishment had connived to conceal them is revealed in the Dominican account book entry 'for claret to treat ye sheriffs in their search, ye 11th … 2s. 6d.'[4]

---

1 A. Hare, *Two noble lives* (1893), 307–8.   2 *Journal of the Irish House of Lords* (1731): session of 6 December 1731, 4 George II.   3 D.D.C. Pochin-Mould, *The monasteries of Ireland* (1976), 122–3.   4 Ibid.

The widespread and continued presence of friars in the vicinity of their former religious houses gave grave cause for concern, as would also the extent of corruption of officials of state, had it been realised, particularly given the continuing Jacobite threat. A survey of the entire Roman Catholic territorial organization on the island of Ireland was consequently ordered and also a hearth money roll that distinguished between the two ethnic communities, Protestant and 'popish'. These surveys commenced in March 1732 and the abstracts of the report were published later that year. The findings of the 'report on popery' regarding the Roman Catholic mass-house network generated the observation that some appeared to be large and pompous buildings,

> particularly one in Tipperary [town], returned by his Grace, the archbishop of Cashel, one in Mullingar, returned by the late bishop of Meath and one in the parish of St Mary Shandon, city of Cork, which by examination of the Revd Mr Dean Ward, minister of the said parish, the Lord's committee find to be a large and expensive building, raised in one of the most conspicuous parts of that great city. Mass-houses are as openly frequented as churches.[5]

It is significant that, of many hundreds of mass-houses surveyed across the entire island, the first of three singled out for special reference lay within South Tipperary. According to the report, the slated mass-house at Tipperary, then nearing completion, was a cruciform structure, measuring 92 feet in length in the nave by 76 feet in transept width. The distribution and foundation dates of mass-houses in South Tipperary, of which there was a total of 48 in use by 1731–2, is shown in map 14.[6] In the northern two-thirds of South Tipperary, comprising that part of the diocese of Cashel and Emly lying within the boundary of the study area, there were 28, mostly (re)built since 1714, while the southern one-third lying within Lismore diocese contained a further 20. In contrast, as may be deduced from map 16, the territorial organization of the Established Church was much less developed, with only 25 active congregations as late as 1760, of which two had been recently formed.

It is evident from the returns sent by rectors that a significant number of mass-houses in the valley of the river Suir – mainly in or adjacent to urban core areas – had been constructed before 1714, the start of the reign of George I. These buildings, which predominated in the south of the study area, were of a more durable nature, indicative of a greater parochial wealth and tolerance by local Protestant interests in these districts than elsewhere in the county. Across mid-Tipperary, mass-houses constructed since 1714 were prevalent, constituting a recent improvement on the part of the rural parishes on earlier meeting facilities, though usually on the site, or in the immediate vicinity, of their predecessors. In the primary towns of the Cashel archdiocese lying within South Tipperary – that is, Cashel, Tipperary and Fethard – the influence of the regular clergy can be noted. At Cashel, the

---

5 *House of Lords Journal* (1732): 'report on the state of popery in Ireland', 5 George II. **6** J. MacCaffrey (ed.), 'Report on the state of popery, 1731: part 4' (1915), 175; see Smyth, 'a colony', 178 for an island-wide perspective.

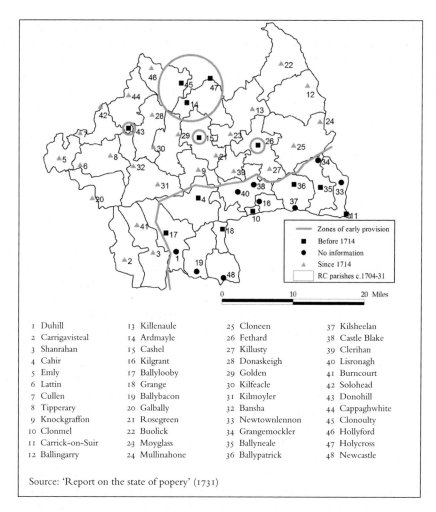

1 Duhill	13 Killenaule	25 Cloneen	37 Kilsheelan
2 Carrigavisteal	14 Ardmayle	26 Fethard	38 Castle Blake
3 Shanrahan	15 Cashel	27 Killusty	39 Clerihan
4 Cahir	16 Kilgrant	28 Donaskeigh	40 Lisronagh
5 Emly	17 Ballylooby	29 Golden	41 Burncourt
6 Lattin	18 Grange	30 Kilfeacle	42 Solohead
7 Cullen	19 Ballybacon	31 Kilmoyler	43 Donohill
8 Tipperary	20 Galbally	32 Bansha	44 Cappaghwhite
9 Knockgraffon	21 Rosegreen	33 Newtownlennon	45 Clonoulty
10 Clonmel	22 Buolick	34 Grangemockler	46 Hollyford
11 Carrick-on-Suir	23 Moyglass	35 Ballyneale	47 Holycross
12 Ballingarry	24 Mullinahone	36 Ballypatrick	48 Newcastle

Source: 'Report on the state of popery' (1731)

Map 14: The foundation of Roman Catholic mass-houses, *c.*1731

thatched mass-house was in a side-street called Chapel Lane, which immediately adjoined the ruined Dominican Abbey and was predominantly staffed by members of that Order throughout the eighteenth century. At Tipperary, the new building of 1731–2 in Mass Lane was constructed on the site of its predecessor, while the lately improved and enlarged mass-house of Fethard was located in Chapel Lane, just outside the walled town. Tipperary, and particularly Fethard, availed of the services of the Augustinian Order as curates; at Clonmel, the urban parish of St Mary availed of the services of the Franciscan friars.[7] In the principal urban centres, therefore, the Roman Catholic Church was already solidly grounded both in terms of buildings and personnel at this early stage.

7 For an illustration of Clonmel mass-house towards the end of its life, see fig. 22.

The Franciscans served the Clonmel, Carrick-on-Suir, Galbally and Cashel hin-terlands, as did the Cistercians at Holycross, the Dominicans at Cashel, and the Augustinians at Fethard and Tipperary. Rural districts were not always so well facil-itated, however, and the opposition of insecure and isolated Protestant families had repercussions for a few specific pockets of South Tipperary. According to tradi-tion, several generations of the Maude family of Dundrum House persecuted priests to the extent that at one stage – at Clonoulty in the 1740s – mass could only be held at night.[8] In the adjoining civil parish of Ballintemple in the north-western corner, the opposition of Maude prevented the construction of a mass-house in the vicinity of his estate village of Dundrum, thus requiring parishioners to travel to Ruan chapel at Donaskeigh, built in 1730, at the other end of the parish. This situation was exceptional in South Tipperary, as it was in most areas outside the province of Ulster, for by 1731, the countryside was well provided with chapels or mass-houses built in the vernacular style.

In general, the penal laws concerning Roman Catholic chapels were not strictly enforced after the death of Queen Anne in 1714, except when foreign invaders in the Jacobite interest actually landed in Britain or Ireland, as occurred in 1715. In that first year of the Hanoverian succession to the throne, the duke of Ormond committed to the Jacobite (Stuart) cause and was consequently attainted and deprived of his estates and lordship of the Tipperary palatinate. At times of perceived danger such as this, the penal legislation against Roman Catholics was enforced and even strengthened, until the immediacy of the threat to the new regime had passed. Increasingly, however, these temporary enforcements became less common and even in the 1731 session of the Irish House of Lords that ordered the 'return on popery', there were signs in evidence that opinion in the Irish Parliament was shift-ing significantly to favour increased tolerance of Roman Catholics. It was reported by a member regarding the proposed repeal of the Sacramental Test Act that 'too many in the House of Commons show a disposition to favour the papists more than is consistent with the Protestant interest here. There was [previously] a very great spirit against popery among the Commons, which I fear I cannot say now'.[9] However, mass-houses were closed for several months in 1734 by the Irish Parliament, in protest against the perceived leniency of the British Privy Council in suppressing recent bills received from Ireland under the terms of Poynings' Law (1494) and as a reminder to the Roman Catholics of their inferior position. Nevertheless, the way was paved for widespread parish re-organization in the ensu-ing two decades, so that by 1743, the preacher of the annual 1641 commemoration sermon before the Irish House of Commons could remark the Roman Catholics

> enjoy the free exercise of their religion in a manner little differing in fact from legal toleration … if any harshness appears in some of our laws with respect to their clergy, it is well known they were intended to prevent treason against the state and are never executed on any account merely religious.[10]

8 W.S. Doyle, *Fragments: scenes and stories of historic Cashel and Emly* (1945), 54, 57; K. Whelan, 'The Catholic parish and village development in Ireland' (1983), 6. 9 Letters of the lord primate, Dr Hugh Boulter, cited in Connolly, *Religion, law and power*, 289. 10 'A sermon preached at St Andrew's church,

These sentiments are echoed in a final reminder of the power of the penal laws, through one last forcible shutting down of the Roman Catholic parish organization for some months in 1744. Yet, ironically, when an actual threat of Jacobite invasion and rebellion appeared the following year, no such measures were taken. Archbishop Arthur Price of Cashel instructed his clergy that Roman Catholics in their parishes 'should be looked upon as part of your flock tho' they are not part of your congregation'.[11] Little hardship was consequently experienced when compared with the Jacobite invasion and repression of 1715.

The hearth money roll of 1732 for Co. Tipperary (see table 7) reveals that there were 1,627 Protestant to 16,465 Roman Catholic households, so that the Protestants represented 9 per cent of the total county population, a proportion of nearly 1:10. In South Tipperary, the 838 Protestant to 10,559 Roman Catholic households gave a slightly lower return of 7.5 per cent. While the figures for South Tipperary were higher in absolute terms, the resilience of the planters of North Tipperary – combined with their proximity to the considerable Protestant marriage field of the King's and Queen's Counties and a significantly lower overall population in the northern baronies – gave them a higher percentage of the total population there. These figures, as with the other counties, did not include garrisons or those living in various state institutions.

Table 7: The hearth money roll of 1732: religious composition[12]

Barony	Protestant families	Protestant percentile	'Popish' families	Total families
Kilnamanagh	30	2.6	1,078	1,108
Iffa and Offa	377	9.3	4,070	4,447
Clanwilliam	206	9.2	2,042	2,248
Middlethird	166	7.8	1,951	2,117
Slieveardagh	59	4.0	1,418	1,477
Total	838	7.5	10,559	11,397

When judged against the last comparable population surveys of 1659–60 and 1666–7 (see fig. 30), it can be seen that the Protestant population, which had been remarkably constant in all five baronies in the period 1659 to 1667, had by 1732 seen considerable overall growth, most particularly in Clanwilliam, where numbers had increased by two-thirds, and also in Iffa and Offa, where numbers had increased by one-tenth.[13] The downward trends already noticeable in the baronies of Kilnamanagh and Slieveardagh by 1666–7 continued. These two baronies had been assigned as payment to Cromwellian soldiers, many of whom sold their land

Dublin, 21 October 1743', cited in ibid., 290. **11** Watson, *Dinner of herbs*, 87. **12** MS 1742/P/8973, Lambeth Palace Library, 'an abstract of the numbers of Protestant and Popish families in the several baronies, counties and provinces of Ireland, 1732'. **13** A multiplier of 5.2 per household is recommended in D. Dickson, 'Hearth tax, household size and Irish population change, 1672–1821' (1982).

allotments to the minority willing to remain in permanent residence and returned to England. By 1732, over 40 per cent of the population of Kilnamanagh recorded in 1660 and 1666–7 had disappeared in this manner, while the decline from 1666–7 in Slieveardagh was over 50 per cent. These figures are even more dramatic for Slieveardagh when compared to the baronial totals for 1660, so that by 1732, the decline was a massive two-thirds.

The negative population growth still displayed by the rural baronies of Kilnamanagh and Slieveardagh – both of which lacked settlement of any significant size – can be largely explained on the grounds that both contained significant upland areas and suffered the economic disadvantages of a peripheral rural location. In the barony of Slieveardagh, once the extensive forests and significant mineral deposits had been exhausted, the frontier may have proved 'hollow' and the Protestant community suffered numerical collapse. There may also have been some contact conversion, with assimilation of Protestants into the Roman Catholic community. In 1732, the barony of Middlethird, containing the important walled towns of Cashel and Fethard and their fertile hinterlands, also exhibited negative growth. This decline by one-quarter on the population of 1666–7 is not readily explicable. There may have been migration to other adjacent areas, such as the barony of Clanwilliam, which exhibited significant growth during the same period. The barony of Middlethird had seen a massive growth of 60 per cent in the early 1660s, at least partly explained by the attraction of rural dwellers to the economic advantages of urban living. The figure recorded for 1732 does compare favourably with the population recorded in 1660, however, in being almost one-fifth higher. As the sale of Cromwellian land grants continued into a second generation of estate consolidation, particularly in the baronies of Kilnamanagh and Slieveardagh, the insecurity of their principal remaining gentry consequently led to the most sustained and ultimately the most successful efforts at estate colony plantation in South Tipperary, in the second half of the eighteenth century. The earliest attempts at the plantation of Protestant colonies took place during the 1740s in the baronies of Clanwilliam and Iffa and Offa, both of which had displayed slow, though consistent growth in the Protestant population.

The frustrations and insecurities of the Protestant establishment in Ireland regarding their numerical inferiority at the beginning of the eighteenth century was such that many of its leading clergy advocated a conversion approach involving the education of the local population, through charitable institutions. As early as 1698, Bishop Foy of Waterford and Lismore had linked the survival of superstition and idolatry among the Irish to 'their wild savage way of living in single cottages and dismal uninhabitable places' and proposed that 'the Irish nation' should be corralled into towns and villages and compelled to attend English-speaking schools.[14] This movement promoting charity schools gathered pace in the 1710s and 1720s and was sharply accelerated by the findings of the 'report on popery' and hearth money roll of 1732, which clearly demonstrated the numerical inadequacies of the Protestant establishment generally and the territorial inadequacies of the Established Church in particular. These findings heightened insecurities accordingly. It was

14 I. McBride, 'The common name of Irishman', 241.

Fig. 12: The Clonmel charter school, built 1748

against this background that the charter schools movement to convert Roman Catholics was launched in 1733. As was the case previously, loyalty to the state was linked to the profession of Protestantism, in particular Anglicanism, and the outbreak of war in 1739 on the Continent led to a fresh return of Protestant householders by the hearth money collectors and also to a rise in conversions from Roman Catholicism in 1740 and 1741.[15]

Conversions to the Established Church – as recorded in the conformity rolls – correspond to the actions of propertied or ambitious individuals who had need to certify their own conformity. The recording of the conversions of 15 married couples in 1747 – mainly farmers and their wives, in the parish of Clogheen – was no accident, and is one of the more prominent examples of a convert landlord family in the process of proving their total dedication to Anglicanism and the establishment.[16] The Jacobite invasion of Britain in 1745–6 was followed by another sharp rise in conversions and a quarter of the 50 charter schools established island-wide were opened in the 1747 to 1749 period, reflecting these waves of fear, uncertainty and insecurity unleashed by the Jacobite incursion. This was also the period of the opening of charter schools at Clonmel (1748) and Cashel (1751) in South Tipperary and at nearby Newport (1751), in North Tipperary. The particular aims of the charter school society reflect all of these concerns, seeking

> *firstly,* the rescuing of the children of the poor natives from that ignorance, superstition and idolatry to which they were devoted from their infancy, to begin with the rising generation, by training up the children of papists in the purity of Christian faith and morals, before the corruptions of popery have taken root

15 Cullen, *Modern Ireland,* 196.   **16** Ibid.

Fig. 13: The Cashel charter school, built 1751

in their hearts; *secondly*, the society proposes to strengthen his Majesty's government and the Protestant interest of Ireland by increasing the number of Protestants in the only Christian and reasonable way; *thirdly*, to cure by degrees that habit of idleness, which is too prevalent among the poor of this kingdom and spread gradually through the kingdom the English spirit of improvement.[17]

The early opening of a charter school at Clonmel was facilitated by the appointment of the prominent local Protestant dissenter and moneylender, John Bagwell, as a collector of subscriptions in the opening years of the Society, 1734–7 and through the bequest in 1743 of £500 to be used to purchase lands for the erection of a charter school. In 1747, a member of the Moore family granted a perpetuity lease of 24 acres at Silversprings and £100 towards the building.[18] The subscribers to the school are of interest and comprised the Moore family of Barne – as corporate patrons of Clonmel – with their junior branches at Chancellorstown and Marlfield; Osborne and Power of Newtownanner; and significantly, the heads of the Bagwell and Perry families, the principals of the Protestant dissenting congregation of the town. At Cashel, the charter school had the backing of the corporation, Archbishop Price and key local families such as Price of Ardmayle (kinsman of the archbishop); Palliser of Derryluskan, Fethard (descendant of a previous archbishop); and Damer of Shronell, a wealthy Unitarian.

The corporation at Cashel granted 21 acres for 99 years to the charter schools society in September 1745, while Archbishop Price donated £50 per annum during his lifetime and left £300 in his will.[19] The schools were initially well-conducted

17 P.J. Kennedy, *The Clonmel charter school, 1747–1886* (1932), 40–2. **18** Ibid., 9. **19 Clonmel**: TCD MS 5789, lease of 23 April 1747; will of 16 January 1743 (admin. granted 9 May 1746), see Kennedy, *Charter*, 32–3; **Cashel**: TCD MS 5789 (leases of 24 September 1745, 2 August 1749); NLI MS 5578,

institutions. In 1752, Bishop Pococke described that of Clonmel as 'a very neat well-regulated charter school, for 20 boys and 20 girls, founded on a legacy left by Mr Dawson', while that at Cashel was 'a sumptuous charter school for 60 children'.[20]

The architecture of both Cashel and Clonmel schools was indeed of mansion proportions and made a huge landscape statement, particularly that of Cashel (see fig. 13). The system was actively promoted by Established Church interests, both clerical and secular, for the charter schools had also an important role to play in industrialization, landscape improvement and the populating of estates with 'civilized' Protestants in the mid-eighteenth century. This is amply illustrated in the writings of Pococke regarding the planned village of Villierstown on the Villiers-Stuart estate at Dromana in north-west Waterford, adjoining South Tipperary.

> I went with Lord Grandison in his chaise half a mile to see a new town he has built called Villers town; the design is two streets crossing each other with a square in the middle for a market and chapel. There are 24 houses built with a garden to each of them and his lordship is bringing in about 80 acres of land at great expense for pasturage for the town, for as they are all [northern] linen weavers, they are not to be diverted by farming: there are above 20 of the charter [school] boys apprenticed to the weavers and my lord settles a curate here and intends to build a chapel. This chapel is since built.[21]

Charter schools continued to open throughout Ireland during the acutely sectarian decade of the 1760s, with a progressive rise in Roman Catholic conversions amid continuing belief among Protestants concerning a Roman Catholic conspiracy. However, the schools did not achieve their stated aim of acting as agents for the advancement of the state religion through the attainment of large-scale conversions, despite the considerable expense laid out in their construction and operation. Converts invariably espoused the aspirations and beliefs of their social class and stood out in Protestant eyes as a distinct and reassuring group in times of political crisis. However, the 1770s witnessed a dramatic falling-off from the religious fervour of the 1760s; the number of children housed in the schools had already peaked and some ten schools actually closed during this decade. The 1760s marked a threshold, with the final manifestations of anti-Jacobite sentiment in Munster.

The principal significance of the charter schools in South Tipperary is as an index of local gentry preoccupations and perceptions. They successfully attracted the involvement of key landed families, including several dissenter dynasties, in the promotion of the school system. The location of the institutions in the south of the county – where Protestantism was weak outside of a few key areas and generally badly distributed when compared with North Tipperary – demonstrates the extent to which these prominent dynasties were prepared to devise strategies to

---

fo. 64; **Fethard**: A school was intended, as its corporation made a grant in perpetuity for that purpose, in 1747, of 42 acres within the town liberties and £400 was donated and £33 subscribed by local benefactors. However, the *report of the incorporated society* (1766) noted no building had yet been erected and none was, in fact, ever built: see NLI MS 5858; RD 154/239/103585.   **20** J. McVeigh (ed.), *Pococke's Irish tours* (1995), 103–4.   **21** Ibid., 102.

augment their minority position. The incorporated urban centres of Clonmel, Cashel and Fethard were the powerhouses of urban, walled ascendancy that were to be the springboard for further efforts to develop and increase Protestantism in the general locality. Additionally, all three had significant Protestant populations in which those attending the charter schools were to be immersed.

Various other schemes for the conversion of the Roman Catholic population gained considerable support among Protestants during the eighteenth century, largely due to the continuing importance of the question of security, or, conversely, the continuing insecurity of the settlers. In addition, there was the widespread conviction among Protestants that Roman Catholicism, with 'its parasitic clergy, its proliferation of holy days and its stifling of individual responsibility', was inimical to economic development.[22] Schemes for the dissemination of Protestantism were thus closely linked to projects for economic development and general social improvement. Conversion was only one way of increasing the Protestant population of a given area. The other method was to bring in Protestants from elsewhere and efforts were made in the provinces of Munster, Leinster and Connaught to establish colonies of Protestants, mainly recruited from the province of Ulster.[23] The motivation behind such ventures was largely economic – either industrial or agricultural – with the general consensus being Protestant tenants of English or Scottish cultural backgrounds were both more reliable and more productive than the Irish. In many cases the importation of Ulster Protestants was also linked with attempts to introduce the spinning and weaving of linen. The introduction of Protestants in this manner to a given locality considerably boosted numbers and aided the physical security and morale of the local Protestant population. However, such measures were only useful in changing the ratio of Protestants to Roman Catholics in a particular locality and did nothing to change the balance in the country as a whole.

In addition to the formal introduction of Protestant tenants to an area by its landlord, there were occasional instances of casual or semi-formal introduction, through the temporary residence of skilled or specialist workmen, usually Protestants from Ulster or Britain. In the construction of Damer Court at Shronell, near Tipperary town, in the 1740s and 1750s, up to 60 Scottish workmen were reputedly imported by Damer, who housed them on his estate.[24] In doing this, Damer was able to avail of specialist skills not readily available in Ireland, and also to swell the ranks of the dissenting congregation to which he belonged in nearby Tipperary town with Scots, who were Presbyterian to a man. While the majority of these workmen invariably moved on following the completion of their contract, they provided marriage partners for the daughters of local settlers and occasionally remained on in the area, thus swelling congregational membership in the longer term.

In South Tipperary in the eighteenth century, however, Roman Catholics dominated the head-tenantry on many of the substantial estates. This was particularly the case in the longer established estates with continuity in ownership from before 1641, which estates had a mere token Protestant presence at this level and also

22 Connolly, *Religion, law and power*, 295.   23 Cullen, *Modern Ireland*, 193–5.   24 Marnane, *Land and violence*, 15.

among the ordinary tenantry. The Butler (Kilcash) estate had just one Protestant tenant in 1730, while the Butler (Cahir) estate had only two in 1750. Even some of the newer Protestant-owned estates – such as those of Bagwell (Marlfield) and Hely-Hutchinson (Knocklofty) – could be sparsely populated with Protestants, with just two and four tenants respectively identified as Protestant in this period, in areas where the former proprietors continued to dominate the head-tenantry.[25]

Some landlords were both persistent and successful in their attempts to develop the numbers of Protestants in their tenantry. An early example was the O'Callaghan estate at Shanbally, newly purchased by this convert family in the 1720s, where subsequent improvement in the 1740s involved introducing a group of Protestant head-tenants, coupled with artisans and craftsmen, who were settled in the revived settlement of Clogheen. Several of these head-tenants also had mercantile links with nearby settlements – particularly Clonmel – which continued to be geographically important as a population centre and a central powerhouse from which Protestantism dispersed throughout the research district, with merchant families investing in its hinterland, settling younger sons on a portion of their country estates and marrying their daughters to existing landowners. Three examples of merchants being given favourable head-tenancies in South Tipperary survive in the registry of deeds concerning the O'Callaghan estate, the first being a three-lives lease for a portion of the estate in the barony of Kilnamanagh with Richard Hammersley of Holycross; the latter two concerning the main estate at Shanbally, Clogheen were contracted with William Miles of Rochestown, near Cahir and Joseph Franklin of Carhunahally, near Tipperary respectively.[26]

Additional landlord activity regarding the increase of Protestantism at Shanbally occurred in the autumn of 1747, when 22 individuals, including 8 couples, converted on this estate. This number included six farmers, the rest being tradesmen or merchants in Clogheen. Of these farmers, the surnames of Curtin, Fennessy, Murphy and Walsh imply a Roman Catholic background, while those of Bradshaw and Burnett would suggest a Protestant background. The pressure on the latter two probably stemmed from the fact their wives were Roman Catholic, a status increasingly incompatible with the new evangelical preferences of the landlord. This demonstrates that the pressure to convert emanated from the landlord and not from a desire among Roman Catholics to gain more advantageous leases than they would legally be entitled to. Newly introduced Protestants dominated this estate with an attendant group of convert farmers, under the direction of a landlord intent on pragmatic changes in the tenancy structure.[27]

Direct or indirect evidence of the artificial introduction of Protestant tenant families to South Tipperary, suggests that the widespread belief among tenants that Protestants were preferred was well founded. Everywhere in Ireland, vigorous estate management went hand in hand with the maintenance or increase of the Protestant population on individual estates. In South Tipperary, where rural Protestant communities were small and less, the effects of these policies of positive discrimination

25 Power, *Land, politics and society*, 148–9. **26** RD: 97/158/67748 (1739); RD: 141/597/93372 (1748); RD: 199/246/132102 (1750). **27** Smyth, 'Estate records', 39–41; Power, *Land, politics and society*, 149–50.

in favour of Protestants were striking when put into practice. Industrial estate colonies, particularly geared to the linen industry, constituted not only experimentation on the part of the local gentry in measures to advance linen making at a time when it was fashionable for their class to do so, but also strategies in furthering of Protestant hegemony. Estate colonies were often attempted in association with the charter schools. At Tipperary, pupils from the Erasmus Smith grammar school were bound as apprentices to craftsmen in the town, including one case in 1722 of apprenticeship to a linen weaver.[28]

The Damer estate introduced a considerable number of Ulster Presbyterian textile workers onto its lands at Shronell, west of Tipperary, in the 1740s. The exact date of their arrival is unknown, although Campbell, writing in 1777, estimated that it was *c*.1740.[29] Damer's initiative may have been triggered by the catastrophic famine of 1740–1, during which one-tenth of the Irish population perished. The famine was most severe in Munster, which prompted 'a gentlemen of the province of Munster' to write an impassioned plea to the Anglican primate under the pseudonym 'Publicola', which was printed at Cashel in May of 1741.[30] Recent research has identified Thomas Dawson of Ballinacourty in the Glen of Aherlow, a near neighbour of Damer, as the likely author of this pamphlet. Dawson argued that

> since, by a moderate computation, very near one-third of the poor cottiers of Munster have perished by fevers, fluxes and downright want, would not this be a very proper time for the gentlemen of this province to give due encouragement to colonies from the north of Ireland, which abounds with people, to come and settle in their room? Would not this turn greatly to the advantage of these gentlemen, by improving their estates, as well as the good of the public, by carrying on the linen manufacture? Would not this serve to strengthen the Protestant interest in this province and prevent many from going to America, to the great detriment of the whole kingdom? I know a popish lord, who intends at a considerable expense, to bring a colony from the north and give them good encouragement to settle on his estate; and I hope Protestant noblemen and gentlemen will not be blind to their own interests, as well as to the general good of their country.[31]

This type of encouragement was much advocated by the [Royal] Dublin Society and Damer's subscription to this philosophy is evident, in that between 1746 and his death in 1768, of 80 deeds registered between him and his tenants, only six were granted to Roman Catholics.[32] In addition, Damer was a Unitarian Presbyterian, a dissenting Protestant denomination closer to Scots Presbyterianism than any other branch of Protestantism, which may have aided the establishment of contact with northern Presbyterians willing to transplant to South Tipperary.[33] As many as 60 families may

28 Smyth, 'Estate records', 45; for Shronell, *The compleate Irish traveller* (1788), ii, 15. **29** T. Campbell, *Survey of the south of Ireland* (1778), 140; Seymour, *Diocese of Emly*, 248. **30** Publicola [T. Dawson], *A letter from a country gentleman in the province of Munster* (1741); also Power, *Land, politics and society*, 231. **31** *Letter from a country gentleman*, 3, 7; also J. Heuston, 'The weavers of Shronell – 250 years ago' (2002), 99–100. **32** RD Grantors register, 1748–68, cited in Heuston, 'Shronell', 100. **33** Power, *Land,*

have originally been planted on the Shronell estate. Some 50 households, with identifiably northern surnames that may have originated in the neighbourhood of Maghera, in south Co. Londonderry, were identified by a descendant of one of the original settler households, on analysis of the return made by the rector of Shronell in the religious census of 1766.[34] Some households may have remained only a few years, before gravitating towards towns and cities. On 6 September 1749, the vestry of Cork Presbyterian Church noted the death of 'Anne Mackense, wife of John, linen weaver. She was admitted to communion with us on 3 July 1743 upon the recommendation of Revd Mr John Mears, at that time minister of Clonmel'.[35]

In 1766, some 64 households of northern origin were clustered in four townlands around the estate core at Shronell, each townland group under the auspices of at least one Protestant head-tenant household. Nearest Damer Court, on the townland of Deerpark, resided 2 of Damer's most prominent head-tenants, White of Ballycohy and Chadwick of Ballinard, with 8 northern settler households; while at adjacent Ballyconree, where Peter Smithwick was head-tenant, there were 6 northern households. These two townlands accounted for barely one-third of the total colony, which was concentrated in the west and south of the estate. In the western townland of Ballynadruckilly (the modern village of Lattin) – where Clement Sadlier was head-tenant – were 22 northern households, while the small civil parish of Bruis to the south – with the head-tenant farms of Richard Waller and Stephen Craddock – contained 28 northern Protestant households. The 8 Protestant families in the civil parish of Cordangan appear to have been English in origin. By 1766, a total of 82 Protestant families were residing at Shronell and five adjoining civil parishes, which was equivalent to some 450 persons, if a multiplier of 5.5 per household is assumed.[36]

It has been noted that in many instances of sponsored migration of linen-weavers from the north of Ireland, enthusiasm for the project did not long survive the passing of the sponsoring landlord.[37] With the death of John Damer of Shronell in August 1768, the settlers lost their benefactor and protector, who had brought them to the locality, provided them with homes and small plots of land, and who had encouraged them in their industry. The heir to the estates was an absentee nephew and there is no evidence to suggest his land agents made any provision or concession to the settlers after Damer's death, so that by 1784, only one settler family of northern origin is recorded on the rent roll of the estate.[38] The exact date of collapse of the weaving colony is unclear, but the settlement of linen weavers by Maude of Dundrum on his estate from 1771 is known to have attracted some households from Shronell.[39] Campbell, writing in 1777, thought the colony had proved ineffectual '[because] the children of the weavers, like the other natives, neither weave nor spin; and in everything but religion are indistinguishable from the general masses. Such is the resiliency of all nature to its original state'.[40] This is a good example of

politics and society, 235. **34** 'Presbyterian householders, Co. Londonderry, 1740', cited in Heuston, 'Shronell', 100–1; NAI, Religious census of Cashel and Emly, 1766. **35** CAI, U87–1, vestry minute dated 6 September 1749. **36** Heuston, 'Shronell'; Religious census; Dickson, 'Hearth tax', 125–81; see also app. VIII. **37** P. O'Flanagan et al., *Rural Ireland, 1600–1900* (1987), 198. **38** Rent roll of the estate of Lord Milton, 1784–98: see Houston, 'Shronell', 109. **39** Information of William Fryday of Dundrum, cited in ibid., 110. **40** Campbell, *A philosophical survey*, 140.

the early stages of contact conversion: within little more than a generation, the colony had become virtually indistinguishable from the locals in all but religion. Many settler households dispersed to tenancies on adjoining estates, of which the tithe applotment books of the 1820s confirm some 6 households on the neighbouring Dawson estate at Ballinacourty in the Glen of Aherlow; 4 on the Maude (Hawarden) estate at Dundrum; 5 on the Massy-Dawson estate at Clonbullogue; and 19 on the Smith-Barry estates at Cordangan, Corroge, Kilshane and Relickmurry.[41] Other surnames were lost through intermarriage with the local population. Some families gravitated to their spiritual homeland of Scotland, while others may well have emigrated to America or Canada, as a cohesive religious group. By 1831, in any case, the number of Protestants in Shronell union of parishes had fallen to 97 persons, just one-quarter of the figure some six decades earlier.

At Cullen, the large number of Protestants dwelling on the Waller estate originated at least in part from an outlier of the Munster Plantation, established around Cullen Castle in the 1610s and 1620s. The surviving families were significantly augmented during the 1740s in much the same manner as the colony at Shronell, through the involvement of the landlord family in linen schemes, and also through the establishment of a charter school on their estate at nearby Newport, in North Tipperary. The redevelopment, modernization and expansion of estate settlements were closely tied to the stimulation of the local economy, which invariably involved an influx of Protestants. The motivation behind such efforts by landlords was therefore partly a desire to increase their rentals and partly a desire to enhance their security through the promotion of Protestant settlement on their estates. The broadly based wealth of South Tipperary and its hinterland, however, was not so much to be found in large mansion houses as in the numerous solid Georgian houses built in every district within its bounds. Each house denoted a resident landowner, whose small estate was prosperous enough to enable him to build a comfortable residence. In addition, there were a significant number of two-storey farmhouses, built by prosperous tenant farmers who, in this period, were for the most part Protestants.

The landlords of South Tipperary were generally slow in the commencement of estate improvements and there is little evidence of a regular investment in estate improvement through the attraction of head-tenants in the first half of the eighteenth century. The notable exceptions were the estates of Mathew at Thomastown, Damer at Shronell, O'Callaghan at Shanbally, Osborne at Newtownanner (near Clonmel), Maude at Dundrum and Barker at Kilcooley, where new tenants were introduced and large-scale remodelling of the landscape through drainage schemes, estate villages and the promotion of model farming methods was undertaken. Even in the early 1750s, this minority of improving landlords in South Tipperary drew attention from travel writers, as with Pococke who noted

> a mile beyond Golding Bridge [Golden] is Mr Mathews fine place at Thomastown, [comprising] 1500 acres within a wall, the great beauty of which is the hernery and duckoy. A little beyond Mr Brombery has a beau-

41 Tithe applotment books 1825–35, barony of Clanwilliam, in Heuston, 'Shronell', 110.

tiful place. Two miles from Tipperary, Mr Daymour has built a fine house and offices and lives in the latter, the house not being finished. New Forest at Aherlow, which belongs to Massey Dawson esq., [is] a beautiful retirement, [with] a fine well-timbered park and ridings cut through the wood. The house is now neglected, not being inhabited by the owner.[42]

Ideas on improvement diffused quickly and easily from Great Britain into Ireland in this period through family linkages, frequent country house visiting, letter writing and the circulation of books, journals, pamphlets and pattern books for the layout of gardens and estates. While initially improvement was seen as a means of increasing the economic value and productivity of estates, it took on additional implications during the eighteenth century.[43] In the Irish context it carried moral, spiritual and political lessons and particularly aimed to demonstrate the superior qualities of Protestantism to Roman Catholic Ireland. Protestantism was seen as the religion of the enlightened; the progressive and the rational and agricultural improvement as a visible outworking of its edifying impact.[44]

The demesne, or area of the estate reserved by the proprietor for his own occupation and use, was in Ireland far more frequently walled in than in England.[45] This was to provide a *cordon sanitaire*, separating the improved landlord landscape from the 'peasant' world outside and also limiting intrusion into this elitist space.[46] In Tipperary, landlord embellishment of demesnes – particularly those surrounding the family seat – was most common in the second half of the eighteenth century. By 1778 there were 184 gentlemen's seats in Co. Tipperary, of which 113, or nearly two-thirds, lay in South Tipperary baronies, viz. Middlethird, 29; Clanwilliam, 27; Iffa and Offa West, 21; Iffa and Offa East, 19; Slieveardagh, 15; Kilnamanagh, 2. The list is not totally exhaustive, as several houses on minor roads were accidentally omitted, such as Killenure Castle, near Dundrum.[47] However, it does reaffirm the crucial importance of the Ormond and York estate sales in the 1690s and subsequently, in the facilitation of a proliferation of country house building in the period 1750–70 in the first four baronies, when compared with Slieveardagh and Kilnamanagh.

Comparatively few gentry seats were built prior to 1750 with many – such as New Park, shown in fig. 14 – erected during the course of the 1750s and 1760s when incomes from estates rose sharply. They were thus largely the product of the previous quarter-century of prosperity and continued to be developed and expanded upon in the succeeding quarter-century, for a travel account of 1797 described the countryside as

> delightful – very handsomely improved and inhabited – abundant in cultivation and richness. We came along by the walls of Mr Pennefather's domain about 3 miles this side of Cashell on the left, called New Park, a fine old seat

42 R. Pococke, *Pococke's tour in Ireland in 1752* (1891).   **43** M. Busteed, 'The practice of improvement in the Irish context' (2000), 19; W.J. Smyth, 'The greening of Ireland' (1997), 55–72.   **44** N.P. Canny, 'Identity formation in Ireland' (1987).   **45** C. Maxwell, *Country and town under the Georges* (1949), 101. **46** R.F. Foster, *Modern Ireland, 1600–1972* (1989), 176; 194; L. Proudfoot, 'Hybrid space?' (2000), 207–8. **47** W. Nolan, 'Patterns of living in Co. Tipperary', 293–4.

Fig. 14: New Park (Ballyowen), Cashel

well wooded – they are remarkably handsome and the situation unrivalled – from hence we rode on good roads and fine country 'till we came to Cashell.[48]

These gentry families were predominantly of the Established Church, though a few enclaves of Roman Catholic and Protestant dissenter gentry remained. The premier rural dissenting community was Presbyterian, with a significant number of gentlemen's seats in the triangular area between Fethard, Killenaule and Cashel, which included landlord families of Cromwellian extraction – such as Jacob and Sankey – as well as more recent head-tenant arrivals.[49] In the case of the Roman Catholics, the primary enclave was that of the Butler (Cahir) estate, with its attendant head-tenant households, while in the district around Tipperary, there was a group of head-tenant families who had been successful in securing leases of large tracts of land.[50] The presence of these families was a significant thorn in the side of insecure elements in the establishment, and their perceived rise in affluence – in South Tipperary and elsewhere – played a significant role in the decision of the establishment to assess its numerical position *vis-à-vis* Roman Catholics and Protestant dissenters, in the religious census of 1766.

The premier indicator of denominational affiliation and distribution in eighteenth century Ireland is the religious census (1766), which resulted from an order issued by the Irish House of Lords to all Anglican ministers to draw up a return of families in their locality, distinguishing between Protestant and 'popish' households.

48 Entry for Friday 11 August 1797 cited in M. Quane, 'Tour in Ireland by John Harden in 1797' (1953), 28. **49 Fethard**: Jacob (Mobarnane), Sankey (Coolmore), Latham; **Killenaule**: Jacob (St Johnstown); **Cashel**: Latham (Ballysheehan) and (Meldrum). Head-tenants included Henderson at Pepperstown and Mobarnane. **50 Cahir**: Butler, Lord Cahir (landlord); Keating, Dogherty, Butler (head-tenants); **Tipperary**: MacCarthy (Springhouse), Dogherty and English (head-tenants). Butler of Ballycarron and Ballyslatteen and O'Meagher of Kilmoyler seem not to be listed.

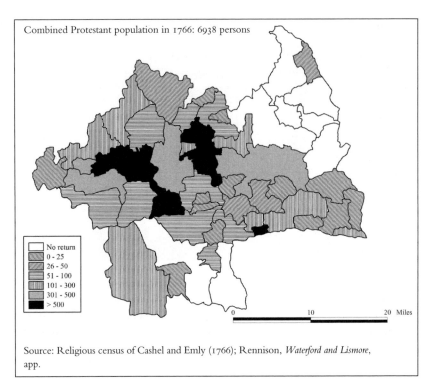

Map 15: The distribution of Protestants in the religious census of 1766

Factors such as the enthusiasm of the individual clergyman, the topography of his parish and his sources of information, all had a bearing on the final figures. Some ministers went to great lengths in detailing the exact composition of households by name, location, religion and social class, while others barely complied with the directive, by simply supplying the total number of Protestant and 'popish' families in their parish unions. Some ministers appear to have defaulted, or their returns may have gone missing, but South Tipperary is fortunate that this deficiency is largely confined to parochial unions in the north-eastern barony of Slieveardagh and also some in Iffa and Offa barony, so that the distribution of Protestantism and Roman Catholicism may be accurately assessed across three-quarters of the county.

The Protestant population distribution in 1766 in accordance with the parochial unions of the Established Church then in operation, is shown in map 15. Three core areas of Protestantism in South Tipperary are readily identifiable, all containing sizable urban centres; namely Clonmel in the south, Cashel in the north-central district and Tipperary in the west. With the exception of the highly compact parish of Clonmel, comprising of only the civil parish of that name, the distribution of Protestantism in these centres was far more concentrated even than the map suggests. In both Tipperary and Cashel parish unions, some five or six civil parishes were grouped with the urban parish for reasons of economy. Protestant settlement was indeed sparse in these areas, being largely confined to the urban centre and its immediate vicinity.

The important urban parish of St John Baptist, Cashel, was the only civil parish in 1766 in all South Tipperary to contain a Protestant majority. Even here – the seat of the Anglican archbishop of Cashel and Emly – the Protestant total of 117 households constituted a by no means overwhelming 54 per cent majority, being just 15 households larger than the Roman Catholic total. However, taking Cashel parochial union as a whole, the Protestant figure falls to 37 per cent, with the implication that while the Protestant population increased by just 43 households when rural districts were included, the Roman Catholic total surged to well over 400. At Clonmel, the Protestants numbered an impressive 320 households, accounted for almost 30 per cent of the urban population, but one-quarter of the entire civil parish. Similarly, at Tipperary, the 97 Protestant households accounted for 24 per cent of the parish, but just under one-fifth of the total population of the union of parishes.

Of the three core districts of Protestantism in South Tipperary, Clonmel was the most important and populous. As the county assize town and a corporate borough, it contained a significant number of administrative services and officials. In addition, it possessed important commercial opportunities, besides educational facilities for families such as a grammar school, an endowed school, a parochial school and numerous private institutions at primary level. Of the parishes which were one-fifth Protestant or greater, most were either urban or suburban in composition, underlining the concentration of the reformed denominations in the towns and their hinterlands. The civil parishes of Kilgrant to the east and Rathronan and Lisronagh to the north consisted of the rural districts in its hinterland and though possessing tiny overall populations, they held above average concentrations of Protestants due to their proximity to the county town. In this way, Kilgrant was 47 per cent, Rathronan 39 per cent and Lisronagh 30 per cent Protestant, ranking as the second, third and sixth most Protestant civil parishes of South Tipperary respectively. Other adjacent civil parishes to Clonmel – such as Inishlounaght to the west and Newchapel to the north-west – were almost 10 per cent Protestant.

The immediate Cashel hinterland was even more emphatically Protestant than that of Clonmel, as it adjoined the important parishes of Mogorban and Fethard to the east, Athassel to the west and the not-inconsiderable Protestant communities of Ardmayle-Ballysheehan to the north and Knockgraffon to the south. Mogorban – an out-parish of Fethard where over one-third of its population was Protestant – held this attribute as a result of the settlement of Protestant head-tenant farmers under favourable leases, including a Quaker community. The parish union of Fethard, itself very extensive, is probably the best example in South Tipperary of a relatively even Protestant distribution over a comparatively large and very fertile hinterland. The 47 Protestant households of the Fethard urban area accounted for over 15 per cent of the total population there, while the 91 families of the entire parish union still made up one-tenth of the total. Fethard had also benefited from the sale of the Ormond and York estates in the 1690s, in that the number of Protestant estates in its hinterland increased significantly with the arrival of many new families, such as the Presbyterian merchant dynasties of Jacob at St Johnstown and Mogorban, and Latham at Meldrum, Ballysheehan and Fethard.

Ardmayle, Ballysheehan and Knockgraffon civil parishes benefited from proximity to Cashel for many of the same reasons of those in the hinterland of Clonmel,
namely the provision of a range of religious, educational and secular services within
easy reach. Consequently, these districts were from 10 to 15 per cent Protestant.
Athassel, lying to the west of Cashel, was a well-populated and fertile rural parish,
whose 20 Protestant households formed just less than 5 per cent of the total population. This parish benefited from the leasing arrangements of the Meade family,
which was responsible for the residence of virtually all of these Protestant households. It may thus be seen that the Cashel core area was more orientated toward
agricultural and ecclesiastical services than Clonmel, which owed much of its
Protestant population to its status of county and assize town.

The last of the core areas, Tipperary, is much more complex. Like Cashel and
Clonmel, the great majority of the Protestant population was concentrated in and
around the town area. However, the rural parishes to its west and north-west –
namely Shronell, Cullen and Donohill-Toem – had experienced considerable
Protestant immigration. Shronell had received an estate colony during the 1740s,
besides having a considerable landlord and head-tenant community. By 1766, it
contained 86 Protestant households, making a significant 30 per cent minority. Both
Tipperary and Shronell contained a number of Protestant dissenters: Unitarian/
Presbyterian at Shronell; Unitarian/Presbyterian and Quaker at Tipperary. Cullen,
a village colony of note, also received renewed Protestant settlement in the 1740s,
so that by 1766 it contained 48 Protestant families, a 10 per cent minority. The circumstances of the Protestant in-migration to the Donohill-Toem district are unclear,
but it is likely to have benefited from proximity to the Shronell, Cullen and
Tipperary colonies, and to have availed of the same Ulster sources for increasing
its Protestant tenantry. Some 28 Protestant families resided in each of Donohill and
Toem by 1766, accounting for 15 per cent of the total population in each district.

Outside these core districts, the parishes of Shanrahan and Cahir are of additional
interest. The former – despite notable efforts at conversion, the introduction of new
Protestant head-tenants in the 1740s, and the development of the estate town of
Clogheen in the 1750s – contained just 23 Protestant families, which in a large, populated rural parish amounted to barely 5 per cent of the total population. On the other
hand, the parish of Cahir – containing the important urban centre and estate town of
that name – was heavily Roman Catholic, largely due to its Roman Catholic landlord,
an almost exclusively co-religionist head-tenantry, the survival of former tenant families in large number, and the consequent lack of incentives to members of the Protestant
establishment to settle there until after the passing of the estate to Anglican cousins in
1788. In 1766, Cahir contained just 19 Protestant households, including several Quaker
families, so that Protestants were fewer than 3 per cent of the parish.

Another aspect of Protestantism that is visible through analysis of surviving returns
of the religious census (1766) is the extent to which Old English and Gaelic Irish
surnames occurred within the Protestant community. This analysis is possible in 12
parish unions across the central districts of South Tipperary, in an area stretching
from Cullen in the west to Fethard in the east, where the returns also included the
surnames of parishioners. In parish unions and civil parishes where Protestants num-

bered few households, there is never more than a single surname of Old English or
Gaelic Irish background. However, it is possible to analyse ethnic diversity within
all of the largest Protestant communities of South Tipperary, except that of Clonmel,
for which only total figures survive (see table 8). It may be seen the Old
English/Gaelic Irish alliance, while accounting for 10 per cent of the total number,
did not constitute a very considerable percentage of the Protestant population, even
in the largest urban and rural settlements. Still, the 12 households of Old
English/Gaelic Irish extraction at Cashel, bearing 11 different surnames, constitute
an interesting concentration. There may have been some limited success in the conversion of the older families of the Cashel hinterland to Anglicanism at this provincial centre of the Established Church, particularly with such surnames as Butler,
Dwyer and Heffernan among the Protestant community there. It can be seen that
local Protestantism generally still owed much to the introduction of families from
Ulster and the conversion of Roman Catholic households, particularly those bearing surnames common in South Tipperary, remained very rare.[51]

Table 8: Ethnic diversity within South Tipperary Protestant communities, 1766

Union	Households	New English	Percent	Old English /Gaelic Irish	Percent
Donohill	28	24	86	4	14
Shronell	86	77	89	9	11
Tipperary	91	82	90	9	10
Cullen	48	41	85	7	15
Cashel	117	105	90	12	10
Fethard	47	39	83	8	17

The returns of the religious census were instrumental in provoking a response
from landlords in the two marginal baronies of Kilnamanagh and Slieveardagh, with
their small, declining Protestant populations. Both registered a very substantial
increase in the 1732 to 1766 period, albeit from a low base, by 115 per cent in
Kilnamanagh barony, and by almost 70 per cent in Slieveardagh. The population of
the barony of Slieveardagh in 1766 is difficult to estimate, owing to the absence of
any return from that barony. A crude estimate of 500 persons is likely, based on the
complete returns for 1732 and 1831 and on a handful of mid-eighteenth population
indicators in estate papers, such as those at Kilcooley. The failure to make a return
is in itself an indicator of the weakness of Protestantism in the district and the lack
of resident clergymen. As the graph and data table in fig. 30 demonstrates, the com-

51 **Donohill**: Corbet (2); Dwyer; Loughlin; **Shronell**: Nowlan; Walsh; Norris; Bourke (2); Collins;
Carroll; Walsh; Nugent; **Tipperary**: English; Doherty (2); Fitzgerald (2); Bourke; Wall; Loughnane;
Hyland; **Cullen**: Moran; Clancy; Dwyer; Furlong (2); Walsh; Grady; **Cashel**: Dempsey; Heffernan;
Fitzpatrick; Healy; Butler; Dwyer; Hickey; Gorman; Phelan (2); McGuire; Doyle; **Fethard**: Carthy;
Fitzgerald (2); Butler; Cahill; Nugent; Ryan; McNamara.

bined Protestant population total for both Kilnamanagh and Slieveardagh baronies, allowing for generous estimates where returns are lacking, was still far behind any single one of the other three in South Tipperary. In 1732, these two baronies had accounted for just 10 per cent of the total Protestant population and by 1766, this figure had increased only slightly, to one-eighth of the total. Both figures fell well short of that recorded a century earlier, when these baronies contained from one-quarter to one-fifth of the total number of Protestants in South Tipperary.

The development from 1767 of the estate village of Dundrum in Kilnamanagh by Sir Thomas Maude, a resident improving landlord, constituted the most immediate response. It relied on the attraction of Protestant settlers, the advancement of the linen industry and the promotion of the latest farming practices. Maude sought 'Protestant manufacturers' for over 270 acres of his estate, which he proposed to let in lots from 5 to 10 acres on 3-lives leases.[52] The scheme was the product of various factors, namely, the sectarian fervour of the 1760s, the desire of the landlord to increase the Protestant population of the district from the very low base enumerated by the religious census, his involvement in county electoral politics and his need of Protestant freeholders, and his desire to improve his estate by importing new tenants possessed of a Protestant work ethic. Certainly in the case of later colonies, their motivation had more to do with the electoral ambitions of the landlord than his concern for the welfare of local Protestantism.[53] But numerical insecurity had much to do with Maude's development, beginning as it did so soon after the religious census (1766) revealed a mere 8 Protestant families residing in Dundrum (Ballintemple) parish and only 16 families in the entire parish union. Using the recommended multiplier of 5.5,[54] this translates to a parish population of 44 and a union population of 88 persons, hardly a Protestant stronghold.

The easing of sectarian tensions during the 1770s, and the death of Maude in 1777, created a situation where the progress of the new settlement under his brother and successor, Sir Cornwallis Maude, was slow. A contemporary measure of the success of the scheme at Dundrum survives in a return of Protestant inhabitants of Ballintemple union, dated 1819, which found 243 parishioners in 40 households, an increase of 275 per cent on 50 years previously. The family of Viscount Hawarden contained 5 individuals, with the promotion of Protestantism still strongly in evidence, in that Dundrum House had 18 servants, the entire number of which was Protestant. The average in each Protestant household at Dundrum was 5.6 persons, safely above the recommended multiplier of 5.5 for rural Ireland. Only 4 of the households had surnames that implied conversion from Roman Catholicism and most seem to have come from Ulster.[55]

The schemes with the most enduring numerical impact on the South Tipperary Protestant community were these later estate colonies initiated in the 1767 to 1780 period, on the Maude (Hawarden) estate at Dundrum, in the extreme north-west, and on the Barker estate at Kilcooley, in the extreme north-east. These estate vil-

---

52 J. Lidwell, *The history of the life and adventures of John Lidwell* (1804), 39; also *Freeman's Dublin Journal*, 10–14 Feb. 1767; RD: 296/461/197728 (1772); Young, *Tour*, i, 392–4. **53** Dickson, *New foundations*, 119. **54** Idem, 'Hearth tax'.

lages became key anchor points of Protestantism. The settlement at Kilcooley involved the attraction of German Palatines from their primary settlement in Co. Limerick, where some 200 families had been settled in 1709. A secondary settlement was established by Sir William Barker of Kilcooley Abbey, who, having briefly contemplated the sale of the Kilcooley estate in 1770, decided to develop the estate through reclaiming its undeveloped uplands, while also increasing the Protestant population of the parish.[56] Not all of the new tenants were of Palatine extraction, but the vast majority were. Only one of the original leases of the Protestant colony survives, but it is sufficient to outline the terms and conditions under which the colonists were settled. A lease dated 20 October 1773, in the possession of the Switzer family of Newpark (fig. 15), was made between Sir William Barker and the heads of five families, viz. Paul Smeltzer, Adam Baker, Daniel Ruckle, John Switzer and Sebastian Lawrence.[57] These tenant families arrived in 1773 and were each required to build a stone house within two years and to reclaim 2.5 acres of wasteland every year for an additional rent of 10s. per acre. The settlement had strongly sectarian overtones, for it was a condition of the lease that the land could not be re-let to any person professing the 'popish' religion, nor could any grazing be let to a 'papist'. The lease was for three lives, with the first two years rent a nominal one of two peppercorns. Thereafter, the rent for the families' lease of 158 acres was to be £29 11s. 0d. The fair distribution of land quality was ensured through strip divisions, so that each family had some good and some bad land. The landlord reserved all hunting, hawking and fishing rights, as well as the coal and mineral mining and stone quarrying. The Palatines were very numerous, with the original Switzer settler at Kilcooley fathering eleven sons: one founded the firm Switzer and Co. in Grafton Street, Dublin, while another became a successful merchant in nearby Kilkenny and founded Protestant alms houses there.

The colony greatly increased the number of Protestant families in Kilcooley from an equally low base to that recorded at Dundrum and many similar leases were subsequently granted so that in time, some 50 tenant families, exclusively Protestant, lived on the uplands of the Barker estate in the Slieveardagh Hills. A list of Protestant freeholders of Co. Tipperary for the election of 1775–6 gives 24 names for Kilcooley district, of which just 9 were Palatines, as there were many households without the necessary leasehold qualifications at this point.[58] However, of the 54 families in the pew allocation of 1829 for the new Anglican parish church at Kilcooley, 21 households bore names to be found among the Limerick Palatines, and many more remained aligned to the local Methodist and Baptist chapels. Though there were 21 families, there were only 10 different surnames, indicating close kinship, viz. Delmege, Uzelle, Glazier, Baker, Miller, Ruckle, Smeltzer, Sparling, Steepe and Switzer.[59] There were many Methodists among the Palatines, such as the several Switzer and Bible households, who would not have been allocated pews in the new parish church, but rather attended the

55 'A return of Protestant inhabitants of Ballintemple union, dated 6 June 1819' in vestry minute book of Ballintemple union, held at Bolton Library, Cashel.   **56** Barker advertised the estate for sale in *Finn's Leinster Journal* during 1770; in March 1772, he advertised for tenants in the same publication: see Neely, *Kilcooley*, 53–4; Power, *South Tipperary*, 94.   **57** Savory, 'The Huguenot-Palatine settlements', 215; Neely, *Kilcooley*, 56.

Fig. 15: Newpark, home of the Switzer family since 1773

meeting-house on Palatine Street, built among the farms of the settlement on the upland townland of Bawnlea. This building of 1790 was rebuilt in 1814. A Baptist church was founded in the adjoining townland of Renaghmore in 1817 and though it had an intermittent existence, resurfaced in the mid-1840s as 'Kilcooley Hills' church.

A similar mistake was made at Kilcooley as at Limerick, where families were crowded into a portion of the estate, without regard to the capacity of the land to support them. By 1820, some 50 Palatine families lived on the hill, with some holding little more than a potato garden and grazing for a cow. Overpopulation led to considerable emigration of these cottiers *c*.1826 to Peel County, at Streetsville outside Toronto, where the same names are to be found as in the pew allocations of 1829 at Kilcooley parish church. A subsequent emigration wave led to a second settlement being established in the early 1830s at Goderich Township, where the church was nostalgically called 'Tipperary'.[60] In a letter dated 25 April 1834, Mrs C.R. Elliott, of a neighbouring Kilkenny gentry family, drew attention to the level of emigration from the district.

> It would astonish you the numbers of people that pass down here daily, going to America – such rich luggage – mostly from the Co. Tipperary. Not the idle and destitute, I suspect, but the wealthy that fear to remain … numbers of them Protestants from Ponsonby Barker's estate.[61]

58 RIA MS 12 D 36: 'A printed list of freeholders of the county of Tipperary, 1776'.   **59** Kilcooley vestry minutes: pew allocation of new church, 1829; Neely, *Kilcooley*, 56, also 'Irish Chronicle' of the *Baptist Magazine* (Older Printed Books, TCD).   **60** Neely, *Kilcooley*, 93.   **61** Mrs Catherine Rose Elliott of Clonmore, Co. Kilkenny, to her son Christopher, living in Colombo, Ceylon, dated 25 April 1834, in R.G. McCutcheon, 'Elliott letters [1834–69]' (2004), 20; similar sentiments were expressed in a letter of 10 June 1836.

It is of interest to observe that in the 1770s the Palatines had come to Kilcooley from Limerick, keenly aware of their German origin, but that 60 years on they perceived themselves to be Tipperary people. Despite this emigration and the fact that the colony was already past its population peak, Barker succeeded in making Kilcooley the parish with the largest Protestant population, urban or rural, in the dioceses of Cashel and Emly in 1834. It accounted for one-tenth of the Protestant population of the united dioceses and, in the whole of South Tipperary, only the large urban centre of Clonmel could surpass Kilcooley numerically.

Isolated efforts to attract Protestant settlement in South Tipperary continued into the late eighteenth century. At Knocklofty, the 2nd Lord Donoughmore, having become a member of the Linen Board, promoted the settlement of Protestant manufacturers on his estate there. In 1781, he built ten houses at Ardfinnan for their accommodation, for which he obtained a grant of three yearly fairs in 1785.[62] The motive behind this and related actions is revealed in a letter of 1794 from his father, urging him to get himself made a trustee of the board as 'the establishment of a small village of [Protestant] manufacturers on the Knocklofty estate would be the means of getting you a seat in parliament upon moderate terms'.[63] Whatever its success in furthering the Donoughmore electoral ambitions, this scheme proved ineffectual in increasing the resident Protestant community in the medium term, having much in common with the Shronell district around Tipperary town, where the large number of Protestant families recorded in 1766 had all but disappeared by 1831. Many of these estate colony experiments would have been forgotten, save for an occasional reference in the registry of deeds, or the published manuscript of a travel writer.

A comparison between the religious census (1766), the *census of Ireland* (1831), and the *First report of the commissioners of public instruction* (1834) is particularly useful in comparing the relative endurance of the several estate colonies of South Tipperary. The five estates proven to have experienced this type of settlement are indicated in table 9. In analysing the changing state of these colonies over seven decades, the following points may be noted. The settlement at Cullen diminished even more significantly than that at nearby Shronell in the period between 1766 and 1831, with similar consequences. At Shanrahan — which had also seen some Protestant plantation in the period prior to 1641 — the introduction of Protestant head-tenants and some tenant conversions in the 1740s resulted in 23 Protestant families, or 127 individuals, living in the parish by 1766. Their number had increased to 200 individuals by 1831, following additional landlord influence over the local population in the area of conversions in the 1782–91 period.[64] It was reported of the landlord *c*.1750 that he had 'encouraged artificers, particularly manufacturers of friezes and ratteens, to settle [at Clogheen]'.[65] This was a smaller, less ambitious

62 Power, *Land, politics and society*, 54.   **63** Hely-Hutchinson to Donoughmore, 2 July 1794, cited in A.P.W. Malcomson, *John Foster* (1978), 272.   **64** 'A roll for conformists kept by the Revd Charles Tuckey of Shanrahan', Shanrahan parish papers collection, RCB Library, Dublin; 13 individuals converted in Shanrahan parish, namely, William Derlyshire (1782); Elinor Adams (1783); Mary Barry (1785); Mary Creed, Denis McCraith (1786); Mary Groody (1787); Thomas Kane, Mary Fenesy (1788); Catherine Rian, Mary Sheehy (1789), Richard Derlyshire (1790), Ellen McCraith, Ally Tobin (1791): only 3 had English surnames.   **65** RIA MS 24 G. 9, fo. 278: Smith's history of Tipperary, Limerick and Clare (*c*.1750).

Table 9: The Protestant population of the South Tipperary estate colonies,
1766–1834

Estate	Location	Foundation	1766	1831	1834
Damer	Shronell	1740s	82 (451)	97	98
Waller	Cullen	1740s	49 (270)	39	56
O'Callaghan	Clogheen	1740s	23 (127)	200	200
Hawarden	Dundrum	1767–77	16 (88)	229	231
Barker	Kilcooley	1772–7	8 (44)*	–	612

* Estimate; – No Return

Sources: Religious census (1766); *Census of Ireland* (1831); *First report of the commissioners of public instruction* (1834).

scheme than either of those employed at Shronell or Cullen, but it was more enduring, and exhibited continued positive growth through the crucial promotion of
conversions among local families by the landlord, himself of a convert family.
Significantly, the final two schemes carried out in the 1770s – those at Dundrum
and Kilcooley – were the most enduring, sponsored as they were with determined
planning by individuals who had a close connection with the sectarianism experienced in the county during the 1760s.

Through detailed analysis of the estate colonies of South Tipperary, it can be
argued with reasonable assurance that few Protestant-owned estates would forego
the opportunity of a Protestant tenant family to replace a Roman Catholic one,
though not so many were prepared to go out of their way to achieve this. A preference for Protestant tenants and the attraction of Protestant outsiders represented
one strategic means of defending and augmenting the Protestant establishment. At
local level, the introduction of loyal freeholder voters who would not be swayed
by nominally Anglican candidates that had converted for the purposes of political
advancement was important. This phenomenon was crucially important to efforts
to preserve Protestant hegemony in the immediate post-emancipation period. Less
common, certainly in South Tipperary, was the approach that involved the conversion of Roman Catholics, despite the backing of draconian penal laws relating
to property. Conversions, as measured by the convert rolls, increased sharply in
years of Jacobite plots or threatened invasions, when Protestant fears were heightened and the social and political pressures leading to conformity were at their most
acute. Ironically, had conversion policy been more successful during the eighteenth
century, the parochial organization of the Established Church would have been
insufficient to meet the demands of a significant church population.

11

'A costly, hollow gesture': late eighteenth-century Anglican expansion and the status of the Protestant dissenters

Anglicanism was a weak and ineffective organization throughout much of the eighteenth century, its problems compounded by its established status. Bishops and archbishops were government nominees, and appointments at every level were enmeshed in the web of patronage and interest which extended through all areas of public life. In rural parishes, there was much non-residence by the lower order of clergy, with many parishes in the care of poorly paid and indifferently qualified curates. Many clergy were pluralists, holding several parish unions at once, so that residence in all of them was impossible. The parish churches were generally in poor repair, even in the principal settlements, and one union in ten had no church at all.[1]

The 1760s saw a gradual improvement of the organizational activity of the Established Church in South Tipperary, with triennial visitations of the archiepiscopal southern province, and a greater self-consciousness through the initiation of the building of a new cathedral church at Cashel.[2] Anglican territorial organization, alongside the distribution and foundation of churches and glebe-houses in South Tipperary in the second-half of the eighteenth century, is illustrated in map 16. It is clear that the vast majority of churches in repair about this time were pre-Reformation buildings. Some 50 per cent had been in virtually continuous use since the Reformation, certainly since the restoration of the monarchy and Established Church in 1660. The most striking feature of the map is the highly symbolic dereliction of the centrally located cathedral at Cashel. This seat of a resident archbishop was dismantled by act of parliament in 1749, using the labour of soldiers of the 22nd regiment of foot quartered in the town.[3] The provision of a new cathedral church on the site of the medieval parish church of St John Baptist took over thirty years, for Irish cathedrals were generally very poorly endowed and totally reliant upon public funding. It was no coincidence that most of them were 'no larger than good-sized parish churches', as that was the basis on which their re-building or building was financed – by parish cess and, if the right conditions were fulfilled and if funds permitted, by grant from the board of first fruits.[4] This was the case in all respects at Cashel where

---

1 S.J. Connolly, *Religion and society in nineteenth century Ireland* (1994), 7. **2** *Freeman's Dublin Journal*, 12–15 February 1763. **3** Malcomson, *Archbishop Charles Agar*, 305. **4** Ibid., 311.

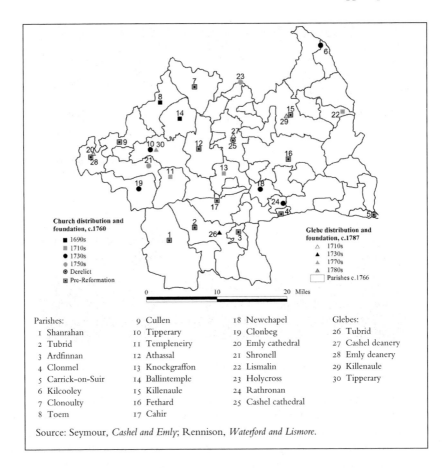

Map 16: Anglican territorial organization in the late eighteenth century

[the foundations of the new cathedral were not laid until] ... 1763, ... and
it was not roofed until 1781. From the demolition of old St John's in 1758
or soon afterwards until the opening of the new cathedral ... [on Christmas
Day] 1783, the Protestants of Cashel were obliged to hold their services in
the courthouse. Lack of funds and inertia on the part of the chapter ... combined to cause this slowness.[5]

From the 1690s, pre-Reformation ruined churches were renovated for use by
Protestant parishioners, usually at the instigation of a significant local landlord family
who wished for ecclesiastical facilities at a local level. In this way, the White and
Maude families initiated the renovation *c.*1690 of the parish churches at Toem and
Ballintemple respectively. Similar developments occurred at the instigation of lead-
ing families at Lismalin (Ikerrin Butler), Templeneiry (Baker) and Knockgraffon

Fig. 16: Knockgraffon church, *c.*1770

(Pyke) in the 1710s; in the 1730s at Clonbeg (Dawson), Newchapel (Moore) and Rathronan (Hamerton), and in the 1750s at Shronell (Damer), while occasional parish churches were renovated or rebuilt by public subscription at the general instigation of the parish, as at Tipperary and Holycross. The parish church of Knockgraffon, near Cahir (fig. 16) – where the chancel was roofed in 1710 and new silverware provided at the instigation of the Pyke family of nearby Woodenstown – is a prime example of a small rural congregation of the Established Church provided with worship facilities by a gentry family, that had until then been associated with the Clonmel Protestant dissenting congregation; both developments should have been co-ordinated by central government. Thus, the gradual extension of Anglicanism was haphazard and intermittent, with little organized provision of parish churches. Consequently, the parish organization was severely limited in the eastern half of the county, which possessed a small Protestant population, and no attempt was made to bring the state church within easy reach of rural dwellers. Indeed, as shown in map 26, one-quarter of parish unions saw no Anglican activity prior to 1800.

There was little adjustment to the territorial boundaries of the Established Church during the eighteenth century.[6] The reasoning behind the few re-arrange-

6 *1712*: Redcity to Fethard; *1750*: St Johnstown to Lismalin; *1776*: Ballingarry to Killenaule; *1783*: Shronell to Cullen; *1801*: St Johnstown and Barrettsgrange to Killenaule, Ballingarry to Lismalin: see Seymour, *Cashel and Emly*; Rennison, *Succession of clergy*.

ments that did occur is not clear, and often appears somewhat haphazard. Ballingarry, for example, was joined to Killenaule union in 1776, then to neighbouring Lismalin between 1801 and 1807, before being erected into a parish in the latter year and having a church and glebe-house built during the 1810s, an arrangement which endured until disestablishment. Several civil parishes erected into cures had, however, long been dependencies of a larger urban parish and, lacking the church population or resources to attract state investment in their ecclesiastical infrastructure (as at Newtownlennon and Graystown), remained anomalies of the Established Church until disestablishment brought their re-integration in the early 1870s.[7]

In many rural parishes, the only religious meeting facilities provided were Roman Catholic, with the result that contact conversion was quite common, where isolated Protestant households were so encircled. In the large arc of territory from Carrick-on-Suir in the south-eastern corner, through Fethard and Killenaule to Kilcooley in the north-east, there were only 5 Anglican parish churches in use, comprising the churches of these named parishes, and that of Lismalin. It can thus be seen that 20 of the 25 Anglican churches were concentrated in the western parishes and only 8 churches lay east of a median line drawn from Holycross in the north to Ardfinnan in the south. In addition, aside from the early eighteenth-century deanery at Cashel, the only other parish union to possess a purpose-built glebe-house for the permanent residence of the incumbent in the first-half of the eighteenth century was Tubrid, the chancellorship of the diocese of Lismore. This did not encourage ministerial residence in rural parishes, and only a few purpose-built glebe-houses were provided prior to the 1780s. However, clergymen in possession of an urban parish could expect to be provided with premises of a standard enjoyed by the gentry. An extract of 1773 from the diary of Dorothea Herbert, daughter of the rector of Carrick-on-Suir, indicates their rectory was a

> villa in the outlets [which] stood in the centre of four beautiful large gardens, a lawn, shrubbery and courtyard which parted it from the high road [with] a very pretty wilderness and a beautiful broad gravel walk shaded half way with yews and elms … The house itself was a venerable old building with two wings and a centre quadrangular fashion. It had once been two houses and had been built a hundred years – King William slept in it after the battle of the Boyne. It had three large parlours, two large halls and three other large rooms below stairs, besides kitchen, larder, housekeeper room and offices innumerable of every sort … above stairs were seven large bedchambers, two closets and a front lobby.[8]

The condition of these old manors varied greatly and the rectory at Carrick – a building over 100 years old – would have been arguably less attractive to an upwardly mobile clerical family than a 'modern' house. The Herberts attempted

---

7 *1754*: Newtownlennon from Carrick (to 1876); *1757*: Shronell from Cullen (to 1783); *1806*: Graystown from Killenaule (to 1871); *1807*: Ballingarry from Lismalin (to 1871); *1874*: Shronell from Cullen (to 1874); ibid. **8** Herbert, *Retrospections*, 20.

Fig. 17: a south-western view of Ardfinnan, by Anthony Chearnley (1744),
copied by Austin Cooper (1785). Note portion of hill-top Anglican church roofed,
constituting a church within a church.

to modernize their residence in 1793, inserting large modern windows to replace
the smaller ones fashionable in the 1670s.[9]

Instances of new church or glebe construction in the Anglican establishment in
the first half of the eighteenth century are exceedingly rare.[10] This is certainly true
of South Tipperary, where of 18 parish churches in repair in the diocese of Cashel
and Emly *c.*1780, 13 were fashioned from the medieval parish church, while in the
Lismore portion, 4 of the 8 in repair were so designed. The incoming archbishop,
Charles Agar, in a letter to Lord Primate Robinson at Armagh, described the state
of his archdiocese on arrival in 1779 as

> very discouraging. I am told that the churches are few and ruinous, that the
> Protestant gentry do not support the clergy in assessing, much less in levy-
> ing, taxes for the repairing of the parish churches, so that in some parishes
> money has not been assessed for this purpose for many years and in others,
> where it has been assessed, the popish interest is so prevalent that church-
> wardens cannot apply for the payment of it but at the hazard of their lives
> and very few indeed are found so hardy as to attempt to *enforce* the payment
> of it. Under these circumstances, a diocese can afford no other prospect than
> that of approaching desolation.[11]

There were exceptions, however, where new churches were provided to replace
the medieval parish church, or the latter was hugely remodelled, as at Bansha (1718),
Kilcooley (1730; 1790), Tipperary (1730), Newchapel (1771), and Kilvemnon (1771)

9 Ibid., 326. **10** De Breffney and Mott, *The churches and abbeys of Ireland*, 118. **11** Agar to Robinson,
24 August 1779, cited in Malcomson, *Archbishop Charles Agar*, 200.

in Cashel and Emly diocese; and at Shanrahan (*c*.1720), Ardfinnan (*c*.1724: see fig. 17), Tubrid and Tullaghmeelan (*c*.1780) in Waterford and Lismore.

As late as 1787, just prior to the beginning of the rejuvenation of the parish organization of the diocese of Cashel and Emly, only three parochial unions had a glebe-house. Under the leadership of Archbishop Charles Agar (1779–1801), some 17 new churches and 22 glebe-houses were provided. This process was considerably aided by his appointment as treasurer to the board of first fruits *c*.1787, coinciding with a major upturn in the fortunes and finances of that institution.[12] This achievement was commendable, however, given that the parochial income of the diocese of Cashel was low relative to its seniority in the hierarchy: 8 dioceses had a higher income and of the 4 presided over by an archbishop, only Tuam had a lower one.[13] Another 20 churches were built or rebuilt and 11 additional glebe-houses provided by 1830. However, new buildings did not necessarily mean higher ecclesiastical standards, as this extract of 1797 reveals.

> On Sunday we went to the new cathedral [at Cashel] and heard service performed, the music and singing delightful, there is as fine an organ as any in Ireland and the choir who chant the service are excelling – the church is a new, plain, but very well finished building internally – after quitting church highly gratified with everything (but the preacher *who was a scandal to the Established Church*) … we once more took to the road.[14]

Ironically, the provision of new churches and the increased residence of rectors in their parishes also caused occasional altercations regarding 'pew politics', where leading families almost came to blows regarding seating accommodation in new churches. Such an instance occurred at the new parish church of Knockgraffon, built in 1788 in the village of New Inn, where in 1789, the daughter of a local peer, despite irregular attendance at church, attempted to force the head pew from the rector's wife. A horsewhipping bout among the gentlemen followed and a duel was narrowly averted.[15]

The period between 1800 and 1830 in the Established Church has been termed 'the era of graceful reform', as it was this period that saw the most effective reorganization of the Church, curbing if not eliminating its most serious abuses.[16] The board of first fruits, set up in the eighteenth century to devote a proportion of ecclesiastical revenues to building and other essential purposes, was reorganized and its resources greatly increased by generous parliamentary grants. As a result, the number of churches island-wide rose by nearly 30 per cent between 1787 and 1832, while the proportion of parish unions with glebe-houses for the accommodation of a minister rose from 32 per cent to 59 per cent.[17] The speed with which dioceses acted on the increased monetary allocations to the board of first fruits varied, with much depending on the attitude of the diocesan. In South Tipperary, the greatest

---

12 Ibid., 186, 221. 13 Ibid., 203. 14 Italics as in original: see Harden's diary entry for Sunday 13 August 1797, cited in M. Quane, 'Tour in Ireland', 28–9. 15 Herbert, *Retrospections*, 186–7. 16 Akenson, *The Church of Ireland*. 17 Ibid.

Fig. 18: St Mary's church, Clonmel, *c*.1790

impact of the reform of the board may be observed in that portion of Lismore diocese lying within its bounds, where a weak Protestant population in the rural
parishes required this sort of financial backing before the extension or improvement of the Church territorial organization could be contemplated.

The condition of parish churches varied greatly in the early nineteenth century.
Some had become hazardous, as at Carrick-on-Suir, when on New Year's Day
1784, the entire steeple and belfry collapsed shortly after the conclusion of morning service.[18] Substantial remodelling was carried out there in 1804, using board of
first fruits funding, the 20-year delay indicative of a lack of other funding. Similarly,
the large medieval parish church at Clonmel (fig. 18) was substantially renovated
in 1805 out of necessity. At Inishlounaght (Marlfield), a small chapel built in 1800
among the ruins of the Cistercian abbey was replaced in 1816–18 following the resolution of the select vestry that its 'walls, roof and other parts are so decayed as to
be unfit for any permanent repair, [and] that the board of first fruits be applied to
for a loan toward the rebuilding of the church'.[19] The board also allowed funding
to complete the rebuilding of Emly cathedral (fig. 19), where the fabric of the
medieval cathedral (inset) had become severely decayed. This facility was open to
abuse, however, as occurred at Cahir, when local interests were desirous of fashionable worship facilities and there was a drive to abandon the architecturally unpre-

18 Herbert, *Retrospections*, 96–7.   **19** Vestry minutes of the parish of Abbey or Innislounaght: entries
for 20 May 1816; 8 April 1817.

Fig. 19: Emly cathedral, built in 1827 with (inset) a representation of the
cathedral in 1769 from the diocesan seal

tentious and indifferently situated medieval parish church. A visitation of Bishop
Stock in 1811 noted the 'church at Cahir easily reparable, if the restless desire of
some of the principal parishioners [i.e. Lord and Lady Cahir] be resisted, as it ought
to be'.[20] The powerful parishioner lobby prevailed, availing of board of first fruits
funding to its fullest extent, and of a free site provided by Lord Cahir, himself the
principal member of the congregation. The royal architect, John Nash, was
employed to design a small, ornate building with a highly pretentious tower and
spire, plasterwork ceiling and carved box pews, so that at £2,307, the whole building cost more than far more substantial parish churches.[21]

   The Anglican churches and glebe-houses of South Tipperary may be divided
into those built before the Act of Union, predominantly relying on private sponsorship and parish subscription; and those built in the three decades following 1800,
predominantly using board of first fruits funding. Most of the pre-1800 modifica-
tion or rebuilding of medieval church buildings and provision of glebe-houses took
place in the northern two-thirds of South Tipperary, the jurisdiction of the archdiocese of Cashel and Emly. In this area, rural Protestant communities were more
numerous and consequential than in the southern-third lying within the diocese
of Lismore. With the advent of a greater availability of board of first fruits loans

20 The episcopal visitation of Bishop Joseph Stock, 1811: Rennison collection, RCB Library, Dublin.
21 Butler, *Cahir*, 12–13.

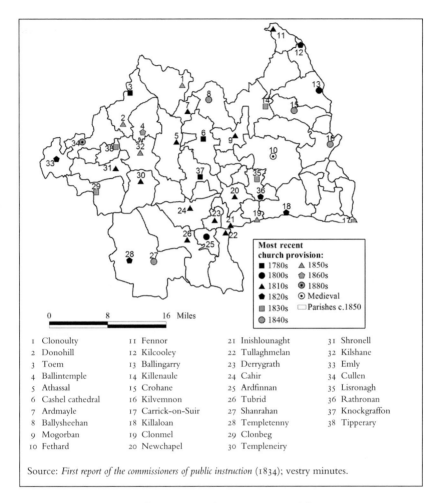

Map 17: Anglican territorial organization at fullest extent

and gifts in the early nineteenth century, the number of rebuilds of existing churches or provision of new ones increased, with some 10 churches modified in this way in both the southern-third and the northern two-thirds of South Tipperary.

Though an equal amount of rejuvenation eventually took place in both areas, the effect was far more dramatic on the more compact territorial organization of the southern-third, and is indicative of the need felt by smaller Protestant communities to raise their profile – amid growing Roman Catholic dominion – in the first two decades of the nineteenth century. However, as map 17 demonstrates, even the provision of some Anglican churches in new areas in this period and subsequently – though extending the parochial organization to a maximum of 38 churches – could not compete effectively with the ubiquitous Roman Catholic chapel network, which at 55 church buildings, was one-third more extensive than the Established Church at the peak of its organization.

Many Anglican parish unions had small Protestant populations, as a detailed analysis of the *First report of the commissioners of public instruction* indicates. Many of these unions were the product of early nineteenth century expansion, when an attempt was made to regularize the anomalies of the Church dating to the pre-Reformation era. The premier example is the erection of the civil parishes that constituted the corps of the archdeaconry of Cashel into cures in 1811, with mixed results. Only Mogorban – which gained a church and glebe-house by 1815 – endured as a parish after disestablishment. Of the others, the union of Tullamain and Redcity was suspended in 1854, while those of Kilmore and Gaile were dissolved at or shortly after disestablishment.[22] None of them developed any ecclesiastical infrastructure: a minute resident Anglican population being the usual reason. From map 18, it may be judged that one-third of parish unions comprised a total church population of less than 50 persons, and that these unions were especially prevalent in the Clonmel hinterland, and in the area west and north-west of Tipperary. The northern two-thirds of the county – that under the jurisdiction of the archdiocese of Cashel and Emly – contained many rural parish unions with church population exceeding 100 persons. This had much to do with the remnants of the estate colonies, particularly in the north-central and north-western unions. This combination was sufficient to outnumber similar unions in the southern-third – which lay under the jurisdiction of the diocese of Waterford and Lismore – by a ratio of 2:1.

Map 18 confirms the Tipperary and Clonmel town hinterlands largely remained the confine of the more sparsely populated parish unions. However, these hinterlands were also those where the membership was most strongly motivated toward church attendance. In the nine parish churches of the Clonmel hinterland, an attendance of greater than 50 per cent was usual in all but one church, while almost half had attendances exceeding three-quarters of their church population. The same trend is in evidence in Tipperary and its hinterland, with all but one of eight churches exhibiting an attendance of greater than half its church population and half of them an attendance of more than 75 per cent. The area with the greatest proportion of low attendance at church lay to the north-east, at Killenaule and its hinterland, where five of six churches had attendances of less than one-half their church population; this area also contained half of all parish churches in South Tipperary exhibiting this tendency.

An examination of map 26 confirms that Anglican Church activity began relatively late in half the parishes of the Killenaule area. In dating the earliest definite Anglican activity in each parish of South Tipperary, this illustrates my earlier findings that following the restoration in 1660, only eight parish churches were in use. All of these were settlement-based, the majority in an urban town context. The beginning of renovation of parish churches in the rural districts – by Protestant landowners requiring church services within easy reach of their estates – has been seen to have occurred after the Williamite victory of the 1690s, when the Protestant Ascendancy was confirmed. This occurred in three parochial unions in the Cashel hinterland, to the north-

---

22 Seymour, *Cashel and Emly*: entries for archdeaconry of Cashel, Tullamain, Redcity, Gaile, Kilmore.

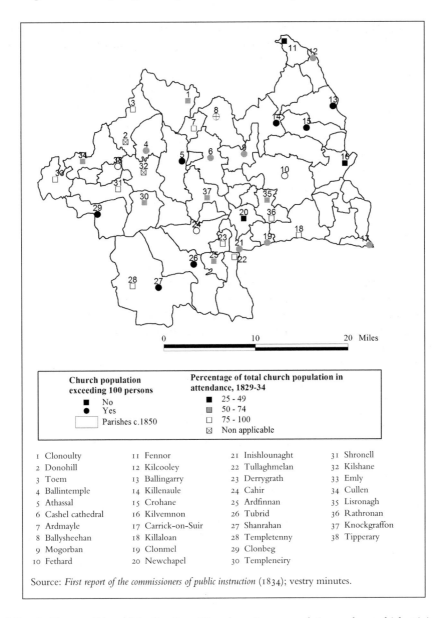

0   10   20 Miles

Church population exceeding 100 persons	Percentage of total church population in attendance, 1829-34
■ No	■ 25 - 49
● Yes	▦ 50 - 74
☐ Parishes c.1850	☐ 75 - 100
	⊠ Non applicable

1	Clonoulty	11	Fennor	21	Inishlounaght
2	Donohill	12	Kilcooley	22	Tullaghmelan
3	Toem	13	Ballingarry	23	Derrygrath
4	Ballintemple	14	Killenaule	24	Cahir
5	Athassal	15	Crohane	25	Ardfinnan
6	Cashel cathedral	16	Kilvemnon	26	Tubrid
7	Ardmayle	17	Carrick-on-Suir	27	Shanrahan
8	Ballysheehan	18	Killaloan	28	Templetenny
9	Mogorban	19	Clonmel	29	Clonbeg
10	Fethard	20	Newchapel	30	Templeneiry

31	Shronell
32	Kilshane
33	Emly
34	Cullen
35	Lisronagh
36	Rathronan
37	Knockgraffon
38	Tipperary

Source: *First report of the commissioners of public instruction* (1834); vestry minutes.

Map 18: The condition of the Anglican Church, *c.*1834 – population and parochial activity

west of the county. The first major refurbishment phase, involving more than a dozen churches, took place in the first three decades of the eighteenth century, the majority about the year 1730. This development was evenly distributed throughout South Tipperary, with the greatest concentration occurring in the suburban parishes around Clonmel. A few churches were also provided in the third-quarter of the eighteenth century, mainly estate church developments.

In Tipperary, the ambitions of the Anglican establishment to erect attractive churches and glebe-houses in the early nineteenth century must be looked upon as 'a costly, hollow gesture' of the kind often encountered in colonial situations.[23] It was a classic reaction to competition for space that failed to sustain or revive parochial life. By contrast with the variety of niches occupied by the Roman Catholic chapel, the Anglican parish church in rural areas was closely associated with the estate system, and was consequently often located within or adjoining the demesne of the local landlord family, a position which highlights its fragile position within Tipperary life as a whole. The last major building phase – contained within the period between the Act of Union and the granting of emancipation to Roman Catholics – involved a landlord-propelled drive by sparsely populated rural parishes to avail of favourable board of first fruits gifts and loans for the provision of Anglican churches where there had not previously been any. This development was especially prevalent in the Clonmel and Cashel hinterlands and involved several newly-landed families of a dissenting background, who had converted to the Established Church within the previous generation for socially conducive reasons.

Clonmel was the greatest centre of Protestantism in South Tipperary – both conforming and non-conforming – at all times in the period covered by this study. In absolute numbers, its combined Protestant population of some 2,000 persons by 1834 was formidable, making it a leading inland centre of Protestantism outside the province of Ulster. Its diversity of reformed Christian congregations was unequalled outside of the largest port cities; in addition to the Established Church, there were six non-conformist places of worship, viz. Quaker (Market Street); Unitarian Presbyterian (Nelson Street); Scots Presbyterian (Anglesea Street); Wesleyan Methodist (Gordon Street); Primitive Wesleyan Methodist (Mary Street); and Baptist (Morton Street). The membership of these congregations was small beyond the Quaker, Presbyterian and Unitarian congregations, but all contained – to some degree – important mercantile and landed interests. The most established of these were the old Unitarian Presbyterian families, who as bankers and premier merchants of Clonmel, bought substantial estates in its hinterland in the first half of the eighteenth century.

Irish Protestant dissenting congregations occupied a middle ground between the Established Church and the Roman Catholic Church throughout this time. They survived the eighteenth century through a combination of three schemes. First, by subscription, an arrangement by which as many members as were able and willing undertook to contribute an annual or quarterly fixed sum towards the minister's salary. This was the most common method used and on the whole worked reasonably well. Often in southern Ireland, the resulting stipend was insufficient for a minister with a family and many served more than one congregation, or where possible, worked as tutors or ran small private academies. Second, by endowment, where the minister's salary was derived in part from interest earned by monies or lands left to the church by leading families of the congregation for that specific purpose. The third method involved freewill offerings, pew rents and other donations.

<hr>

23 Jones-Hughes, 'Landholding and settlement'.

The precarious financial position of most dissenting congregations in Ireland during the eighteenth century forced them to rely heavily on the subscriptions of the principals of the membership. As these families rose in circumstance, they often, through influence of intermarriage or as a result of material and social affluence, converted to the persuasion of their marriage partner, invariably that of the Established Church. In addition, conversion to the state church arguably removed many financial commitments from leading dissenting families.

Each of the satellite Anglican congregations of Clonmel had a principal family associated with it: at Rathronan, Hamerton (subsequently Gough) of Rathronan demesne; at Inishlounaght, Bagwell of Marlfield House; at Killaloan, Osborne of Newtownanner demesne; at Newchapel, Moore of Barne demesne; at Tullameelan, Hely-Hutchinson of Knocklofty demesne; and at Derrygrath, Perry of Woodrooffe House. Of these, Bagwell, Hutchinson and Perry were originally aligned to the Unitarian Presbyterian congregation, the original Protestant dissenting congregation of the town. The Established Church there may be seen to have already benefited substantially from a considerable influx of dissenter families, and also some Roman Catholics by the close of the eighteenth century, as noted in vestry minute references and pew-allocations. Two pew lists survive from the key urban parish of Clonmel in the early nineteenth century: in 1805, using surname analysis, there were 13 convert families with pews in the parish church, viz. 9 Roman Catholic, one Unitarian and 3 Quaker; in 1820, there were 15, the Unitarian number having tripled. In this way one-quarter of the pews in the parish church were owned by convert families. Perhaps the close identification of the parish church with the local establishment – well emphasized at Clonmel, where up to the renovation of 1805, a portion of the north gallery was reserved for the corporation and emblazoned with its arms – had a role in this.[24]

In contrast to the more vigorous parochial unions surrounding the archiepiscopal seat of Cashel, all of the hinterland parishes of the great Protestant dissenting centre of Clonmel, and all but one of those surrounding Tipperary, held communion services quarterly or six times per annum. This can be taken as indicative of the dominance of a low-church tradition in each particular Anglican parish, as this matter was governed by the rector and select vestry. The promotion of a low-church ethos indeed indicated a willingness to promote inter-marriage with the Protestant dissenters, with the explicit aim of denominational assimilation and the further strengthening of the Protestant interest. The infrequent holding of communion services in particular mirrored the low-church approach of the Presbyterians, and also made Anglicanism more palatable to the Quakers of the district.

Upward social mobility among the Protestant dissenters tended towards their assimilation to the Established Church. Arguably the best example is the Quakers, whose concentration in the south of the county – around the towns of Clonmel

24 Roman Catholic (1805): Keating; Slaughtery; O'Brien; Farrell (2); Ryan; Flanagan; Kelly; Leary; (1820): Keating; Slaughtery; O'Brien; Farrell (2); Flanagan; Leary; Hogan; Casey; **Unitarian** (1805): Riall (1); (1820): Riall (3); **Quaker** (1805): Collett (2) Harvey; (1820): Collett (2); Harvey. See vestry minutes of St Mary's, Clonmel, fos. 1–2; Watson, *A dinner of herbs*, 110–11.

and Cahir – was such that until the mid-eighteenth century they were the second largest dissenting denomination in the area, after the Presbyterians. Though their community numbered fewer than twenty households at this point, it contained diversity from an early date. In the urban context, at Clonmel, member families were significant textile merchants, while households in the Cahir and Cashel hinterlands held large farms on long leases. There was an upturn in their population in the second-half of the eighteenth century as a result of their involvement in the prosperous flour milling industry. This led to a vast increase in their birth rate from 14.2 per decade in 1700–50 to 51 per decade in 1751–1800, and their overtaking the Presbyterians during the 1750s as the premier dissenting denomination (numerically and soon economically) in South Tipperary.[25] These statistics were greatly enhanced by the influx of several Quaker families to the district in the years after 1750, attracted by economic opportunity, who then proceeded to monopolize the corn industry and related trades at the period of their greatest prosperity. New families at Clonmel included those of Richard Sparrow from Wexford, Solomon Watson from Carlow, John Malcomson from Lurgan, Robert Dudley, Thomas Rigg, and several others. Between 1763 and 1828, 23 mills were in operation at Clonmel, making it the largest milling centre in Ireland, while from 1770, Tipperary was the third county in Ireland in terms of the corn trade.[26]

In this period, the Quaker population of South Tipperary, as elsewhere on the island, became heavily concentrated in urban areas and their immediate hinterlands. By 1787, though accounting for no more than 3 per cent of the town population, some 36 of the 154 Clonmel businesses listed have identifiably Quaker surnames, so that members of Clonmel congregation operated some 20 per cent of the businesses there.[27] Indeed, at this time, it was remarked 'they seem to live like princes of the earth more [so] than in any country I have seen, [as evidenced by] their gardens, horses, carriages and various conveniences, with the abundance of their tables'.[28] Successful Quaker families invested heavily in country estates and in 1780 it was remarked, 'the Quakers be very cunning and the devil a bad acre of land will they hire'.[29] Although the Collett family, founders of Clonmel Quakerism in 1661, had defected to Anglicanism before 1778 – for they are listed as pew-owners in vestry minutes of that year – sufficient membership remained that new meeting-houses were constructed at both Cahir and Clonmel, exclusively using the wealth of the local Societies. Cahir had been a movable house-meeting, held wherever the greatest proportion of the membership resided. Worship was held in various houses in Kilcommon between 1660 and 1775, until the ending of the last Quaker lease in that area. It moved in 1775 to the townland of Garryroan, in the vicinity of which most of the membership then resided and where a small meeting-house was constructed in 1789, at a cost of £101 16s. 8d.[30] By the 1830s, the member-

25 FHL, Tipperary monthly meeting births register. **26** Burke, *Clonmel*, 296. **27** R. Lucas, 'General directory of the kingdom of Ireland, 1788' (1966), 468–76, also Burke, *Clonmel*, 133–5; RIA MS 12 D 36, 'A printed list of [Co. Tipperary] freeholders (1776)' lists 12 households with Quaker surnames of a total 78 for Clonmel. **28** Extract from the journal of William Lavery, 1 January 1792, written while at Clonmel. **29** Young, *Journal*, 26; 194. **30** FHL, Grubb collection S1856, MS Box 56, 'Clonmel subscribers towards building the meeting-house at Garryroan, 1789'.

ship was largely resident in Cahir town; following a period of meetings for worship being held in Cahir Abbey House, a new, larger meeting-house was constructed at nearby Abbey Street in 1833, using subscriptions to the value of £838.[31]

The meeting at Clonmel was relocated, c.1800 from its meeting-house of 1700 – built in a laneway off Main Street – to larger premises converted for this purpose, in an area of town subsequently named Meeting-House Lane (now Market Street). This affluence had a negative impact internally in the religious society, and a growing concern about the inherent problem associated with wealth and indifference moved a leading member of the Clonmel meeting, Margaret Grubb, to comment that 'although things are low in our religious society, there is some prospect of revival, even among the youth, some of whom are not ashamed to confess Christ before men, with earnest desires that the number may increase'.[32] These concerns were timely, but they did not prevent many leading families of longstanding affiliation converting to the Established Church, a system of worship more suitable to their new affluence and status. This was a problem that affected all social levels in dissenting congregations, whether Quaker, Presbyterian or Baptist. Decline was so widespread among the Baptists during the eighteenth century, that in 1749, all congregations of the denomination – many of them subsisting in no more than name – presented a petition to the lord lieutenant listing the disadvantages their clergy experienced through a lack of governmental encouragement and support, protesting 'want of proper encouragement for the clergy of our persuasion' and asking

> for a share in his Majesty's royal bounty, that we might have in our power, in a more extensive manner, to promote, strengthen and extend the Protestant interest and true zeal, loyalty and love to his Majesty's royal person and court, in several places in this kingdom, where popery mostly prevails.[33]

This represented an effort on the part of the Baptist denomination to gain access to the *Regium Donum* – the annual royal grant to the various Presbyterian congregations – through appealing to the governmental bias in favour of Protestantism. Of the 12 Baptist congregations then in Ireland, 5 had a resident pastor, 3 were supply stations of these congregations and 4 were destitute of all preaching supplies.[34] They felt themselves to be third-class Protestants, shunned even by the Presbyterians, who as the premier dissenting denomination in Ireland obtained the lion's share of the annual royal grant.

On the whole, therefore, Protestant dissenters occupied a delicate in-between position between the Established Church and Roman Catholics, a position that led

---

31 FHL, Grubb collection S90, 'Cahir meeting-house subscription list', lists 31 subscribers from Clonmel meeting and 13 from Cahir, who combined to add £628 3s. 9d. to the £200 legacy of William Connor of Cahir for this purpose; G.W. Grubb, *The Grubbs of Tipperary* (1972). **32** FHL, Grubb collection S1856, MS Box 56, portfolio 72, doc. 72, 'Letter of Margaret Grubb to the youth of Co. Tipperary monthly meeting, 1 June 1826'. **33** Kirtland, *Historical sketch of the Baptist denomination in Ireland*, 15–16. The congregations were Dublin (2); Waterford, Ormond (Cloghjordan); Westmeath (Rahue); Wexford; Enniscorthy; Lismortagh (nr. Killenaule); Clonmel; Cork; Kilkenny; Rich Hill, Co. Armagh. **34** Cork church book, fo. 88.

many to defect to the Established Church to escape continued inferiority. This can also be seen as a development that was encouraged by an emphatically low-church Anglican tradition. There are no prominent examples of dissenter defections to the Roman Catholic Church, as this would usually have meant an even lower status in the mentality of the establishment than that available by remaining within the dissenting community. The status of this Roman Catholic group was by no means clear-cut, however, incorporating as it did a gradually diminishing number of gentry and aristocratic families, a steadily increasing number of wealthy merchants and substantial leaseholders, as well as a rapidly expanding poorer population.

12

Renewal and response: inter-church rivalry
and the carving out of territory

The eighteenth century was a period in which Protestants of all ranks and creeds in general still viewed the Roman Catholic denomination with the greatest distaste and its followers with the greatest distrust. Their spiritual link with the pope in Rome caused them to be termed 'popish', 'papist' or 'romish' by members of the Protestant denominations. Such bigoted attitudes continued in the eighteenth century, as with the author of this mid-century pamphlet, who deplored the presence of

> popish priests [who] swarm over the whole kingdom at present [while the papists] resort to mass-houses [in a manner] as public and unrestrained as [we do] to our churches. The religious orders of monks, friars, Jesuits and nuns have their nests in many places and are perfectly well known in the vicinity.[1]

It may be seen that both diocesan clergy and religious orders were compared with swarms of insects and portrayed as less than human, due to Protestant Ascendancy fears of their powerful influence over the ordinary people. Immense social pressures were placed on clergy in the first half of the eighteenth century in particular and a few serving in key towns were induced to convert, as with the Revd John Connor of Cahir, in 1739, and the Revd William Daniel of Clonmel, in 1747.[2] Surviving sources reveal that local government despaired of ever having sufficient armed force with which to censor the priests as they 'have such an influence on the people'.[3] Several note the injuries suffered by companies of soldiers, attacked by vast stone-throwing mobs while transporting a priest to prison. The intimidation experienced by the high sheriff, Jonathan Lovett, was such that he left his home at Kingswell, near Tipperary, to dwell in the safety of the town itself. The Ashe family – Cromwellians with an upland seat in the Glen of Aherlow (fig. 20) – had twin sentry posts installed at the entrance of their small estate. Joseph Damer of Shronell, a neighbouring magistrate, complained that 'the common papists are insolent and provide themselves with arms. We hope the lord chief justice in his charge to the grand jury will let the county know their duty and raise the spirits of the now insulted poor Protestants'.[4] Support and reassurance of some significance was supplied, for presentments were made to the grand jury on several occasions in the 1760s at the Clonmel assizes, regarding the activities of 'popish'

---

1 *The ax[e] laid to the root or reasons humbly offered for putting the popish clergy in Ireland under some better regulations* (Dublin, 1749), cited in Burke, *Irish priests*, 461.   2 See *Convert rolls*.   3 Burke, *Irish priests*, 461.   4 Joseph Damer to Dublin Castle, dated 6 April 1754, cited in Burke, *Irish priests*, 362.

Fig. 20: Ashgrove, Glen of Aherlow

priests in South Tipperary. These ongoing insecurities led to an increased military presence in the landscape.

As a means of shoring up the Protestant interest in the towns after 1690, Roman Catholics were excluded from urban trade in a variety of by-laws enacted for the trade guilds in each corporate town, where none but 'reputable persons and these being Protestants' were admitted as members.[5] This strategy of law, therefore, had the result that no Roman Catholic shopkeeper or artisan had a right to trade in urban Ireland; if he was there, he was a trespasser in a strictly Protestant preserve and was fined accordingly. At Clonmel, for example, when a Roman Catholic entered the town or opened shop, he paid 'intrusion money', from 5s. to 10s. 6d. and upwards, and if he remained, paid each quarter a tax called 'quarterage', from 6d. to 3s., according to his capacity. This remained the situation throughout Ireland from the 1690s until the 1760s, when a lawsuit between a Cork merchant and the mayor of that city – in which damages were obtained against the mayor for imprisonment on account of quarterage – gave impetus to the campaign for the abolition of the quarter tax.[6]

In 1764, the Roman Catholic merchants at Clonmel began an agitation against the payment of this tax, which led to the increasingly insecure corporation sending a petition to parliament early in 1766, wherein it pleaded the purpose of the tax for a variety of charitable causes, including the relief of reduced merchants and the provision of proper insignia and regalia for each guild company. The Roman

5 Burke, *Clonmel*, 145–6. **6** Ibid.; M. Wall, *Catholic Ireland in the eighteenth century* (1989).

Catholic party sent a counter petition the following month, highlighting the unlaw-ful nature of the tax on them as 'peaceful and loyal subjects'. Though it was not explicitly mentioned in either petition, some of the quarterage was apparently spent in the following way.

> Clonmell, 12th July 1767. This day being the anniversary of the battle of the Boyne fought by King William (of ever glorious and immortal memory), the morning was ushered in with ringing of bells, the ensigns or standards of the different companies of this corporation were displayed from the Tholsel and the mayor, bailiffs, burgesses, freemen and gentlemen of the dif-ferent corporations, with orange cockades, proceeded at six o'clock in the morning to perambulate the liberties and franchises according to ancient custom; and the evening concluded with bonfires, illuminations and other public demonstrations of joy.[7]

The expending of this sort of tax in sectarian celebrations was nothing short of an incitement to protest and unrest. In addition, Tipperary was a county where a far larger than average portion of the countryside remained in Roman Catholic hands and where as a result, the tension between the Protestant establishment and lead-ing Roman Catholic families reached its zenith. The single greatest reason for this was the failure of the colonial administration to convert sufficient branches of the Butler dynasty – the largest landowners in Co. Kilkenny and among the largest in Co. Tipperary – to the Established Church. In Tipperary especially, these families were vehemently anti-establishment, with the Cahir branch refusing any form of nominal conversion, and persisting in directing many of its younger sons and daugh-ters into religious orders on the Continent. Lord Cahir was president of the Confraternity of St Paul during the first half of the eighteenth century, the society with responsibility for nominating the parish priest of Clonmel; two of his daugh-ters were nuns at Ypres, Belgium, while a son was a Jesuit in England.

Tipperary had a large number of Roman Catholic gentleman tenants, who leased from the remaining gentry of their denomination and Protestants alike. This strong Roman Catholic landed interest, which was at its most powerful in the southern districts of Tipperary, created an interface between an active Protestant interest in the north-west and in the south, along the lower reaches of the river Suir and its tributaries. Indeed, the county constituted an almost physical frontier between the largely Butler lands stretching from Kilkenny across Tipperary to Cashel and Cahir and the 'quite rabid' flanking regions of predominantly Protestant landownership on either side.[8]

The entry of some of the more prominent Roman Catholic families into power and politics through nominal conversion to the Established Church swiftly wors-ened an already deteriorating situation. The initial political flashpoint was the con-tested Tipperary election of 1761 between the evangelical Maude at Dundrum and his neighbour Mathew of Thomastown and Annfield, whose conformity to the

---

7 *Freeman's Journal*, 14–17 July 1767, cited in Burke, *Clonmel*, 146–7. **8** Cullen, *Modern Ireland*, 122–3.

Established Church was in doubt. These tensions quickly spread to the upper classes along the lower Suir valley, where the Butler (Cahir) estate bounded that of O'Callaghan (Shanbally). The latter was a newly purchased, recently extended estate, in the ownership of a convert family which sought to identify wholly with the establishment, to the extent of socially engineering the religious composition of their estate from the 1740s. Before analyzing the hegemonic flows between Protestant and Roman Catholic, however, it is necessary to consider the source of Protestant insecurity in this period, namely the territorial organization and power of the resurgent Roman Catholic Church, and its principal support in the landed classes.

The number of Roman Catholic aristocratic and gentry families dwindled gradually during the first half of the eighteenth century, as penal legislation impeded the transfer, intact, of their estates from one generation to the next. Their wealth and status remained significant, however, with several estates surviving virtually intact and many more continuing as head-tenants on their former estates. Already, by the mid-1730s, numerous Roman Catholic families of aristocratic, gentry and mercantile background were subscribing to contemporary publications. These voluntary subscription lists provide a window into Roman Catholicism of this period, which belies the myth of the total degradation of leading families of the denomination, while revealing an availability of surplus funds for philanthropic and leisurely pursuits. There are several examples from this period, such as *Botanalogia Universalis Hibernica* (1735)[9] and *Zoologia Medicinalis Hibernica* (1739).[10] The former volume is particularly relevant, being printed in Cork, from where it drew subscriptions from the entire province of Munster, and also Co. Kilkenny. Of some 370 subscribers, one-third was identifiably Roman Catholic, a remarkable statistic and indicative of the lifestyle many dynasties were able to maintain. In South Tipperary, there were 9 subscribing Roman Catholic households, viz. Lord and Lady Cahir (2); Mathew (2); McCarthy of Springhouse (2); Mandeville of Ballydine (2); Purtill of Killusty; Kearney of Cashel; Keating of Cahir (2); Hiffernan MD; Ryan MD; and 7 Protestant households, viz. Clutterbuck of Fethard; Callaghan of Clogheen; Moore of Clonmel (3); Prendergast of Ardfinnan; Pennefather of Cashel; Perry of Clonmel; Le Hunt of Cashel: together, the former actually outnumbered the latter, both in terms of households subscribing and numbers of copies taken.

The situation concerning land inheritance remained difficult, however, as penal legislation was such that any of the sons of an estate could inherit if the eldest refused to conform to the Established Church, and if all refused their estate was at the mercy of Protestant discoverers within a year. A prominent example was the Butlers of Kilcash, where the head of the family died in 1738 and the eldest son found himself in the position of having to conform to save the family estates in 1739. John Butler of Kilcash was sole male heir and his conversion was not only intended to keep the Kilcash estate intact, but also to make him eligible to inherit the remnant of the Ormond estates, as stressed in the public notices of his conversion. As he left

---

9 J. Keogh, *A general Irish herbal account* (Cork, 1735). Keogh was son of an Anglican clergyman, sometime dean of Killaloe.   **10** Idem, *A treatist shewing the medicinal virtues of birds, beasts, fishes, reptiles and insects* (Dublin, 1739). I am indebted to Mr K.W. Nicholls, dept. of History, UCC for this reference.

no heir on his death in 1766, his first cousin, Walter Butler of the Garryricken branch, whose only son, John, had converted in 1764, succeeded him.[11]

Other aristocratic families, through a combination of astuteness and good fortune, managed to retain their estates and their religion. The premier Irish examples were Browne, Viscount Kenmare, in-law of the Kilcash Butlers and Butler, Lord Cahir, their kinsman. The Browne family were fortunate in that for three generations, a single male heir inherited. The evasion by the Butlers of Cahir of penal legislation is still more interesting. They were exempt from the early stages of the penal laws, in that a single male heir succeeded before 1703, thus postponing the requirement that all Roman Catholic estates be equally divided between all male heirs to the next succession. Their problems did not therefore become acute until 1744, when the five sons of Lord Cahir had equal rights of inheritance to an estate of over 10,000 acres. This was avoided through the vesting of the estate in trustees and its repeated mortgaging during the 1750s, with the proviso that it was not to revert to the owner until the borrowed money had been repaid. The heir, James, lived for most of his life outside Ireland – either in Suffolk, England or in France – giving long leases of his lands to provide ready income. However, as he lacked an heir and his surviving brothers were either unmarried or in the Church, the estate passed on the death of the last of them, in 1788, to the Glengall branch of the family, which had, ironically, recently conformed: Richard Butler, Lord Cahir (later 1st earl of Glengall), had been baptized at Curraghscateen on 26 December 1775, by the Revd John Byrne, PP of Freshford and Tullaroan.[12] The improvements to town and estate begun by the last Roman Catholic Lord Cahir, following the relaxation of penal legislation in the 1770s, were rapidly accelerated under his Anglican successors.[13]

In addition to these key gentry survivors, a numerous group existed at the level of head-tenant, with the majority located in that portion of South Tipperary stretching from south of Cahir to north of Cashel, and also in the hinterland stretching northwards from Clonmel and Carrick-on-Suir. McCarthy of Springhouse and Keating of Garranlea, noted priest protectors, each held lands extending to several thousand acres, which brought them to the attention of the travel writer, Arthur Young, in the 1770s.[14] The gentry-style refinement of these households can be further observed in their subscribing to notable publications as early as the 1730s. Keating of Knockagh, Nagle of Garnavilla (fig. 21) and Mulcahy of Corabella (fig. 28) dominated the head-tenantry on the Butler (Cahir) estate, where the bulk of the tenants were Roman Catholic.

Throughout the south county, several former landowners whose ancestors had been expropriated in the seventeenth century maintained their position by secur-

---

11 *Freeman's Journal*, 29 December 1764: 'John Butler esq., only son of Walter Butler of Garryricken, renounced the errors of the church of Rome in the parish church of Golden, diocese of Cashel'. **12** W. Carrigan, *History of the diocese of Ossory* (1905); a silver chalice, in possession of Sandymount parish, Dublin is inscribed on one side 'Given by the first earl of Glengall to his relative, P. Everard, archbishop of Cashel' and on the other 'Pray for the soul of James, lord Baron Cahir, 1776'; see also GO MS 176. **13** Butler, *Cahir*, 6–7; Power, *Land, politics and society*, 107. **14** A. Young, A *tour in Ireland*, i (1780), 388–91.

Fig. 21: Garnavilla House, Cahir

ing advantageous leases. A sympathetic landlord was essential. In 1729, in addition
to bequeathing 30s. towards the upkeep of Cahir mass-house, Robert Keating of
Knockagh bequeathed 'to my Lord Cahir's eldest son, a young grey mare, now
grazing on the lands of Knocknefalling, as a token of my love to him and his
father'.[15] This flattery obviously paid dividends, for by 1767 the Keatings held over
3,000 acres on lease. Kinship to the landlord was another distinct advantage, as evidenced by the presence of several Butler families renting substantial farms on long
tenancies in the manors of Rehill and Castlegrace on the Cahir estate, before the
last quarter of the eighteenth century.[16] On the townland of Kilroe, Edmond Butler
held a tenancy of 265 acres from March 1781, for five lives or 80 years, whichever
should last the longer; at nearby Clogheenafishoge, adjoining the Butler family seat
at Rehill, James Butler held a very substantial 378-acre farm for three lives, or 61
years, from the same month, while at Munroe, James Butler held 187 acres from
March 1799; a similar tenancy of 85 acres was granted James Butler of Killaidamee
from May 1784, in the manor of Castlegrace, so that between them, these four
families held over 900 acres on favourable terms.[17]

  The pattern of marriage among major Roman Catholic families, as with the
Protestant dissenters, was one of integration, with many close kinship ties. In a blur-
ring of social distinctions, landowners forged marriage ties with members of large
middleman families both within and without the county. There were few signifi-

15 Will of Robert Keating, dated 12 April 1728 in H.D. Walsh, 'Index to Irish wills in the Carrigan
manuscripts' (1970), 225; Whelan, 'Catholic mobilisation, 1750–1850' (1991). 16 See Butler, 'House
of Rouskagh' (2003). 17 NAI MS 976/3/4/1: Cahir estate rental, 1826–43.

cant inter-church marriages, even between nominal convert families and Protestants, the sole example in the landed class of South Tipperary being the Mathew family, relatives of the Butler dynasty. This family's range of marriage partners was not confined to those of their own religious persuasion, but rather diversified into matches with members of the establishment interest, to which they were nominal conformists, which brought substantial financial and connective benefits.

Three successive members of the Butler family held the premier church office in Munster, the archbishopric of Cashel, in the period 1712–91, which is a measure of the confidence the Church held in the religious pedigree of the various branches of this family and also their ability to increase the perceived respectability of the denomination among Protestants. Christopher Butler, of the Kilcash branch, was archbishop from 1712 to 1747, during which time he held mass ordinations at chapels on the Mathew estates at Thurles (in 1728, 1731, 1734 and 1742) and Thomastown (1741) for a total of 50 priests. His successor, Archbishop James Butler I, was of the Dunboyne branch, while Archbishop James Butler II was of the Ballyraggett, Co. Kilkenny branch. The survival of a book of some diocesan visitations undertaken by James Butler I in Cashel and Emly is of unique significance. They give 'a definite impression of a church going through a period of reform and renewal, not a church existing as a secret underground force struggling for survival', a phase which the archbishop's secretary, Dr John Butler, PP Ardmayle, noted as returning to its 'old form'.[18] It shows that rural church buildings were modest in size and furnishings, but numerous and that improvements were continually in progress with several newly built or renovated chapels noted in the years covered by the reports. Even villages had decent chapels, as at Killenaule by 1754, where Butler noted 'a chapel built in the form of a T, [with] a stone wall 7 foot high, 4 gable ends [and] 20 couples well tha[t]ched, 6 glass windows, altar, rails and pulpit of dale [*sic*] boards, [and] 3 large cisterns of stone to hold holy water'.[19] Butler provides details of 50 chapels in all, about half of which lay within South Tipperary. In this largely rural portion of countryside, they were predominantly barn-like structures with clay floors, whitewashed stonewalls and a low thatched roof.

Though the Church was still lacking in material resources, it was becoming better organized, with a wide parochial structure well established by the 1750s. The mass-houses of the towns were significant buildings – particularly those of Clonmel and Tipperary – and were envied by rural Protestants still lacking a church or resident rector. The writer Charles Smith visited Clonmel during the 1750s, where he noted 'the Romanists have a very neat mass-house, pleasantly situated on the side of the Suir and adorned with a grove of trees, it being a few years ago splendidly rebuilt with many others in Munster by large contributions raised in Spain'.[20] A side-view of this building, drawn in the 1840s toward the end of its life, is depicted in fig. 22. While showing just one side of the substantial, T-shape building, its size and durability is obvious. There was a number of very large leaded glass windows, a slated roof and

---

18 C. O'Dwyer (ed.), 'Archbishop Butler's visitation book, i' (1975), 5. The visitation book, composed of parochial visitations for the years 1752, 1754, 1758, 1759, 1760 and 1764, is written almost entirely in English, with only a few words in Latin or Irish. **19** Visitation of Killenaule chapel, dated 11 July 1754, in ibid., 68. **20** RIA MS 24 G 9, History of Co. Tipperary (*c*.1750), fo. 277.

Fig. 22: St Mary's mass-house, Irishtown, Clonmel (side-view)

three galleries all accessed by outside steps, very much in the vernacular style of architecture favoured by the Presbyterians and Roman Catholics during the eighteenth century. In addition, an impressive array of vaults contained the remains of previous parish priests. Clerical numbers were well maintained, with the older religious orders continuing to maintain a token community presence near the site of many of their ancient foundations, thus playing an important role in assisting the parochial clergy in surrounding districts. South Tipperary continued to have an above average spread of assistance from this element of the Church, with the more established orders continuing their ministry as curates at Fethard, Cashel, Clonmel and Carrickbeg. These were joined by new orders from the early nineteenth century, by invitation of the parochial clergy and episcopacy. The earliest Co. Tipperary foundation was that made by the Ursuline Order at Thurles in 1787; in South Tipperary, foundations were made by the *Christian Brothers*: Carrick-on-Suir (1805), Clonmel (1847), Tipperary (1868), Cashel (1869); *Presentation Sisters*: Carrick-on-Suir (1813), Clonmel (1813) and Cashel (1830), Fethard (1862), Ballingarry (1871), Dundrum (1908); *Sisters of Charity*: Clonmel (1845); *Sisters of Mercy*: Cahir (1863), Tipperary (1864), Drangan (1872), New Inn (1879), Cashel, Clogheen, Clonmel district hospitals (1884), Clogheen (1886), Ballyporeen (1887); *Holy Ghost Fathers*: Rockwell College, Cashel (1864); *Patrician Brothers*: Fethard (1873); *Loreto Sisters*: Clonmel (1881); *Institute of Charity (Rosminian)*: Ferryhouse industrial school, Clonmel (1884).

Map 19 illustrates in full the Roman Catholic chapel network of South Tipperary, detailing the vintage of the earliest modern chapel-building throughout all parishes, also whether a change of site was involved in the upgrade from mass-house to chapel, and the status of the chapel network both in 1800 and in 1834. In rural parishes, these buildings were often towerless and cruciform, erected on sites that were more related to the convenience afforded by an expanding arte-

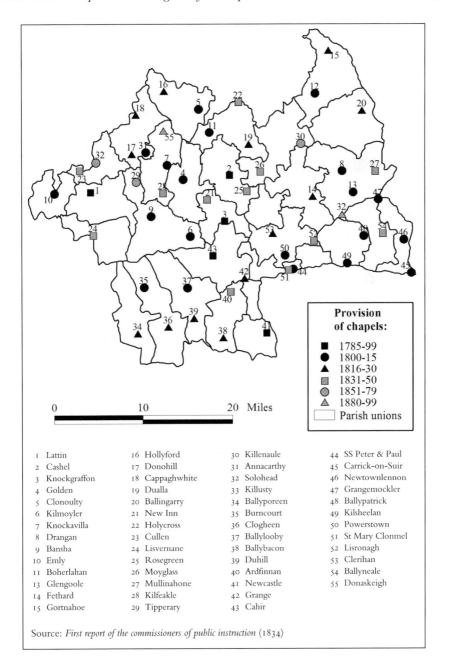

Provision
of chapels:

■ 1785-99
● 1800-15
▲ 1816-30
▨ 1831-50
◉ 1851-79
△ 1880-99
☐ Parish unions

0   10   20 Miles

1 Lattin	16 Hollyford	30 Killenaule	44 SS Peter & Paul
2 Cashel	17 Donohill	31 Annacarthy	45 Carrick-on-Suir
3 Knockgraffon	18 Cappaghwhite	32 Solohead	46 Newtownlennon
4 Golden	19 Dualla	33 Killusty	47 Grangemockler
5 Clonoulty	20 Ballingarry	34 Ballyporeen	48 Ballypatrick
6 Kilmoyler	21 New Inn	35 Burncourt	49 Kilsheelan
7 Knockavilla	22 Holycross	36 Clogheen	50 Powerstown
8 Drangan	23 Cullen	37 Ballylooby	51 St Mary Clonmel
9 Bansha	24 Lisvernane	38 Ballybacon	52 Lisronagh
10 Emly	25 Rosegreen	39 Duhill	53 Clerihan
11 Boherlahan	26 Moyglass	40 Ardfinnan	54 Ballyneale
13 Glengoole	27 Mullinahone	41 Newcastle	55 Donaskeigh
14 Fethard	28 Kilfeakle	42 Grange	
15 Gortnahoe	29 Tipperary	43 Cahir	

Source: *First report of the commissioners of public instruction* (1834)

Map 19: The Roman Catholic chapel network at fullest extent

rial road network rather than to the intrinsic appeal of the many historic Christian sites.[21] In rural districts of South Tipperary, Roman Catholic chapels gathered new villages around them at Ballylooby, Boherlahan, Clerihan, Dualla, Knockavilla and Grange, and to a lesser extent in a further eight parishes. In the towns, however, chapel building was of a far more affluent nature. In 1824, the chapel erected in 1790–1 at Cahir was described as 'a large plain building and, what is an uncommon circumstance, has a handsome lofty spire', while in 1831, just prior to the building of the present church, it was described as 'a very graceful structure'.[22] The site at Cahir had no ecclesiastical significance prior to 1790, but at Cashel and Thurles, the site of both the mass-house and succeeding chapel were on or adjoining the site of the monastery of a religious order. At Cashel, the new chapel of 1795 was built on the site of the Franciscan friary, but this was insufficient to quell the dissatisfaction of the parishioners. Such was their sense of identification with and attachment to the old thatched chapel adjoining the ruined Dominican priory in Chapel Lane, that it was razed in 1798 on the orders of the parish priest, Very Revd Edward Cormack VG, in defiance of their opposition to the new site and building in Friar Street, to which he had contributed substantially from his own Palmers Hill estate.[23]

The territorial organization of the Roman Catholic Church at this time was still largely that created in the later seventeenth century, and parish boundaries were significantly redrawn in just four locations within South Tipperary in the period prior to the mid-nineteenth century. Three of these boundary revisions came about through a realization that current arrangements were too extensive to serve the needs of the parishioners. The earliest change occurred in 1804 in the archdiocese of Cashel and Emly, just beyond the north-western fringe of South Tipperary, when a total of six civil parishes were taken from surrounding parochial unions to create the new upland parish of Kilcommon. The area was again affected when, in 1821, the adjacent union of Cappaghwhite and Hollyford was dissolved: Hollyford was joined to Kilcommon, Cappaghwhite was constituted a one-church parish, and replacement chapels were constructed at new locations in all three, so as to better reflect the new arrangements.

Another territorial boundary change almost contemporaneous with the initial creation of the parish of Kilcommon occurred on the eastern boundary. Drangan – which constituted a portion of the parish of Mullinahone until 1806 – was joined with Cloneen to create the new parish of Drangan and Cloneen, and a chapel was also built at Drangan in that year. The other two boundary revisions reflecting population growth occurred along the southern boundary. In 1816 the civil parish of Templetenny was separated from the vast union of Shanrahan, Templetenny and Ballysheehan and erected into a parish. In 1828 the thatched chapel of Templetenny – located at Carrigavisteal – was replaced by a church in the nearby estate village of Ballyporeen and the parish was renamed after this new settlement. A final boundary realignment also directly related to a growing population involved the building in 1810 of a chapel-of-ease to St Mary's, Clonmel, dedicated to SS Peter and

21 Jones-Hughes, 'The historical geography of Ireland from *c.*1700', 158; 163.   **22** *Pigot and Co. commercial directory of Ireland, 1824*, 225; NLI MS 3452, 'newspaper cuttings, compiled by Lord Dunboyne, *c.*1880'.   **23** Dunboyne, ibid.

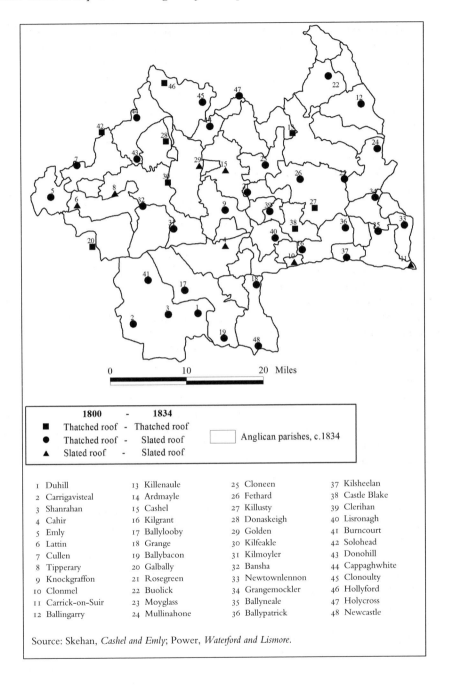

	1800	-	1834
■	Thatched roof	-	Thatched roof
●	Thatched roof	-	Slated roof
▲	Slated roof	-	Slated roof

☐ Anglican parishes, c.1834

1	Duhill	13	Killenaule	25	Cloneen	37	Kilsheelan
2	Carrigavisteal	14	Ardmayle	26	Fethard	38	Castle Blake
3	Shanrahan	15	Cashel	27	Killusty	39	Clerihan
4	Cahir	16	Kilgrant	28	Donaskeigh	40	Lisronagh
5	Emly	17	Ballylooby	29	Golden	41	Burncourt
6	Lattin	18	Grange	30	Kilfeakle	42	Solohead
7	Cullen	19	Ballybacon	31	Kilmoyler	43	Donohill
8	Tipperary	20	Galbally	32	Bansha	44	Cappaghwhite
9	Knockgraffon	21	Rosegreen	33	Newtownlennon	45	Clonoulty
10	Clonmel	22	Buolick	34	Grangemockler	46	Hollyford
11	Carrick-on-Suir	23	Moyglass	35	Ballyneale	47	Holycross
12	Ballingarry	24	Mullinahone	36	Ballypatrick	48	Newcastle

Source: Skehan, *Cashel and Emly*; Power, *Waterford and Lismore*.

Map 20: Progression from thatched to slated Roman Catholic chapels, 1800–34

Paul, on a heretofore non-ecclesiastical site in Johnston (now Gladstone) Street. This chapel was erected into a parish in 1836. All these developments involved expansion or improvement. Only one mass-house was abandoned and not replaced – that of Castle Blake – which served the civil parish of Mora and constituted a chapel-of-ease within the union of Powerstown-Lisronagh. This thatched chapel was abandoned during the 1840s, owing to a falling population, and was fully integrated in the union of parishes, the memory of its presence being continued through the use of its engraved silver chalice at Lisronagh church.[24]

From map 19, it can be judged that the earliest period of chapel-building occurred about the last decade of the eighteenth century, and was largely confined to five central and southern parishes. The two main phases of chapel building actually occurred in the pre-emancipation period, with 20 chapels built in the first fifteen years of the nineteenth century, this zone of early development predominantly in parishes in or adjacent to the valley of the river Suir. A further 13 chapels were built in the decade before emancipation, mainly in the southern-most parishes and in isolated parishes of the north-east and north-west. Post-emancipation chapel building can be divided into two main phases, namely the period from emancipation to the Famine and the period from the Famine to the end of the nineteenth century. In the first period, 11 chapels were constructed, mainly concentrated in parishes of the central district, but influencing all areas; a further 4 chapels were built after 1850.[25]

The strongest adherence to the site originally chosen for the thatched mass-house occurs in the southern-most parishes, particularly in the heavily Roman Catholic jurisdiction of the diocese of Waterford and Lismore. In the great swathe of territory to the north of this area – the jurisdiction of the archdiocese of Cashel and Emly – retention of the original mass-house site was the exception rather than the rule. This would seem to indicate the existence of a generally more favourable climate for the prominent placement of mass-houses in the early eighteenth century in the southern-most parishes. Here, a large number of comfortable Roman Catholic tenant farmers and merchants, together with the survival of a number of gentry, allowed the Roman Catholic denomination to establish itself on favourable sites at an earlier period than their brethren in Cashel and Emly archdiocese to the north.

The premier local example of chapel-site improvement occurred in the border-village of Galbally, in the archdiocese of Cashel and Emly (fig. 23), where the thatched cruciform mass-house of 1717 – separated from the village by a river and located at the end of a side street – was superseded in 1836 by a large slated chapel and schoolhouse. This was symbolically placed at the heart of the old plantation settlement of Lowe's Town. The glebe-house demesne, complete with medieval ruined church, still occupied the ancient ecclesiastical site of the settlement. However, the extent of the identification of the entire settlement with the Roman Catholic Church from 1836 led the Anglican establishment to relocate its parish church to the village in the early 1850s, to a prominent site at the street junction

---

24 For full details of these parishes, a comparison with others and list of sources used, see app. VII.
25 See app. X for the order of construction of modern Roman Catholic chapels in South Tipperary.

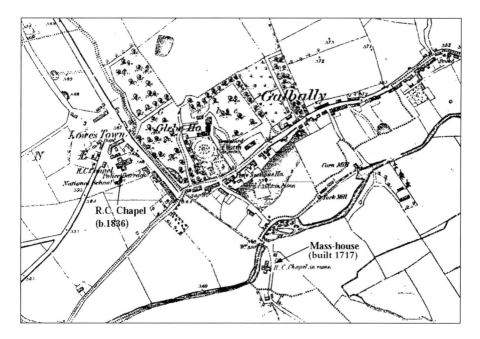

Fig. 23: Chapel relocation in Galbally village

next to the entrance to the glebe-house. The estate church of the Massy family at Duntrileague, which had served the parish union since the Restoration, was then dismantled. Roman Catholic mass-houses were generally thatched structures and prior to the building of the first modern chapels in South Tipperary, only the important urban parishes of Clonmel, Carrick-on-Suir and Tipperary possessed a slated mass-house. Map 20 shows the thatched roof still prevailed on all but 7 of the chapels in existence in 1800. A striking indicator of the seismic transition from thatched chapel to slated chapel in little more than three decades is the fact that, by 1834, only 8 parishes continued with a thatched chapel. They were predominantly backward, rural parishes, in which this deficiency was not remedied for many decades. It is significant, however, that all but one of these churches lay within the bounds of Cashel and Emly, with its significant and enlarged Protestant rural communities, and with Roman Catholic tenant farmers of a less affluent nature than their brethren in the diocese of Lismore to the south.

In the first half of the eighteenth century, prior to the easing of penal legislation, Roman Catholic houses of worship were termed 'mass-houses', while those of the Protestant dissenters were called 'meeting-houses'. They shared a second-rate status and were invariably located in side streets and less desirable obscure locations. In the last quarter of the century, both were somewhat upgraded in the eyes of the establishment as 'chapels', while the term 'church' remained reserved for the buildings of the Established Church alone.[26]

---

26 See Butler, 'The meeting-house of the Protestant dissenter'.

The location of Roman Catholic chapels was determined by a number of factors, such as site sponsorship by a local family, and the co-operation or otherwise of the principals of the local Protestant establishment. Surviving Roman Catholic gentry and head-tenants had been most important in the provision of the rudimentary mass-houses of the early eighteenth century, as at Cahir, where the mass-house stood by the demesne gates of the Butler estate, and Kilcash and Thomastown, where it was within the demesne itself. In the 1790 to 1830 period, these families played a less significant but still important role in individual parishes, as at Kilfeakle (Scully), Lattin (Moore of Mooresfort) and Kilmoyler (Meagher). The changing role of some of the older families is best demonstrated through the removal of the mass-house from the gates of Cahir Park demesne in 1790–1, just two years after the succession of distant Anglican cousins to the estate and the building of a new church at a respectable distance.

The co-operation of the local Protestant landlord in chapel-building was forthcoming in many instances in early nineteenth century South Tipperary. In the important corporation town of Fethard, for example, William Barton of Grove gave a prominent Main Street site rent-free, in spite of considerable criticism from his co-religionists, and subsequently laid the foundation stone for the present parish church. Similarly, William Latham of Meldrum – whose family were stalwarts of Fethard Presbyterian congregation – gave the site for the chapel at Dualla.[27] However, these instances of goodwill were countered in two other parishes by serious bigotry regarding the granting of a chapel site. At the chapel village of Knockavilla, it had proved impossible to buy or lease a site from the landlord, Maude of nearby Dundrum House, until a site was given by his co-religionist, Cooper of Killenure Castle, in 1806. At Bansha, matters were taken much further, when the principal landlord, Baker of Lismacue, refused to grant a chapel site in the village. He was usurped by Mr O'Brien-Butler of Bansha Castle, a fellow Protestant and lesser landlord, who in 1807 granted a site for the new chapel that directly adjoined the Anglican parish church. O'Brien-Butler had Roman Catholic relatives in his immediate family, and consequently this development was vehemently opposed by several leading Protestant families – notably the Bakers of Lismacue and Ballydavid and the Smithwicks of Barnlough – who successively petitioned Lord Lieutenant Hardwicke and the chief secretary, Sir Arthur Wellesley. However, after enquiries by the Dublin administration, the building of the chapel was continued with the active financial support of O'Brien-Butler and several other Protestant gentlemen.[28]

Villages and towns were battlegrounds between the two traditions. The Roman Catholic chapel was usually located well away from the church, reflecting the deep-seated dualism common in a colonial setting. Indeed, by the mid-nineteenth century, the location of various institutional buildings in many towns and villages reflected both the dominance of the Anglican establishment and the subordinate status of the Roman Catholic majority. This concept of churches at opposite ends

27 Skehan, *Cashel and Emly*, entries for Fethard-Killusty and Boherlahan-Dualla. **28** Ibid.: entries for Knockavilla-Donaskeigh and Bansha-Kilmoyler.

of a village or town, gathering each to its own, often at the end of a single thor-oughfare, underlined 'the most blatant symbols of the powerful undercurrents that bedevilled this polarized society'.[29] The dichotomy of the market square and fair green appeared to be a well-developed characteristic of villages and small towns, which served as centrepieces of estate cores.

The square or main street displayed the planned arrangements of institutions and functions which satisfied the needs and tastes of the landlord, including his own townhouse (if he had one), a market and court house, the assembly rooms, the church and the school. In association with the fair green, on the other hand, were usually found the more casual and menial needs of the countryman: a smithy, a ball alley, a pound, a police barrack, a bridewell, a public house, a medical dispensary, a national school, a 'big chapel' and a priest's house. The estate town of Cahir (fig. 24) was unique in South Tipperary and exceptional in southern Ireland, in that in addition to being a fine example of the above phenomenon, it also developed three distinct denominational spheres of influence. A great swathe of territory to the north and west of the town was leased by the Quaker milling dynasties, with the country estates of Cahir Abbey (Grubb), Alta Villa (Going) and Mill View (Walpole) adjoining their family's mills of Abbey, Suir and Cahir respectively. The great cen-tral zone was occupied by the Anglican establishment, with a church, parochial school, glebe-house, bridewell, police barrack, courthouse and market place all adjoining the landlord's seat, Cahir House. The Roman Catholic zone of influ-ence was miniscule by 1840, with its chapel and national school boxed in on all sides by landlord-owned property. Ironically, this was a direct reversal of influence enjoyed prior to 1788, when the sphere of Roman Catholic interest adjoined the Quaker properties – leaseholders of a Roman Catholic landlord – and the Anglican zone of influence was confined to its medieval churchyard.

The town of Cahir was the exception in South Tipperary during this period, where the reorganization of the Roman Catholic Church was closely linked to the emergence of an articulate and mobilized middle class of that denomination. The presence of this grouping has been demonstrated through analysis of the Tipperary entries under the test oaths 1775–6 and the Tipperary names recorded on the Catholic qualification rolls of 1793, noting that 300 of the 364 entries for Tipperary in 1775–6 were of persons of intermediate rank such as farmer, gent, merchant, priest, cloth-ier, publican, esquire and shopkeeper; a similar proportion was continued in 1793.[30] These findings conflict strongly with the carefully promoted myth of a church funded by the pennies of the poor, though the folk memory still retains a strong sense of the association of the church with its wealthier parishioners, particularly in the survival of the oft-quoted phrase, 'high money – high mass, low money – low mass; no money – no mass'. The relaxation of restrictions on chapel-building in 1793 led to an immediate response in the rebuilding and renovation of chapels, particularly in urban areas of South Tipperary, but rural parishes had also responded well by the time of emancipation in 1829, with comparatively few exceptions.

29 Jones-Hughes, 'Village and town in mid-nineteenth century Ireland' (1981), 158. **30** Whelan, 'The Catholic Church', 221–3.

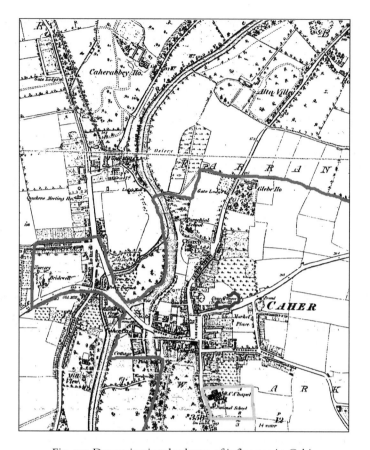

Fig. 24: Denominational spheres of influence in Cahir

Further evidence of the competition for space between Anglican and Roman Catholic institutional churches in the early nineteenth century can be observed on examination of the dates of construction or renovation of parish churches in both communities.[31] It can be established that in eight South Tipperary parishes where Roman Catholic chapels were (re) built, the local Anglican establishment retorted – on average within five years – by substantially rebuilding or replacing their own premises. This competition was even more pronounced in a further four parishes, where within a year of the Anglican parish church being (re)built, the local Roman Catholics responded even more promptly by providing new church premises, usually within four years. In 15 of 36 parishes – or 42 per cent of those with an Anglican Church – the Roman Catholics relocated to an alternative location within the civil parish. A chapel village often grew at this new location, usually to the detriment of the original settlement. The premier examples in South Tipperary, with the old settlement in brackets, are Ballylooby (Tubrid); Boherlahan (Ardmayle); Grange (Tullaghmelan) and Knockavilla (Ballintemple). In several rural Anglican parishes,

---

31 See app. IX.

the insecurities resulting from the relaxation of penal legislation from the 1770s led to an upgrading of the visibility of the parish church, usually in the form of the addition of a tower or steeple. This occurred at Shanrahan (1793–4); Rathronan (1797), Shronell (1808), Bansha (1814) and Tullaghmelan (1814) and was also addressed in the building of fashionable new churches, as at Knockgraffon (1788), Derrygrath (1815), Cahir (1817–8), Tubrid (1819–20), Emly (1827) and Tipperary (1830) to name a few. The success of the Church in occupying central urban sites in the post-emancipation period also prompted the movement of the Established Church from the medieval church site to the settlement itself, as occurred at Mullinahone (1843), Clogheen (1846) and Galbally (1850).

Despite this competition for space, cordial relations were in evidence in several parishes. At a local level, theological issues often had little bearing on inter-church co-operation; in the heavily Roman Catholic town of Carrick-on-Suir, the chief builder of the new chapel was Mr Richard Clarke, 'a good, honest Protestant'.[32] In 1819, at Clogheen, following the completion of the new parish church, the vestry resolved that

> the materials from the old church, that is, windows, wainscoting, seats, railings, stairs, the two galleries, roof, slates and floors (except the steeple roof), be given [to] Revd Mathias Casey, Messrs. Henry and Francis O'Brien and Messrs. Denis and Jeremiah McGrath in trust for the use of the new [Roman Catholic] chapel intended to be erected in the town of Clogheen.[33]

This was a significant change from the attitude in evidence in that parish during the 1740s, and the fact that 7 of the 33 households in the congregation pew-allocation of 1820 had local surnames may have had a bearing on this munificent gift.[34] However, the exclusion of the steeple from this ecumenical gesture signifies that the Anglican community, while still comfortable in its ascendancy, was averse to being lorded over by Roman Catholics, most particularly with materials of their own provision. The steeple at Shanrahan, a comparatively recent erection of 1793–4 that aimed to raise the profile of the Established Church on its detached medieval church site, one mile from the town of Clogheen, was instead left in position. Nevertheless, this gesture was of the utmost significance, given its location in a district that had seen some proselytising during the 1740s and widespread anti-establishment violence from the 1760s, resulting in the execution of the parish priest in 1766 at the peak of sectarian tensions.

---

32 P. Power (ed.), 'Notes from a Carrickman's diary, 1787–1809' (1913), 26. **33** Shanrahan vestry minutes, ii (1797–1849): entry for 27 December 1819. **34** Ibid., entry for 16 June 1820; the surnames: Butler, Collins, Meany, Keogh, Burke (2) and Prendergast.

13

Confrontation and consequence: the orchestration of anti-establishment resistance and the defence of Protestant Ascendancy

In times of economic hardship, violent resistance had a strong agrarian basis in South Tipperary. This was particularly true of the 1690s to 1720s period, when the activities of Tories and Raparees successfully disrupted the commercial life of the county. In the subsequent period up to 1750, a scattering of instances of rural outrage are on record, but these appear to be largely associated with more general criminal activity or else, if agrarian in nature, were localized and uncoordinated, and therefore not symptomatic of widespread grievances. An early example occurred with the robbery and attempted murder of the Revd Peter Hickes, rector of Kilcooley, in 1727, whose son was actually murdered during the raid.[1] From the mid-eighteenth century, however, violence was definitely an anti-establishment strategy of the Roman Catholic community, indicative of the increasing confrontation and competition for space between the two communities.

In the 1750s, there is evidence that agrarian unrest expressed itself in two ways: the killing or maiming of livestock, and the forcible possession of land. Of the two serious instances recorded in Co. Tipperary during this time, the first occurred in 1750 in the northern part of the county, the second in 1751 in the south, when a brace of deer in the deer park of John Damer of Shronell were killed. Both incidents occurred on Protestant-owned estates and neither elicited a proclamation from central government, though local rewards were offered. The Damer case is of particular note, in that it is contemporary with the settlement of a Protestant colony on the estate there, and may have been an act of local displeasure at the preferential treatment by the landlord of the artificially introduced northern weaver colony. The contention gains added authority in that the offenders were suspected to be disaffected locals, including a poacher, Buckston Hayes, and former territorial lords of the area, particularly O'Dwyer of Solohead and Ryan of Bruis. Crucially, the motive was reported to be only partly financial. The crime was seen as a protest against the enclosure of common lands and an effort to provoke hostility between the landlord, Damer, and his head-tenant, Richard Chadwick of Ballinard, a Protestant, on whose lands some of the deer were slaughtered, 'with a design to prejudice my interest and good neighbourhood with Mr Damer'.[2]

The construction of turnpike roads and toll houses were important factors which influenced the spatial occurrence and spread of agrarian outrages, as they were obvi-

---

1 Power, *Land, politics and society*: app. III. 2 Ibid.

ous instruments of the extension of central governmental control through the provinces. South Tipperary was a centrally located area, positioned at the cross-roads of Munster. As a consequence of this, eleven acts of parliament were passed in the course of the eighteenth century regarding the construction of roads in the area and there was an upsurge in this activity from the early 1750s, when a number of acts were amended and new ones passed. Of necessity, the new lines of road disturbed existing tenancy arrangements, reducing and dividing tenant holdings. However, it was the erection of toll-houses for the collection of tolls on produce and the transportation of animals, which provoked the greatest reaction. In South Tipperary, toll-houses or gates were constructed at eight locations along the north-eastern, eastern and southern flank of the county, at Urlingford, Knockboy, Longford Pass, Nine-Mile-House, Ballypatrick, Twomilebridge, Marlfield and Clogheen.[3] These control centres became the focus of attack by agrarian groups and such attacks were often signals whereby unrest was disseminated to wider areas.

The wrath of agrarian agitation groups was invariably directed against landlords, or at least against landed property. There was a large group of vehemently Protestant families in Clonmel and district, some of whom were quite rabidly anti-Roman Catholic. The zeal of these settler families, which included a considerable body of Protestant dissenters, is best indicated through the endowment of three charter schools in South Tipperary. This underlying inter-communal bitterness erupted in the early 1760s into the infamous support by the Tipperary Protestant gentry of the allegation of a 'popish plot', which was directed against Roman Catholic landowners and minor gentry. This episode can be viewed as a strategy of containment employed by the establishment, '[in] consequence of tension between [the] two rival groups within the county's landed class and as having the purpose of totally undermining the social position of the Roman Catholic group'.[4] Their numerical inferiority clearly influenced the chronically insecure attitude of the Protestants in Tipperary, a factor recognized by a visitor to the area in 1760, when he remarked 'the Protestants here are what we should call in England 'red-hot Protestants', [for] the smallness of their number makes it necessary for them politically to be so'.[5] This numerical situation was confirmed just 6 years later, in the religious census (1766). In combination with the continual and increasing contestation by Roman Catholics of the penal laws, this would lead to loss of life, most notably that of Fr Nicholas Sheehy of Clogheen.

The agrarian secret society known as the Whiteboys began its operations in 1761 in South Tipperary, the epicentre of their early actions being Clogheen.[6] Here, the enclosure of the common lands, the preferential introduction of Protestant head-tenants and landlord-sponsored conversion schemes during the 1740s overflowed into sectarian violence. The Whiteboy name itself derived from its members' practice of wearing white linen over-shirts, normally used as farming overalls

---

3 Power, *South Tipperary*, 150.   **4** Cullen, *Modern Ireland*, 50.   **5** Letters of Chief Baron Wiles, BL Add. MS 29252, fos. 38–40: transcripts in Canon W.P. Burke collection, Mount Mellary abbey, Cappoquin, Co. Waterford.   **6** Power, *South Tipperary*, 96; J.S. Donnelly, 'The Whiteboy movement, 1761–5' (1978).

over their clothes, during their nocturnal activities. With the suspension of restrictive cattle acts in 1758–9 that had prohibited the export of Irish beef since the late seventeenth century and with rising consumer demand in Europe, investment in pasture became more profitable. Landlords re-let to graziers who in turn curtailed traditional access to commons by smaller tenants. The Whiteboys attempted to defend these customary rights and devised strategies that channelled local resistance into a group that tore down – or 'levelled' – fences, hedges and walls, by filling in ditches and digging up pasture and by maiming or 'houghing' cattle at dead of night. This movement spread from South Tipperary into much of eastern Munster, as well as Co. Kilkenny.

The primary grievance of the Roman Catholic population was the payment of tithes to the Established Church. Tithe was usually paid in kind – corn or potatoes – and, after 1735, pasture was exempt from payment. These exactions were inflated by the machinery of collection, which constituted a corps of tithe-proctors and tithe-farmers who, at a price, administered the system on behalf of the clergy. Such 'middlemen' were a constant Whiteboy target. Between 1761 and 1765, Whiteboys were active in Cos. Waterford, Cork, Limerick and Kilkenny, where the scale of the outbreak is indicated by the introduction of the Whiteboy Act in 1765, a key provision of which made the administration of oaths by threat of violence – the defining characteristic of Whiteboyism – a capital offence.

The timing of the outbreak, during the first half of the 1760s, is significant. A number of additional issues related to Roman Catholicism were attracting the increased attention of the establishment in Ireland generally and Tipperary particularly about this time, most notably the collection of tithe from members of that denomination, which was being resisted at parish level, and the nominal conversion of several leading Roman Catholic landed families in order to qualify to run for Parliament.[7] Since the Whiteboys drew their members and support (but not their leadership) from lower-class Roman Catholics and since most of the bigger landlords were Protestants of the Established Church, allegations of sectarian motives were almost inevitable. Charges of French intrigue and popish conspiracy were made against the background of the Seven Years War (1756–63), which betrayed establishment fears of a French invasion. Local Protestant paranoia ensured that the agitation of social and economic questions was quickly sucked into the political arena. In Tipperary, gentry reaction to the Whiteboy troubles was sharpened by a bitterly contested county election in which the successful candidate – Thomas Mathew, a member of a convert family – had been stigmatized as a representative of the 'popish' interest. The local detail is crucial because the Dublin government at this time disregarded reports of the Whiteboys as 'papist' insurgents. It is in the area of local or regional politics, for example, that the explanation for the trial and execution of the Clogheen parish priest, Nicholas Sheehy lies. Sheehy had 'probably [been] mixed up' in the disturbances in Tipperary, but it seems clear that he was the victim of sectarian animus and judicial murder.[8] In 1761, Thomas Mathew of Thomastown (a nominal Anglican) opposed Sir Thomas Maude of Dundrum

---

7 Donnelly, 'The Whiteboy movement'.   8 J. Smyth, *The men of no property* (1992).

(an ardent Anglican evangelical) for return as MP for Co. Tipperary. The declaration in favour of Mathew was challenged by Maude, on grounds based on Mathews' closet Roman Catholicism, an argument given added impetus by the fact his wife and children openly professed it. The result was allowed to stand, though a duel later ensued between the representatives of each party, when Gahan, Maude's agent, killed Prendergast, a supporter of Mathew, at Clonmel. Maude, along with other Anglican Protestants, suspected the local Roman Catholic leadership to have a principal role, which attitude led in great measure to the Fr Nicholas Sheehy incident.

Whiteboyism was never a confessional movement inspired and maintained by the slogans and organization of Irish Roman Catholicism. Indeed, if anything, the Whiteboy movement presented 'a challenge to the Church leadership and ultimately showed that the whole membership of the Church – whose unity was supposedly consolidated by a shared experience under the penal laws – was not necessarily the sum total of its component parts'.[9] Though no direct evidence survives, certainly in relation to South Tipperary, it is likely that the Whiteboy movement utilized the parish network of the Roman Catholic Church as a vehicle for the dispersal of ideas, particularly during the informal gatherings after church on Sunday. The leading Church laity tended to condemn the activities of the Whiteboys and all other secret oath-bound agrarian-protest societies, as did also their clergy in their mission to avoid all confrontation with the Anglican ruling elite and so avoid drawing their wrath down upon the Church. The days of priest hunting and exile by the authorities were over, but the clergy and episcopacy were still very cautious. This is best illustrated in South Tipperary by the mid-eighteenth century removal of the seat of the Roman Catholic archbishop of Cashel and Emly from that of Anglican dominated Cashel to the heavily Roman Catholic town of Thurles. Similarly, the selection by the bishop of Waterford and Lismore of the heavily Roman Catholic town of Carrick-on-Suir as his seat in this period – above the more populous but substantially Protestant towns of Waterford, Clonmel and Dungarvan – further illustrates this point. Thus, the known presence of Sheehy at the levelling of fences on farms in his parish, his vehement opposition to tithe collection, and his generally anti-establishment disposition in sermons and otherwise, were not welcomed by his Church, for the hostile attention it drew from the more evangelical of the local Anglican establishment.[10]

Dr Pierce Creagh, bishop of Waterford and Lismore and Dr William Egan, parish priest of Clonmel and successor to Creagh, are accused in popular folklore of having betrayed Fr Sheehy. In 1762, Creagh had written a pastoral against the Whiteboys, forbidding his priests from absolving them, while Egan, an influential figure, refused to come forward when called as a witness for his fellow priest. Indeed, as Sheehy's corpse was taken away from the place of execution in Clonmel, the procession stopped at Dr Egan's parochial house, where blood was scattered on the door and the phrase inscribed 'Aodhagán is Créach a dhíol tú, Bagwell agus Maude a chráigh an croí ionat', which translates 'Egan and Creagh sold you, Bagwell and

9 M.J. Bric, 'The Whiteboy movement, 1760–80' (1985), 168.   10 S. Ó Cadhla, 'Captaen na bhFear mBán: Father Nicholas Sheehy in history/folklore' (2002).

Maude tormented you'.[11] Sheehy 'became at once the supreme victim of the anti-
Catholic frenzy of the 1760s and a rallying-point for his oppressed parishioners'.[12]
It would indeed appear that he was hunted down because fears for the security of
land titles, combined with 'apprehensions that lands would be overrun by a foreign enemy in league with an internal Whiteboy force led by prominent [Roman]
Catholics', drove Protestants to desperate measures.[13] A measure of this ascendancy
fear is in evidence throughout this period, when Dublin Castle was in constant
receipt of unsolicited letters and reports from Protestant country gentlemen that
they were about to be slaughtered in their beds, or that French agents had been
seen in their neighbourhood.[14]

The fury of the Protestant Ascendancy was further aroused by the failure of
Chief Justice Aston to convict more than a handful of 500 imprisoned Whiteboys
during the course of a special commission which held trials at Limerick, Clonmel,
Waterford and Cork. At Clonmel, to the great mortification of the assembled magistrates and gentry, no one was capitally convicted and, apart from one Whiteboy
who was sentenced to a year in prison, no other was found guilty of an offence.
Consequently, as Aston left Clonmel, 'both sides of the road were lined with men,
women and children who, as he passed along, kneeled down and supplicated heaven
to bless him as their protector and guardian angel'.[15] Against this background of
embarrassment, it becomes much easier to understand the twisted psychology of
the Protestant gentry of Tipperary who, thirsting for revenge and recovery from
disgrace, construed Whiteboy misdemeanours as high treason and set the scene for
the grand-jury indictments and show trials of 1765–7, culminating in the execution of Fr Nicholas Sheehy in 1766.

Sheehy was perceived within his own denomination as an outspoken young
parish priest who attracted the unwelcome attention of the authorities. A contemporary Roman Catholic historian described him as

> the outspoken, socially committed young parish priest, giddy and officious,
> but not ill-meaning, with something of a quixotish cast of mind towards
> relieving all those within his district whom he fancied to be injured or
> oppressed and setting aside his unavoidable connection with these rioters,
> several hundred of whom were his parishioners, he was a clergyman of unim-
> peached character in all other respects.[16]

The Protestant community saw him as 'a very capital ringleader of those insurgents
and the very life and soul of those deluded [Roman Catholic] people' and thus a
threat to be eradicated.[17] Between 1762 and 1766, there had been 50 instances of
Whiteboy violence in South Tipperary. Sheehy was the object of sustained harassment from the local ascendancy and magistrates, most notably William Bagnell of
Marlhill, Ardfinnan; John Bagwell of Marlfield; Sir Thomas Maude of Dundrum

11 Ibid.; also Donnelly, 'The Whiteboy movement'. 12 Bric, 'The Whiteboy movement', 153. 13 Power, *Land, politics and society*, 258. 14 Marnane, *Land and violence*, 11. 15 Donnelly, 'The Whiteboy movement', 46. 16 Dr John Curry, founder of the Catholic committee, cited in Corish, *The Catholic community*, 123. 17 Ibid.

and the Revd John Hewetson of Suirville, Co. Kilkenny, who held the tithes for several Tipperary parishes and was a curate anxious for promotion in the Established Church.[18] Sheehy was charged in 1763 with two others for general connection with the Whiteboys and, having escaped conviction, was again charged in 1764. This indictment sent him into hiding, which was taken as an admission of guilt and a proclamation was issued in 1765, calling on all officials of the realm to arrest him and put him in jail. Sheehy hid in the Shanrahan district, at one time in the two-storey mausoleum of the O'Callaghan family in Shanrahan churchyard. He eventually surrendered to the local landlord, O'Callaghan, who had him escorted to Dublin for trial, for it was thought that a Tipperary trial would be too highly charged. Sheehy was released on bail and at his trial in early 1766 was declared innocent of the leadership of a criminal conspiracy, of exercising men under arms, of swearing them to be loyal to the king of France, and of inciting them to rebellion. On release he was re-arrested, the prosecution moving that he be brought to Clonmel to stand trial for the murder of John Bridge. Of this he was convicted, through the use of trumped-up evidence. One of the chief witnesses against him was a woman whose sexual conduct he had publicly denounced from the altar; Molly Dunlea, bribed to bear false witness against Nicholas Sheehy, was of the parish of Dundrum. This act of bribery is reputed to have occurred in 1766, at a spot where a bridge crosses the river bordering the Maude estate, called 'Black bridge'.[19] His conviction and execution were motivated by the authorities' desire to be rid of him.

In 1767, the year after Sheehy's death, the Bagnells of Cork – brothers of William Bagnell of Ardfinnan – republished Sir John Temple's and Archbishop William King's famous works on the 1641 rising and the state of the Protestants under King James. These were presented as an intellectual and historical justification for the actions of the Tipperary gentry in 1765–6.[20] The Tipperary gentry were among the main subscribers to these publications, with John Bagwell taking five copies and William Bagnell, Matthew Bunbury and Mathew Jacob taking four copies each.[21] While these works kept passions inflamed within the Protestant community, the act of execution itself had a similar, more lasting effect on the Roman Catholics. As with the clerical martyrs of the late sixteenth and mid-seventeenth centuries, Sheehy was executed in the urban garrison centre of Clonmel, instead of at the alleged scene of the crime, as the authorities could not guarantee order beyond the confines of the county town. Within three years of his death, Sheehy was perceived as a martyr, as by 1769 there were daily pilgrimages of 'poor misguided papists' to Shanrahan churchyard.[22] The extent of popular outrage is underlined by the stoning to death of his executioner by a mob in 1770, which was reported as follows:

---

18 Bric, 'The Whiteboy movement', 169–76.   **19** Power, *South Tipperary*, 87–8; Doyle, *Cashel and Emly*, 72.   **20** These were Temple's *Irish rebellion or the history of the beginning and first progress of the general rebellion raised within the kingdom of Ireland upon the three and twentieth day of October 1641* and King's *State of the Protestants of Ireland under the late King James's government*; Power, *Land, politics and society*, 254. The Bagnells were dissenters; on 4 June 1749, the minutes of vestry of Cork Presbyterian meeting-house noted 'Phineas Bagnell, bookseller, lately settled in Cork and admitted to our communion, but to procure a cert. from the Revd Mr Dennison of Waterford': see CAI, U87–1.   **21** Burke, *Clonmel*, 366.   **22** Bric, 'The Whiteboy movement', 161.

> On Thursday the 6th inst, a man was executed at Philipstown [King's County] for murder; during the execution the mob (which was very great) were remarkably quiet, but as soon as it was over, they stoned the hangman to death and the body lay for two or three days under the gallows. This unfortunate creature was the person who hung Sheehy the priest, which is supposed to be the reason of this outrage.[23]

The execution of Sheehy testified to the continued strength of sectarian animosities in Tipperary, a county where Roman Catholic landed proprietors had survived in relatively large numbers alongside the Cromwellian planters.[24] Increasingly from the 1760s, confrontation of the establishment by the ruled Roman Catholic majority became commonplace and strategies of resistance began to focus on taxes paid to support the state church.

The guerrilla activities of Tories and Rapparees, and settler insecurities, led to the establishment of a network of government-sponsored garrisons in rural redoubts and urban barracks in the early eighteenth century. In combination with the nature of the terrain, this dictated that a higher than average number of redoubts were provided at this time in mountainous and upland areas bordering and encircling South Tipperary. Many were indifferently constructed and their condition was such that, by the mid-eighteenth century when speaking of standing barracks, all that was meant was that they 'were still on the [military] establishment' and 'had a right to stand, if they were able'.[25] By 1750 many barracks, particularly redoubts in upland areas of Ireland, had become surplus to requirements and were abandoned. This situation extended to the vicinity of South Tipperary, for in 1752 Pococke could write of

> the road from Cappoquin to Clonmel [where I] passed by an old redou[b]t for soldiers against Rapparees, now an alehouse called Ballinamult in the parish of Seskin. Ascending the hill beyond this place, I had a glorious view of the fine country of Tipperary and of the river Suir, which runs towards Clonmel.[26]

Map 21 illustrates the distribution of garrisons in South Tipperary and adjacent districts about the year 1780, distinguishing between types of troop companies and the actual size of each detachment. Lying at the heart of south-central Ireland, South Tipperary can still be seen to contain a higher number of garrisons than any of the surrounding districts, including that of Waterford, if that regional urban centre is separated from the county at large. The Cashel garrison covered the north-central and north-western districts, Fethard the eastern, Clogheen the western, Carrick-on-Suir the south-eastern and Clonmel the central areas and also the county as a whole.

A number of issues combined in the last three decades of the eighteenth century to militarize the landscape in a manner that equalled and which, by the early nine-

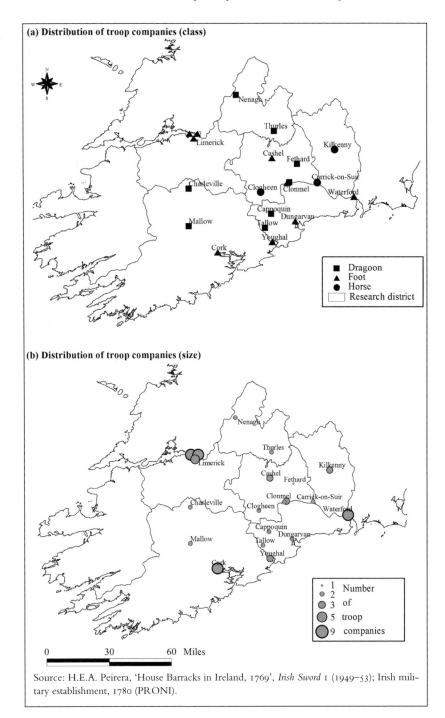

(a) Distribution of troop companies (class)

Nenagh

Thurles

Limerick

Cashel Fethard Kilkenny

Charleville Clogheen Clonmel Carrick-on-Suir Waterford

Cappoquin Dungarvan
Mallow Tallow
Youghal

Cork

■ Dragoon
▲ Foot
● Horse
☐ Research district

(b) Distribution of troop companies (size)

Nenagh

Thurles

Limerick

Cashel Fethard Kilkenny

Charleville Clonmel Carrick-on-Suir
Clogheen Waterford

Cappoquin
Mallow Tallow Dungarvan
Youghal

Cork

1 Number
2
3 of
5 troop
9 companies

0   30   60 Miles

Source: H.E.A. Peirera, 'House Barracks in Ireland, 1769', *Irish Sword* 1 (1949–53); Irish military establishment, 1780 (PRONI).

Map 21: The garrisons of South Tipperary and adjoining districts, *c*.1780

teenth century, surpassed that of the era of the Raparees. The first issue is related to
agrarian unrest, rebellion and an associated deterioration in the stability of rural society. At Clogheen, as a direct result of Whiteboy agrarian disturbances and the Fr
Sheehy affair of the 1760s, a permanent limestone-built cavalry barrack was provided
in 1770 on the Main Street of the estate town, with accommodation for 56 men, all
ranks and 60 horses.[27] It is ironic that discontent and rebellion, which had long caused
the migration of Protestants and otherwise negatively affected their mentalities and
sense of security, was now brought to have some positive impact on their numerical distribution, through the increased deployment of military detachments.

The second set of issues leading to a military build-up can be divided between
overseas military commitment and the threat of invasion from abroad. The
American War of Independence drew heavily on England's resources, above all on
its military strength. As troop numbers in Ireland diminished, Whiteboy disturbances forced the ruling classes and landowners in general to consider an independent means of defence. From 1776, as part of a strategy of containment, volunteer corps formed throughout Ireland, founded, officered and financed by the
ruling classes. These corps had decorative uniforms and frequently paraded and
drilled in shows of strength. Some sixteen companies were founded within South
Tipperary in 1776–81, with Protestant-dominated corps at Dundrum, Kilcooley,
Cashel, Clonmel, Clogheen, Fethard and Tipperary and Roman Catholic dominated corps at Carrick and Cahir.[28] It is interesting to note the predominance of
urban centres in the mobilising of volunteer corps and also that the only non-urban
centres to raise corps for their protection were the estate colonies at Dundrum and
Kilcooley. Many of the urban corps were also estate-driven. At Tipperary town,
the earl of Derby, whose estate lay within four miles of the town, formed a regiment and had twenty Englishmen brought over to officer it. The local Protestant
community benefited as several of these officers later settled in Tipperary as tenants of the Derby estate. Although a small settlement in 1788, Tipperary became
an important market town in the early nineteenth century through the agricultural
and mercantile entrepreneurial skills of these Hansard, Le Barte, Evans, Armstrong,
Lamphier, Robinson, Hodges and Wilkinson dynasties.[29]

The rebellion of 1798 caused great panic among Protestants. They were made
even more aware of how few they were and their insecurity increased accordingly.
This was particularly the case in upland rural districts of the barony of Slieveardagh,
where in an isolated instance, Springhill, seat of the Hemphill family, was burned.[30]
Several of the county gentry, most notably descendants of Cromwellian soldiers
such as Despard of Killaghy Castle and Langley of Coalbrook, reacted to every
rumour of rebellion for decades after and were responsible for a near constant stream
of letters to Dublin Castle. Despard's residence lay close to Slievenamon, the upland
locality where an abortive, localized offshoot of the 1798 rebellion occurred.[31]

27 W.J. Bergin, 'Military barracks, Cahir and military barracks, Clogheen' (1984), 243–4. **28** W.J.
Hayes, *Tipperary in the year of rebellion, 1798* (1998), 13–15. **29** R. Lucas, 'General directory of the
kingdom of Ireland, 1788': entry for Tipperary town; *Clonmel Chronicle*, 11 April 1896. **30** See NLI
MS 3452. **31** Neely, *Kilcooley*, 73–5; Hayes, *Tipperary*.

There was also the threat of invasion, particularly from France. Even in peacetime, there were regular encampments of the Irish army, designed to give the troops and companies who were normally divided and housed in barracks some experience of working together in the field. The early realization by the military establishment of the strategic importance of the southern portion of Tipperary was in evidence in the concentration of garrisons there, from where a defending army could be concentrated to deal with a landing at any point on the coast between the river Shannon at Limerick and the river Suir at Waterford. Consequently, South Tipperary was where the majority of these encampments took place, at locations such as Clonmel, Cahir, Cashel and Ardfinnan. In 1779, the entire Irish army was encamped there, with the bulk of the force, comprising 5 regiments of cavalry and 5 of infantry distributed about Cahir and Cashel.[32] This system was continued during the Napoleonic Wars and by the autumn of 1798, troop numbers were so high that all barracks were overcrowded, though supplemented by rented accommodation.[33]

A contemporary Protestant view of this military landscape is provided through the late eighteenth-century memoir of Dorothea Herbert, daughter of an Anglican clergyman. The Herbert family spent nine months of each year at the urban centre of Carrick-on-Suir and three summer months at Knockgraffon, a village near Cashel. Herbert continually mentions the particular garrison quartered each year in both districts, although seemingly more out of care to note their important role in society, than out of a sense of insecurity. Protestant society in particular made the most of their presence and Herbert hailed the positive effect the company of innumerable officers had on the social set in South Tipperary by the 1790s.

> Knockgraffon was now become a martial scene by the continual passing of the army to and from the camp of Ardfinnan, a romantic village eleven miles distant. The Co. Kilkenny militia had been stationed in Carrick some time – their officers were mostly all related to us. When the Kilkenny regiment went, the South Cork came in its place and with them [its colonel] Lord Barrymore and Lady Barrymore. Besides this set, we had Mr Hutchinson, a recruiting officer who was a universal genius. His chief forte was spouting plays with which he amused his acquaintance. Altogether it was a very gay jumble of regimental scraps. We had nothing but band playing, singing, leaping and cutting apples with the sword's point [and] in this manner we spent the latter end of the year 1794.[34]

The peripatetic military population swelled the numbers attending the parish churches and also the Protestant birth rate, as birth and marriage registers attest. At Cahir, for example, an important garrison town with a small resident Anglican population, the garrison accounted for half of the births in the parish in the first thirty years of the nineteenth century. This was true of many garrison towns and military stations. At Clonmel, with its large resident merchant and gentry population, the military establishment with its separate cavalry, infantry and artillery barracks, in combination with

32 Ferguson, 'The army in Ireland', 102; 148; 184. **33** Ibid., 101. **34** Herbert, *Retrospections*, 329; 338–9.

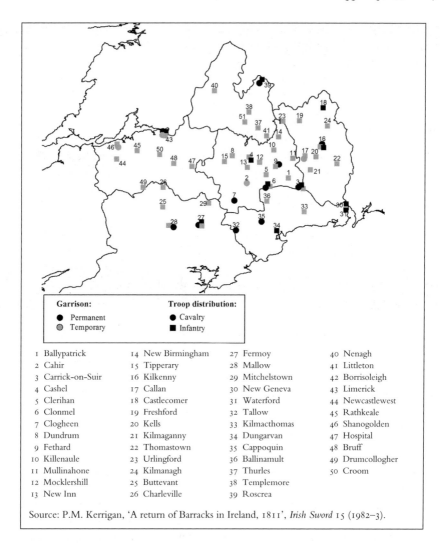

Garrison:
- ● Permanent
- ● Temporary

Troop distribution:
- ● Cavalry
- ■ Infantry

1 Ballypatrick	14 New Birmingham	27 Fermoy	40 Nenagh
2 Cahir	15 Tipperary	28 Mallow	41 Littleton
3 Carrick-on-Suir	16 Kilkenny	29 Mitchelstown	42 Borrisoleigh
4 Cashel	17 Callan	30 New Geneva	43 Limerick
5 Clerihan	18 Castlecomer	31 Waterford	44 Newcastlewest
6 Clonmel	19 Freshford	32 Tallow	45 Rathkeale
7 Clogheen	20 Kells	33 Kilmacthomas	46 Shanogolden
8 Dundrum	21 Kilmaganny	34 Dungarvan	47 Hospital
9 Fethard	22 Thomastown	35 Cappoquin	48 Bruff
10 Killenaule	23 Urlingford	36 Ballinamult	49 Drumcollogher
11 Mullinahone	24 Kilmanagh	37 Thurles	50 Croom
12 Mocklershill	25 Buttevant	38 Templemore	
13 New Inn	26 Charleville	39 Roscrea	

Source: P.M. Kerrigan, 'A return of Barracks in Ireland, 1811', *Irish Sword* 15 (1982–3).

Map 22: The distribution of garrison stations in the district, 1811

some households employed in aspects of the provincial civil service, still accounted for half of all Anglican births in the period from 1766 to 1830.[35]

Map 22 displays the distribution of garrison stations in South Tipperary and surrounding districts, *c.*1811. This period was one of intense military activity, toward the end of the Napoleonic Wars. The number of military stations within South Tipperary is itself striking, with 23 garrisons in 16 locations, comprising one-third of the 68 barracks in the districts mapped.[36] The spread of barracks in the three decades since 1780

---

35 Baptism and marriage registers of Cahir parish (1801–30); baptism and marriage register of St Mary's Clonmel (1766–1830), both held at the parish office, St Mary's church, Clonmel, Co. Tipperary. **36** See app. XI for full details of all garrisons mapped. Several of the temporary barracks, viz. those at

Fig. 25: The collection of tithe at Knockgraffon parsonage, *c.*1790

is obvious, most particularly in South Tipperary, where a military presence was restored to many of the upland areas and lesser settlements which had been garrisoned in 1704. Its 8 infantry (foot) barracks may be seen to outweigh the distribution of any surrounding district and to equal any three districts combined, while the same is the case with the cavalry (horse) troop distribution. Indeed, the concentration of five permanent barracks in South Tipperary far exceeds that of any other surrounding district, indicating the strategic importance of its central location, its spread of significant urban centres, the need for the security of these areas and their hinterlands and the successful arguments of the local Protestant establishment for this defence.

While the Napoleonic wars raged, there was a constant suspicion – not entirely unreasonable given Ireland's recent history – that disorders in the Irish countryside were part of an organized conspiracy aiming, with French assistance, to overthrow the whole system of government. A teeming correspondence poured into Dublin Castle, month after month, from county after county, on the disturbed 'state of the country', with magistrates, peers, landowners, clergy, police officers and military commanders providing a steady stream of reports whose contents outlined seemingly endless attacks on officials, robbery and destruction of property, intimidation and assault, murder, rescue of prisoners and assassination of hostile witnesses.[37] There were alarmists in every section of the ruling establishment and in the letters coming into Dublin

Ballinamult, Cahir, Charleville, Nenagh, New Inn and Templemore, were constituted permanent barracks by 1824–5: see PRO, WO: 44/100: 'A list of the permanent barrack stations in Ireland, 20 December 1824' and L. Thomas, 'List of the several rents paid by the ordnance dept. in Ireland, 3 August 1825'. I am grateful to Dr Jacinta Prunty of dept. of History, NUI Maynooth for furnishing me with copies of these documents. **37** N. Gash, *Mr Secretary Peel* (1961), 168; 170.

Castle there was a clear tendency to maximize each potential situation. Riot or outrage was invariably reported, or if there was none and all was quiet, this very quiet-
ness was interpreted as suspicious evidence of organization and conspiracy. On the
subject of French agents working with dissident Roman Catholic priests, in particular, the reports from the provinces were apt to be exaggerated and prejudiced.

Lawlessness in Co. Tipperary, a phenomenon closely connected with agrarian
problems and anti-establishment protest from the mid-eighteenth century, wors-
ened in the early nineteenth century as the Roman Catholic ruled majority population increasingly turned to strategies of visible resistance. A key aspect of this
unrest was opposition to the payment of tithes – a tax levied on agricultural produce for the support of the clergy of the Established Church (the payment of which
is shown in fig. 25) – which was economically and religiously motivated.[38] The
basis of religious hostility to this tax was the fact the majority of those liable for
payment – Roman Catholics – derived no benefit from it. In addition, there was
considerable resentment at having to support the Established Church as a state institution. The importance of tithe as a strategy of resistance to the Anglican establishment in an area depended to a great extent on the personality of the parish
incumbent and the history of tithe in that parish. Initially, violence focused on the
tithe proctor, as the nominee of the parish incumbent for the collection of tithes
was termed. Tithe-related agitation was already prevalent by the 1770s, when it
manifested itself in the southernmost baronies of South Tipperary, the heartland of
Whiteboyism. At Clonmel, a vestry minute of 1774 reveals considerable unrest at
parish level, with the rector recording 'the disorderly behaviour of mobs, particularly at funerals and marriages and other parts of divine service, to ye great annoy-
ance and disturbance of ye congregation and inhabitants and the manifest injury of
ye church'.[39] The same year, the tithe proctor of Carrick-on-Suir had his crops
burned and the caretaker of his lands was attacked and left for dead. The tithe proctor of Knockgraffon was similarly attacked.[40]

A second, more widespread, phase of anti-tithe agitation commenced in the 1810s,
which was strongly related to the fall in agricultural prices from 1815, in the aftermath of the Napoleonic wars. The resulting economic hardship contributed to the
need to withhold payment of tithes. Established Church property was increasingly
the target of abuse, as at Marlfield near Clonmel, where repayment of the board of
first fruits loan for rebuilding Inishlounaght church was levied off the parish through
increased taxation, leading to a display of discontent in the vandalizing of windows
in the newly finished building.[41] Many tithe proctors were physically attacked and
several murdered. These events were especially prevalent in the north-west, where
the Clonoulty proctor was murdered in 1815, as was his replacement in 1817.[42]

In 1831, in an action undoubtedly related to the plantation of a Protestant colony
on the estate there, the proctor of the adjoining parish union of Ballintemple was

38 P. O'Donoghue, 'Causes of the opposition to tithes' (1965), 7–28. **39** Vestry minute of 14 April
1774, cited in *Clonmel Chronicle*, 11 May 1907. **40** T. McGrath, 'Interdenominational relations in pre-
Famine Tipperary' (1985), 269–70. **41** Vestry minutes of the parish of Abbey or Innislounaght: entry
for 1 February 1819. **42** McGrath, 'Interdenominational relations', 270–1.

killed and the rector's son shot and seriously wounded within the demesne of the landlord at Dundrum.[43] This frenzy of anti-tithe violence reached its zenith in 1832, following several years of local tithe proctors being attacked and murdered, with the murder of the rector of neighbouring Athassel. This clergyman was stoned to death near his glebe, for unreasonably demanding the full £1,400 payment of his tithe despite an offer of £1,000 under the Tithe Composition Act (1823) from the inhabitants of his three parishes.[44] Opposition was not to the payment of tithe as such, but rather was directed against those who were thought to be unreasonable. This can be seen by the immunity of the succeeding incumbent, who, through a combination of personality and precaution, managed to survive for forty years as rector. However, the precautions taken were indeed significant, as it was written of Athassel rectory in 1866 that each evening at dusk – even in summer – the servants put bulletproof shutters on every window in the house.[45]

Despite these protests, good relations could exist between Anglican clergy and their Roman Catholic parishioners, as at Ardfinnan, where in 1837 the farmers of the parish sowed six acres of wheat for the Revd Mr Kettlewell in gratitude for his humanity in the matter of tithe collection.[46] However, many parishes withheld the payment of tithe, so that great economic hardship was imposed on the rural clergymen who depended upon it. A valuable insight from the diocese of Waterford and Lismore may be obtained from letters written by the rector of Rathronan. Though adjoining the great urban centre of Clonmel, his parish itself contained only twenty parishioners. He was reportedly 'in great [economic] distress', while the neighbouring rector of the churchless union of Donoughmore and Kiltegan – conscious of the great danger of isolation amidst a hostile Roman Catholic populace – was 'obliged to remove with his family into the town [of Clonmel] for safety'.[47] Incumbents of rural parishes were easy victims, readily identified and located by anti-tithe and anti-establishment agitators.[48]

In addition to tithe, a vestry tax or church cess was imposed on all the inhabitants of a parish, regardless of religious affiliation, for the maintenance of the fabric of the Anglican parish church, the payment of church officers (usually a parish clerk and sexton) and the provision of the requisites for divine service. During the course of the early 1830s, this taxation was steadfastly opposed and as failure to pay could result in prosecution, the campaign against cess was a violent, bitter one. This opposition was by no means confined to urban areas and was at its most intense in rural areas, particularly where the Anglican Church population was sparse. At Killaloan, a parish in the rural hinterland of Clonmel, opponents of vestry tax broke the windows of the newly built church and many parishes in the adjoining rural districts were similarly affected.[49] The struggle against parish cess, although an intense one, was of short duration, being resolved by the Church Temporalities Act (1833), where the right of a vestry to tax a parish for Anglican religious purposes was abolished. The parish churches subsequently

43 Ibid. 44 Ibid.; Marnane, *Land and violence*, 50. 45 R. ffolliott, *The Pooles of Mayfield* (1958), 85. 46 Power, *Waterford and Lismore*, 67. 47 Revd W. Giles of Rathronan to Col. W.S. Curry, 14 March 1833 and 22 March 1833; Revd S. Dickson of Donoughmore and Kiltegan to Col. W.S. Curry, 15. Mar. 1833: see NAI Outrage papers, 29/1 (1833). 48 N. Higgins, 'The 1832 clergy relief fund for Co. Tipperary' (2004). 49 RCB Library, Dublin: Rennison MSS, 'History of Waterford and Lismore', fo. 26.

had to rely on voluntary contributions and, in this sense, were disestablished, while the vestry became solely a religious unit, no longer retaining any civil functions.[50]

With the success of the agitation against the payment of tithes and parish cess, the strategic attention of the Roman Catholic agitators turned to non-payment of rents and, since landlords were mainly Protestant, this continued to foster sectarian dissension and enable the intensification of a Protestant siege mentality. Landlords' agents and rent collectors, in the place of tithe proctors, now became the target of attacks. It was in this context that the murder of two land agents, Cooper and Wayland, took place at Donaskeigh, Tipperary in 1838,[51] despite the diffusion of state institutions of defence and control that aimed to contain insurrection and defend the establishment interest.

In the adjoining barony of Middlethird, a number of agrarian protest groups terrorized the district between 1811 and 1813, particularly targeting Protestants, with the effects spreading into neighbouring Cos. Waterford and Kilkenny.[52] The drain on military resources caused by the Napoleonic Wars meant that the army could not cope with police demands in Ireland. This led to the establishment of a peace preservation force, under the Peace Preservation Act (1814), recruited from members of the demobbed army and county militias. The first police force in Ireland was allocated to the barony of Middlethird, which in September 1814 had been proclaimed to be in a disturbed state, following a succession of agrarian outrages, culminating in the assassination of one of the county magistrates. A chief magistrate and a force of twenty ex-cavalry sergeants, operating from a base in Cashel, patrolled day and night along changing routes. The barony was quickly brought under control and initial success in South Tipperary led to calls for the establishment of the force in all parts of Ireland. The paramilitary nature of the force made it universally disliked by the ruled population. Darby Ryan, poet, farmer and hedge-schoolteacher at Bansha, forever connected it to its original pilot area through the composition of a popular ballad around 1830 entitled 'The Peeler and the Goat'.[53]

By the end of 1815, seven Tipperary baronies had been proclaimed and placed under the Insurrection Act. This was a more severe version of the Peace Preservation Act, which amounted to martial law, and the government paid for the force sent to implement it, not the proclaimed barony. The same year, a house hired as a barrack at Dundrum in Kilnamanagh barony was destroyed and a notice posted threatening that similar houses would suffer the same fate.[54] The culprits were the O'Dwyer's, who had been barons of Kilnamanagh prior to 1641 and their actions may be interpreted as a distinct change from accommodating themselves to their ruled situation and as a violent reaction to this unprecedented intrusion of the forces of the state into rural districts.[55] The panic of the ruling minority establishment continued unabated and by the end of 1821, terror-stricken letters were flooding into Dublin Castle from Tipperary gentlemen and magistrates, torn between conflicting desires to preserve

50 Akenson, *Church of Ireland*, 172; 177.   51 Marnane, *Land and violence*, 53–8; *Tipperary Constitution*, 22 January 1836, 'attack on Richard Long esq. of Longfield'; NAI Official papers: (1836) 27/590; (1837): 27/1; 27/86; 27/202; 27/386; 27/509; (1838) 27/15.   52 D.J. O'Sullivan, *The Irish constabularies, 1822–1922* (1999), 26.   53 O'Sullivan, ibid., 27; J. Herlihy, *The royal Irish constabulary* (1997), 29; 31.   54 V. Crossman, *Politics, law and order in nineteenth century Ireland* (1996), 22–3.   55 NAI Outrage papers, 1682 (26).

their local influence and authority, or to preserve their lives and property. The weakness of their local influence was acknowledged by the very fact of writing to Dublin; but the result was the maintenance of regular garrisons in rural outposts.

Much of this agrarian unrest manifested itself in anti-establishment protest, which eventually led to tithe atrocities. The level of intimidation was such that the gentlemen of the Slieveardagh rural district resolved to provide a garrison at Killenaule at their own charge.[56] Charles Langley of Coalbrook explained to the chief secretary at Dublin Castle that the Palatine tenants had 'for their private protection a good many stand of arms' and recommended that 'before disarming them, a small detachment [ought] to be placed among them', as it would be 'impossible' to leave them unprotected.[57] In the continuing unrest, the Protestant population was encouraged to uncover the machinations of rebel agents and other conspirators. Crime and the presence of secret societies were seen as further evidence of this conspiracy, though in actual fact much of the crime stemmed from the presence of a far larger population than the agricultural economy could support.

By the 1820s, unrest was such that the gentry in some areas had to keep to their homes after dark and had to be guarded through the night. This led to the creation of small temporary military posts, as at Newtownlennon, north of Carrick-on-Suir, where the gentry were particularly isolated and the number of Protestants especially low.[58] Ironically, the increased military presence caused further agitation, with harassment and boycotting of those locals in any way involved with supplying services to the garrisons. These developments combined to ensure that a network of constabulary barracks was spread quickly throughout South Tipperary. Map 23 demonstrates that by 1830 – little more than a decade after the first Irish constabulary pilot scheme was in operation at Cashel – there were 53 barracks covering virtually all districts.[59] Their very designation 'barracks' emphasized the paramilitary nature of the force and their close relationship with the colonial administration.

Constabulary barracks were often placed outside of settlements to guard strategic uplands and crossroads and to protect isolated estates and Anglican rectories: while 33 of the 53 constabulary stations were settlement based, another 20 stations, a substantial 38 per cent, were charged with the protection of elements of the Protestant establishment. The constabulary stations at Clonkelly, Fennor, Tubrid and Ballybeg protected the adjacent rectories of the parishes of Ballintemple, Fennor, Tubrid and Tullaghmeelan. Barracks were constructed in or adjacent to seven estate demesnes, as at Woodrooffe (Perry), Harley Park (Poe), Lisnamrock (Langley), Mobarnane (Jacob), New Park (Pennefather), Thomastown (de Chabot) and Greenfield (Purefoy). At Greenfield House, Cappaghwhite (fig. 26), the need for security was taken to an extremity by the construction of the district police barrack in the courtyard of the household. This situation continued for some time, for when land agent William Wilson Holmes 'arrived at Greenfield [in January 1847]'; he 'found six police stationed in the stable yard.'[60]

56 Neely, *Kilcooley*, 93.   **57** NAI Outrage papers (1815); 1722 (66).   **58** Power, *South Tipperary*, 100.
59 See app. XII for full details of constabulary barracks in South Tipperary and surrounding districts.
60 D.G. Marnane, '"Such a treacherous country": a land agent in Cappawhite, 1847–52' (2004), 236.

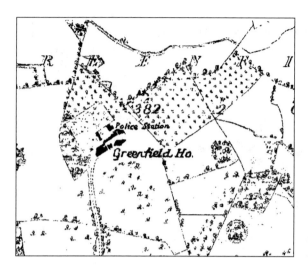

Fig. 26: Constabulary barrack
in courtyard of Greenfield
House

The Purefoy household was descended from a Cromwellian grantee, while
Langley and Poe were insecure alarmists and well practised letter-writers to Dublin
Castle. A further nine constabulary barracks were placed at strategic, mainly upland
locations, including Araglin in the extreme south-western Knockmealdown mountain area bordering Co. Cork and Glamaskeogh in the north-eastern Slieveardagh
Hills; while four barracks maintained vigilance at crossroad locations – often with
the twin role of protecting nearby rural demesnes – as at Camas and Peake in the
north-central area, Hymenstown and Donegal in the south-central district, Rehill
in the south-west, and at Cullen and Carragheen in the west.

   Augmenting the constabulary barrack network and largely contemporary with
them was a large network of bridewell prisons. The provision of bridewells was an
important function of the Protestant-dominated grand jury, with site selection and
the scale of construction expenditure at the discretion of each head-landlord. These
bridewells were often formidable structures in the context of early nineteenth-century provincial town architecture and had the dual aim of keeping the masses of
the population in awe of the local establishment, while providing extra holding
places as a release valve for the county gaol. Tipperary had a county gaol at Clonmel
at least since Cromwellian times, which was rebuilt in 1700 and enlarged on two
subsequent occasions prior to the mid-nineteenth century. By the late eighteenth
century there were also rudimentary holding centres at the larger urban centres of
Carrick-on-Suir, Cashel and Tipperary. These were essentially fortified rooms in
the basement of the courthouse or civic offices and, from the early nineteenth century, were replaced by architect-designed bridewells.

   During the course of the 1810s in particular and also in the 1820s, bridewells
were constructed at Tipperary town, Cashel, Cahir, Carrick-on-Suir, Clogheen
and New Birmingham (Glengoole), also a new county gaol at Clonmel, named
HM Richmond Prison, after the duke of Richmond. Many of these buildings saw
considerable subsequent enlargement and improvement in the first half of the nine-

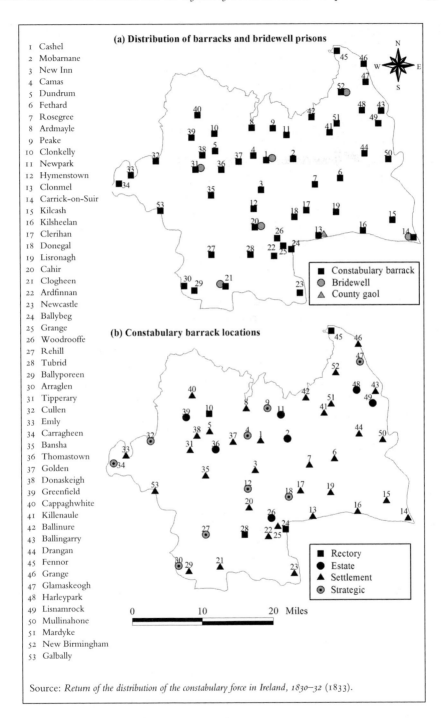

(a) Distribution of barracks and bridewell prisons

1 Cashel
2 Mobarnane
3 New Inn
4 Camas
5 Dundrum
6 Fethard
7 Rosegree
8 Ardmayle
9 Peake
10 Clonkelly
11 Newpark
12 Hymenstown
13 Clonmel
14 Carrick-on-Suir
15 Kilcash
16 Kilsheelan
17 Clerihan
18 Donegal
19 Lisronagh
20 Cahir
21 Clogheen
22 Ardfinnan
23 Newcastle
24 Ballybeg
25 Grange
26 Woodrooffe
27 Rehill
28 Tubrid
29 Ballyporeen
30 Arraglen
31 Tipperary
32 Cullen
33 Emly
34 Carragheen
35 Bansha
36 Thomastown
37 Golden
38 Donaskeigh
39 Greenfield
40 Cappaghwhite
41 Killenaule
42 Ballinure
43 Ballingarry
44 Drangan
45 Fennor
46 Grange
47 Glamaskeogh
48 Harleypark
49 Lisnamrock
50 Mullinahone
51 Mardyke
52 New Birmingham
53 Galbally

Constabulary barrack
Bridewell
County gaol

(b) Constabulary barrack locations

Rectory
Estate
Settlement
Strategic

0   10   20 Miles

Source: *Return of the distribution of the constabulary force in Ireland, 1830–32* (1833).

Map 23: The constabulary barracks and prison network, *c*.1830

Fig. 27: The bridewell of Cahir

teenth century.[61] The bridewells were district-holding centres for the temporary confinement of offenders, pending trial at the petty sessions or transferral to the county gaol at Clonmel. They were generally two-storey stone structures, comprising of 5 to 12 cells, dayrooms, airing yards and living accommodation for a keeper. Most adjoined the courthouse for convenience, the exception in South Tipperary and district being the castellated bridewell at Cahir (fig. 27), built on a hilltop site overlooking the town. This represented a powerful attempt to regulate, police and discipline with the likely deliberate intention of overawing the majority ruled population in town and district.[62] Incredibly, in the 1830s, the disturbed nature of Tipperary was such that officials of the prison establishment alleged that the overall expenditure on the 12 prisons of its combined northern and southern districts exceeded that of the other 31 counties combined, and that committals to Tipperary prisons exceeded that of the entire province of Ulster.[63]

This heavy investment of central resources in the maintenance of law and order and defence of Protestant colonial hegemony, while tightening government control of the local population at the micro-parish level, served only to protract the decline of Protestant Ascendancy *vis-à-vis* the Roman Catholic ruled majority, with the reluctant granting of religious and political emancipation to the latter community.

---

61 50 George III, c.103, Act of Parliament dated 20 June 1810; Power, *South Tipperary*, 126. **62** B. Hindess, *Discourses of power*, 96–123. **63** See *reports on the general state of prisons in Ireland* (1830–7).

The gradual decline of Protestant hegemony: establishment reform in the aftermath of Roman Catholic emancipation

The outbreak of war between Britain and her continental enemies was invariably accompanied by a drive, however brief, to enforce the statutes against Roman Catholics. From the 1760s onwards these events provided opportunities for Roman Catholics to proclaim and emphasize their loyalty to the establishment through drawing up addresses of support, as at Cahir, on 18 December 1775, when

> a respectable number of the Roman Catholics gave testimony of their allegiance before James Butler of Kilcommon and William Hayes esqrs., two of his majesties justices of the peace, who obligingly attended upon this occasion. Dr Egan and all the clergy of the neighbourhood, Edmond Power of Garnevella, Richard Butler of Keylogue, Richard Dogherty of Loughlora esqrs. and all the principal gentry hereabouts who were not in the way to take the oath at Clonmell last assizes, took it and subscribed it here, with the utmost cheerfulness.[1]

This had the effect of undermining the previous arguments of Irish Protestants regarding Roman Catholic untrustworthiness and constituted the immediate background to the Roman Catholic Relief Act (1778). The rebellion of the American colonies, closely followed in 1778 by war with France and Spain, overstretched British military resources and impelled the British government to turn to Irish Roman Catholics as a manpower resource for the British army. Legislation allowing Roman Catholics to hold land on almost the same terms as Protestants was forced through the Irish Parliament in the hope that it would persuade their priests and surviving gentry to endorse the recruitment drive. Even at this point in the later eighteenth century, Irish Roman Catholics were prominent in the armies of the Roman Catholic powers of continental Europe and marriages were taking place between gentry, farming or merchant families in Ireland and the Irish officer class in foreign service. A contemporary local example was the marriage of 'Edward d'Alton esq., lieut. colonel in the Austrian service and one of her imperial majesties

---

1 *Freeman's Dublin Journal*, 31 December 1775, also 20 December 1775 for Cashel district; *Dublin Evening Press*, 15 September 1779 for Clonmel district, also 7 June 1798, declaration of loyalty from the Roman Catholics of Carrick-on-Suir (106 signatures) and 12 June 1798, declaration of loyalty from the Roman Catholics of Clonmel, signed by Revd Thomas Flannery PP.

chamberlains, to Miss McCarthy, daughter of John McCarthy of Springhouse, Tipperary'.² To a great extent, Britain was successful in redirecting and expanding this Irish tradition of military service abroad towards British imperial purposes.

It was no coincidence that further concessions were made to Roman Catholics in 1782 with regard to freedom of worship and religious orders, at the very time when Irish Protestants were clamouring for legislative independence and parliamentary reform.³ These and subsequent concessions deftly undermined this campaign in the medium term. After the passing of the Catholic Relief Acts of 1792–3, Protestants living in provincial Ireland were swiftly reminded of the change in their relationship with the London government, as Roman Catholics began to be admitted to offices in local government. At the grand jury summer assizes of 1793, the names of four Roman Catholics – Ulick Alleyn, James Scully, Laurence Smith and Denis Meagher – appeared out of a total of 23 names for Co. Tipperary; at the same time, the improvement of their places of worship commenced, often with the support of selected Protestant landlords. In 1790, it was noted 'the marquis of Waterford is now building at Curraghmore, a handsome chapel for the use of his servants … several other noblemen and gents in different parts of Ireland have done the same'.⁴

Tipperary led the introduction of Roman Catholics to the grand jury system of local government; the same year it became the first county in which a Roman Catholic was appointed to the commission of the peace, when on 4 March 1793, John Ryan of Ballyvisteen was installed.⁵ The central importance of the Cahir (Butler) estate in the maintenance of suitably qualified households continued when, in May 1793, Thomas Mulcahy of Neddans, Ardfinnan, a head-tenant on that estate (whose seat is depicted in fig. 28), was appointed deputy governor of the county, the first Roman Catholic to hold such a position in Ireland.⁶ With these developments, Protestant dynasties generally perceived their status to be in rapid decline and their influence under direct threat from a resurgent Roman Catholic population, to the extent that the historic partnership between the Protestant Ascendancy and the British in the government of Ireland was threatened with disruption. Already in 1802, almost three decades before full emancipation was granted to the Roman Catholics, the South Tipperary gentry and head-tenantry of the denomination accounted for a high proportion of the gentlemen licensed to bear arms for the killing of game.⁷ The majority registered at Clonmel and were largely residents of the Cahir and Carrick-on-Suir districts, where they accounted for 48 of 153 (one-third) of those listed, while they accounted for just 2 of 44 (one-twentieth) at Cashel and 6 of 29 (one-fifth) at Tipperary town. Thus it is clear that Clonmel, Cashel and Tipperary remained districts with a large majority of Protestant gentry, while Cahir and Carrick-on-Suir continued as strongholds of the Roman Catholic gentry and merchant classes.

2 *Hibernian Journal*, 1 July 1771.   3 Bartlett, *An account of the Whiteboys*, 10–11.   4 *Clonmel Gazette*, 23 July 1793; *Dublin Chronicle*, 13 November 1790.   5 *Clonmel Gazette*, 6 March 1793.   6 Power, *Waterford and Lismore*, 140: this office came into being under the Militia Act of 1793.   7 'A list of the names and places of abode of the several persons who have taken out certificates for killing game … between 25 March and 1 August 1802', *Clonmel Herald*, 11 August 1802 in R. ffolliott, 'Some game licenses of 1802' (1976).

Fig. 28: Corabella House, near Newcastle

At an ecclesiastical level, the intensity of the competitive relationship between the Roman Catholic clergy and the clergy of the Established Church increased following the relaxation of the penal laws. Controversy came from both sides, as when Thomas Hussey, Roman Catholic bishop of Waterford and Lismore, attempted to cause anti-establishment disturbance among his clergy and by extension, among their congregations. In a pastoral letter of 1797 to his clergy, he alleged a high proportion of Roman Catholic soldiers were going to service with their Protestant colleagues and exhorted them that

> if in any of your districts, the Catholic military frequent Protestant places of worship, it is your duty to expostulate with them and to teach them how contrary to the principles of the Catholic faith it is, exteriorly to profess one faith and interiorly to believe another … an Irish soldier ought not to be ashamed of openly professing the Catholic religion, the religion of Irishmen.[8]

The epistle of Hussey was a clear attempt to involve the Established Church in heated debate, through hinting that his Church, in holding the allegiance of the majority of Irish people, was the true Established Church of the land. The publishing of epistles and pamphlets by both sides was popular from this time until the granting of emancipation to the Roman Catholics. In the Protestant upper and middle classes, this was reflected in the popularity of inflammatory works, such as those which positioned the rebellion of 1798 in the heritage of Irish rebellions and

8 T. Hussey, *A pastoral letter to the Catholic clergy of the united diocese of Waterford and Lismore* (1797), 3.

presented it as a primarily religious movement, connived at and actively encouraged by the Roman Catholic clergy.[9]

Although a considerable amount of tolerance and co-operation was practised between the two communities and their clergy in the early nineteenth century, several of the more evangelical church educational societies wreaked havoc with this accord over the course of the 1810s and 1820s. The moderate Kildare Place Society, founded in 1811 to provide elementary education for the common people, initially included prominent Roman Catholics on its board of management, until their clergy disowned this practice.[10] This was as a result of the presence of several even more evangelical church educational societies, whose widely publicized and deeply held conviction was that the main source of Ireland's economic, social and political problems was the Roman Catholic religion. It was regarded by them as a pernicious faith, based on superstitions and heresies, these being perpetuated by a priesthood steeped in ignorance, whose members held a tyrannical sway over their congregations.[11] Education was therefore seen as the primary means of freeing the masses from the yoke of Roman Catholicism.

In South Tipperary, *c.*1826, in addition to the parochial schools of the establishment – many of which received a portion of their income from an evangelical educational society – were also 39 private schools, mainly urban-based, which contained a significant percentile of Protestant pupils, or were run by a Protestant (see map 24). These private schools proliferated in the urban centre of Clonmel in particular, and in Fethard, Tipperary, Cashel and Killenaule to a lesser extent. They were often small institutions and represented the most extreme form of religious segregation, with exclusively Protestant private schools in operation at Tipperary (2), Fethard (3) and Clonmel (1). In general, this was true of all urban schools: at Clonmel, 9 of 12 schools with Protestant involvement were more than 50 per cent Protestant, while 5 of 7 schools at Cashel, 5 of 8 at Tipperary, 3 of 5 at Fethard and half of the schools at Carrick-on-Suir fell into this category. This was even more the case in the Roman Catholic schools, with only a small minority containing even a handful of Protestants. These were highly sectarian times, when even menial posts were filled on a denominational basis. There is much evidence of two parallel communities who had little unnecessary interaction.[12]

The most widely distributed school system was the parochial network, which comprised twenty schools totally dependent on endowments or Anglican subscriptions, besides as many more receiving the greater portion of their income from one or more of five church educational societies. Schools relying solely on local congregational funding were mainly confined to the western and north-western districts of the county, while those under the auspices of one or more church societies enjoyed a distribution covering even the more isolated rural districts. Of this latter category, that with the widest distribution was the Kildare Place Society, with nine schools

9 McGrath, 'Interdenominational relations'.   10 *Second report of the commissioners of Irish education inquiry*, HC 1826–7 (12), xii, 164–5.   11 E. Broderick, 'The Famine and religious controversy in Waterford, 1847–50' (1996), 12.   12 *Tipperary Constitution*, 17 October 1837: 'wanted: an outdoor servant who is a Protestant' and 8 November 1839: 'wanted: a lady's maid: must be a Protestant. Clonmel town'.

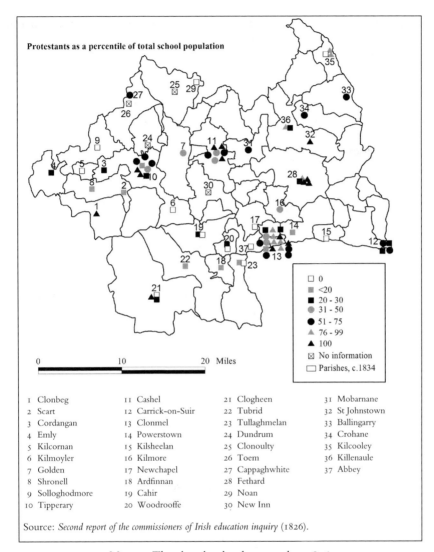

Protestants as a percentile of total school population

35

25 29

27

26

33

34

36

32

9

24

7

11

31

4

5

3

28

8

2

10

1

6

30

16

19

17

14

15

12

20

37 13

22

18 23

21

□ 0
▨ <20
■ 20 - 30
● 31 - 50
● 51 - 75
▲ 76 - 99
▲ 100
⊠ No information
▢ Parishes, c.1834

0   10   20 Miles

1	Clonbeg	11	Cashel	21	Clogheen	31	Mobarnane
2	Scart	12	Carrick-on-Suir	22	Tubrid	32	St Johnstown
3	Cordangan	13	Clonmel	23	Tullaghmelan	33	Ballingarry
4	Emly	14	Powerstown	24	Dundrum	34	Crohane
5	Kilcornan	15	Kilsheelan	25	Clonoulty	35	Kilcooley
6	Kilmoyler	16	Kilmore	26	Toem	36	Killenaule
7	Golden	17	Newchapel	27	Cappaghwhite	37	Abbey
8	Shronell	18	Ardfinnan	28	Fethard		
9	Solloghodmore	19	Cahir	29	Noan		
10	Tipperary	20	Woodrooffe	30	New Inn		

Source: *Second report of the commissioners of Irish education inquiry* (1826).

Map 24: The church schools network, *c.*1826

covering a wide area of the south-eastern and south-western districts of South Tipperary, besides joint sponsorship of a further three schools in the north-western district with the London Hibernian Society. The five schools of the Association for the Discountenance of Vice were mainly confined to the eastern district, while the Incorporated (Charter School) Society and the Baptist Irish Society maintained a presence at Clonmel and Cashel and at Kilcooley respectively. These last three societies were strongly evangelical in character, but as their locations were in comparative Protestant strongholds, Protestants comprised significantly in excess of 50 per cent of pupils in six of the eight combined schools. Inter-communal school-related strife, in the few instances in which it arose, was invariably associated with the strongly evangelical London Hibernian Society's charge of schools where the Roman Catholics comprised all or most of the students, as at Solloghodmore and Tipperary town. In the mid-1820s, the joint school of the Kildare Place and London Hibernian Societies at Tipperary was burned for sectarian reasons, as three-quarters of the 100 pupils were Roman Catholic, giving rise to suspicions of proselytism.[13]

There is certainly some evidence of elements within the Established Church locally continuing attempts to redress the numerical imbalance in this period immediately prior to the granting of Roman Catholic emancipation. At Fethard in 1827, rioting broke out and the communion service was interrupted when the rector initiated his 'Reformation crusade on the Farnham plan' by displaying 14 converts in his church.[14] In addition, the Orange celebration of the battle of the Boyne was another potential source of interdenominational aggravation. At Tipperary town, on 12th July 1827, soldiers of the 34th Regiment wore orange lilies on the anniversary of the battle of the Boyne, which display of their political affiliations led to a furious riot. The soldiers were obliged to retire to their barracks where they were required to hold fire, though assailed with stones. Subsequent violence was entirely directed against the Protestant inhabitants of the town. The doors and windows of 25 Protestant houses were broken, the sexton's house 'demolished' and the Protestant church only saved from attack when it was pointed out to the rioters that if they damaged the church they would be required to pay for its repair.[15] Such violent responses from the Roman Catholic population to acts of symbolic commemoration in this tense period of community re-definition led to the foundation of Protestant defence associations and an extension in the distribution of existing ones.

The formation of the Brunswick Constitutional Club of Ireland in August 1828 at Dublin was the response of ultra-Protestant conservatives to the threat presented by the emancipation campaign. It had the primary aim of 'maintaining the *status quo*, namely their privileged status in the social hierarchy and impressing upon the government the hazard of conceding equality'.[16] These clubs were composed of aristocrats, gentry and, to a lesser extent, working class Protestants. Their leading membership was often heavily involved in the church educational societies of the New Reformation and the organization of anti-emancipation petitions were their main reason for existence.[17] Tipperary Cromwellian dynasties were especially likely to petition the government not to grant emancipation, an interesting continuation of the anti-Roman Catholic attitude of previous generations of planters. A petition of March 1827, circulated in Mullinahone and Ballingarry and published in the *Tipperary Free Press*, attracted 24 signatures, predominantly from members of the Despard, Langley, Cooke and Going dynasties and led to the formation of the Slieveardagh Brunswick Club.

Sectarian strife was narrowly averted at the first meeting of the Club, held in the petty sessions court house at Ballynonty in November 1828, when the magistrates

---

13 Marnane, *Land and violence*, 46.   **14** *Dublin Evening Post*, 18 April 1827, cited in McGrath, 'Interdenominational relations', 258. The 'Farnham plan' refers to the proselytising of the Maxwell family on their estate at Cavan town, the head of whom held the title Lord Farnham.   **15** *Tipperary Free Press*, 18 July 1827, cited in ibid., 261.   **16** H. Senior, *Orangeism in Ireland and Britain, 1795–1836* (1966), 226.   **17** I. d'Alton, *Protestant society and politics in Cork, 1812–44* (1980), 138.

Ponsonby Barker and Charles Langley, leading Barker's Protestant tenants, the Palatines of Kilcooley, were met by a large and hostile Roman Catholic contingent.[18] The liberal *Tipperary Free Press* depicted the Palatine tenantry as 'proverbially ugly and deformed', while the unionist *Clonmel Herald* praised the establishment of the Slieveardagh Brunswick Club as a defence against the 'viler portion of the people'.[19] At Ballynonty, violence was averted through the intervention of the parish priest and energies diverted here, as elsewhere, into the prompt establishment of a liberal club, in this case the Slieveardagh Friends of Civil and Religious Liberty.

In response to this series of abortive strategies for the augmentation of Protestant hegemony, areas with significant Protestant populations turned to membership of the loyal Orange institution as a means of community defence and solidarity and 'the bringing together of many Protestants, for the indulgence of conference and companionship, so comforting to Protestants at such a season of gloom and trouble'.[20] Orange lodges were already widespread in all 9 Ulster counties by 1834 and there were lodges in 9 Leinster counties (including many in Dublin), and in 4 Connaught counties. In Munster, where Cork reached a peak of 32 lodges in 1834; Limerick 10, Tipperary 4 (with a further 3 recently dormant[21]) and Waterford 2, it was remarked of Co. Tipperary at the annual meeting of the grand lodge of Ireland that 'not so much crime has been perpetrated in the province of Ulster in the last 35 years as has been perpetrated within two years in this county. There are a number of Orange lodges, but few Orangemen in this county.'[22]

South Tipperary had at least three lodges at various times. An Orange lodge was working in the county town of Clonmel some time prior to 1831 – in which year its warrant was renewed[23] – and a second was established by 1833 on the Ponsonby-Barker estate at Kilcooley. The tithe war had fostered bitterness and compounded Protestant fears and insecurities and the Orange lodge in each of these substantially Protestant centres was, in its essence, a Protestant defence association. The Established Church was particularly targeted at Kilcooley, and by 1832 its curate could report to the landlord that

> every Sunday evening there is a great, most disorderly assembly at your gate, whose great object seems to be to annoy the poor old persons who have charge of the gate and to interrupt our evening service in church. Their number is weekly increasing and last evening it amounted to more than 100. Three entered the church and stamped their feet during the service.[24]

18 McGrath, 'Interdenominational relations', 265. **19** *Tipperary Free Press*, 5 November 1828; *Clonmel Herald*, 5 November 1828; *Tipperary Free Press*, 24 December 1828, cited in ibid. **20** d'Alton, 'A contrast in crises', 75. **21** LOL 365 (a Clones, Co. Monaghan warrant) worked briefly in Co. Tipperary c.1834; LOL 538 (a Dublin warrant in 1800), working in Tipperary in 1829, but on becoming dormant, was renewed to Belfast in 1834; LOL 539 worked briefly in Co. Tipperary between 1829 and October 1835, when surrendered and renewed to Florence Court, Co. Fermanagh, and LOL 1092 granted instead. No details of LOL 1902 survive, other than that it was dormant by 1856: see MS registries of the loyal Orange institution, 1834 and 1856. **22** *Reports of the select committee on Orange lodges in Ireland*, HC 1835 (377). **23** Schomberg LOL 778, warrant renewed 24 June 1831, MS registries of the loyal Orange institution. **24** Revd J. Whitty to W. Ponsonby-Barker, 23 July 1832, cited in Neely, *Kilcooley*, 96.

The membership at Kilcooley lodge consequently included not only the Protestant tenants of Kilcooley, but also those on the neighbouring St George estates at Balief and Woodsgift, Co. Kilkenny. There was a peak membership of 124 persons in 1834, with Ponsonby-Barker as master and the curate as chaplain of the lodge. A subscription list for the purchase of arms for the defence of the membership survives in the minute book of the lodge.[25] The minute book shows that in the autumn of 1838, however, meetings of the lodge ceased without advance warning after perhaps five years operation, probably as a result of hints from Dublin Castle that such activity was dangerously provocative to the neighbouring populace in that upland, rural district. The Clonmel lodge however – situated within that well-garrisoned and significantly Protestant county seat of administration and symbolically dedicated to the duke of Schomberg who headed the Williamite armies into the town in 1690 – remained working until *c.*1880.[26]

There would appear to have been several other lodges working in South Tipperary: a second Clonmel lodge – LOL 1859[27] – was established during the 1830s, and still worked there in 1856; in addition, the warrant of LOL 1061 was titled 'First Cashell lodge' in 1800, suggesting that at that time, several lodges may have worked in that town.[28] Details of few early southern lodges survive, other than tantalizing references, such as the above.

The foundation of these clubs and lodges was due to the Protestant establishment being firmly opposed to emancipation, as it meant a fundamental undermining of their perceived rights and superiority *vis-à-vis* Roman Catholics. In small rural communities, these feelings of superiority were accentuated, helping to compensate for paucity of numbers in a sea of Roman Catholicism. Evidence of such mindsets in this period survives through testimony given by the agent of an estate adjoining South Tipperary, who argued that 'Catholics in every class of society feel inferior to Protestants. I am perfectly convinced that there is a feeling generally of superiority among the Protestants; that even [in] the lower orders, Protestants consider themselves as superior to Catholics'.[29] In the lead-up to the granting of emancipation in 1829, Protestants sought sinister motives in every Roman Catholic action, with full use made of the violent state of society by the gentry in reporting their precarious and vulnerable state to Dublin Castle. This consciousness of numerical inferiority led to ultimately successful calls for increased troop allocations and the provision of additional police barracks throughout the south and west of Ireland. However, the presence of Roman Catholics among the police and the magistrates gave rise to repeated Protestant allegations to the Dublin administration informing

<hr>

25 Minute book of LOL 806 (warrant renewed 21 November 1833), meeting at Kilcooley Abbey, cited in ibid.   **26** 'Address to the Revd Gordon, chaplain of the Schomberg LOL 778, meeting at Clonmel, 1850': Hoey and Denny Parcel 82, NAI, Dublin. The lodge warrant was transferred to Nenagh, 5 August 1882, where it was still working in 1891. It became dormant in the early years of the twentieth century.   **27** The warrant of LOL 1859 – originally issued to John A. Quenton – was renewed in September 1848 to J.A. Aldwell, master.   **28** The lodge warrant, dating from 1800, was issued to J.D. White, master. By 1835, it was working in Borrisokane district (renewed 25 February 1835 to Revd William B. Fry), and still working there in 1856.   **29** *Minutes of evidence taken before the select committee of the House of Lords appointed to inquire into the state of Ireland*, HC 1825 (181), ix, 187: agent's evidence, Curraghmore estate, Co. Waterford.

them that, in the event of inter-communal clashes, such individuals could not be counted upon to act against their own brethren. Protestants had no hesitation in overstating their fears in order to obtain the desired results and the distribution of constabulary barracks certainly increased in the years and decades after emancipation, until every crossroads and settlement of note maintained a police presence.

The erosion of Protestant hegemony can thus be seen to have commenced prior to the granting of Roman Catholic emancipation, but as Archbishop Richard Lawrence of Cashel and Emly aptly deposed to a House of Lords committee in 1825, the general Protestant apprehension was that this primary concession to the Roman Catholics would lead to a tidal wave of further demands.[30] This fear was swiftly justified, as the reforms of the Established Church and local government effected by parliament in the 1830s were a consequence of emancipation. Once Irish Roman Catholics were represented in significant numbers in the House of Commons, it was inevitable that attention would focus on the reform of the Established Church. Under the terms of the Church Temporalities Act (1833), the archbishoprics of Cashel and Tuam were to be reduced to bishoprics when next they fell vacant and five sees were to be abolished and united to others on the same basis. The reaction of Protestants to these developments is difficult to gauge, but the scattered nature of their church population and parochial organization militated against a prompt response. There being a vacancy in the diocese of Waterford and Lismore due to the death of the bishop late in 1832, that diocese, and consequently South Tipperary, was the first area in Ireland to experience the effect of the Act. The speed of its implementation may have eased the situation. The decision of the archbishop to reside in Waterford, the largest population centre of the now united dioceses of Cashel, Emly, Waterford and Lismore, removed the possibility of vocal opposition from Protestants in Waterford and Lismore, while the continuity under his stewardship aided acceptance in predominantly rural Cashel and Emly.

At parochial level there was also considerable rationalization as a direct result of the Church Temporalities Act. From 1835, a number of parishes were suspended, the most illustrative example being the tiny civil parish of Brickendown, near Cashel, which was constituted a parish in 1822, only to be suspended due to non-viability in 1836. A reasonably successful attempt to eradicate long-standing anomalies in the territorial organization of the Established Church was made under the Act: several parishes were suspended pending full official integration and the church population of these parishes placed under the care of a nearby rector as curate-in-charge.[31] At local parochial level, tiny Anglican populations doubtless interpreted these developments as further evidence of the decline in the hegemony of the state church and a new form of appeasement to the Roman Catholics.

The campaign for the reform of local government also commenced in the 1830s, in continuation of a seemingly endless slide in Ascendancy power, as Protestants perceived it. The early stages of this reform – particularly the abolition in 1831 of

30 Watson, *A dinner of herbs*, 114, 119, 123; *House of Lords reports* (1825), ix, 276. **31** *1835–6*: Brickendown, Erry, Redcity, Tullaghorton; *1843*: Ballysheehan; *1854*: Kiltinan and Tullamain: see Seymour, *Cashel and Emly*.

county governorships unique to Ireland and their replacement with lieutenancies on the English model – generated a storm of protest from within the Ascendancy ranks. The Whig government took the opportunity that this reform afforded them to replace governors who were their political opponents with lieutenants who were their political supporters. The flagrant political motivation behind most of the appointments gave the Irish Tories a field-day in the House of Commons. They demanded to know why, if a Tory who was the obvious choice had not been appointed to Waterford because he would not be of age for a few months and consequently could not immediately act, had a Whig been appointed to Tipperary who 'suffered from paralysis, was bed-ridden, unable to walk or to attend to public business ... Was this appointment to be an exception because Tipperary was the arcadia of Ireland, remarkable for its internal peace and tranquillity? ...'[32] This was deeply ironic, given the consistently disturbed nature of Co. Tipperary and it appears the appointment was a result of a sincere, though probably misguided, belief that magnates of a high Tory or Orange complexion could not be trusted to administer justice impartially between Protestants and Roman Catholics.

The corporations or governing bodies of the corporate walled towns were still self-perpetuating bastions of Protestant symbolism and ascendancy at this time, which maintained an influence on the politics of central government through each electing a member of parliament. In 1835 the Tory government introduced a Municipal Reform Bill, the first stages of which passed in April 1836. Lord Leitrim, a participant in the debate, was moved to comment, 'the Tories are going to establish a most sweeping municipal reform, much more [than was] ever intended. The Whigs merely wished to *reform* the corporations, but the Tories say they will have *no corporations at all*. How it will end is more than I can foresee.'[33] The bill was eventually enacted in 1840, after stalling tactics employed by the conservative House of Lords on no fewer than six occasions. The change was significant. In the last corporation elected at Clonmel prior to the Act, Roman Catholics comprised 4 of the 23 members. The first reformed corporation was the inverse of this, with just 4 Protestant members.[34] This inversion was repeated across Munster, as at Waterford; where 2 of 40 councillors had been Roman Catholic, now only 4 were Protestant.[35]

The reform of parliamentary electoral politics, while a setback, was of secondary importance as far as members of county Protestant society were concerned. Of far greater personal importance to them were the local offices of deputy-lieutenants, justices of the peace, grand jurors and members of the boards of guardians. In this local sphere, still enjoying state backing as the Established Church, southern Anglicanism sought most fiercely to maintain its power and prestige in the period after emancipation. In assessing the condition of the post-emancipation Established Church, the *First report of the commissioners of public instruction* (1834) is of central

32 Newspaper cutting reporting the appointment of the earl of Donoughmore and non-appointment of the marquess of Waterford, cited in A.P.W. Malcomson, *John Foster*, 251–2. I am grateful to Dr Malcomson for information about this reference. **33** Lord Leitrim, Grosvenor Square to Lady Leitrim, Killadoon, 26 April 1836: Killadoon papers, NLI MS 36,034/39: emphasis as in original letter. **34** Burke, *Clonmel*, 180; 228–9. **35** E. Broderick, 'Waterford's Anglicans: religion and politics, 1819–72' (PhD, UCC, 2000).

importance, in its collation of a diverse array of statistics concerning the general state of religion in Ireland, over the years 1829 to 1834. Through this survey, it may be seen that while some Anglican parishes recorded significant Protestant presences in 1834, others had, quite literally, little or no Protestant population. Percentile figures by parish union can be deceptive, serving to flatter the strength of Protestantism in general and Anglicanism in particular. In some tiny civil parishes, the small Anglican population comprised a large proportion of a total parish population not greatly exceeding its own total. Even parish unions recording from 80 to 100 Anglicans can hardly be regarded as strongholds of the establishment. The commissioners of public instruction observed

> it will accordingly be found that there are some benefices [parish unions] in which there are no members of the Church of England; that there are others in which there are but a few; while, in others, more especially in the large towns, their number is considerable. It is also observable that in some instances, from the great extent of the benefice, the members of the Established Church are widely scattered among the other inhabitants.[36]

This summary is accurate regarding the distribution of membership of the Established Church in South Tipperary in the nineteenth century, as may be seen on examination of map 18. The status of the congregations and therefore the Anglican community in the period 1829 to 1834, as also the provision of weekly and communion services, is shown in map 25. In the main, congregations increased in this crucial period for Protestant confidence, coming immediately after Roman Catholic emancipation. However, a series of 11 rural congregations, 6 in the Tipperary hinterland and 5 in the area around Clonmel, were stationary, indicative of factors cancelling out growth. Even more ominously, 3 satellite congregations of these Protestant core population areas were already in actual decline.

The population of the rural parish unions was usually quite small and consequently, attendance was modest and the provision of services minimal. The largest congregation attendances remained those in the garrisoned, urban population centres – the largest being Clonmel, followed in order of precedence by Tipperary, Cashel, Fethard, Cahir, Carrick-on-Suir and Killenaule. The only rural parishes to have a large attendance were the more recently planted Protestant colonies of Kilcooley and Dundrum, due entirely to the efforts of their respective landlords. Aside from these, no rural parish union – even one containing a substantial village – possessed a congregation with an attendance of greater than 100 persons. Numerically, a viable Anglican community was therefore lacking in wide areas of South Tipperary by the 1830s. The provision of weekly church services was, as a result, usually no greater than the minimum service required each week. This was the case in two-thirds of the parish churches and while a second (evening) service was provided in a considerable number of churches, usually ones possessing a settlement of note, the 5 parishes offering three or more services per week were all urban based.

---

36 *First report of the commissioners of public instruction*, 7; see app. XIII.

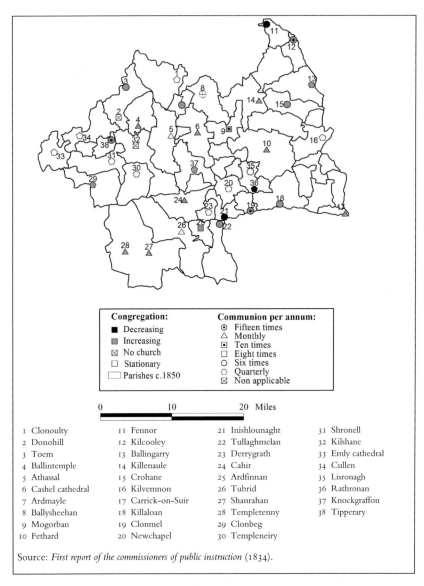

Map 25: The condition of the Anglican Church, *c.*1834 – levels of parochial activity

In South Tipperary in 1834, 25 of the 62 parish unions had a Protestant population comprising at least one person in forty.[37] Clonmel town itself (see fig. 29)
contained one-quarter of Protestants of all reformed Christian denominations in
that year, or 1,987 persons out of a South Tipperary peak total of 8,151. This figure
included a considerable body of 250 Protestant dissenters, so that the total number
of Anglicans was 1,737 persons. The number of Anglicans in the towns, however,

37 See app. XIII.

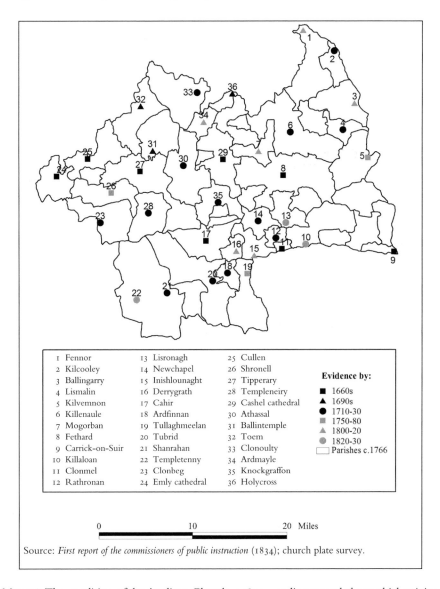

1 Fennor	13 Lisronagh	25 Cullen
2 Kilcooley	14 Newchapel	26 Shronell
3 Ballingarry	15 Inishlounaght	27 Tipperary
4 Lismalin	16 Derrygrath	28 Templeneiry
5 Kilvemnon	17 Cahir	29 Cashel cathedral
6 Killenaule	18 Ardfinnan	30 Athassal
7 Mogorban	19 Tullaghmeelan	31 Ballintemple
8 Fethard	20 Tubrid	32 Toem
9 Carrick-on-Suir	21 Shanrahan	33 Clonoulty
10 Killaloan	22 Templetenny	34 Ardmayle
11 Clonmel	23 Clonbeg	35 Knockgraffon
12 Rathronan	24 Emly cathedral	36 Holycross

Evidence by:

■ 1660s
▲ 1690s
● 1710-30
■ 1750-80
▲ 1800-20
● 1820-30
☐ Parishes c.1766

0   10   20 Miles

Source: *First report of the commissioners of public instruction* (1834); church plate survey.

Map 26: The condition of the Anglican Church, *c.*1834 – earliest recorded parochial activity

was considerable in relation to their presence in other parts of the country. Munster Protestants were more urbanized than their Roman Catholic neighbours and in the 1830s, 40 per cent of them lived in or near sizeable urban settlements.[38] D'Alton, in his study of Cork Protestants, has written of 'the existence of "clusters" or large groups of Protestants in small areas'.[39] Commenting on Co. Longford, around 1841, Kennedy observes

---

38 P. O'Flanagan, 'Urban minorities and majorities' (1988), 125. **39** d'Alton, *Protestant society*, 13.

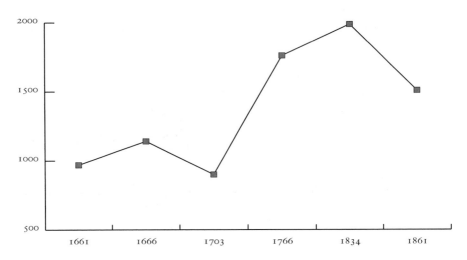

Fig. 29: The Protestant population of Clonmel town, 1661–1861

some clustering of Protestants in relation to the 'big houses' of the gentry; they tended to be concentrated in the more fertile districts of the region; were likely to be found in areas characterized by village or town settlements; and were well represented where the local economy had (or once had) a significant industrial base.[40]

There was a considerable decline in the Anglican population in the period immediately prior to emancipation, which seems to have been disproportionately borne by the poorer elements and the tradesmen of that community.[41] Population decline seems to have accentuated the tendency of Protestantism to concentrate in urban dominated areas and by 1834, 40 per cent of the Protestant population of South Tipperary was concentrated in the southern-most barony of Iffa and Offa, rising to 50 per cent by 1861. Combined with a considerable Protestant dissenter community at Clonmel and at Cahir, this Anglican core area had increased by an average 100 persons per decade since 1766. A further one-quarter of the Protestant community lived in Middlethird barony, predominantly in the urban centres of Cashel, Fethard, Killenaule and their hinterlands. These two baronies, in combination, contained over two-thirds of the Protestant community by 1834. Elsewhere in South Tipperary, the Protestant population of the three baronies of Clanwilliam, Kilnamanagh and Slieveardagh was in decline, though this is somewhat masked in the last two, particularly in Slieveardagh, as a result of the plantation of estate colonies of Protestants.

A massive demographic surge in the Roman Catholic community commenced

---

40 L. Kennedy, 'The long retreat: Protestants, economy and society, 1660–1926' (1996), 12–13. **41** O'Flanagan, 'Urban minorities and majorities'.

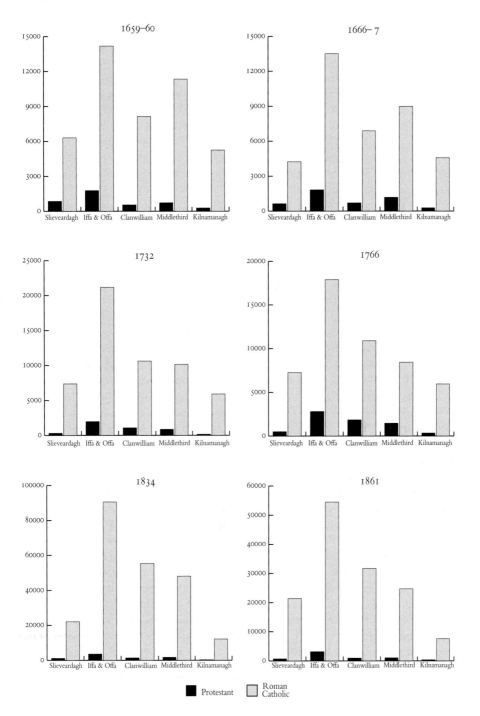

Fig. 30: The Protestant and Roman Catholic population of South Tipperary, 1660–1861

in the early nineteenth century, which greatly increased the ratio of Protestants to Roman Catholics in all five baronies in South Tipperary (see fig. 30). Nowhere was this more pronounced than in the eastern barony of Slieveardagh, which contained significant upland areas of marginal land. Throughout the second-half of the seventeenth century, while forestry and mineral resources were available for exploitation, the ratio of Protestants to Roman Catholics remained a respectable 1:8. The exhaustion of these commercial resources, in combination with moderate Roman Catholic population increase during the eighteenth century, resulted in this proportion dipping to 1:25 by 1732, before improving slightly to 1:20 by 1766. Population increase in the Roman Catholic community in this barony was such that between 1766 and 1834 the population tripled from some 7,000 persons to in excess of 22,000 persons, with the result that the ratio of Protestants to Roman Catholics more than doubled to 1:41 by 1834. In the barony of Iffa and Offa, the Roman Catholic population surged from under 20,000 to in excess of 90,000 persons in this period, a more than 4-fold increase. Similarly, the baronies of Clanwilliam and Middlethird saw increases in their Roman Catholic populations of five-fold and six-fold respectively. Here, as elsewhere, pre- and post-Famine emigration comprised a larger proportion of members of the Roman Catholic community than of the Protestant community. The Roman Catholic communities of the baronies of Iffa and Offa, Clanwilliam, Kilnamanagh and Middlethird all declined by between 40 and 50 per cent between 1834 and 1861. In South Tipperary as a whole, the Roman Catholic population declined by almost 90,000 persons, or 40 per cent, while the Protestant population declined by some 6,000 persons, or 25 per cent, in this period. Thus, part of the ground lost by the Protestant community to Roman Catholicism was recovered.

Emigration was the main factor in Protestant population decline in the pre-Famine period. Protestant predated Roman Catholic emigration by several decades, in extending from the 1820s to the onset of the Famine in 1847, and beyond. Between 1834 and 1861, population loss of substantially in excess of 300 Protestants was recorded at Tipperary town, while the Palatine colony at Kilcooley suffered an equal decline. Almost 500 were lost to the Protestant community at Clonmel over the same period and smaller losses of up to 100 were made among the Protestant farming communities at Athassel, Shanrahan and Killenaule. Great swathes of territory experienced smaller population losses, particularly in the eastern and central parishes and also in the western extremity. Small increases in population were made in the north-western rural parishes, but the majority of gains, albeit nominal ones, were confined to the extended Clonmel hinterland, testifying to a removal of residents from that urban centre to nearby country residences. The only parish in the entire county to substantially increase its Protestant population in this period was Cahir, which may be directly attributed to the massive expansion of the cavalry headquarters near that town.

The decline in the number of Munster Protestants was noted and explained as early as 1826, when a regional newspaper of the Protestant community claimed

> a personal knowledge which enables us to state that where emigration had taken place from certain districts it was largely made up by the emigration

of Protestants; and from universal, concurrent testimony, we apprehend there can be no doubt generally that the disposition to quit the country exists more strongly among Protestants than among Roman Catholics.[42]

Economic factors were an important determinant in relation to Protestant emigration, as they also were for Roman Catholics, though to a slightly lesser extent. Agricultural prices fell sharply after the ending of the Napoleonic Wars in 1815, during which they had been artificially inflated. Many Protestant households, seeing wartime prosperity and rising expectations giving way to recession, feared a decline in living standards. In the voluminous petitions to the government for free passage to the colonies in the years after Waterloo, concern regarding economic prosperity was the most frequent citation.[43] It is significant that these petitioners were disproportionately Protestant.[44]

A changing political climate, in which it appeared that Roman Catholics were making advances at the expense of Protestants, was a primary stimulus to emigration before the Famine. The fears experienced by Protestants were accentuated by their sense of isolation and intimidation among an overwhelmingly Roman Catholic majority. The passage of Roman Catholic emancipation further eroded the confidence of Protestants and confirmed their belief that concessions to Roman Catholics would subsequently be unstoppable. The Tithe War of the 1830s appeared to confirm this, for

> even when the physical dangers seemed remote, the psychological impact of sustained, successful Roman Catholic agitation was devastating for Protestants accustomed to unquestioned dominion and unlimited submission … many could scarcely contemplate living in an Ireland were they would no longer be masters.[45]

It was estimated by Protestant sources in 1832 that 60,000 co-religionists had emigrated since 1829, the year of Roman Catholic emancipation.[46]

In 1834, the British government initiated an enquiry into the condition of the small tenantry in Ireland, which among other things sought to ascertain the extent of emigration from selected parochial unions in every barony, over the previous three years.[47] The respondents were invariably clergy or gentlemen resident within each district and the value of their perspectives is thus considerable. Their evidence confirms that the pre-Famine Protestant population was more likely to emigrate than their Roman Catholic neighbours and particularly from rural areas of considerable Protestant settlement. In North Tipperary, there is evidence of a significant exodus from these areas at this time, particularly in the rural parish of Modreeny, where the rector regretted that 'within the last three years about 200 Protestants

---

42 *Waterford Mail*, 9 August 1826. 43 Cullen, *An economic history of Ireland since 1660*, 109. 44 Kennedy, 'The long retreat', 16. 45 Miller, *Emigrants and exiles*, 233–4. 46 *Waterford Mail*, 15 February 1832. 47 *Royal commission on the condition of the poorer classes in Ireland*, app. F, xxxix (260). I am grateful to Dr Andy Bielenberg, dept. of History, UCC, for drawing my attention to this source.

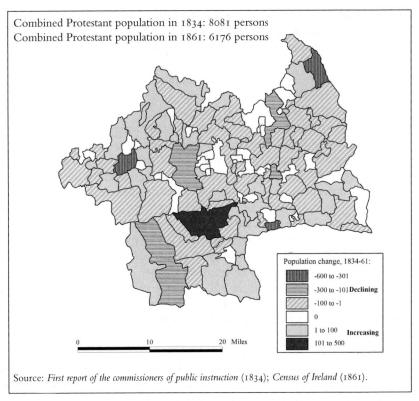

Combined Protestant population in 1834: 8081 persons
Combined Protestant population in 1861: 6176 persons

Population change, 1834-61:

-600 to -301
-300 to -101 **Declining**
-100 to -1
0
1 to 100 **Increasing**
101 to 500

0   10   20 Miles

Source: *First report of the commissioners of public instruction* (1834); *Census of Ireland* (1861).

Map 27: The changing distribution of Anglicans, 1834–61

have left, [who were] generally in comfortable circumstances and industrious persons; [but] only one Roman Catholic and he [was] a person of bad character'.[48] At Terryglass, the parish priest reported that 'thirteen or fourteen families [emigrated], half of them Protestants [and] the most of them were small farmers', while in the urban parish of Templemore, the rector emphasized the loss of 'several *respectable Protestant families, much disgusted* at the situation they were in, unprotected from lawless aggression of mobs and deserted by government; *such were their complaints:* they went to Canada'.[49]

In the fertile lowlands of South Tipperary, pre-Famine emigration by all creeds was extremely limited in comparison to the marginal agricultural areas of the south and west of Ireland. There are constant references to the fact that 'not many' or 'few' had emigrated from its parochial unions, with a few important exceptions. Here, as elsewhere, Protestants needed little persuasion to emigrate and as map 27 demonstrates, this was particularly the case in the less fertile areas to the north-east, which also possessed a considerable, artificially introduced Protestant community,

---

48 Ibid., Revd William Homan, rector of Modreeny, 247. **49** Ibid., Revd Ambrose Bowles, P.P. Kilbarron, Terryglass and Finoe, 246; Revd William N. Faulkner, rector of Templemore, 234: his emphasis.

in a location that had recently witnessed emancipation-related sectarian strife. At Ballingarry, the emigrants were noted to be 'mostly Protestants of a better description [and] they have gone to America', while in the adjoining parish of Kilcooley, the landlord reported the emigration of 'a few Protestant families [to] Upper Canada and America'.[50] It is true to say these households, being Palatines, had larger families than was normal among Irish Protestants, which explains the response of the parish priest of Fennor and Kilcooley, that 'there have been many emigrants, most of which were Palatines and very well settled at home, who sold off their properties here to try and better themselves in America'.[51]

The numerical and visible strength of establishment Protestantism *vis-à-vis* Roman Catholicism was a crucial matter for Anglicans throughout the nineteenth century, because the number of adherents to Roman Catholicism and Protestantism was a central element in the political struggle between the emerging democracy and Protestant Ascendancy. The years 1836 to 1841 in South Tipperary saw a particularly significant amount of church (re)building and upgrading, as the Anglican community rid itself of several medieval parish churches, preferring for a new and fashionable statement of redefinition on the landscape. Protestants became involved in so-called 'political algebra', in efforts to reconcile their own (in)security with the demands of democracy. Issues of emigration and decreasing community vitality consequently received increased coverage in the Protestant media in the 1820s and 1830s, when proposals were circulated regarding methods of holding and increasing the Protestant interest. The philosophy of the 1830s returned to the idea of Protestant estate colonies and a Protestant Colonization Society of Ireland was formed, its purpose being to establish settlements throughout the country, so as to prevent 'the dispersion of poor Protestants in regions beyond the reach of the means of grace'.[52] Protestant colonies were still regarded as a positive response to emigration, yet ironically, it was from these strongholds that emigration was subsequently greatest, as at Kilcooley.[53]

In South Tipperary, the legacy of mentalities surrounding proponents of this and related societies can be seen in a final successful effort at Protestant settlement in the later 1830s at Dundrum, where the landlord, Maude, further increased his Protestant freehold tenantry in the spirit of his ancestors and the hope of electoral advancement. The Protestant *Tipperary Constitution* declared itself 'glad to see Viscount Hawarden increasing his Protestant tenants and hopes to see them in Clonmel at the next election, as they are good to a man'.[54] Hawarden evicted 200 Roman Catholic families, comprising 1,300 persons, from his estate at Dundrum during the decade after emancipation. Although anxious to extend his demesne and enlarge his grazing pastures, existing tenants were replaced by Protestants, who were also favoured in all matters of trade and employment in the estate village. The ensuing county election of 1841 is a barometer of the consequences artificial

50 Ibid., A. Going esq. J.P., Ballingarry, 250; William Ponsonby J.P., Kilcooley, 251. **51** Ibid., Revd Michael Meghan P.P., Fennor and Kilcooley, 250. **52** *Waterford Mail*, 18 June 1832. **53** Neely, *Kilcooley*, 93. **54** *Tipperary Constitution*, 27 September 1839; McGrath, 'Interdenominational relations', 277.

Protestant plantation at Dundrum and Kilcooley, in this and earlier periods, had on the political landscape of South Tipperary. Both landlords were reluctant to witness hegemonic transfer to the Roman Catholics, and their successful attraction of considerable numbers of freehold voters gave them electoral advantage in this era of limited franchise. The electoral contest of 1841 is worthy of inclusion in this narrative for its similarity to the earlier contest of 1761, and as a worthwhile indicator of the consequent level of ethnic and sectarian hostility in South Tipperary at the conclusion of this study.

Both Co. Tipperary parliamentary seats were contested in July 1841, with two Liberal candidates opposing two Conservative candidates. The ancestors of both Conservative candidates, Maude of Dundrum and Ponsonby-Barker of Kilcooley had direct involvement with the trial of Fr Sheehy in 1766, and Maude's ancestor was also a contestant in the infamous election of 1761. Barker was an Orangeman, whom the parish priest of Fethard further alleged was sworn 'to wade knee-deep in Catholic blood'.[55] The county polling station at Clonmel was open for 14 days in the period of the annual Orange commemoration, during which time the town was filled with sectarian rivalry. The added symbolism of the involvement of Maude's ancestor with the hanging of Fr Sheehy at Clonmel in 1766, combined with his introduction of Protestant Palatine tenants in the 1770s and 1780s as part of a strategy to seek election in the same constituency, haunted his canvass, and harassment varied from defacement of his carriage to verbal taunts of 'Who hung the priest?'.[56]

It was widely alleged that Ponsonby-Barker's forebear had brought in the Palatines to his estate as 40s. freehold voters to further the political ambitions of his dynasty; he certainly provided carriages to bring his thirty leasehold voters to Clonmel. The Kilcooley electors, despite their police escort, were attacked en-route to Clonmel by hundreds of stone-throwing protestors at New Birmingham. One lost an eye, another later died from his injuries and the Palatines were forced to retreat to Kilcooley, which contributed significantly to Ponsonby-Barker losing the election.[57] The electors in the northern part of the county, comprising many Protestant tenant farmers certain to vote Conservative, were also prevented from travelling to vote at Clonmel, through threatened and actual damage to persons, goods and property. Conservative voters who did travel were attacked and harassed while passing through Cashel, and in Bansha, police opened fire on the crowd attacking voters, killing one man. At Clonmel, the town experienced extensive rioting between nationalists and unionists, with the former gathering in the street shouting and throwing stones outside the hotel where the Conservative voters were barricaded.[58]

The election of 1841 represents the final great push of Protestant political influence in nineteenth century South Tipperary, after which time the Protestant interest never again represented the county in parliament. The intensity of the Roman Catholic reaction to the previous century of artificial plantation of Protestants in estate colonies, which this study has identified as the prevalent strategy between the 1740s and 1830s

55 *Tipperary Free Press*, 14 July 1841; McGrath, 'Interdenominational relations'. 56 Ibid. 57 NAI Official papers (1841): 27/15287; 27/10547; 27/13330; 27/5061; 27/4401. 58 Ibid., 27/10455; 27/1061; 27/10339; 27/10379.

of increasing Protestantism numerically and extending its political interest, left the establishment in no doubt as to the impossibility of continuing in this manner. The impact of the estate colonies and other strategies for the growth and extension of the Protestant community, while successful in the medium term, had little long-term significance beyond a severe deterioration in inter-church relations. In 1660, the core area of Protestant settlement was Clonmel and rural Protestantism was sparsely and unevenly distributed. In both 1766 and 1834, the cores of Protestantism were the three urban centres of Clonmel, Tipperary and Cashel, each containing a population in excess of 500 persons, with the addition of rural Kilcooley by 1834. However, even at this stage, the amalgamation of parish unions was such that much of the ongoing decline in urban and rural civil parishes is hidden. Even in 1834, at its overall Protestant population peak, South Tipperary may be seen to contain considerable districts with less than 50 resident members of the reformed Christian Churches. By 1861, population decline had visibly reduced the number of Anglican parish unions, the centrality of Clonmel as sole Protestant population core was reasserted, and evidence of a return to a population distribution similar to that of 1660 becomes apparent. The groundwork for full church disestablishment was already laid.

Conclusion

This study has sought to address the nature of the changing relationship between the Protestant and Roman Catholic communities of South Tipperary, from their earliest divergence *c*.1570 to the culmination of the post-emancipation readjustments in 1841. Three major themes have been explored in its empirical chapters, viz., first, how the New English Protestant ruling minority carved out spaces of dominion in South Tipperary in the pre-Cromwellian period, *c*.1570 to 1649; second, how this ruling establishment then proceeded to devise strategies to maintain and consolidate their territorial control, *c*.1650 to *c*.1730; and finally, how this Protestant ruling class sought to contest hegemony *vis-à-vis* the Roman Catholic ruled majority population from this time to 1841. In short, the aim has been to identify – through a case study examination of South Tipperary – the spatial strategies employed by the ruling Protestant minority in Ireland in a colonial context in order to gain and retain power and dominion *vis-à-vis* the ruled Roman Catholic majority. It has further sought to show how this ruled majority progressively challenged and devised counter-strategies of resistance that increasingly dominated and undermined the ruling minority in South Tipperary.

From the outset, a key research question was to seek to explicate the territorial strategies devised and utilized by the Protestant establishment as a ruling minority to gain power, maintain and consolidate control and stem hegemonic decline. Part one identified an early strategy that enabled the gaining of power by the New English minority, involving the joint agency of the Irish court of wards and New English land law, in undermining the titles of Gaelic Irish and Old English gentry to their ancestral lands. This policy became increasingly successful during the 1620s and 1630s, but in turn undermined and delayed the advance of New English hegemony, by acting as a catalyst for both the partial unification of Gaelic Irish and Old English communities – under the common banner of Roman Catholicism – against the New English now perceived as a common enemy and their joint response to increasing New English hegemony in the rebellion of 1641–2.

A second strategy employed by the New English to gain control of land and property centred on the Cromwellian military campaign of terror in 1650–4, during which 6 priests and 13 gentry, besides many ordinary people, were executed at Clonmel, the administrative hub of the study area. I have interpreted these actions to have been carried out in reaction to the killing of some 70 Protestants in the study area during 1642. Many of those killed early in 1642 – particularly those at Cashel and Golden – were themselves targeted in retaliation to the heavy-handed reaction of Sir William St Leger, lord president of Munster, in killing 16 Roman Catholics in the countryside between Cashel and Golden in November 1641, without trial and at random. These actions stemmed from a frustration when the culprits responsible for the ruin of his lands and livestock and those of his brother-in-law, William Kingsmill, at Ballysheehan (north of Cashel), could not be identified. This strategy was followed by the imposition of anti-Roman Catholic legislation and the transplantation of the Roman Catholic landowners of South Tipperary to

Cos. Clare and Galway, while those locals remaining were forcibly involved in the expansion of Cromwellian power and knowledge as assistants to the surveyors engaged in itemizing and mapping the forfeited lands in the 'civil survey' and 'down survey'. The sense of injustice and desperation emanating from the majority population, forcibly uprooted from their ancestral lands, became most evident in the guerrilla activities of the dispossessed. This in turn led to the need for the provision of state and privately funded garrisons, so as to enable the New English ruling minority to defend and safely colonize the landscape of new properties.

Part two also established a link between the siege mentality of the colonial New English elite and the urban settlement bias exhibited by that community from the mid-seventeenth century. Those settlers who did venture into the hinterlands of the walled towns and places of strength sought fortified country residences, usually the tower-houses of the former landowners. The settlers of the study area were, prior to *c*.1740, particularly slow to improve their estates and build modern seats. Their numerical inferiority *vis-à-vis* the majority population and, in particular, the continuation of a substantial Roman Catholic landed gentry and development of a middleman grazier class, seem to have impacted upon this attitude. Commencing in the early seventeenth-century state papers and continuing in the writings of Sir William Petty, the colonial administration continually despaired of the preponderance of Roman Catholicism among and growing demographic power of, the Irish population. Although no local or central government directives survive (if they ever existed), part three has further demonstrated how this sense of insecurity amid the overwhelming numerical prevalence of the Roman Catholic 'other' led the Protestant establishment to seek formal strategies of community consolidation.

A primary strategy of consolidation that would seem to have originated in the early seventeenth century and which was repeatedly utilized in the economic and numerical strengthening of the Protestant community from the mid-seventeenth century, involved the attraction of Protestant head-tenants by landlords and the dispensing of favourable leases to Protestant tenants. Some estates also promoted the importation of colonies of Protestant dissenter weavers. This concept was pioneered in the 1670s in four of his estate towns by the 1st duke of Ormond, of which Clonmel and Carrick-on-Suir lay within the bounds of South Tipperary. This scheme, whereby the duke imported Huguenot and Walloon weavers from their primary settlement at Canterbury, set an important precedent and underlined the economic potential of attracting Protestant colonies to individual estates. This strategy for the augmentation of the Protestant community in the south and west of Ireland became inextricably linked with the charter school movement from the 1730s, whereby some of the students were apprenticed to weavers from the estate colonies. It aided the local Protestant community through not only increasing the local population of their co-religionists, but also the field of potential marriage partners.

Part three in particular uncovered a link between the attraction of colonies of Protestants to individual estates and the political ambitions of their landlords. In two instances – on the Dundrum and Kilcooley estates – the landlords reacted to the small, declining Protestant population recorded in their respective parochial unions and baronial districts in the religious census of 1766 and explicitly sought to acquire political power through obtaining considerable quantities of Protestant freeholder tenants, who acted as 'colonies of voters'. In this way, they adopted a three-fold strategy of improving their political prospects, augmenting their income through the economic advantage of having 'improving' Protestant tenants and also increasing the Protestant population of their respective districts. This section further established a connection between the siege mentality of the ruling minority establishment and the evidence of both the hearth roll of 1732 and religious census of 1766, which indicated the extent of the demographic advantage enjoyed by the Roman Catholic population in large areas of the island of Ireland. From *c.*1690 until *c.*1730, the Protestant establishment was reasonably secure in its ascendancy, but these religious returns heightened insecurities and confirmed its worst fears. In South Tipperary, the survival of a large number of significant Roman Catholic landholders – particularly several cadet branches of the Ormond Butler family – constituted an additional thorn in the side of the establishment. There was deep suspicion in the local Protestant establishment of those Roman Catholic families that had converted to the Established Church in an apparently nominal sense, particularly the Mathew dynasty of Thurles (also Annfield and Thomastown), the majority of whom continued in the 'old faith' and the head of which, in 1761, contested a parliamentary seat for Co. Tipperary. This adaptable conformity for material and political gain, in combination with an upsurge in agrarian and political agitation by the Roman Catholics in the first-half of the 1760s, has been shown to have been interpreted by an increasingly insecure local Protestant establishment as constituting a direct challenge to its hegemony and the execution of Fr Nicholas Sheehy can be directly attributed to this chain of events.

The sectarian bigotry and polarized atmosphere of 1760s South Tipperary, in combination with unfavourable returns in the religious census of 1766, led to the establishment of two largely successful estate colonies at Dundrum and Kilcooley, which constituted the last major attempt to correct Protestant numerical inferiority *vis-à-vis* Roman Catholicism in the county. However, while these estate plantations of Ulster and immigrant Protestants proved locally significant and enduring, they were of little benefit to the Protestant establishment at county-level in the medium-to-long term. Indeed, they generally led to a further deterioration in inter-church relations during the first-quarter of the nineteenth century, when church education societies, Brunswick clubs and Orange lodges developed, particularly in these localities, as a Protestant initiated counter-strategy to the growing establishment perception of threatened Roman Catholic dominion. These clubs and lodges were established as part of an attempt to redefine Protestant identities, in reaction to campaigns that led inexorably toward the granting of Roman Catholic emancipation in 1829; the Church Temporalities Act of 1834 effectively laid the groundwork for full disestablishment, while the Municipal Reform Act of 1840, removed the Protestant monopoly of the corporations and parliament and reduced the political power of the Protestant community to the grand juries, the predecessors of the county councils.

In addition to explicit strategies of community extension and consolidation, this study has demonstrated that the Protestant establishment also utilized implicit strategies. These proved more difficult to ascertain but some evidence was uncovered in last testament provisions of individual landowners, where various stipulations concerning future marriage partners for heirs to estates were outlined. Generally, strict boundaries were constructed between Protestants and Roman Catholics, in that intermarriage was not allowed or even contemplated between the two communities. South Tipperary had a high number of 'in-between' people, such as where Roman Catholics were targeted for conversion to the Established Church on selected estates, the premier example in the study area being the O'Callaghan estate at Clogheen. On this estate between the 1740s and 1780s, the landlord, himself of a convert family, applied sporadic pressure to key artisan and farming households – particularly those where inter-church marriages had taken place – to conform to the Established Church. This philosophy would appear to have been widely practiced; conversions to the Established Church in Co. Tipperary as a whole constituted one of the highest numbers in the entire convert rolls. In addition, potential unions between members of the Established Church and Protestant dissenters were generally encouraged, particularly from the early eighteenth century. This study uncovered evidence of a concerted effort to attract Protestant dissenters into the Established Church, which constituted a change from the initial strategies of exclusion and intolerance in evidence in the immediate aftermath of the restoration of the monarchy and establishment in 1660, as realization swiftly dawned that a united Protestant community was needed to confront Roman Catholicism.

Through the course of writing this research, the central exploration has been the explication of the changing geographical relationship between the Protestant and Roman Catholic communities of South Tipperary, c.1570 to 1841, particularly as a consequence of English colonial activities in Ireland. Based on the evidence of this study, it would be incorrect to allude to the continuous presence of two monolithic forces, Protestant and Roman Catholic, for during the eighteenth century in particular (as the convert rolls attest) a considerable number of Roman Catholics and Protestant dissenters conformed to the Established Church. These 'in-between' people were often landowners of note or aspiring politicians, the integrity of whose estates, or whose future social status, was threatened by their continuing profession of their birth church. This study highlighted the (occasionally nominal) conversion of the heads of key Roman Catholic gentry and mercantile dynasties, when often branches of their immediate family continued in the 'old faith'. Such moves were usually for material reasons rather than out of religious conviction.

Evidence was also uncovered in early nineteenth century pew lists and vestry minutes, of the conversion of key upwardly-mobile Unitarian, Presbyterian and Quaker dynasties to the Established Church by this time, as a system of worship more suitable to their new affluence and status. The promotion of a low-church ethos indicated a willingness on the part of the Anglican establishment to promote inter-marriage with the Protestant dissenters, with the explicit aim of denominational assimilation and the further strengthening of the Protestant interest. The infrequent holding of communion services in particular mirrored the low-church approach of the Presbyterians and also made Anglicanism more palatable to the Quakers of the district. The general shunning of all decoration in Anglican parish churches, the practice of quarterly communion in many rural parishes of the study area and the dominance of members of the Established Church in the Protestant marriage field combined in drawing many prominent dissenting dynasties – Presbyterian, Baptist and Quaker – toward membership of the Established Church during the eighteenth and nineteenth centuries.

In part one, I argued that the Protestant Reformation was ultimately unsuccessful in the study area because the Established Church was rendered ineffective in the crucial second-half of the sixteenth century by a combination of unwieldy territorial structures, a lack of central funding, the prevalence of lay proprietorship, the activities of maverick clergy such as Archbishop Miler Magrath and general inertia. Despite evidence of Church reform during the early Stuart administration through the introduction of increasing numbers of university-educated English clergy, the loss of indigenous clerical families of Gaelic Irish and Old English stock led to the clergy of the Established Church being unable to speak the vernacular of the majority and to its becoming a colonial Church. The strategic rationalization of the territorial and parochial organization *c.*1670 (largely carried into effect by *c.*1704) constituted an attempt to better mould the ineffective territorial structures inherited from the pre-Reformation Church to the modern needs of the small Anglican population. However, as the second and third parts of this book testify, problems of inertia and incompetence continued to haunt the Established Church as an institution into the early nineteenth century, during which time its ungainly territorial inheritance placed it at a continual disadvantage.

The subtle, almost invisible adaptation of the Roman Catholic Church to its proscribed situation by 1730, through building thatched barn-like chapels with stonewalls and clay floors in the vernacular style in rural districts and locating urban chapels discreetly on side streets behind the existing street frontage, effectively merged them with the landscape. Commencing in the 1760s and increasingly from the 1780s, the Church (particularly in the south-east of Ireland) raised its profile through constructing more visible chapels, often on prominent sites. As part three has established, the upgrading and extension of the church and glebe-house network of the Established Church in the study area during the last quarter of the eighteenth and first quarter of the nineteenth centuries can be definitely linked to a growing realization of, and reaction to, visibly growing Roman Catholic territorial hegemony.

The spread of military garrisons and detachments in barracks and redoubts throughout the main urban centres and strategic rural upland locations of the study area constituted a positive spin-off for the Protestant minority establishment. The construction of permanent stone barracks in the years after 1700 gave rise to the orderly distribution and continued presence of considerable numbers of officers and men, all of them Protestant (particularly Anglican), prior to the 1770s recruitment of Roman Catholics into the army. The presence of large numbers of Protestant soldiers had a positive spin-off for the wider Protestant minority community, for even after 1780, the majority of soldiers in the Irish military establishment remained Protestant and the subsequent provision of additional barracks – at Clonmel, Clogheen, Cahir, New Inn and Tipperary – served to further augment the Established Church community in these districts.

The difficulties encountered by the local Protestant establishment in containing growing Roman Catholic disquiet for democracy and equality led to the development of a further strategy of containment. This scheme, first piloted in the study area, involved the carving up of territory into constabulary districts, at the centre of which was placed a constabulary barrack of police, the very name 'barrack' indicating the paramilitary nature of the force. This force was backed by an extensive array of bridewell prisons and county gaols, of which South Tipperary contained one of the highest concentrations on the island of Ireland, in a county where the expenditure on prisons by the 1830s exceeded that for the entire province of Ulster. However, while the force was ultimately successful in containing and reducing insurrection and rebellion, it served only to stem, rather than halt, the hegemonic decline of the Protestant ruling establishment. External factors, not least the government of Ireland from Westminster, combined to overrule local Protestant concerns in favour of British Empire interests. Against a backdrop of growing concessions by Westminster to Irish Roman Catholics and the obvious failure of various implicit and explicit strategies employed to alter the denominational ratio and so arrest the decline of their hegemony, Protestants increasingly advocated emigration to Protestant strongholds, particularly Canada, as a way of maintaining their sense of community and cultural difference.

The reasons for this outcome are tied into my second major research question, which sought to examine how, or indeed whether, the 'underground' Roman Catholic Church of the majority population first accommodated itself to a 'ruled' situation in the colonial context and then how it progressively challenged the establishment through devising counter-territorial strategies of resistance to increasingly dominate and undermine the ruling minority. This study has emphasized the symbolic and practical significance that a relatively small number of leading Old English and Gaelic Irish elite families had in opposing New English colonialism in Ireland and in sustaining and revitalising the territorial structures of the Roman Catholic Church throughout the penal era. Early in this work, I detailed evidence of widespread anti-establishment sentiment among the leading urban mercantile families by the last quarter of the sixteenth century, particularly at Clonmel, where there were many prominent recusants, most notably the White mayoral dynasty. The selection of Clonmel by the New English colonial administration as a site of public execution for clerical recusants from the 1580s, in an effort to enforce the concept of *cuius regio, eius religio*, played a key role in turning this core population centre of the south-east and its hinterland against both the religious and secular arms of the establishment. In Ireland, where the majority population was of the same religion as the condemned, the effect of public executions was dangerously inverted, aiding the propagation of *fama martyrii*, the fame of martyrs. This must be placed within a wider European context, where the deterioration in diplomatic relations between England and the Roman Catholic states of Europe – most notably France and Spain – in conjunction with the availability in Ireland by the 1590s of Counter-Reformation preachers trained in these countries, brought about an insistence by the New English colonial administration that the Irish population declare in favour of Anglicanism, the religion of state. I have argued that, inspired by these urban martyrdoms, the Roman Catholics moved to openly resist and reject the Protestant Reformation, while the anti-recusancy endeavours of the colonial administration served only to further antagonize their premier mercantile and gentry dynasties and urge their founding of Irish colleges on the European continent, where scions of these families were trained for the Irish 'mission'.

The crucial significance of the commencement of the Observant movement among the religious orders in facilitating resistance to the Protestant Reformation has also been highlighted. This 'back to basics' movement among the Franciscans, Dominicans and Augustinians prepared these religious communities for their crucial pastoral role in the 'hidden' or 'underground' Roman Catholic Church in Ireland. In a subtle adaptation to ongoing state surveillance, they adopted the strategy of non-visibility by living in merchant and gentry households disguised as servants, by providing private house masses therein, thus proving largely invisible to and impenetrable by the colonial authorities. In these activities, both religious orders and secular clergy were greatly aided – particularly from the 1570s to the 1620s and between 1662 and 1715 – by the existence of the palatinate of Tipperary, under the princely jurisdiction of the earl of Ormond, wherein these clerical figures were largely beyond the reach of the colonial authorities. The connivance of the earl of Ormond with some of the religious orders is illustrated at Holy Cross abbey, where their ownership from 1540 of the monastic estate enabled the continuation of the Cistercian community there, even to the extent of their being granted leases of their former lands. Following the restoration of the monarchy in 1660 and the elevation of the earl of Ormond to the dukedom of Ormond and lord lieutenancy of Ireland, his guarded tolerance of Roman Catholicism among the cadet branches of his family (although he himself was emphatically a Protestant) and his influence in the restoration of key Roman Catholic dynasties to all or part of their ancestral lands in the study area and beyond, proved crucial for the post-Cromwellian revival of the Roman Catholic Church as an institution. As my research of state papers has shown, the Tipperary palatinate in the 1630s was noted as a 'receptacle and den for all ill-affected persons' which quite possibly would 'infect our other loving subjects' and by the 1660s, Ormond was in receipt of direct enquiries from the colonial authorities.[1] After the restoration of the monarchy and Established Church, the territorially uprooted Roman Catholic Church was forced to accommodate itself to its proscribed situation in a more permanent way. The endurance of the Ormond palatinate created the conditions for the development of a network of safe-houses for the clergy and episcopacy among the gentry of the study area and district and was crucial to the continuation of their pastoral mission in the difficult first quarter of the eighteenth century and their proving all but invisible and impenetrable to the state.

This study uncovered no evidence of the Roman Catholic community seeking a religious accommodation with the New English colonial administration, following the excommunication in 1570 of Queen Elizabeth by Pope Pius V. On the contrary, from this time forward there were two increasingly separate religious

1 *Cal. SP (Ireland), 1647–60: addenda*, 160.

communities, united under a temporal monarch, but increasingly divided over the issue of her spiritual rule. The Roman Catholic community of the study area, as in south-eastern Ireland in particular, was blatantly recusant from the Established Church from the earliest discernible divergence between Protestant and Roman Catholic in the last quarter of sixteenth century. Evidence of this turning against what the Roman Catholics increasingly saw as the church of the colonial New English alone (despite its continued use of the medieval parish church territorial organization), was uncovered in the royal visitations record of the targeting of the infrastructure of the Established Church by the Roman Catholics as early as the Desmond rebellion of the 1580s.

There was some evidence of a political accommodation, however, particularly just prior to the failed rebellion of 1641 when some of the Gaelic Irish and Old English gentry of Tipperary sought arms and state support from the lord president of Munster, Sir William St Leger, for their campaign to put down the early rising by some of the more base elements of society. His rejection out of hand of their offer symbolized the distrust of the New English colonial administration of all elements of the Gaelic Irish and Old English landed classes and the designs which it held on their estates. This distrust was not without foundation, for the composition in *Foras Feasa ar Éirinn* of a common origin legend for both Gaelic Irish and Old English communities under the common banner of Roman Catholicism by South Tipperary Counter-Reformation cleric, Dr Geoffrey Keating, helped lay the groundwork for the joint rising of the Gaelic Irish and Old English in the rebellion of 1641–2, in the face of the growth of New English hegemony. Keating's manuscript helped establish the political, cultural and military alliance of these two communities and the pre-emptive actions of St Leger acted as a catalyst for their rebellion.

Strategies of resistance to the colonial administration employed by dispossessed Roman Catholic guerrillas from the second half of the seventeenth to the first quarter of the eighteenth century directly led to an increased garrisoning of the landscape. The largely invisible and surprisingly durable Roman Catholic Church was well organized territorially by the last quarter of the later seventeenth century and had already adapted to its changed circumstances, as a detailed examination of the correspondence of Archbishop John Brenan revealed. By this time it was in a position to effectively resist total obliteration at the hands of the colonial authorities and already possessed a more comprehensive territorial lattice than the Established Church. The possession of a strong and enduring mercantile and gentry-led Roman Catholic community facilitated the early granting of sites for the building of mass-houses and chapels, so that by 1731, all districts of the study area were adequately served.

From its position of unassailable numerical strength, the Roman Catholic community of the study area was to the forefront in challenging the hegemony of the Protestant minority-ruling establishment in Ireland, particularly that of Co. Tipperary itself, variously described as 'red-hot' and 'rabid' by contemporary sources. From the 1760s, with the successful contestation of issues of urban mercantile taxation (quarterage) behind them and the ultimately successful rural campaigns of Whiteboy agrarian and anti-tithe agitation well under way, the Roman Catholic community played upon the growing realization by the British of the endlessly insecure Irish Protestant establishment, particularly in the amplification of riots and allegations of French intrigue to their own ends. Allegations of conspiracies with France and the presence of French agents in Ireland were not unfounded, given the impact of the French democratic revolution on late eighteenth-century Europe and on the British North American colonies. There was great concern in the Protestant establishment that this revolutionary atmosphere would feed into the democratic drive by Irish Roman Catholics, which fear proved well founded with the arrival of a French expeditionary force in Ireland during the 1798 rebellion. The connection of Irish Roman Catholics with France had long been feared by the colonial administration, for it was in the Irish colleges of France that the majority of sons of merchants, gentry and aristocracy received their clerical education, under oath of return to serve on the Irish 'mission'. This study has shown that while a constant stream of epistles from Protestant alarmists to Dublin Castle continued and ultimately achieved their aim of the increased provision of military and constabulary detachments in the study area, the local Protestant establishment ultimately weakened its position by demonstrating its incapability of containing insurrection with existing resources.

Perhaps the main addition of this study to the wider literature of the historical geography of colonial Ireland is in its examination of the territorial strategies utilized by the Anglican ruling minority establishment in the gaining, consolidation and maintenance of hegemony and contestation of hegemony *vis-à-vis* the Roman Catholic majority population and, equally, in analysing the counter-territorial strategies employed by this ruled majority in progressively challenging and eventually overcoming that hegemony. Throughout, the imperative has been to visualize processes where strategies of colonial advancement were created and to identify the myriad of Protestant and Roman Catholic responses to their changing situation. There were indeed deliberate strategies employed by the Protestant establishment with the aim of consolidating its hegemony and resistance to the decline of that hegemony over the Roman Catholic majority population. Furthermore it has exposed the varied and evolving counter-strategies of initial accommodation and of subsequent resistance employed by the Roman Catholics themselves in contesting and overcoming this hegemony. South Tipperary has proved to be very much an area of hegemonic contestation, a 'zone of confrontation and conflict', where both communities sought continually 'to gain the upper hand and thus create the hegemony of a fundamental social group over a subordinate group'.[2]

While it was relatively easy to establish that strategies of colonial advancement and dominion and counter-strategies of accommodation and resistance were constituted, a paucity of contemporary source documentation – partly as a result of the incineration of the contents of the Public Record Office in 1922 and perhaps partly because such schemes were seldom formally committed to paper – frustrated the exploration of some key evolutionary aspects, particularly relating to the organization and foundation – haphazard or otherwise – of each particular scheme. Some of the schemes of domination and resistance have proved so 'hidden' and 'under-

2 A. Gramsci, *Selections from the prison notebooks of Antonio Gramsci* (1971), 12; 181–2.

ground' as to be all but invisible to the historical record. In the case of the development of estate colonies, for instance, it can probably never be definitively established what, if any, formal channels of communication existed between the Protestant landlords of the study area and the Protestant dissenting weavers of the province of Ulster, owing to a lack of direct evidence. The researcher is left pondering, for example, how contact was established with groups? How many originally arrived and how long did they prevail? How many of them subsequently emigrated? In addition, the difficulty of conceptualising the emergence of modern Ireland becomes more difficult as the research progresses, as the political landscape becomes coloured by controversy and inflected by the search for historical antecedents for the legitimacies of contested identities of the present. It could be argued the approach of this study in treating of the period from the 'report on popery' (1731) to just after the *Report of the commissioners of public instruction* (1834) in one major section masks the tumultuous political events surrounding the 1798 rebellion; it possibly also obscures the shift in the Roman Catholic political movement from one that was fairly conservative and largely led by aristocrats and the landed classes up to the 1760s, to one which had become more radical and included significant middleclass elements by the 1780s. However, it is felt that ongoing establishment insecurities and state-sponsored surveillance, commencing with the 'report on popery' (1731) and religious query in the hearth money roll (1732), continuing with the religious census of 1766, and ending with the first definitive religious census of Ireland, published in the *Report of the commissioners of public instruction* (1834), constitutes a vital thread of continuity which narrative would not benefit from interruption.

Notwithstanding the above, this interpretation has aimed to enhance understanding of the early modern period by addressing the limitations of a generalising colonial perspective on early modern Ireland, *c.*1570 to 1841. This has been achieved through exploring the strategies employed by the Protestant minority–ruling establishment in South Tipperary in both secular and religious fields, while simultaneously analysing the varied Roman Catholic responses. An achievement of this work is perhaps the detailed interrogation, analysis and GIS mapping of the documents of conquest and colonization to reveal zones of establishment inertia and peripheral zones from where the Roman Catholics increasingly dominated. This has been achieved through a historical geographical analysis of the changing strategies employed by the Protestant ruling minority to maintain control and contest hegemony *vis-à-vis* the Roman Catholic population and the varied responses of that ruled majority to the changing socio-economic and political environment.

It is important to recognize the trauma of the past identified here, without obscuring the very intricacies and contradictions which make this period so revealing and consequential for our understanding of the present, particularly in the northern Irish context. In bringing this study to a close, it is appropriate to return once more to the outset, where hegemony was noted as 'a process of struggle, a permanent striving, a ceaseless endeavour to maintain control over the "hearts and minds"

---

3 R. Miliband, *Capitalist democracy in Britain* (1984), 76.

of subordinate classes [that] is never done'.[3] It may be seen in this study that on the one hand, even to the end, the ruling Protestant minority establishment never ceased to struggle to retain the hegemony to which it had grown accustomed and without which it could see no purpose for itself; on the other hand, the Roman Catholic majority continually strived for the religious, social and economic ascendancy it saw as its God-given right.

Appendices

Appendix I: The religious houses of South Tipperary district

Location	House	Status after 1540	Owner by 1541
Athassel, Golden	Augustinian Canons abbey	Dissolved in 1550; extinct thereafter	James Butler, earl of Ormond.
Cahir	Augustinian Canons priory	Extinct, but mention of a monk living here in the late 1500s.	Sir Thomas Butler, baron of Cahir
Carrickbeg	Franciscan friary	Revived 1644–9; in continuous use from 1669	James Butler, earl of Ormond.
Carrick-on-Suir	St Thomas (Acon)	Extinct.	James White, gent. Carrick-on-Suir
Cashel	Cistercian: Hore abbey	Extinct, but mention of a monk living here in 1620.	Edmund Heffernan, clerk
	Dominican friary	In continuous use until abandoned in first-half of nineteenth century	Walter Houth, gent
	Franciscan friary	Friars remained until 1550, returning 1618–47 and again from 1658 until their 1740s removal to Thurles.	Edmund, archbishop of Cashel.
Clonmel	Dominican friary	Extinct, but failed attempts at revival by the Order in 1726.	George, archbishop of Dublin.
	Franciscan friary	Continuous 'underground' presence, in Irishtown 1649–58, in friary 1658–90, in Irishtown from 1690 until friary restored in 1828.	James Butler, earl of Ormond
	Carmelite friary	Extinct.	James Butler, earl of Ormond
Fethard	Augustinian friary	Continuous 'underground' presence, until restored to friary in 1823.	Edmund Butler, baron of Dunboyne
Galbally, Co. Tipperary	Franciscan friary	Friars remained, burnt out in 1570, returned 1645–9, 1658–80 and 1684–1748 until removal to Mitchelstown.	John FitzGerald, brother to the earl of Desmond
Holy Cross	Cistercian abbey	Continuous presence to 1649, then in charge of parish until 1750; extinct.	James Butler, earl of Ormond.
Inishlounaght, Clonmel	Cistercian: Suir abbey	Extinct, revived 1641–9 and extinct thereafter.	Sir Thomas Butler, baron of Cahir
Kilcooley	Cistercian abbey	Extinct, revived 1622–49 as the novitiate, extinct thereafter.	James Butler, earl of Ormond
Lady Abbey, Ardfinnan	Carmelite friary	Extinct.	Robert Butler of Knockgraffon
Molough, Newcastle	Benedictine nunnery	Extinct.	Robert Butler of Knockgraffon
Tipperary	Augustinian friary	Continuous presence; succession of priors continued into the 1830s	Dermot Ryan of Tipperary

Source: Bradshaw, *The dissolution of the religious orders in Ireland under Henry VIII*; Conlan, *Franciscan Ireland*; Flynn, *Irish Dominicans*; White, *Extents of Irish monastic possessions, 1540–1*.

Appendix II: Fair patents granted to South Tipperary, 1607–1814

Location	Founder	Date of patent	Subsequent grants
Knockorden	Geoffrey Sall	1607	
Fethard	Corporation	1607	
Graystown	James Laffin	1607	Epaphroditus Marsh*/ Matthew Jacob* 1705
Kilknocken	Sir John Everard	1607	William Barton* 1773
Knockkelly	Sir John Everard	1607	
Killerke	Sir John Everard	1607	
Clonmel	Corporation	1608	John Bagwell* 1811
Tipperary	William Ryan	1609	
Solloghodhead	William Ryan	1609	
Cahir	Thomas, Lord Cahir	1614	Lord Cahir 1776
Ballyboy	Sir Patrick Murry*	1615	
Lissinsky	William O'Meara	1615	
Drohid (Clogheen)	Sir William Fenton*	1619	
Toem	Sir James Craige*	1627	
Cullen	William Warter*	1634	
Cashel	Corporation	1637; 1639	
Clonyharpa	Francis Bolton*	1658	(near Clonoulty)
Kilcooley	Sir Hierom Alexander*	1673	
Clogheen	Viscount Sidney*	1693	O'Callaghan* 1758
Ballinacourty	John Dawson*	1706	
Carrick-on-Suir	Countess of Tyrone*	1711	
Killenaule	Edward Worth*	1728	
Cappagh White	Richard Nutley*	1729	
Roesgreen	William Roe*	1729	
Emly	John Damer*	1731	
Golden	Sir Richard Meade*	1739	
Ballysheehan	Robert O'Callaghan*	1745	
Ballyporeen	Lord Kingston*	1752	
Holycross	William Armstrong*	1756	
Mullinahone	Riggs Falkiner*	1760	
Ardfinnan	John Hely-Hutchinson*	1785	
New Birmingham	Sir Vere Hunt	1802	
New Inn	John Cooke*	1810	
Grangemockler	Stephen Moore*/Robert Cashin	1814	

* Protestant landowners; source: Lodge MSS.
Fairs were also held at Ballingarry, Ballyclerihan, Bansha, Cloneen, Dundrum, Nine-Mile-House, Kilcash and Molough; their founders are not now known.

Appendix III: Burses open to South Tipperary students in the Belgian Netherlands

Legacy of	Foundation	Endowment	Eligible seminarians
John Normel	1653	993 florins	Natives of Lismore and Clonmel
Thomas Stapleton	1688	325 francs	Natives of Fethard, Co. Tipperary
Thomas Hurley	1697	3200 florins	Natives of Limerick and Tipperary
Michael Hennessy	1730	Unknown	Natives of Fethard, Co. Tipperary
John Kent	1778	7002 florins	Waterford and Lismore diocese

Source: Walsh, *Irish continental colleges*: app. III.

Appendix IV: The ranking of Protestant landholders in South Tipperary, 1640

Rank	Landholder	Total estate	Annual valuation
1	Earl of Ormond*	22,517	£1,214
2	Countess of Ormond*	8,466	£682
3	Sir William Fenton	4,715	£228
4	Gamaliel Warter	4,680	£518
5	Sir Philip Percival*	3,311	£351
6	Hierom Alexander*	2,130	£94
7	Archbishop of Cashel	1,974	£162
8	Lord Laurence Esmond*	1,654	£148
9	Sir Hardress Waller*	1,386	£281
10	Thomas Baker	1,054	£180
11	William Kingsmill*	918	£70
12	Greenvill Halls	890	£50
13	Sir William St Leger*	840	£60
14	Bishop of Waterford*	734	£111
15	Thomas Grove	664	£122
16	Earl of Cork*	553	£32
17	Earl of Thomond*	500	£120
18	Robert Cox*	346	£73
19	Robert Powell	294	£40
20	William Young	176	£14
21	Parson Kittlebee/Vicar Cox	32	£5

* = non-resident; source: Simington, *Civil survey of Co. Tipperary*

Appendix V: Lands held by Protestants in South Tipperary, 1640

Barony	Parish	Protestant acreage	Leased from the estate of	Protestant landholder	Annual valuation
Middlethird					
	Ballysheehan	840	In fee	Sir William St Leger*	£60
		274	Sall of Cashel	William Kingsmill*	£25
		518	Hackett of Ballysheehan	Archbishop of Cashel	£40
		356		Sir Philip Percival*	£25
	Cloneen	9	In fee	James, earl of Ormond*	10s.
	Cooleagh	290	The crown	Sir Philip Percival*	£15
	Crompsland	122	In fee	James, earl of Ormond*	£12
	Erry	303	Sall of Cashel	William Kingsmill*	£25
	Gaile	272	Church lands	Archbishop of Cashel	£15
		241	In fee	James, earl of Ormond*	£12
	Holycross (part of)	968	In fee	James, earl of Ormond*	£66
	Kilconnell	331	Hackett	Sir Philip Percival*	£15
		289	In fee	James, earl of Ormond*	£20
	Kiltinan	47	In fee	James, earl of Ormond*	£3
	Knockgraffon	69	Church lands	Earl of Cork*	£3
		345	Church lands	Sir William Fenton	£28
		491	In fee	James, earl of Ormond*	£37 10s.
	Mogorban	449	In fee	James, earl of Ormond*	£32
	Moorstownkirk	316	Church lands	Bishop of Waterford*	£30
	Rathcoole	103	In fee	James, earl of Ormond*	£7 10s.
	Redcity	294	Church lands	Robert Powell	£40
	St John Baptist Grange	140	In fee	James, earl of Ormond*	£7 10s.
	St Patrick's Rock	1171	Church lands	Vicars Choral	£102
		341		William Kingsmill*	£20
		176		William Young*	£14
		8,755			£655
Iffa and Offa					
	Ardfinnan	20	Church lands	Earl of Cork*	£3
	Ballybacon	12	Church lands	Earl of Cork*	£3
	Ballyclerihan	9	Church lands	Chapter of Cashel	£1
		140	In fee	James, earl of Ormond*	£21
	Cahir	58	Keating of Moorstown	Robert Cox of Bruff*	£8
	Carrick-on-Suir	500	In fee	James, earl of Ormond	£60
	Derrygrath	106	Keating of Moorstown	Robert Cox* of Bruff	£15
		69	Shea of Kilkenny	John Grove, Rochestown	£8
	Donoughmore and Kiltegan	395	Church lands	Bishop of Waterford*	£80
		72	In fee	James, earl of Ormond*	£20
	Inishlounaght	182	Keating of Moorstown	Robert Cox* of Bruff	£50
	Kilgrant	3	Church lands	Earl of Cork*	10s.
		185		Lord Esmond*	£28

Barony	Parish	Protestant acreage	Leased from the estate of	Protestant landholder	Annual valuation
	Killaloan	120	In fee	Lord Esmond*	£24
	Kilmurry	221	In fee	James, earl of Ormond*	£30
	Kilsheelan	200	Shea of Kilkenny	John Grove, Rochestown	£45
		20	In fee	James, earl of Ormond*	£3
	Mortlestown	10	Church lands	Earl of Cork*	£1 10s.
	Neddans	4	Church lands	Vicar Cox	10s.
	Newchapel	28	Church lands	Earl of Cork*	£4 10s.
	Newcastle	12	Church lands	Parson Kittlebee and Vicar Cox	£2
	Newtownlennon	433	In fee	James, earl of Ormond*	£53
	Rathronan	11	Church lands	Earl of Cork*	£1 10s.
		239	In fee	James, earl of Ormond*	£50
	Rochestown	395	Wyse estate, Waterford	John Grove, Rochestown	£69
	Shanrahan	4,370	In fee	Sir William Fenton	£200
		1	Church lands	Lord Esmond*	5s.
	Tubrid	20	Church lands	Dean of Lismore*	£5
	Tullaghorton	3	Church lands	Bishop of Waterford*	5s.
	Tullaghmeelan	16	Church lands	Parson Kittlebee and Vicar Cox	£2
		7,854			£789
Clanwilliam					
	Bohercrow	400	Ryan of Solloghodbeg	Gamaliel Warter	£120
	Clonbeg	400	In fee	Earl of Cork*	£15
	Clonbullogue	800	In fee	Countess of Ormond*	£30
	Cordangan	400	Ryan of Solloghodbeg	Gamaliel Warter	£120
	Corroge	200	In fee	James, earl of Ormond*	£30
	Cullen	1,500	Earl of Thomond*	Gamaliel Warter	£100
	Donohill	296	In fee	Countess of Ormond*	£50
		88	Countess of Ormond*	Sir Hardress Waller*	£18
		220	James, earl of Ormond*	Sir Hardress Waller*	£47
	Emly	1,100	In fee	Bishop of Emly	£80
		1,100	Church lands	Gamaliel Warter	£86
	Kilcornan	180	Church lands	Gamaliel Warter	£12
	Kilfeakle	3,000	In fee	Countess of Ormond*	£280
	Killardry	460	In fee	Countess of Ormond*	£30
	Kilmucklin	120	Burke of Shanballymore	Sir Hardress Waller	£30
	Kilshane	120	In fee	Countess of Ormond*	£20
	(Swiffin)	600	In fee	James, earl of Ormond*	£50
	Lattin	938	Heffernan and Magrath, Lattin	Thomas Baker	£160
	Rathlennon	148	James, earl of Ormond*	Sir Hardress Waller*	£36

Barony	Parish	Protestant acreage	Leased from the estate of	Protestant landholder	Annual valuation
	Rathlennon	460	Richard Butler of Kilcash	Sir Philip Percival*	£175
	Relickmurry	6,585	In fee	James, earl of Ormond*	£273
		1,250	In fee	Countess of Ormond*	£50
		500	Thomond estate*	Sir Philip Percival*	£20
	Solloghodbeg	158	English of Solloghodbeg	Thomas Baker	£30
	Templenoe	660	Countess of Ormond*	Sir Hardress Waller*	£140
	Tipperary	200	In fee	Countess of Ormond*	£20
		150	Burke of Shanballymore	Sir Hardress Waller*	£24
		22,033			*£2,046*
Kilnamanagh					
	Aghacrew	32	Archbishop of Cashel	Sir Philip Percival*	£3
	Clogher	137	O'Dwyer of Ballagh	Sir Philip Percival*	£17
	Clonoulty	890	Magrath of Ballymore	Greenvil Halls	£50
		469	Archbishop of Cashel	Lord Esmond*	£50
		508	O'Dwyer of Ballagh	Sir Philip Percival*	£32
	Oughterleague	493	Archbishop of Cashel	Sir Philip Percival*	£45
	Toem	4	Archbishop of Cashel	Sir Philip Percival*	10s
		2,533			*£197 10s.*
Slieveardagh					
	Ballingarry	2,500	In fee	James, earl of Ormond*	£70
	Buolick	1,200	In fee	James, earl of Ormond*	£40
	Crohane	500	In fee	James, earl of Ormond*	£26
	Fennor	300	In fee	Countess of Ormond*	£15
		430	In fee	James, earl of Ormond*	£25
	Graystown	1,180	In fee	Countess of Ormond*	£37
		1,900	In fee	James, earl of Ormond*	£70
	Grangemockler	879	In fee	Lord Esmond*	£46
	Kilcooley	2,130	In fee	Hierome Alexander*	£94
		918	In fee	James, earl of Ormond*	£45
	Killenaule	200	The crown (forfeiture)	Sir Philip Percival*	£3
		1,600	In fee	James, earl of Ormond*	£80
	Lismalin	200	In fee	Countess of Ormond*	£10
		1,600	In fee	James, earl of Ormond*	£70
		15,537			*£631*
Total		**56,712**			**£4,319**

Source: Simington, *Civil survey of Co. Tipperary.*

Appendix VI: Registration of 'popish' clergy, 1704: archdiocese of Cashel (part of)

Modern parish	Former parish union/benefice	Parish priest	Age	Ordained	Residence	Known protector
Anacarthy & Donohill	Donohill, Kilpatrick, etc.	Teige Ryan	60	Lisheen, Bansha	Knockroe, near Barnastook	A native son of the parish
Ballingarry	Ballingarry, Crohane, etc.	William Kelly	72	Ferbane	Graguagh, near Ballingarry	Butler, Viscount Ikerrin
Bansha & Kilmoyler	Templeneiry, Killardry, etc.	Thomas Grace	38	Garryricken	Kilshane	McCarthy of Springhouse
Boherlahan & Dualla	Ardmayle/Erry, Ballysheehan	Philip Coleman	53	Irish college, Lisbon	Gortmakellis	
Cashel & Rosegreen	St John Baptist and St Patrick's Rock	Edward Sall	52	Irish college, Salamanca	Cashel	A native son of the parish
Clerihan	Kiltinan, Colman, etc.	Geoffrey Sall	51	Liege	Killusty	A native son of the parish
Clonoulty & Rossmore	Clonoulty, Clogher and Moyaliff	Richard Butler	38	Kilkenny	Gatterstown	Butler, 'baron' of Ardmayle
Drangan & Cloneen*	Cloneen, Drangan, etc.	Michael Tobin	60	Perques	Mullinahone	Tobin of Killaghy
Emly	Emly	Eustace Browne	60	Portugal	Emly	Browne, Viscount Kenmare
Fethard & Killusty	Fethard	James Kearney	72	Rouen	Fethard	Kearney of Cashel
Galbally & Aherlow	Galbally and Clonbeg	John Finaghty	56	Dublin	Galbally	
Golden & Kilfeakle	Relickmurry	Darby Berkery	40	Kilkenny	Rathduff, nr. Thomastown	Matthew of Thomastown
Gortnahoe & Glengoole	Fennor, Kilcooley	Matthew Cahill	60	Longford	Fennor	
Holycross & Ballycahill	Holycross	Edmond Lahy, O. Cist.	56	Lisheen, Bansha	Holy Cross Abbey	Butler of Ormonde
Killenaule & Moyglass	Killenaule, Graystown, etc.	Thaddeus O'Donoghue	50	Gascoigne, France	Killenaule	
Knockavilla & Donaskeigh	Ballintemple, Oughterleague, Kilfeakle, etc.	William Dwyer	50	Lisheen, Bansha	Dundrum	A native son (O'Dwyer of Dundrum)
New Inn & Knockgraffon	Knockgraffon, Boytonrath	John Devane	74	Paris	Masterstown	
Solohead & Oola	Solloghodmore/Solloghodbeg	John Casey	40	Cashel	Ballygodoon	
Tipperary	Tipperary, Lattin, Shronell	William O'Meara	31	Cork	Ballinleenty	A native son of the parish

* In 1776, Mullinahone was separated from Drangan, while about this time Lattin and Cullen were separated from Tipperary.

diocese of Lismore (part of)

Modern parish	Former parish union/benefice	Parish priest	Age	Ordained	Residence	Known protector
Ardfinnan, Grange & Ballybacon	Ardfinnan, Ballybacon and Neddins	William Hearn	35	Rehill	Ardfinnan	Mulcahy, head-tenant of Lord Cahir (Corabella)
See Ardfinnan (Grange)	Tullaghmelan	Gerard Prendergast	42	Paris	Garnavilla	James Nagle, head-tenant of Lord Cahir (Garnavilla)
Ballylooby & Duhill	Tubrid, Tullaghorton	William English II	60	Lisheen, Bansha	Knockane	A native son
Ballyporeen	Templeteny	James Holane	72	Nantes	Carrigavisteal	
Cahir	Cahir, Derrygrath, etc.	Dennis Fogarty	38	Carricktwohill	Knockagh	Keating of Knockagh
Carrick-on-Suir	Carrick-on-Suir	Daniel Duggan	60	Paris	Carrick-on-Suir	Butler of Ormond
Clogheen & Burncourt	Shanrahan and Ballysheehan	James Hyland Jr.	36	Rehill	Rehill	Butler of Cahir/Rehill
Clonmel	Clonmel	Edward Tonnery	50	Kilkenny	Irishtown, Clonmel	A native son
		Luke White	67	Nantes	Irishtown, Clonmel	A White of Clonmel
Grangemockler	Grangemockler, Kilmurry	William Boulger	57	Kilkenny	Bleanaleen	Butler of Garryricken
Kilsheelan & Kilcash	Kilcash, Kilsheelan, etc.	James Butler	56	Kilkenny	Shanbally	A Butler of Kilcash
Lisronagh	Lisronagh, Rathronan, etc.	William Bourke	57	Lisheen, Bansha	Kilmore	
Newcastle	Newcastle and Innislounaght	James Daniel	56	Waterford	Inishlounaght or Glasha	
Powerstown	Kilgrant	Edward Butler	46	Cregne	Redmondstown	A Butler of Kilcash

Source: Ó Fiaich, 'The registration of the clergy in 1704', *Seanchas Ard Mhacha* 6 (1971).

Appendix VII: Mass-house – barn chapel – slated chapel progression in South Tipperary

Portion of Lismore diocese

Ardfinnan,	No chapel in the village, until the building of a chapel-of-ease in 1838.
Ballybacon,	A thatched chapel was built in the early eighteenth century; the present chapel was built up around it in 1829–30 and the old chapel demolished.
& Grange	A thatched chapel was built in the early eighteenth century and replaced in the same manner as Ballybacon, by the present chapel of 1829.
Ballylooby &	The present chapel was built in 1813 on the site of an eighteenth-century thatched chapel; it was renovated and virtually rebuilt in 1929.
Duhill	The present chapel was built 1829–30, near its eighteenth-century thatched predecessor. It was also heavily renovated in 1929.
Grangemockler	The early eighteenth-century thatched chapel was located a short distance from the present chapel, which was built in 1805 and renovated in 1897.
& Ballyneale	A thatched chapel roofed in 1654, noted as the private chapel of O'Neill of Ballyneale; it was replaced *c.*1785 by a church at Curraghdobbin, on which site is the present church of 1840.
Ballyporeen	A mass-rock site 'the old altar' at an ancient crossroads tree and in the adjoining Coolagarranroe townland at 'clair an aifrinn' (mass-trench). A thatched chapel-of-ease to Clogheen was erected at 'an sheana séipéal' (old chapel), Carrigavisteal, in the early eighteenth century. Ballyporeen was declared an independent parish in 1816 and the chapel site moved to the village; the present church was erected in 1828.
Cahir	In the Ballingeary-Poulmucky area, there is a tradition of 'clair an aifrinn' (mass-trench), a depression where mass may have been celebrated in penal times. In addition, the 'priest's road' area leading from the town to this district is reputed to have contained the abode of the parish priest – likely the middle section of 'Suirvale House'. No chapel-of-ease developed; the town of Cahir had a thatched chapel before 1700 – located on the Ardfinnan Road, adjoining what later became Cahir House demesne gates – which was renovated in 1722. The mass-house was replaced by a modern chapel in 1790–1 further up the road towards the town on the present site, replaced by the present church in 1833–9 and extensively renovated 1888–9.
Carrick-on-Suir	Bishop Creagh of Waterford and Lismore lived 1747–76 in a house in a laneway off Main Street, near the penal chapel. A slated church 82 feet by 62 feet was erected in 1804 on the site of the penal chapel, containing three galleries and seating 1,500 persons; replaced by the current church in 1880.
& Newtownlennon	At Poulmaleen is a penal site, 'clairin an aifrinn' (little trench of the mass), a quarry-like depression. A thatched early eighteenth-century chapel was replaced by a slated church in 1804; it was replaced by the current church in 1880.
Clogheen	In Doon townland is 'gleanntán an tsagart' (the priests little glen), a possible mass-site or place of refuge in penal times. A thatched chapel was built in 1740 at Chapel Lane, Clogheen; it was replaced in 1820 by a slated church on Main Street, on the site of the present church of 1862–4.
& Burncourt	A thatched penal chapel was built *c.*1740 at Scart, which survives in the place-name 'an sheana séipéal' (the old chapel); it was used by Fr Sheehy. This building became Ballysheehan chapel-of-ease and was replaced by a church on the present site in the village of Burncourt in 1810–14, which was extensively renovated in 1874.
St Mary, Clonmel	A thatched mass-house was built on present church site *c.*1670, which was slated and extended to include three galleries in the 1720s. It continued as

the parish church, with several renovations, until the building of the current church up and around it (1836–50) and final demolition in 1850. A parochial house was built nearby during the 1770s.

SS Peter and Paul,   A chapel-of-ease to the above was built in Johnson (now Gladstone) Street in 1810 and constituted an

Clonmel   independent parish in 1836. The present church was built in several stages during the period 1885–1936.

Kilsheelan   A thatched early eighteenth-century chapel was located opposite the present church site, on the townland of Gambonsfield, a name still retained. The present church was erected in 1810; it was rebuilt in 1885.

& Kilcash   A tradition of a mass-rock persists at Ballypatrick, but there was a thatched chapel by 1654 at Kilcash Castle, replaced by another in the early eighteenth century on the present church site. The current Ballypatrick church was built in 1810; it was rebuilt in 1885.

Newcastle   A mass-rock site at 'cnoicín an aifrinn' (little hill of the mass), in Clashganny, 3½ miles from Newcastle village. Other nearby districts were served from 'Knockanaifrinn' (hill of the mass) in the Nire Valley, Comeragh Mountains. A thatched chapel was erected in the early eighteenth century at 'sheana séipéal' (old chapel) in Middlequarter; it was replaced by another built in 1793 for the parish union, located in the font field at Pastorville. With the building of Four-Mile-Water church in 1826, the need for a central church diminished; a small slated chapel was built in Newcastle village about this time, which was entirely rebuilt in 1879. Pastorville became the parochial residence during the 1820s.

Powerstown   A thatched early eighteenth-century chapel was replaced by the current church on the same site in 1810. There was a thatched chapel-of-ease at Castle Blake until the 1840s, serving the parish of Mora, which was then abandoned owing to falling population.

& Lisronagh   A thatched early eighteenth-century chapel was located at Quarryhole, to the north of the present site; it was replaced by present church in the village in 1832, which was rebuilt in 1860.

Portion of Cashel & Emly archdiocese

Tipperary   'St John's church', noted in the 'report on popery' of 1704, was replaced in 1731 by a new slated cruciform chapel 92 feet by 76 feet in Mass Lane, close to current church. The present church – on a site obtained in the 1820s – was commenced in the 1840s, but was delayed by the crash of the town bank; it was finally completed in 1859.

Cashel   A thatched chapel was built before 1710 in Chapel Lane, adjoining the Dominican abbey and supplied by the Dominicans. The current church, built in 1795, is on site of the Franciscan friary in Friar Street.

& Rosegreen   There was a thatched chapel here by 1731. The current chapel-of-ease was built on the same site in 1838.

Emly   A small thatched chapel was built at north end of village in 1729, within 100 yards of the Anglican cathedral church of St Ailbe. It was replaced by a slated church in 1809 on new site to the east. The present church site adjoins the old churchyard and was selected when the current church was built in 1883. The 1809 building is used as the parochial hall.

Clonoulty   A thatched mass-house was built before 1714, which was replaced by another on the same site in 1752. A slated church was built in 1805–6 on a new site, which is also that of the current church of 1883.

(& Rossmore)	Rossmore (North Tipperary portion) received a church in 1831.
Holycross	The monks obtained the position of parish priest, and portion of the abbey was thatched for use as the parish church and parochial residence by the early seventeenth century. This structure served, with renovations, until the building of a church in 1832, adjoining the abbey graveyard.
(& Ballycahill)	Ballycahill church was built 1819–20; it replaced a thatched building.
Donohill	A thatched mass-house was built before 1710. In 1783, a chapel was built at the moat of Donohill. The current church was built in 1824, on a new site; it was enlarged in 1861.
& Annacarthy	A church was first built here in 1813, which was converted into the school-house in 1870, when the present church was built on a new site.
Clerihan	A thatched chapel was built at Newchapel in 1729; it was called Orchardstown chapel by 1754. This site continued until the present church was completed in 1820 in Clerihan village.
Drangan	An out-parish of Mullinahone until 1806, when united to Cloneen. A chapel was built at Drangan in 1806, replaced by the current one in 1850.
& Cloneen	A thatched chapel at Cloneen by 1731; the present church was built in 1815 on the same site.
Gortnahoe	A thatched chapel at Buolick by 1731, then the only parish chapel. A new chapel was built in 1758, on Cahill's Hill, near the village. The present church was built on a new site in 1820.
& Glengoole	A chapel-of-ease was built at Glengoole before 1754, which was replaced by the present church built in the nearby estate village of New Birmingham (now Glengoole) in 1813–15 by Sir Vere Hunt, the landlord.
Ballingarry	This parish had a mass-rock at Rathanaiffrin (mass-fort). A thatched mass-house was built by 1731 at Kilbeheen; it was replaced in 1798 by another chapel on the same site. The current church dates to 1828.
Killenaule	A mass-rock site at 'gleann na caillighe', a T–junction where the road divides to Fethard and Drangan. There was a thatched mass-house at Killenaule by 1731, which in 1752 was 'a good chapel, thatched, with walls 7 foot high'. This building served until replacement in 1859–65 by the present church on a new site nearby.
& Moyglass	A thatched mass-house by 1731, replaced by current church in 1838, on a new site one mile away; the old chapel became the parish schoolhouse.
Mullinahone	A mass-rock at 'carraig an aifrinn' (hill of the mass) in the townland of Kylatlea, on Slievenamon's northern slope, just above the 600 foot contour; a possible priest-shelter of that district – 2½ miles west of the mass-rock – was Poulataggert waterfall (priests hollow), 1,100 feet above sea-level. A thatched chapel dedicated to St John was built before 1731 behind the stone castle in Carrick Street in the village centre. A thatched chapel was built on a new site *c.*1800, near the Callan Road, about 250 yards from the old site. In 1838, Wright of Killaghy Castle bestowed unsolicited three acres of his pleasure garden to be annexed to the chapel yard as a burial ground. A new slated church was constructed around the old building in 1838–9, using portion of this new plot of ground.
Fethard	A thatched chapel built in Chapel Lane in 1731, subsequently enlarged and improved. It was replaced by the present church in 1818–19, on an adjoining site donated by Barton of Grove, who laid the foundation stone.
& Killusty	A thatched chapel was built before 1731 by the Purcell family of Killusty, which continued as chapel-of-ease to Fethard until its replacement by the current building, on the same site, in 1883.

Boherlahan	A thatched chapel was in use at Ardmayle before 1710; it continued in use until the 1770s, when it was abandoned in favour of a new site at Boherlahan. The current church was built in 1810 on a nearby site, halfway between Lower Nodstown and Boherlahan, beside a mass path.
& Dualla	The first church here was built in 1826–30, on a site given by Oliver Latham of Meldrum and London, a local Protestant gentleman.
Lattin	A thatched chapel was provided by 1731, located in Mote Field, 200 yards from Lattin village. A slated church was built in the mid-1780s, on an elevated site in the present church grounds, the earliest of its period in South Tipperary; it was replaced in 1865–9 by the present church.
& Cullen	A thatched chapel was provided by 1731, which was replaced by a slated church, on the same site, in 1833–4.
Solohead	A thatched church was provided at Ballyfireen (Oola) before 1752. A thatched church was provided at Solohead shortly after; both were in good repair in 1819. The present church at Solohead was built in 1872–87 on the same site.
(& Oola)	The present Oola church was built c.1836.
Cappaghwhite	This union with Hollyford was called 'Carnahalla and Losset' during the eighteenth century and constituted the ancient parish of Toem with Hollyford. The chapel for Carnahalla was located at the 'fox cover' in Knockanavar, where it bounds Shanacloon, while that for Hollyford was at Losset. In 1821, Hollyford was separated from Cappaghwhite and a new church built, while Losset chapel was abandoned that year. At Cappaghwhite, a new thatched chapel was temporarily erected on the present site in 1821, until the completion of a slated chapel in 1826.
Hollyford (with Rearcross & Kilcommon)	This parish was carved out of six adjacent ones in 1804; in 1821, Hollyford was taken from Cappaghwhite and added; its church was built that year. Kilcommon church was built in 1821 and rebuilt 1875–87; a chapel-of-ease of timber and iron was built, c.1894, at Rearcross.
Knockavilla	The first chapel of this new settlement was built in 1759; it was thatched. The present church was completed in 1806, on a site given by Mr Cooper of Killenure Castle, despite opposition from Maude of Dundrum House.
& Donaskeigh	A thatched chapel was built at Ruan before 1730, which continued in various forms as the principal chapel, until the 1806 chapel was opened at Knockavilla. Ruan chapel continued until replacement by the present church in 1901, on a new site about 1½ miles north-east of the old chapel.
(Galbally)	A thatched mass-house was erected in 1717, replaced by a small thatched chapel erected in 1776 on the townland of Ardrahan, just outside Galbally village. This was in turn replaced by a slated church in 1836–8, one mile north, on the present site in the heart of Galbally village.
& Aherlow	Lisvernane church was built in 1835; no previous chapel here.
Knockgraffon	The original thatched mass-house was built in 1725. In 1799, a chapel built on a new site at Knockakillian, near Knockgraffon; it was replaced by the current church in 1846; a tower was added in 1874.
& New Inn	A mass-house was built in this new settlement in 1759, serving until the completion in 1832 of the current church, on a new site.
Golden	A thatched chapel was provided by 1731 at Athassal, which was replaced by one in the village by 1766. The present church was built on this site in 1801 and renovated extensively in 1840.
& Kilfeakle	A thatched chapel was provided by 1731, also called Rathduff or Thomastown; it was situated within the demesne walls of Thomastown Castle and hosted ordinations during the 1740s. The present church was built in 1837–45, on a nearby roadside site at Kilfeakle.

Bansha	The thatched eighteenth-century chapel was located at Bansha West, in a swampy glen. The present church was built in 1807, on a site given by Mr O'Brien-Butler, a Protestant, despite opposition from several of his co-religionists that it was built adjoining their parish churchyard.
& Kilmoyler	The present church was built in 1805, at the expense of the local head-tenant family, Meagher of Kilmoyler House.

Sources: Doyle, *Fragments*; Whelan, 'The Catholic Church'; Power, *Placenames of Decies*; Power, *Waterford and Lismore*; Skehan, *Cashel and Emly*.

Appendix VIII: Protestant percentiles in Anglican parishes of South Tipperary, 1766

Parish or union	Protestant families	Popish families	Per cent
Cashel ^ +	117	102	54
Kilgrant ^	7	15	47
Rathronan ^	5	13	38.5
Mogorban	17	46	37
Cashel union ^ +	160	430	37
Lisronagh ^	6	20	30
Shronell union #	86	291	29.5
Clonmel ^	320	1126	28.5
Clonmel union ^	337	1369	25
Tipperary ^	97	406	24
Rathronan union ^	29	140	21
Tipperary union ^	107	552	19.5
Ardmayle	12	22	16.5
Fethard ^	47	05	15.5
Donohill	28	190	15
Fethard union ^	91	836	11
Ardfinnan	41 persons	334 persons	12
Cullen union #	48	469	10
Templeneiry	12	139	9
Newchapel	47 persons	544 persons	9
Ballysheehan	11	32	9
Inishlounaght ^	16	202	8
Knockgraffon	12 (66 persons)	160 (986 persons)	7.5
Ballintemple union	16	216	7.5
Clonoulty	7	108	6.5
Clonbeg	14	228	6
Shanrahan #	23	428	5

Source: Religious census of 1766.
Key: ^ urban parish; + ecclesiastical centre; # planted area.

Appendix IX: Correlation between Anglican churches and Roman Catholic chapels
in South Tipperary, *c*.1730–*c*.1830

Anglican parish	Church	Glebe-house	Roman Catholic chapel
Ardfinnan	M (1724); 1807	1818–19	1830 Ballybacon
			1838 Ardfinnan
Ardmayle	M (<1815)	1822	*1810 Boherlahan*
Athassel (Golden)	M (<1760); 1807	1819	*1801* Golden
			1837–45 Kilfeakle
Ballingarry	1807–11	1814	1828
Ballintemple	M (<1695); 1862	1797	1806 *Knockavilla*
(Dundrum)			1730; 1901 Donaskeigh
Ballysheehan	1844	–	1826–30 *Dualla*
Bansha	M (1718), 1814	1793	*1807* Bansha
			1805 Kilmoyler
Cahir	M; 1816–20	1816	1791; 1833–9
Carrick-on-Suir	M; 1804; 1839	1816	*1804*; 1879–80
Cashel	M (to 1749); *1783*	1730–2	1795 Cashel
			1838 Rosegreen
Clonbeg	M (<1731); 1837	1788	*1835* Lisvernane
Clonmel	M; 1805; 1857–8	1805–06	1660s; *1850–60*
			1810 SS Peter and Paul
Clonoulty	M (<1730);1783;1856	1797	1803; 1878
Cullen	M (<1615); 1878–80	1819	1834; (Oola 1836)
			1872–87 Solohead
Donohill	1855	1880	1813; 1870 Annacarthy
(formerly Toem)	1700	1790	1821 Hollyford
			1824 Donohill
			1826 Cappaghwhite
Emly	M; 1790; 1827	1783/1796	1809; 1883
Fennor	1815	1824	*1813–15* Glengoole
Fethard	M (<1609)	1797	1818–19 Fethard
			1883 Killusty
Inishlounaght	M (1800); 1818	–	United to Clonmel
Kilcooley	M (<1730); 1829	1818	*1820* Gortnahoe
Killaloan	1825–7	–	1810 Kilsheelan
			1810 Kilcash
Killenaule	M (<1762); 1839	1780	1859–65
Kilshane	1859–60	–	–
Kilvemnon	M (1771); 1843	1788–93	1805 Grangemockler
			1839 Mullinahone
			1840 Ballyneale
Knockgraffon	M (1712); to New Inn, 1788	1788	1832 New Inn
			1799; 1846 Knockgraffon
Lismalin/Crohane	M (1716); *1846–7*	–	1806; 1850 Drangan
			1815 Cloneen
Lisronagh	*1831–2*	1818	1832; 1860
Mogorban	1807–16	1812	1838 Moyglass
Newchapel	M (<1771); *1819*	1791–2	1820 *Clerihan*
Outeragh	–	1825	United to Cahir
Rathronan	M (1730);1797;1825	–	1810 Powerstown

Anglican parish	Church	Glebe-house	Roman Catholic chapel
Shanrahan	M (<1723); *1819*; to Clogheen 1846	–	1740; 1820; 1862–4 1810 Burncourt
Shronell	M (1757); 1808	1829	1780; 1863–4 Lattin
Templetenny	*1827*	–	1828 Ballyporeen
Tipperary	M; *1730*; 1830	1784	1731; 1845–59
Tubrid	M (<1744); 1819	<1744; 1793	*1813 Ballylooby* 1829–30 Duhill
Tullaghmelan	*c.1780*	1817–18	1793; 1879; Newcastle 1829 *Grange*

M = church in continuous use since the Reformation.
M ([<] date) = church in Anglican use by this date.

Key: subsequent dates in same column indicate substantial remodelling or rebuilding; a date in bold *italics* may be seen as the instigation of renewal and dominant denomination in that particular parish and district; a location in ordinary *italics* is an example of a chapel village.

Sources: Seymour, *Cashel and Emly*; idem, *Diocese of Emly*; Skehan, *Cashel and Emly*; Wyse-Jackson, 'Old church plate'; Whelan, 'The Catholic Church'; Doyle, *Fragments*.

Appendix X: The order of construction of Roman Catholic chapels in South Tipperary

Portion of Cashel and Emly archdiocese		Portion of Waterford and Lismore diocese	
Lattin	1785; 1863–4	Cahir	1790–1; 1833–9; 1889
Cashel	1795	Newcastle	1793; 1879
Knockgraffon	1799; 1846	Carrick-on-Suir	1804; 1879–80
Golden	1801	Newtownlennon	1804; 1880
Clonoulty	1803; 1883	Grangemockler	1805; 1897
Kilmoyler	1805	Burncourt	1810
Knockavilla	1806	Kilcash	1810; 1885
Drangan	1806; 1850	Kilsheelan	1810; 1885
Bansha	1807	Powerstown	1810
Emly	1809; 1883	SS Peter and Paul	1810
Boherlahan	1810	Ballylooby	1813
Glengoole	1813–15	Clogheen	1820; 1862–4
Cloneen	1815	Ballyporeen	1828
Fethard	1818–19	Grange	1829
Gortnahoe	1820	Duhill	1829–30
Clerihan	1820	Ballybacon	1830
Hollyford	1821	Lisronagh	1832; 1860
Donohill	1824	Ardfinnan	1838
Cappaghwhite	1826	Ballyneale	1840
Dualla	1826–30	St Mary, Clonmel	1850
Ballingarry	1828		
New Inn	1832		
Holycross	1832		
Cullen	1833–4		
Lisvernane	1835		
Rosegreen	1838		
Moyglass	1838		

Portion of Cashel and Emly archdiocese

Mullinahone	1839
Kilfeakle	1845
Tipperary	1859
Killenaule	1859–65
Annacarthy	1870
Solohead	1872–87
Killusty	1883

Sources: Doyle, *Fragments*; Skehan, *Cashel and Emly*; Whelan, 'The Catholic Church'.

Appendix XI: A return of military barracks of South Tipperary and adjoining districts, 1811

South Tipperary

QUARTERS	PERMANENT					TEMPORARY				
	CAVALRY			INFANTRY		CAVALRY			INFANTRY	
	Officers	*men*	*horses*	*Officers*	*men*	*Officers*	*men*	*horses*	*Officers*	*men*
Ballypatrick										12
Cahir									30	812
Carrick-on-Suir	2	46	46	3	124				4	192
Cashel				5	228					100
Clerihan									1	22
Clonmel	15	132	132	4	183				28	1008
Clogheen	8	68	96							
Dundrum									1	30
Fethard	7	110	135							188
Killenaule										80
Mullinahone									3	50
Mocklershill									2	50
New Inn									1	20
New Birmingham									2	50
Tipperary									8	250
Total: 15 outposts	*32*	*356*	*409*	*12*	*535*				*80*	*2864*

388 cavalry and 3491 infantry = 3879 troops.

Kilkenny

QUARTERS	PERMANENT					TEMPORARY				
	CAVALRY			INFANTRY		CAVALRY			INFANTRY	
	Officers	*men*	*horses*	*Officers*	*men*	*Officers*	*men*	*horses*	*Officers*	*men*
Callan*						12	12		1	23
Castlecomer			8	164						
Freshford										20
Kells										20
Kilkenny	2	72	72	17	134				7	420
Kilmaganny										12
Kilmanagh										14
Thomastown										16
Urlingford*			3	75						30
Total 9 outposts	*2*	*72*	*72*	*28*	*373*	*12*	*12*		*8*	*555*

86 cavalry and 964 infantry = 1050 troops.

North Cork

QUARTERS	PERMANENT					TEMPORARY				
	CAVALRY			INFANTRY		CAVALRY			INFANTRY	
	Officers	*men*	*horses*	*Officers*	*men*	*Officers*	*men*	*horses*	*Officers*	*men*
Buttevant										250
Charleville									5	100
Fermoy	26	144	168	98	1992					188
Mallow	6	86	99						46	1000
Mitchelstown*									6	100
Total 5 outposts	*32*	*230*	*267*	*98*	*1992*				*57*	*1638*

262 cavalry and 3785 infantry = 4047 troops.

Waterford

QUARTERS	PERMANENT					TEMPORARY				
	CAVALRY			INFANTRY		CAVALRY			INFANTRY	
	Officers	*men*	*horses*	*Officers*	*men*	*Officers*	*men*	*horses*	*Officers*	*men*
Ballinamult*									2	50
Cappoquin*	4	3	56							
Dungarvan				6	96					
Kilmacthomas										100
Waterford City				20	576					
New Geneva				62	1728					
Tallow	8	68	76							
Total 7 outposts	*12*	*71*	*132*	*88*	*2400*				*2*	*150*

83 cavalry and 2640 infantry = 2723 troops.

North Tipperary

QUARTERS	PERMANENT					TEMPORARY				
	CAVALRY			INFANTRY		CAVALRY			INFANTRY	
	Officers	*men*	*horses*	*Officers*	*men*	*Officers*	*men*	*horses*	*Officers*	*men*
Borrisoleigh										40
Cappawhite*									1	40
Littleton*										50
Nenagh									2	636
Roscrea	1	21	16	8	345					
Templemore										60
Thurles*									3	150
Total 7 outposts	*1*	*21*	*16*	*8*	*345*				*6*	*976*

22 cavalry and 1335 infantry = 1357 troops.
Source: Kerrigan, 'A return of barracks in Ireland, 1811', *Irish Sword* 15 (1982).
* = barracks within 5 miles of South Tipperary county boundary

Appendix XII: A return of constabulary stations of South Tipperary
and adjoining districts, 1830–2

District	Station	Chief Constables		Constables		Sub- Constables		Total men in each station	
South Tipperary									
Cashel	Cashel	1	(1)	4	(3)	21	(19)	25	(22)
67 men	Mobarnane	–		1	(1)	2	(3)	3	(4)
11 stations	New Inn	–		1	(1)	4	(4)	5	(5)
	Camas	–		1	(1)	3	(2)	4	(3)
	Dundrum	–		1	(1)	4	(5)	5	(6)
	Rosegreen	–		1	(1)	5	(5)	6	(6)
	Ardmayle	–		1	(1)	3	(3)	4	(4)
	Peake	–		1	(–)	3	(3)	4	(4)
	Clonkelly	–		–		2	(–)	2	(–)
	Newpark	–		–		4	(4)	4	(4)
	Hymenstown	–		–	(1)	5	(3)	5	(4)
Clonmell	Clonmell	1	(1)	1	(1)	12	(9)	13	(10)
45 men	Carrick	–		1	(1)	5	(3)	6	(4)
8 stations	Kilcash	–		1	(1)	3	(3)	4	(4)
	Kilsheelan	–		1	(1)	3	(3)	4	(4)
	Clerihan	–		–	(1)	4	(3)	4	(4)
	Donegal	–		1	(1)	3	(2)	4	(3)
	Lisronagh	–		–	(1)	4	(3)	4	(4)
	Fethard	–		1	(1)	5	(4)	6	(5)
Caher	Caher	1	(1)	1	(1)	8	(7)	9	(8)
48 men	Clogheen	–		1	(1)	4	(3)	5	(4)
11 stations	Ardfinnan	–		–	(1)	4	(3)	4	(4)
	Newcastle	–		1	(1)	3	(3)	4	(4)
	Ballybeg	–		1	(1)	3	(2)	4	(3)
	Grange	–		–	(–)	4	(4)	4	(4)
	Woodrooffe	–		1	(1)	5	(4)	6	(5)
	Rehill	–		1	(1)	3	(3)	4	(4)
	Tubrid	–		1	(1)	2	(3)	3	(4)
	Ballyporeen	–		1	(1)	3	(3)	4	(4)
	Arraglin	–		–	(–)	1	(2)	1	(2)
Tipperary	Tipperary	1	(1)	1	(2)	9	(11)	10	(13)
58 men	Cullen	–		–	(1)	3	(3)	3	(4)
10 stations	Emly	–		1	(1)	4	(6)	5	(7)
	Carragheen	–		1	(1)	5	(5)	6	(6)
	Bansha	–		1	(1)	3	(4)	4	(5)
	Thomastown	–		1	(1)	5	(5)	6	(6)
	Golden	–		1	(1)	5	(5)	6	(6)
	Donaskeigh	–		1	(1)	4	(3)	5	(4)
	Greenfield	–		1	(1)	8	(5)	9	(6)
	Cappaghwhite	–		1	(1)	3	(3)	4	(4)
Killenaule	Killenaule	1	(1)	1	(1)	6	(8)	7	(9)
52 men	Ballinure	–		1	(1)	3	(3)	4	(4)
12 stations	Ballingarry	–		1	(1)	3	(3)	4	(4)
	Drangan	–		1	(1)	4	(4)	5	(5)
	Fennor	–		1	(1)	4	(3)	5	(4)

District	Station	Chief Constables	Constables	Sub-Constables	Total men in each station
	Grange	–	1 (1)	3 (3)	4 (5)
	Glamaskeogh	–	1 (1)	3 (3)	4 (4)
	Harleypark	–	– (–)	4 (4)	4 (4)
	Lisnamrock	–	– (1)	4 (3)	4 (4)
	Mullinahone	–	2 (2)	2 (3)	4 (5)
	Mardyke	–	1 (1)	2 (3)	3 (4)
	New Birmingham	–	1 (1)	3 (4)	4 (4)
5 districts	52 stations	5 (5)	45 (50)	212(212)	270(263)
Waterford					
Carrickbeg	Carrickbeg*	1 (1)	1 (1)	11 (5)	12 (6)
(part of)	Clonmel*	–	1 (1)	2 (2)	3 (3)
	Kilmanahan*	–	1 (1)	2 (3)	3 (4)
	Four-Mile-Water* 1	–	1 (1)	3 (3)	4 (4)
	4 stations	1 (1)	4 (4)	18 (13)	22 (17)
North Cork					
Mitchelstown	Mitchelstown*	1 (1)	1 (1)	7 (6)	8 (7)
(part of)	Mountain Barrack*	–	1 (2)	2 (2)	3 (4)
	Arraglin*	–	–	2 (2)	2 (2)
	3 stations	1 (1)	2 (3)	11 (10)	13 (13)
Limerick					
Nicker	Dromkeen*	–	1 (1)	3 (2)	4 (3)
(part of)	Cappamore*	–	1 (1)	5 (5)	6 (6)
	Castlelloyd*	–	1 (1)	3 (4)	4 (5)
	Doon*	–	1 (1)	5 (5)	6 (6)
Bruff (part of)	Galbally*	–	1 (1)	6 (4)	7 (5)
	Kilbehenny*	–	1 (1)	2 (3)	3 (4)
	6 stations	–	6 (6)	24 (23)	30 (29)
North Tipperary					
Thurles	Thurles	– (1)	2 (1)	12 (19)	14 (20)
	Ballycahill*	–	1 (–)	5 (6)	6 (6)
	Horse and Jockey*–	–	–	3 (3)	3 (3)
	3 stations	– (1)	3 (1)	20 (28)	23 (29)

Source: *Return of the number and distribution of constabulary force in Ireland, 1830–2* (1833).
* = station within 5 miles of South Tipperary county boundary

Figures for 1832 are recorded in brackets. Those barracks adjoining South Tipperary are listed below by district, for their importance in controlling upland areas and routes of communication.

Appendix XIII: Anglican population percentiles in parochial unions
of South Tipperary, 1834*

Parochial union	Per cent	Persons
Kilcooley	15.6	612
Mogorban	11.5	101
Clonmel	11.1	1,945
Erry	6.8	53
Ballintemple	5.0	230
Tipperary	4.8	614
Inishlounaght	4.2	182
Cashel	4.1	529
Fethard	4.1	414
Killenaule	4.0	339
Ardfinnan	3.7	63
Shronell	3.7	38
Cahir	3.5	269
Holycross	3.3	106
Lismalin/Crohane	3.2	152
Lisronagh	3.2	32
Tullaghmelan	3.0	30
Carrick-on-Suir	2.8	211
Athassel	2.7	197
Clonbeg	2.7	152
Fennor	2.7	58
Ballysheehan	2.5	72
Knockgraffon	2.5	92
Shanrahan	2.5	252
Toem	2.5	88

Source: *First report of the commissioners of public instruction.*
* Ballingarry (2.2: 126), Templeneiry (1.4: 135) and Tubrid (1.3: 116), though containing Anglican communities exceeding 100 persons, were below the minimum criteria for inclusion.

Bibliography

MANUSCRIPT SOURCES

Belfast
Grand Orange Lodge of Ireland, Schomberg House, Cregagh Road
MS registry of the loyal Orange institution in Ireland, 1834.
MS registry of the loyal Orange institution in Ireland, 1856.
Reports of proceedings of the Grand Lodge of Ireland at general half-yearly meetings.
Presbyterian Historical Society of Ireland, Church House, Fisherwick Place
Diary of the Revd John Cooke, 1700–5.
Extracts from the minutes of the transactions of the southern association of Protestant dissenting ministers (comprising the united presbyteries of Dublin and Munster), commencing in the year of Our Lord, 1809, by the Revd G.T.C. Clements, 1929.
Sketches of the history of Presbyterianism in Ireland by the Revd Dr William Campbell DD, written in the year 1803, while minister of Clonmel (1789–1805).

Cashel
Diocesan Archive of Cashel and Emly, Bolton Library, John Street
O'Callaghan estate (Shanbally Castle) papers: Mr Timothy Looney collection.
Ballintemple baptism and marriage register, 1805–44; communion attendance 1805–19; census of Ballintemple union of parishes, 1819; vestry minutes, 1805–71.
Cullen baptism, marriage and burial register, 1775–1911; church attendance, 1839–52.
Shronell vestry minutes, 1757–1833.
MS 10, Extract from 'Anne R[egina], an establishment or list containing all payments to be made for civil affaires from the twenty fifth day of March in the third year of our reigne, 1704'.

Chichester
West Sussex Record Office, County Hall, Orchard Road
Petworth House (Egremont) papers, deriving from the 3rd earl of Egremont,
PHA 6500 A book of maps of the estate of the Rt. Hon. Henry, earl of Thomond in the kingdom of Ireland, dated 1703, surveyed by Thomas Moland.
PHA 9342 A book of reference to the survey of the estate of Rt. Hon. Henry, earl of Thomond in the kingdom of Ireland by Thomas Moland, dated 1703.

Clonmel
Clonmel Union Parish Office, Old St Mary's Church, Mary Street
Cahir baptisms, 1801–30; marriages, 1804–30; burials, 1801–30.
Inishlounaght vestry minutes, 1804–72; Newchapel vestry minutes, 1806–72.
St Mary, Clonmel baptisms, 1766–1830; marriages, 1766–1830; burials, 1766–1830; vestry minutes, 1817–60; pew allocation of 1805 and 1820.
Tipperary (S.R.) County Museum, Emmet Street
1991.14, Map of Clonmel, the estate of John Bagwell, esq., surveyed by S. Chaloner, 1815.
1989.469, Map of Clonmel for Bagwell estate office, by P. Leahy and Sons, Clonmel, 1832.
1983.154, Minister's money account for Clonmel [Clonmel Incumbent booke], 1703.
D619, Minute book of the Clonmel Unitarian Church, Nelson Street, 1825–1923, with loose folios for 1757–1814.

Cork
Cork Archives Institute, Christ Church, South Main Street
MS U87-1, Minutes of vestry and other meetings of Cork Presbyterian meeting-house, Princes Street, Cork, 1717–1830.

Cork Baptist Church, MacCurtain Street
Cork Baptist Church book, 1653–1875.
Trinity Presbyterian Manse, Rochestown
Clonmel baptism register, 1833–42.
Special Collections, Boole Library, University College
Microfilm Neg. No. 823, Records of the births, marriages and burials of the Quakers of Co.
Tipperary monthly meeting, 1655–1859.

Dublin
Friends Historical Library, Swanbrook House, Bloomfield Avenue, Donnybrook
Grubb collection.
Deed and pamphlet collections.
Journal of William Lavery.
Grand Lodge of Freemasons, Molesworth Street
Membership registers of lodges: Cahir, no. 485; Carrick-on-Suir, nos. 268, 308; Cashel, nos. 95,
541, 770; Clonmel, nos. 44, 96, 279; Fethard, no. 484.
Irish Architectural Archive, Merrion Square
Box files of photographic material of Co. Tipperary, nos. 1–13.
National Archives of Ireland, Bishop Street
Cahir estate papers.
Grubb collection.
Outrage papers.
Ordnance survey collection.
Religious census of 1766 for Cashel and Emly dioceses.
National Library of Ireland, Kildare Street
The 'down survey' baronial maps.
Manuscript maps collection.
Registry of Deeds, Henrietta Street
Memorials of registered deeds.
Representative Church Body Library, Braemor Park, Churchtown
MS 33, Copy of 1607 royal visitation of Waterford, Lismore, Cashel and Emly.
MS 40, The Revd W.H. Rennison collection.
MS D 9, Waterford and Lismore rural deanery report, 1820.
MS D 10, Lismore diocesan visitation, 1836.
P4, Fethard vestry minutes, 1804–1904.
P79, A roll for conformists, kept by the Revd Charles Tuckey, Shanrahan, 1782–91.
P79 Shanrahan vestry minutes, 1725–96, 1797–1849.
Royal Irish Academy, Dawson Street
MS 12 D 36, A printed list of freeholders of the county of Tipperary, 1776.
MS 24 G 9, History of Cos. Limerick, Clare and Tipperary, by Charles Smith, c.1750.
Trinity College Manuscripts Department, College Green
MS 566, visitations of 1588, 1591, 1607.
MS 808, documents commission, 1622.
MSS 820–1, depositions of 1641–2; examinations of 1652–60.
MS 1066, Reeves copy of visitation of 1615.
MS 1067, Reeves copy of visitation of 1634.
MS 948, Bishop Stock visitation diary, 1811.

London
Lambeth Palace Library
MS 1742/P/8973, An abstract of the numbers of Protestant and Popish families in the several
baronies, counties and provinces of Ireland, 1732

Private Custody
A Plymouth Brethren memoir, by Evangeline Maud Mandeville, written in 1975, when in her 92nd year
(Mr Geoffrey Mandeville, Anner Castle, Clonmel).

Baptism and marriage register of Clonmel Unitarian congregation, Nelson Street, commenced July 1825, with loose folios for 1808–14 (Mr Steven ffeary-Smyrl, Dublin).

Deeds of conveyance (1720–1900), relating to Lismoynan and Peppardstown, formerly part of the Jacob estate (Mrs Heffernan-Delany, Parsons Hill House, Fethard).

Family reminiscences of the Jellico(e)s of Co. Tipperary, Ireland, compiled by Richard Carey Jellicoe (1875–1961), *c.*1950 (Mrs Sara Jellicoe-Cobley, England).

Thurles

Kilcooley Rectory, Grange, Barna

Kilcooley vestry minute book: pew allocation of 1829.

Waterford

Mount Melleray Abbey, Cappoquin

The Very Revd William P. Canon Burke collection.

Municipal Library, Waterford

Diary of James Ryan (1757–1809), Carrick-on-Suir.

Diary of Patrick Hayden (1774–1851), Carrick-on-Suir.

PARLIAMENTARY PAPERS

Account of number of parishes, benefices, churches and glebe houses in Ireland, 8 (1802–3)

Returns presented to the House of Commons, in pursuance of their orders of the 5th June 1805, from the several dioceses in Ireland, 14 (1806)

A list of the parishes in Ireland, with the names of their respective incumbents and distinguishing those parishes in which the incumbent is not resident, 11 (1824)

Minutes of evidence taken before the select committee of the House of Lords appointed to inquire into the state of Ireland, 9 (1825)

Second report of the commissioners of Irish education inquiry, 12 (1826–7)

First report of the royal commission on ecclesiastical revenue and patronage in Ireland, 21 (1833)

Return of the number and distribution of the constabulary force in Ireland, 1830–2, 32 (1833)

Second report of the royal commission on ecclesiastical revenue and patronage in Ireland, 23 (1834)

First report of the ecclesiastical commissioners of Ireland on the temporalities of the Church of Ireland, 22 (1835)

First report of the select committee on Orange lodges, associations or societies in Ireland: minutes of evidence and appendices, 15 (1835)

Second and third reports of the select committee on Orange lodges, associations or societies in Ireland: minutes of evidence and appendices, 15 (1835)

First report of the commissioners of public instruction, 46 (1836)

Third report of the royal commission on ecclesiastical revenue and patronage in Ireland, 25 (1836)

Royal commission on the condition of the poorer classes in Ireland, 39 (1836)

Fourth report of the royal commission on ecclesiastical revenue and patronage in Ireland, 21 (1837)

Return of sums appropriated by the ecclesiastical commissioners to repair and rebuilding of churches in Ireland, 1834–7, 41 (1837)

A return of the number of churches and chapels built or rebuilt or enlarged in Ireland since September 1833, 43 (1844)

Correspondence between Irish government and congregation of Clonmel, in connexion with general assembly of Presbyterian Church and presbytery of Cork, respecting withholding Regium Donum, 49 (1847–8)

Correspondence between moderator of general assembly of Presbyterian Church in Ireland and Irish government, relative to stoppage of Regium Donum of minister of Clonmel, July 1848–50, 51 (1850)

Primary valuation of tenements in the South Riding of Co. Tipperary in August 1850, as surveyed by Richard Griffith, 51 (1850)

Report of the commissioners to enquire into the state of fairs and markets in Ireland, 41 (1852–3)

Return of lands and houses belonging to the Established Church in Ireland, 58 (1854)

Calendar of state papers relating to Ireland, 1509–1670 (1860–1912: 24 vols)
Return of number of parishes in the dioceses of Cashel and Waterford, 44 (1864)
Return of names of churches built and repaired by ecclesiastical commissioners in Ireland, 1834–65, 54 (1867)

PRINTED SOURCES
♦ denotes primary sources

Acheson, A., *A history of the Church of Ireland, 1691–1996* (Dublin, 1997)
Adams, W.F., *Ireland and Irish emigration to the new world from 1815 to the Famine* (Baltimore, 1980)
Agnew, D.C.A., *Protestant exiles from France in the reign of Louis XIV, or the Huguenot refugees and their descendants in Great Britain and Ireland* (London, 1871–4: 2nd ed.)
Ahern, M., 'The Quaker schools in Clonmel', *Tipperary Historical Journal* 3 (1990), 128–32
—, 'Clonmel charter school', *Tipperary Historical Journal* 5 (1992), 148–52
—, 'Clonmel grammar school', *Tipperary Historical Journal* 6 (1993), 128–34
—, 'Clonmel model school', *Tipperary Historical Journal* 9 (1996), 110–16
A history of congregations in the Presbyterian Church in Ireland, 1610–1982 (Belfast, 1982)
Akenson, D.H., *The Church of Ireland: ecclesiastical reform and revolution 1800–85* (New Haven, Conn., 1971)
—, *Small differences: Irish Catholics and Irish Protestants, 1815–1922* (Montreal, 1991)
Allen, F.N.A. et al. (eds), *Atlas of the Irish rural landscape* (Cork, 1997)
♦*An alarm to Protestant princes and people, who are struck at in the popish cruelties at Thorn and other barbarous executions abroad* (London, 1725)
Annacarthy-Donohill history (Tipperary, 1997)
Andrews, J.H., 'Geography and government in Elizabethan Ireland' in Stephens and Glassack (eds), *Irish geographical studies* (Belfast, 1970), 178–91
—, *History in the ordnance map: an introduction for Irish readers* (Dublin, 1974)
—, *A paper landscape: the ordnance survey in nineteenth century* Ireland (London, 1975)
—, 'Land and people, *c.*1685' in Moody, Martin and Byrne (eds), *A new history of Ireland*, iii (1976), 454–77
—, *Plantation acres: a historical study of the Irish land surveyor and his maps* (Belfast, 1985)
—, 'Land and people, *c.*1780' in Moody and Vaughan (eds), *A new history of Ireland*, iv (1986), 236–64
—, *Shapes of Ireland: maps and their makers, 1564–1839* (Dublin, 1997)
—, 'Plantation Ireland: a review of settlement history' in Barry (ed.), *A history of settlement in Ireland* (2000), 140–57
—, 'The mapping of Ireland's cultural landscape, 1550–1630' in Duffy et al. (eds), *Gaelic Ireland, c.1250–c.1650* (2001), 153–80
♦Archdall, M., *The peerage of Ireland, or a genealogical history of the present nobility of that kingdom, by John Lodge esq., revised, enlarged and continued to the present time by Mervyn Archdall* (Dublin, 1789)
Bagwell, R., *Ireland under the Tudors: with a succinct account of the earlier period* (London, 1885–90: 3 vols)
Baker, A.F., 'The Bakers of Lismacue: a family chronicle', *Tipperary Historical Journal* 7 (1994), 115–28
♦Bale, J., *The vocacyon of John Bale to the bishoprick of Ossorie* (Basel, 1563; repr. New York, 1990, for Renaissance English Text Society, ed. by P. Happe and J.N. King)
Banham, T., 'The Non-Subscribing Presbyterian Church of Ireland' in Richardson (ed.), *A tapestry of beliefs* (1997)
Barnard, T.C., 'Planters and policies in Cromwellian Ireland', *Past and Present* 61 (1973), 31–69
—, *Cromwellian Ireland: English government and reform in Ireland, 1649–60* (Oxford, 1975)
—, 'Crises of identity among Irish Protestants 1641–85', *Past and Present* 127 (1990), 39–83

—, 'Protestants and the Irish language, *c.*1675–1725', *Journal of Ecclesiastical History* 44 (1993), 243–72

—, '1641: A bibliographical essay' in B. MacCuarta (ed.), *Ulster 1641: aspects of the rising* (Belfast, 1993), 173–86

—, 'The Protestant interest, 1641–60' in Ohlmeyer (ed.), *Ireland from independence to occupation* (1995), 36–50

—, 'Protestantism, ethnicity and Irish identities, 1660–1760' in Claydon and McBride (eds), *Protestantism and national identity* (1998), 206–35

—, 'The origins of Empire' in W.R. Louis and N.P. Canny (eds), *The Oxford history of the British Empire, vol. I: British overseas expansion to the close of the seventeenth century* (Oxford, 1998), 309–27

Barry, T. (ed.), *A history of settlement in Ireland* (London, 2000)

Bartlett, T., 'The origins and progress of the Catholic question in Ireland, 1690–1800' in Power and Whelan (eds), *Endurance and emergence* (1990), 21–48

—, 'An account of the Whiteboys from the 1790s', *Tipperary Historical Journal* 4 (1991), 141–8

—, 'Informers, informants and information: the secret history of the 1790s', *History Ireland* 6:2 (1998), 23–6

Bateman, J., *The great landowners of Great Britain and Ireland* (New York, 1971)

◆Beard, J. (ed.), *Unitarianism: its actual condition* (London, 1846)

◆Beaufort, D.A., *Memoir of a map of Ireland* (London, 1792)

Beckett, J.C., *Protestant dissent in Ireland, 1687–1780* (London, 1948)

—, *The making of modern Ireland, 1603–1923* (London, 1966)

—, *The Anglo-Irish tradition* (Belfast, 1982)

—, 'Eighteenth century Ireland: an introduction' in Moody and Vaughan, *A new history of Ireland,* iv (1986), pp xxxiv–lxvi

—, 'The Anglo-Irish' in P. Loughrey (ed.), *The people of Ireland* (Belfast, 1988)

◆Belehar, J., *The Baptist Irish society: its origins and prospects* (London, 1845)

Bence-Jones, M., 'The trust of landowning' in Townend (ed.), *Burke's genealogy and heraldic history of the landed gentry* (London, 1965: 18th ed.)

—, *Twilight of the ascendancy* (London, 1987)

—, *A guide to Irish country houses* (London, 1990: 2nd revised ed.)

Bergin, W.J., 'Military barracks, Cahir and military barracks, Clogheen', *An Cosantóir* (July 1984), 243–4

Biggs-Davidson, J., *Catholics and the Union* (Belfast, 1972)

Bliss, A., *Spoken English in Ireland, 1600–1740* (Dublin, 1979)

Boal, F.W., J.A. Campbell and D.N. Livingstone, 'The Protestant mosaic: a majority of minorities' in P.J. Roche and B. Barton (eds), *The Northern Ireland question: myth and reality* (Belfast, 1991)

Bossy, J., 'The Counter-Reformation and the people of Catholic Ireland, 1596–1641' in T.D. Williams (ed.), *Historical studies 8: papers read before the Irish conference of historians, Dublin, 27–30 May 1969* (Dublin, 1971), 155–69

Bottigheimer, K.S., *English money and Irish land: the adventurers in the Cromwellian settlement of Ireland* (New York, 1971)

—, 'The Reformation in Ireland revisited', *Journal of British Studies* 15:2 (1976), 140–9

—, 'The failure of the Reformation in Ireland: une question bien posée', *Journal of Ecclesiastical History* 36:2 (1985), 196–207

— and U. Lotz-Heumann, 'Ireland and the European Reformation', *History Ireland* 6:4 (1998), 13–16

Bottigheimer, K.S., 'The Irish Reformation in the European perspective', *Archive for Reformation History* 89 (1999), 268–309

Bourke, M., 'Erasmus Smith and Tipperary grammar school', *Tipperary Historical Journal* 2 (1989), 82–99

—, 'Guide to Tipperary newspapers (1770–1989): a supplement', *Tipperary Historical Journal* 3 (1990), 204

—, 'Journal of the Cork historical and archaeological society: an index to Tipperary material', *Tipperary Historical Journal* 5 (1992), 57–62

◆Bowden, C.T., *A tour through Ireland in 1790* (Dublin, 1791)

Bowen, D., *Souperism: myth or reality?* (Cork, 1970)

—, *The Protestant crusade in Ireland, 1800–80: a study of Protestant-Catholic relations between the Act of Union and disestablishment* (Dublin, 1973)

—, *History and shaping of Irish Protestantism, vol. 4: Irish studies* (New York, 1994)

Bowen, K., *Protestants in a Catholic state: Ireland's privileged minority* (Montreal, 1983)

Boyce, D.G., *Ireland, 1828–1993: from ascendancy to democracy* (Oxford, 1992)

—, R. Eccleshall and V. Geoghegan (eds), *Political discourse in seventeenth and eighteenth century Ireland* (London, 2001)

Boyle, P., *The Irish college in Paris, 1578–1901* (London, 1901)

Braddick, M.J. and J. Walter (eds), *Negotiating power in early modern society: order, hierarchy and subordination in Britain and Ireland* (Cambridge, 2001)

Bradshaw, B., *The dissolution of the religious orders in Ireland under Henry VIII* (London, 1974)

—, 'Fr Wolfe's description of Limerick, 1574', *North Munster Antiquarian Journal* 17 (1975), 47–53

—, 'The Edwardian Reformation in Ireland, 1547–53', *Archivium Hibernicum* 34 (1977), 83–98

—, 'Sword, word and strategy in the Reformation in Ireland', *History Journal* 21:3 (1978), 475–502

— (ed.), 'A treatise for the Reformation of Ireland, 1554–5', *Irish Jurist* 16 (1981), 299–315

—, 'The Reformation in the cities: Cork, Limerick and Galway, 1534–1603' in Bradley (ed.), *Settlement and society in medieval Ireland: studies presented to Francis Xavier Martin OSA* (Kilkenny, 1988), 445–76

—, 'Robe and sword in the conquest of Ireland', in C. Cross, D. Loades and J.J. Scarisbrick (eds), *Law and government under the Tudors: presented to Sir Geoffrey Elton ... on the occasion of his retirement* (Cambridge, 1988)

— et al., *Representing Ireland: literature and the origins of the conflict, 1534–1660* (Cambridge, 1993)

Bradshaw, B., 'Geoffrey Keating: apologist of Irish Ireland' in Bradshaw et al., *Representing Ireland,* 166–90

— and J. Morrill (eds), *The British problem, c.1534–1707: state formation in the Atlantic archipelago* (London, 1996)

— and P. Roberts (eds), *British consciousness and identity: the making of Britain, 1533–1707* (Cambridge, 1998)

—, 'The English Reformation and identity formation in Ireland and Wales', in Bradshaw and Roberts, *British consciousness and* identity (1998), 43–111

Brady, C., 'Court, castle and country: the framework of government in Tudor Ireland', in Brady and Gillespie (eds), *Natives and newcomers* (1986)

Brady, C. and R. Gillespie (eds), *Natives and newcomers: essays on the making of Irish colonial society, 1534–1641* (Dublin, 1986)

◆Brady, J., 'Catholics and Catholicism in the eighteenth century press: appendix', *Archivium Hibernicum* 16 (1951), 1–112

—, 'The Irish colleges in Europe and the Counter-Reformation', *Proceedings of the Irish Catholic Historical Committee* (1957), 1–8

◆—, 'Proposals to register Irish priests, 1756–7', *Irish Ecclesiastical Record* 47 (1962), 209–22

—, *Catholics and Catholicism in the eighteenth century press* (Dublin, 1965)

Breathnach, C., 'Archbishop John Brenan (1625–93): his life and work', *Tipperary Historical Journal* 6 (1993), 148–159

◆Brewer, J.N., *The beauties of Ireland, being the original delineations, topographical, historical and bibliographical of each county* (London, 1825–6: 3 vols)

Bric, M.J., 'The Whiteboy movement, 1760–80' in Nolan and McGrath, *Tipperary: history and society* (1985)

Broderick E., 'The Famine and religious controversy in Waterford, 1847–50, *Decies* 51 (1996), 11–24

—, 'Waterford's Anglicans: religion and politics, 1819–72' (PhD, UCC, 2000)

Broeker, G., *Rural disorder and police reform in Ireland, 1812–36* (London, 1970)

Brown, T., *The state of the Protestant minority in Ireland: a social and cultural history* (Dublin, 1981)

—, *The whole Protestant community: the making of a historical myth* (Derry, 1985)

Buchanan, R.H., 'Historical geography of Ireland, pre–1700' in Herries Davies (ed.), *Irish geography* (1984)

—, 'Towns and plantations, 1500–1700' in Nolan (ed.), *The shaping of Ireland* (1986), 84–98

◆Buckley, J., 'A tour in Ireland in 1672–4', *JWSEIAS* 10 (1904), 85–100

◆Buckley, J., 'A vice-regal progress through the south and west of Ireland in 1567', *JWSEIAS* 12 (1909), 61–76; 132–46; 179–84

Buckley, P. and G. Riordan, *History of a Tipperary parish: Lattin-Cullen* (Tipperary, 1984)

Burke, J., *Burke's peerage and baronetage* (London, 1970: 105th ed.)

◆Burke, T., *Hibernia Dominicana* (Cologne, 1762)

◆Bush, J., *Hibernia curiosa: collected in a tour through the kingdom in the year 1764* (Dublin, 1769)

Burke, W.P., *History of Clonmel* (Waterford, 1907)

—, *Irish priests in the penal times* (Waterford, 1914)

Butler, D.J., 'An historical geography of the Irish Baptist churches, 1650–1870', *Chimera: UCC Geographical Journal* 13 (1998), 56–62

—, 'The meeting-house of the Protestant dissenter: a study of design, layout and location in southern Ireland [mainly Cork and South Tipperary]', *Chimera: UCC Geographical Journal* 14 (1999), 118–24

—, *Cahir: a guide to heritage town and district* (Cahir, 1999)

—, 'Presbyterianism in the Fethard district, c.1690–1919: part 1', *Tipperary Historical Journal* 13 (2000), 64–72; part 2, *Tipperary Historical Journal* 14 (2001), 129–37

—, 'The Jehovah's witnesses in Ireland: origins, settlement, distribution and territorial organization', *Chimera: UCC Geographical Journal* 15 (2000), 30–7

—, 'Representing Christianity in Ireland: the literature of the origin legend', *Chimera: UCC Geographical Journal* 16 (2001), 92–100

—, 'Beyond Roman Catholicism: other aspects of Christianity in Carrick-on-Suir since the Reformation', *Tipperary Historical Journal* 15 (2002), 127–43

—, 'A survival of the fittest': Protestant dissenting congregations in Cork, Waterford and Tipperary, c.1660–1810', *Chimera: UCC Geographical Journal* 17 (2002), 86–96

—, 'Butler of Rouskagh, Co. Tipperary', *Journal of the Butler Society* 4:3 (2003), 453–61

—, 'Presbyterianism in Clonmel, 1650–1977', *Tipperary Historical Journal* 16 (2003), 81–101

—, 'Historical background to the Fair of Cahir – patent granted in 1614' in *The Fair of Cahir Meets Scarborough Fair Commemorative Magazine* (2003), 13–15.

—, 'House of Rouskagh: the obscuring of a cadet branch of the Butlers of Cahir', *Irish Genealogist* 11:2 (2003), 118–34

—, 'Contesting hegemony: the historical geography of the Protestant and Roman Catholic communities of South Tipperary, c.1570–c.1841' (PhD, UCC, 2003), abstract in *Irish Economic and Social History* 31 (2004), 74–6

—, 'Defence from the dispossessed: the state-sponsored garrisoning of the South Tipperary landscape, c.1650–c.1730', *Irish Sword* 24:95 (2004), 45–56

—, 'Controlling insurrection: garrisons, police barracks and bridewells in South Tipperary, c.1750–c.1840', *Irish Sword* 25:97 (2005), 291–301

Butlin, R.A., 'Land and people, c.1600' in Moody, Martin and Byrne (eds), *A new history of Ireland*, iii (1976), 142–67

— (ed.), *The development of the Irish town* (London, 1977)

Caball, M., 'Providence and exile in early seventeenth century Ireland', *IHS* 29:114 (1994), 174–88

—, 'Faith, culture and sovereignty: Irish nationality and its development, 1558–1625' in Bradshaw and Roberts (eds), *British consciousness and identity* (1998), 112–39

Cairns, A., 'The Independents in Ireland' (PhD, QUB, 1952)

Cairns, D. and S. Richards, *Writing Ireland: colonialism, nationalism and culture* (Manchester, 1988)

Caldicott, C.E.J. et al. (eds), *The Huguenots and Ireland: anatomy of an emigration* (Dun Laoghaire, Co. Dublin, 1987)

◆Campbell, T., *A philosophical survey of the south of Ireland in a series of letters, 1775–7* (Dublin, 1778)

Canny, N.P., *The Elizabethan conquest of Ireland: a pattern established, 1565–76* (Brighton, 1976)

—, 'The permissive frontier: the problem of social control in English settlements in Ireland and Virginia, 1550–1650', in K.R. Andrews, N.P. Canny and P.E.H. Hair (eds), *The westward enterprise: English activities in Ireland, the Atlantic and America, 1480–1650* (Liverpool, 1978)

—, 'Dominant minorities: English settlers in Ireland and Virginia, 1550–1650' in Hepburn (ed.), *Minorities in history: Historical Studies 12* (1978), 51–69

—, 'Why the Reformation failed in Ireland: une question mal posée', *Journal of Ecclesiastical History* 30:4 (1979), 423–50

—, 'Edmund Spenser and the development of an Anglo-Irish identity' in Hunter and Rawson (eds), *The Yearbook of English Studies, vol. 13: colonial and imperial themes special number* (London, 1983), 1–19

—, 'Migration and opportunity: Britain, Ireland and the new world', *Irish Economic and Social History* 12 (1985), 7–32

—, 'Protestants, planters and apartheid in early modern Ireland', *IHS* 25:8 (1986), 105–15

—, *From Reformation to Restoration: Ireland, 1534–1660* (Dublin, 1987)

—, 'Identity formation in Ireland: the emergence of the Anglo-Irish' in N. Canny and A. Pagden (eds), *Colonial identity in the Atlantic world, 1500–1800* (Princeton, 1987), 159–212

—, 'Early modern Ireland, c.1500–1700' in R. Foster (ed.), *The Oxford illustrated history of Ireland* (Oxford, 1992), 88–133

—, 'The 1641 depositions: a source for social and cultural history', *History Ireland* 1:4 (1993), 52–5

—, 'The attempted Anglicization of Ireland in the seventeenth century: an exemplar of "British History"', in R.G. Asch (ed.), *Three nations – a common history?: England, Scotland, Ireland and British history, c.1600–1920* (Bochum, 1993)

—, 'English migration into and across the Atlantic during the seventeenth and eighteenth centuries' in N.P. Canny (ed.), *Europeans on the move: studies on European migration, 1500–1800* (Oxford, 1994)

—, 'What really happened in Ireland in 1641?' in Ohlmeyer (ed.), *Ireland from independence to occupation* (1995), 1–25

—, *Making Ireland British, 1580–1650* (Oxford, 2001)

Cappamore: a parish history (Cappamore, 1992)

◆Carleton, S.T., *Heads and hearths: the hearth money rolls and poll tax returns for Co. Antrim, 1660–9* (Belfast, 1991)

Carlin, D., 'Extreme or mainstream?: the English Independents and the Cromwellian reconquest of Ireland, 1649–51' in Bradshaw et al., *Representing Ireland* (1993), 209–26

◆Carlisle, B., *A topographical dictionary of Ireland* (London, 1810)

◆Carr, J., *The stranger in Ireland, or a tour in the southern and western parts of that country in 1805* (London: 1806, repr. Shannon, 1970)

Carrigan, W., *The history and antiquities of the diocese of Ossory* (Dublin, 1905: 4 vols)

◆Carrigan, W., 'Catholic episcopal wills (province of Dublin), 1683–1812', *Archivium Hibernicum* 4 (1915), 66–95

◆Carte, T., *An history of the life of James, duke of Ormond, from his birth in 1610, to his death in 1688, wherein is contained an account of the most remarkable affairs of his time ... in two volumes, to which is added, for the satisfaction of the curious, in another volume, a very valuable collection of letters* (London, 1735–6: 3 vols; repr. Oxford, 1851: 6 vols)

◆Chetwood, W.R., *A tour through Ireland in several entertaining letters by two English gentlemen* (Dublin, 1748)

Chapman, A., 'The Religious Society of Friends (Quakers) in Ireland' in Richardson (ed.), *A tapestry of beliefs* (1997)

Christmas, B., 'Some Protestant settlers in Ireland, 1662–1737', *Irish Genealogist* 7:3 (1988), 349–57

Clarke, A., 'Colonial identity in early seventeenth century Ireland' in T.W. Moody (ed.) *Nationality and the pursuit of national independence: historical studies 11* (Belfast, 1978), 57–71

—, 'Ireland, 1534–1660' in Lee (ed.) *Irish historiography* (Cork, 1981), 34–55

—, 'The Irish economy, 1600–60' in Moody, Martin and Byrne (eds), *A new history of Ireland*, iii (1976), 168–86

— and R. Dudley-Edwards, 'Pacification, plantation and the Catholic question, 1603–23' in *A new history of Ireland*, iii (1976), 187–232

Clarke, A., 'The breakdown of authority, 1640–1' in *A new history of Ireland*, iii (1976), 270–88

—, 'Colonial attitudes in Ireland, 1640–60', *PRIA* C 90:2 (1990), 357–75

—, 'Varieties of uniformity: the first century of the Church of Ireland, 1618–48', *Journal of Ecclesiastical History* 2 (1989), 202–21

Clark, J.C.D., 'Protestantism, nationalism and national identity, 1660–1832', *History Journal* 43:1 (2000), 249–76

Clarkson, L.A., 'The Carrick-on-Suir woollen industry in the eighteenth century', *Irish Economic and Social History* 16 (1989), 23–41

Claydon, T. and I. McBride (eds), *Protestantism and national identity: Britain and Ireland, c.1650–c.1850* (Cambridge, 1998)

— (eds), 'The trials of the chosen peoples: recent interpretations of Protestantism and national identity in Britain and Ireland' in Claydon and McBride, *Protestantism and national identity* (1998), 3–32

Cockton, P., *Subject catalogue of the House of Commons parliamentary papers, 1801–1900, vol. 4: Ireland* (Cambridge, 1988)

Coles, M., 'The Congregational union of Ireland' in Richardson (ed.), *A tapestry of beliefs* (1997)

Comerford, R.V. et al. (eds), *Religion, conflict and co-existence in Ireland* (Dublin, 1990)

◆Comyn, D. and P.S. Dineen (eds), *Foras feasa ar Éireann: the history of Ireland (c.1633) by the Revd Dr Geoffrey Keating* (London, 1902–14: 4 vols)

Conlan, P., *Franciscan Ireland* (Cork, 1978)

Connolly, J., 'The parish community and the mystical body in rural Ireland', *Economic and Social Review* 1 (1961), 531–54

Connolly, S.J., *The published record: sources for local studies in the Public Records Office of Ireland* (Dublin, 1982)

—, *Priests and people in pre-Famine Ireland, 1780–1845* (New York, 1982: repr. Dublin, 2000)

—, *Religion and society in nineteenth century Ireland: studies in Irish economic and social history 3* (Dublin, 1985)

—, *Religion, law and power: the making of Protestant Ireland, 1660–1760* (Oxford, 1992)

—, et al., *Conflict, identity and economic development: Ireland and Scotland, 1600–1939* (Lancashire, 1995)

— (ed.), *The Oxford companion to Irish history* (Oxford, 1998)

—, *Kingdoms united?: Great Britain and Ireland since 1500: identity and divergence* (Dublin, 1999)

—, *Political ideas in eighteenth century Ireland since 1500: identity and divergence* (Dublin, 2000)

Cook-Meyers, A., *The emigration of the Irish Quakers to Pennsylvania, 1682–1747* (Pennsylvania, 1902)

Coombes, J., 'The beatified martyrs of Ireland (5): Maurice MacKenraghty', *Irish Theological Quarterly* 65:1 (2000), 57–64

Corish, P.J., 'The rising of 1641 and the Catholic confederacy, 1641–5' in Moody, Martin and Byrne (eds), *A new history of Ireland*, iii (1976), 289–316

—, 'Ormond, Rinuccini and the confederates, 1645–9' in Moody, Martin and Byrne (eds), *A new history of Ireland*, iii (1976), 317–35

—, 'The Cromwellian conquest, 1649–53' in Moody, Martin and Byrne (eds), _A new history of Ireland_, iii (1976) 336–52

—, 'The Cromwellian Regime, 1650–60' in Moody, Martin and Byrne (eds), _A new history of Ireland_, iii (1976), 353–86

—, 'The rising of 1641 and the Catholic confederacy, 1641–5' in Moody, Martin and Byrne (eds), _A new history of Ireland_, iii (1976), 289–316

—, 'Irish ecclesiastical history since 1500' in Lee (ed.), _Irish historiography_ (1981), 154–72

—, _The Catholic community in the seventeenth and eighteenth centuries_ (Dublin, 1981)

—, _The Irish Catholic experience: a historical survey_ (Dublin, 1985)

Corkery, D., _The hidden Ireland: a study of Gaelic Munster in the eighteenth century_ (Dublin, 1967)

Coughlan, P. (ed.), _Spenser and Ireland: an interdisciplinary perspective_ (Cork, 1989)

Cowman, D., 'The Reformation bishops of the diocese of Waterford and Lismore or notes for the Atherton file, _c._1540–_c._1640', _Decies_ 27 (1984), 31–7

◆Crofton-Croker, T. (ed.), _The tour of M. de la Boullaye le Gouez in Ireland, 1644_ (London, 1832)

Cromie, A.S., _Controversy amongst southern Presbyterians_ (Belfast, 1999)

Crookshank, A., 'The visual arts, 1603–1740' in Moody and Vaughan (eds), _A new history of Ireland_, iv (1986), 471–98

—, 'The visual arts, 1740–1850' in Moody and Vaughan (eds), _A new history of Ireland_, iv (1986), 499–541

—, and The Knight of Glin, _The watercolours of Ireland: works on paper, in pencil, pastel and paint, c.1600–1914_ (London, 1994)

Crookshank, C.H., _Days of revival, being the history of Methodism in Ireland, 1747–1859_ (Clonmel, 1994)

Crossman, V., _Politics, law and order in nineteenth century Ireland_ (Dublin, 1996)

Cullen, L.M., _An economic history of Ireland since 1660_ (London, 1972)

—, 'Economic trends, 1660–91' in Moody, Martin and Byrne (eds), _A new history of Ireland_, iv (1976), 387–407

—, 'Eighteenth century flour milling in Ireland', _Irish Economic and Social History_, 4 (1977), 5–25

—, _The emergence of modern Ireland, 1600–1900_ (London, 1981)

— and F. Furet (eds) _Ireland and France, 17th century to 20th century: towards a comparative study of rural history_ (Paris, 1981)

Cullen, L.M., 'Incomes, social classes and economic growth in Ireland and Scotland, 1600–1900' in Devine and Dickson (eds), _Ireland and Scotland, 1600–1850: parallels and contrasts in economic and social development_ (Edinburgh, 1983), 248–60

—, 'Economic development, 1691–1750' in Moody and Vaughan (eds), _A new history of Ireland_, iv (1986), 123–58

—, 'Economic development, 1750–1800' in Moody and Vaughan (eds), _A new history of Ireland_, iv (1986), 159–95

—, _The economic history of Ireland since 1600_ (London, 1987: 2nd ed.)

—, 'The Catholic social classes under the penal laws' in Power and Whelan (eds), _Endurance and emergence_ (1990)

Cunningham, B., 'Native culture and political change in Ireland, 1580–1640', in Brady and Gillespie (eds), _Natives and newcomers_ (1986), 148–70

—, 'Geoffrey Keating's _Eochair sqiath an aifrinn_ and the Catholic Reformation in Ireland' in Sheils and Wood (eds), _The churches, Ireland and the Irish: studies in church history_ vol. 25 (Oxford, 1989), 133–43

— and R. Gillespie, 'Englishmen in sixteenth-century Irish annals', _Irish Economic and Social History_ 17 (1990), 5–21

Cunningham, B., 'The culture and ideology of Irish Franciscan historians at Louvain, 1607–50' in C. Brady (ed.), _Ideology and the historians_ (Dublin, 1991), 11–30

— and R. Gillespie, 'The most adaptable of Irish saints: the cult of Saint Patrick in the seventeenth century', _Archivium Hibernicum_ 49 (1995), 82–104

Cunningham, B., _The world of Geoffrey Keating: history, myth and religion in seventeenth century Ireland_ (Dublin, 2000)

—, 'Representations of king, parliament and the Irish people in Geoffrey Keating's *Foras Feasa ar Éirinn* and John Lynch's *Cambrensis Eversus* (1662)' in Ohlmeyer (ed.), *Political thought in seventeenth-century Ireland* (Cambridge, 2000), 131–54

Currie, D., 'The Christian Brethren' in Richardson (ed.), *A tapestry of beliefs* (1997)

Curtis, E. and R.B., McDowell, *Irish historical documents, 1172–1922* (London, 1968)

Dalsimer, A.M. and V. Kreilkamp, *Visualising Ireland: national identity and the pictorial tradition* (London, 1993)

d'Alton, I., 'A contrast in crises: southern Irish Protestantism, 1820–43 and 1885–1910' in Hepburn (ed.), *Minorities in history: historical studies 12* (1978), 70–83

—, *Protestant society and politics in Cork, 1812–44* (Cork, 1980)

◆Danaher, K. and J.G. Simms (eds), *The Danish force in Ireland, 1690–1* (Dublin, 1962)

Darmody, W.C., 'The Franciscans in Clonmel' in O'Connell and Darmody (eds), *Siege of Clonmel commemoration* (1950), 52–6

de Breffney, B. and G. Mott, *The churches and abbeys of Ireland* (London, 1976)

◆Deighan, P., *A complete treatise on the geography of Ireland* (Dublin, 1810)

◆De Latocayne, *Rambles through Ireland by a French emigrant* (Cork, 1798)

Dickson, D., 'Property and social structure in eighteenth century south Munster' in L.M. Cullen and F. Furet (eds) *Ireland and France* (Paris, 1981), 129–38

— et al., 'Hearth tax, household size and Irish population change, 1672–1821', *PRIA C 82:6* (1982), 125–81

—, *New foundations: Ireland, 1600–1800* (Dublin, 1987)

—, *Arctic Ireland: the extraordinary story of the great frost and forgotten famine of 1740–1* (Belfast, 1997)

◆Dodd, J. S., *The traveller's directory through Ireland* (Dublin, 1801)

Donnelly, J.S., 'The Whiteboy movement, 1761–5', *IHS 21:81* (1978), 20–54

—, 'Pastorini and Captain Rock: millenarianism and sectarianism in the Rockite movement of 1821–4' in Clark and Donnelly (eds), *Irish peasants: violence and political unrest, 1780–1914* (Dublin, 1983), 102–39

— and K.A. Miller (eds), *Irish popular culture, 1650–1850* (Dublin, 1998)

Donovan, B.C. and D. Edwards, *British sources for Irish history, 1485–1641: a guide to manuscripts in local, regional and specialized repositories in England, Scotland and Wales* (Dublin, 1997)

Doyle, T.G., 'The politics of Protestant Ascendancy: politics, religion and society in Protestant Ireland, 1700–10' (PhD, UCD, 1996)

Doyle, W.S., *Fragments: scenes and stories of historic Cashel and Emly* (Tralee, 1945)

Drudy, P.J. (ed.), *Ireland: land, politics and people* (Cambridge, 1982)

Dryasdust [J. Nelson], 'Clonmel: a congregational memoir, part 1', *Non-Subscribing Presbyterian* 1084 (1997), 7–8; part 2, *Non-Subscribing Presbyterian* 1086 (1997), 50–1

Duffy, P.J., 'Eighteenth century estate maps', *History Ireland 5:1* (1997), 20–4

—, D. Edwards and E. Fitzpatrick (eds), *Gaelic Ireland, c.1250–c.1650: land, lordship and settlement* (Dublin, 2001)

Duffy, S. and M. O'Dowd, *Sources for early modern Irish history, 1534–1641* (Cambridge, 1985)

Duffy, S. et al., *An atlas of Irish history* (Dublin, 1997)

Dunlop, R., 'The plantation of Munster, 1584–9', *English Historical Review 3* (1888), 250–69

◆Dunlop, R (ed.), *Ireland under the Commonwealth, being a selection of documents relating to the government of Ireland from 1651–9*, vol. ii (Manchester, 1913)

Dunne, T.J., 'The Gaelic response to conquest and colonization: the evidence of the poetry', *Studia Hibernica 20* (1980), 7–30

Eagar, A.R., *A guide to Irish bibliographical material: a bibliography of Irish bibliographies and sources of information* (London, 1980)

◆Eakins, L.E., 'Papal bull of Pius V against Elizabeth' in *Electronic primary source texts and documents of Tudor history, compiled by Lara E. Eakins* (1995–2002), http://tudorhistory.org/primary/papalbull.html

◆Edmundson, W., *A journal of the life, travels, sufferings and labour of love in the work of the ministry of William Edmundson who departed this life, 30 June 1712* (London, 1715)

Edwards, D., 'Beyond reform: martial law and Tudor Ireland', *History Ireland* 5 (1997), 1–5

Elliott, B.S., *Irish migrants to the Canadas: a new approach* (Belfast, 1988)

Ellis, S.G., *Tudor Ireland: crown, community and the conflict of cultures, 1470–1603* (London, 1985)

—, 'Economic problems of the church: why the Reformation failed in Ireland', *Journal of Ecclesiastical History* 41:2 (1990), 239–65

—, 'Writing Irish history: revisionism, colonialism and the British Isles', *Irish Review* 19 (1996), 1–21

Ellison, C.C., 'Going of Munster', *Irish Ancestor* 9:1 (1977), 21–43

Elmes, R.M. et al., *Catalogue of Irish topographical prints and original drawings* (Dublin, 1975)

◆Erck, J.C., *An account of the ecclesiastical establishment subsisting in Ireland, with an ecclesiastical register* (Dublin, 1830)

Erskine, J., 'The Presbyterian Church in Ireland' in Richardson (ed.), *A tapestry of* beliefs (1997)

◆Eustace, P.B. (ed.), *Registry of deeds, Dublin–abstracts of wills, vol. I: 1708–45* (Dublin, 1956)

◆Eustace, P.B. (ed.), *Registry of deeds, Dublin–abstracts of wills, vol. II: 1746–85* (Dublin, 1954)

◆Eustace P.B. and E. Ellis (eds), *Registry of deeds, Dublin–abstracts of wills, vol. III: 1785–1832* (Dublin, 1984)

Evans, R.J.W., *The making of the Habsburg monarchy* (Oxford, 1979)

Eversley, D.E.C., 'The demography of the Irish Quakers, 1650–1850' in Goldstrom and Clarkson (eds): *Irish population, economy and society* (Oxford, 1981)

Fahy, G., 'The English perception of Ireland and the Irish: a geographical analysis and explanation', *Geographical View* 17 (1988), 24–38

Falkiner, C.L., *Illustrations of Irish history and topography, mainly of the seventeenth century* (London, 1904)

Fennessy, I., 'A supplement to the report on the state of popery in Ireland in 1731: an anti-fraternal bias', *Collectanea Hibernica* 42 (2000), 66–84

Fenning, H., 'A guide to the eighteenth century reports on Irish dioceses in the archives of Propaganda Fide', *Collectanea Hibernica* 11 (1968), 19–35

—, *The undoing of the friars of Ireland: a study of the novitiate question in the eighteenth century* (Louvain, 1972)

—, *Publications of Irish Catholic interest, 1700–1800* (Rome, 1973)

—, *The Irish Dominican province, 1698–1797* (Dublin, 1990)

—, '*Brevis et summaria relatio*: an unpublished account of Dominican martyrs and exiles, 1656', *Collectanea Hibernica* 34 and 35 (1992–3), 34–58

—, 'Cork imprints of Catholic interest, 1723–1804: part 1', *JCHAS* 109 (1995), 129–48; part 2, *JCHAS* 110 (1996), 115–42

◆Fenning, H., 'The last speech and prayer of Blessed Terence Albert O'Brien, bishop of Emly, 1651', *Collectanea Hibernica* 38 (1996), 52–8

Fenning, H., 'Dublin imprints of Catholic interest, 1701–39', *Collectanea Hibernica* 39 and 40 (1997–8), 106–54; '1740–59', 41 (1999), 65–116; '1760–9', 42 (2000), 85–119; '1770–82', 43 (2001), 161–208

Ferguson, K.P., 'The army in Ireland from the Restoration to the Act of Union' (PhD, TCD, 1980)

ffolliott, R., *The Pooles of Mayfield and other Irish families* (Dublin, 1958)

—, 'Houses in Ireland in the seventeenth century', *Irish Ancestor* 6:1 (1974), 16–21

—, 'Some game licenses of 1802', *Irish Ancestor* 8:1 (1976), 35–47

—, 'Irish naming practices before the Famine', *Irish Ancestor* 18:1 (1986), 1–4

Finegan, F., 'The Irish college of Poitiers, 1674–1762', *Irish Ecclesiastical Record* 104 (1965), 18–35

—, 'Rectors of the Irish college, Salamanca, 1705–67', *Irish Ecclesiastical Record* 110 (1968), 231–49

Finke, R. et al., 'Turning pews into people: estimating nineteenth century church attendance', *Journal for the Scientific Study of Religion* 23 (1986), 180–92

Finn, A., *Cashel and its ancient corporation* (Dublin, 1930)

Fitzpatrick, B., *Seventeenth century Ireland: the war of religions* (Dublin, 1988)

Fitzpatrick, T., *Waterford during the civil war, 1641–53* (Waterford, 1912)

Fletcher, A.J. and R. Gillespie (eds), *Irish preaching 700–1700* (Dublin, 2000)

Flood, J. and P., *Kilcash: a history, 1190–1801* (Dublin, 1999)

Flynn, T.S., *The Irish Dominicans, 1536–1641* (Dublin, 1993)

Ford, A., J. McGuire and K. Milne (eds), *As by law established: the Church of Ireland since the Reformation* (Dublin, 1995)

Ford, A., *The Protestant Reformation in Ireland: 1590–1641* (Dublin, 1997: 2nd ed.)

—, 'James Ussher and the creation of an Irish Protestant identity' in Bradshaw and Roberts, *British consciousness and identity* (1998), 185–212

Forristal, D., *Seventeen martyrs* (Dublin, 1990)

Foster, R.F., *Modern Ireland, 1600–1972* (London, 1988)

— (ed.), *The Oxford illustrated history of Ireland* (Oxford, 1989)

Foucault, M., *The archaeology of knowledge* (London, 1972)

—, 'Power and strategies' in C. Gordon (ed.): *Michel Foucault: power/knowledge, selected interviews and other writings, 1972–77* (Brighton, 1980), 134–45

Fraser, A.M., 'The Damer family in Co. Tipperary', *Clonmel Historical and Archaeological Society Journal* 1:2 (1953), 52–4

Freeman, T.W., 'Historical geography and the Irish historian', *IHS* 5:18 (1946), 139–46

—, 'John Wesley in Ireland', *Irish Geography* 8 (1975), 86–96

Froude, J.A., *The English in Ireland in the eighteenth century* (London, 1872)

Fulton, J., *The tragedy of belief: division, politics and religion in Ireland* (Oxford, 1991)

Gahen, D., 'Religion and land tenure in eighteenth century Ireland' in Comerford (ed.), *Religion, conflict and co-existence in Ireland* (1990), 99–117

Gallwey, H.D., 'Proprietors of Fethard, Co. Tipperary, 1641–63', *Irish Genealogist* 6:1 (1980), 5–8

Gardiner, M.J. and T. Radford, *Soil associations of Ireland and their land use potential* (Dublin, 1980)

Gash, N., *Mr Secretary Peel: the life of Sir Robert Peel to 1830* (London, 1961)

General alphabetical index to the townlands and towns, parishes and baronies of Ireland: based on the census of Ireland for the year, 1851 (Baltimore, 1984)

◆Giblin, C., 'Ten documents relating to Irish diocesan affairs, 1740–84 from the Franciscan library, Killiney', *Collectanea Hibernica* 20 (1978), 58–88

◆Gilbert, J.T., *A Jacobite narrative of the war in Ireland, 1688–91* (Shannon, 1971)

Gillespie, R., *The transformation of the Irish economy, 1550–1700: studies in Irish economic and social history 6* (Dundalk, 1991)

—, 'Explorers, exploiters and entrepreneurs: early modern Ireland and its context, 1500–1700' in Graham and Proudfoot (eds), *An historical geography of Ireland* (1993), 123–57

—, *Devoted people: belief and religion in early modern Ireland* (Manchester, 1997)

—, 'Popular and unpopular religion: a view from early modern Ireland' in Donnelly and Miller (eds), *Irish popular culture, 1650–1850* (1998), 30–49

— and M. Hill, *Doing Irish local history: pursuit and practice* (Belfast, 1998)

Gillespie, R., 'Political ideas and their social contexts in seventeenth-century Ireland', in Ohlmeyer (ed.), *Political thought in seventeenth-century Ireland* (2000), 107–30

Gillingham, J., 'The English invasion of Ireland' in Bradshaw et al., *Representing Ireland* (1993), 24–42

Gimlette, T., *The history of the Huguenot settlers in Ireland* (Waterford, 1888)

Godkin, J., *Ireland and her churches* (London, 1867)

—, *The religious history of Ireland: primitive, papal and Protestant* (London, 1873)

Goldstrom, J.M. and L.A. Clarkson (eds), *Irish population, economy and society* (Oxford, 1981)

Goodbody, O.C., *Guide to Irish Quaker records, 1654–1860* (Dublin, 1967)

◆Gough, J., *A tour in Ireland in 1813/14/16 by an Englishman* (Dublin, 1817)

Gowen, M.M., 'Irish artillery fortifications, 1550–1700' (MA, UCC, 1979)

Graham, B.J. and L.J. Proudfoot (eds), *An historical geography of Ireland* (London, 1993)

Graham, B.J. and C. Nash (eds), *Modern historical geographies* (London, 2000)

Gramsci, A., *Selections from the prison notebooks of Antonio Gramsci* (New York, 1971)

Greeves, J.R.H., 'Records of the Society of Friends in Ireland', *Irish Genealogist* 2:6 (1948), 177–9

Greaves, R.L., *God's other children: Protestant non-conformists, 1660–1700* (California, 1998)

Grey, W.R. 'The vanishing Protestants', *Focus* 9:10 (1966), 1–11

Gribbon, H.D., 'The Cork church book, 1653–1875', *Irish Baptist Historical Society Journal* 1 (1968), 5–18

—, 'Some lesser known sources of Baptist history', *Irish Baptist Historical Society Journal* 6 (1973), 61–73

—, 'Sources of Baptist history', *Irish Baptist Historical Society Journal* 8 (1975), 14–26

—, 'Irish Baptists in the nineteenth century: economic and social background', *Irish Baptist Historical Society Journal* 16 (1983), 4–18

—, 'Prominent Irish Baptists of the eighteenth century', *Irish Baptist Historical Society Journal* 29 (1996), 25–44

Griffen, B., 'Religion and opportunity in the Irish police forces, 1836–1914' in Comerford (ed.), *Religion, conflict and co-existence* (1990), 219–34

Griffin, I.J. and S. Lincoln, *Drawings from the Irish architectural archive* (Dublin, 1993)

Grubb, G.W., *The Grubbs of Tipperary: studies in heredity and character* (Cork, 1972)

Grubb, I., 'Social conditions in Ireland in the seventeenth and eighteenth centuries: an analysis of the role of the Society of Friends' (MA, University of London, 1916)

—, *Quakers in Ireland, 1654–1900* (London, 1927)

Grubb, J.E., 'County Tipperary Friends schools', *Journal of the Friends Historical Society* 1 (1903), 110

—, 'County Tipperary Friends records', *Journal of the Friends Historical Society* 2 (1905), 90

—, 'The three Sarah Grubbs of Clonmel', *Journal of the Friends Historical Society* 16 (1919), 95–6

Gulliver P.H. and M. Silverman, *Approaching the past: historical anthropology through Irish case studies* (New York, 1992)

Gurrin, B., *Pre-census sources for Irish demography* (Dublin, 2002)

Hadfield, A., 'Translating the Reformation: John Bale's Irish *Vocacyon*' in Bradshaw et al., *Representing Ireland* (1993), 43–59

— and J. McKeogh, *Strangers to that land: British perceptions of Ireland from the Reformation to the Famine* (London, 1994)

◆Hall, J., *A tour through Ireland, particularly the interior and least known parts* (London, 1813)

◆Hall, S.C., *Ireland: its scenery and character* (London, 1834: 10 vols)

◆Harbison, P., *Beranger's views of Ireland* (Dublin, 1991)

Hare, A., *The story of two noble lives, being memorials of Charlotte, Countess Canning and Louisa, marchioness of Waterford* (London, 1893)

Harries, E.G. and E. Turner (eds), 'The Church of Ireland' in Richardson (ed.), *A tapestry of beliefs* (1997)

Harrington, J.P. (ed.), *The English traveller in Ireland: accounts of Ireland and the Irish through five centuries* (Dublin, 1991)

Hassett, J. and R. Fitzgerald (eds), *The history and folklore of Killenaule-Moyglass* (S.n., 1990)

◆Haydon, C., *Anti-Catholicism in eighteenth-century England, c.1714–80* (Manchester, 1993),

Hayes, J.C., 'Guide to Tipperary newspapers (1770–1989)', *Tipperary Historical Journal* 2 (1989), 1–16

Hayes, R.J., *Manuscript sources for the history of Irish civilization* (Boston, Mass., 1970)

Hayes, W.J., *Tipperary in the year of rebellion, 1798* (Dublin, 1998)

Hayes-McCoy, G.A., 'Conciliation, coercion and the Protestant Reformation, 1547–71' in Moody, Martin and Byrne, *A new history of Ireland*, iii (1976), 69–93

—, 'The completion of the Tudor conquest and the advance of the Counter-Reformation, 1571–1603' in Moody, Martin and Byrne, *A new history of Ireland*, iii (1976), 94–141

—, 'The royal supremacy and ecclesiastical revolution, 1534–47' in Moody, Martin and Byrne, *A new history of Ireland*, iii (1976), 39–68

Hayton, D., 'From barbarian to burlesque: English images of the Irish, *c*.1660–1750', *Irish Economic and Social History* 15 (1988), 5–31

Hechter, M., *Internal colonialism: the Celtic fringe in British national development, 1537–1966* (London, 1975)

Helferty, S. and R. Refausse (eds), *Directory of Irish archives* (Dublin, 1992)

◆Hemphill, W.D., *Stereoscopic illustrations of Clonmel and the surrounding countryside* (Dublin, 1860)

Hempton, D.N., 'The Methodist crusade in Ireland, 1795–1845', *IHS* 22 (1980), 33–48

—, 'Methodism in Irish society, 1770–1830', *Transactions of the Royal Historical Society* 35 (1986), 18–33

—, 'Religious minorities' in Loughrey, *The people of Ireland* (1988), 155–68

Henderson, G., 'Landscape is dead: long live landscape', *Journal of Historical Geography* 24:1 (1998), 95–100

Henry, J.M., 'An assessment of the social, religious and political aspects of Congregationalism in Ireland in the nineteenth century' (PhD, QUB, 1965)

Hepburn, A.C. (ed.), *Minorities in history: historical studies 12* (London, 1978)

—, 'Minorities in history' in Hepburn (ed.), *Minorities in history* (1978), 1–10

Herbert, D., *Retrospections of ..., 1770–1806, [with] accompanying commentary by L.M. Cullen* (new ed., Dublin, 1988)

Herlihy, K., 'The Irish Baptists, 1660–1780' (PhD, TCD, 1992)

—, 'The early eighteenth century Irish Baptists – two letters', *Irish Economic and Social History* 19 (1992), 71–3

— (ed.), *The Irish dissenting tradition, 1650–1750* (Dublin, 1995)

—, *The religion of Irish dissent, 1650–1800* (Dublin, 1996)

—, *The politics of Irish dissent, 1650–1800* (Dublin, 1997)

—, *The propagation of Irish dissent, 1650–1800* (Dublin, 1998)

Herries-Davies, G.L. (ed.), *Irish geography: the geography society of Ireland golden jubilee, 1934–84* (Dublin, 1984)

Heuston, J., 'The weavers of Shronell – 250 years ago', *Tipperary Historical Journal* 15 (2002), 97–112

◆Hewitt, E. (ed.), *Lord Shannon's letters to his son: a calendar of the letters written by the 2nd earl of Shannon to his son Viscount Boyle, 1790–1802* (Belfast, 1982)

Hick, V., 'The Palatine settlement in Ireland' (PhD, UCD, 1994)

◆Hickson, M., *Ireland in the seventeenth century or the Irish massacres of 1641–2: their cases and results* (London, 1884: 2 vols)

Higgins, N., 'Genealogical sources for Co. Tipperary', *Tipperary Historical Journal* 4 (1991), 181–9

Hill, J.R., 'National festivals, the state and 'Protestant Ascendancy' in Ireland, 1790–1829', *IHS* 24:93 (1984), 30–51

—, 'Convergence and conflict in eighteenth century Ireland', *Historical Journal* 44:4 (2001), 1039–63

Hindess, B., *Discourses of power: from Hobbes to Foucault* (Oxford, 1996)

◆Hoare, E.N., *Practical observations on Church reform, the tithe question and national education in Ireland* (Dublin, 1838)

◆Hogan, E., *The description of Ireland and the state thereof as it is at this present in anno 1598: now for the first time published from a manuscript preserved in Clongowes Wood College* (Dublin, 1878)

◆Hogan, E. (ed.), *Hibernia Ignatiana: manuscripts of the Society of Jesus* (London, 1880)

◆Hogan, E., *Distinguished Irishmen of the seventeenth century* (London, 1894)

Holdsworth, D.W., 'Historical geography: the ancients and the moderns – generational vitality', *Progress in Human Geography* 26:5 (2002), 671–8

◆Holmes, G., *Sketches of some of the southern counties of Ireland, collected during a tour in the autumn of 1797, in a series of letters* (Dublin, 1801: repr. Whitegate, Co. Clare, 1987)

Hoppen, K.T., 'Landlords, society and electoral politics in mid-nineteenth century Ireland', *Past and Present* 75 (1977), 62–93.

Howard, L., 'Irish Catholic education II, 1669–85', *Studies* 58 (1969), 309–23

Howell, P., 'Foucault in Ireland', *Chimera: UCC Geographical Journal* 17 (2002), 30–5

Hunter, G.K. and C.J. Rawson (eds), *The Yearbook of English Studies, vol. 13: colonial and imperial themes special number* (London, 1983)

◆Hussey, T., *A pastoral letter to the Catholic clergy of the united diocese of Waterford and Lismore* (Waterford, 1797)

Hussey de Burgh, U.H., *The landowners of Ireland: an alphabetical list of the owners of estates of 500 acres or £500 valuation and upwards in Ireland* (Dublin, 1878)

◆Inglis, H.D., *A journey throughout Ireland during the spring, summer and autumn of 1834* (London, 1835: 2 vols)

Irish Manuscripts Commission, *Catalogue of publications, 1928–66* (Dublin, 1967)

Irwin, C.H., *A history of Presbyterianism in Dublin and the south and west of Ireland* (London, 1890)

◆Jacob, A.A. and J.N. Glascott, *An historical and genealogical narrative of the families of Jacob* (S.n., 1875)

James, F.G., *Lords of the ascendancy: the Irish House of Lords and its members, 1600–1800* (Dublin, 1995)

James, P.E., *Ireland in the empire, 1688–1770: a history of Ireland from the Williamite Wars to the eve of the American Revolution* (Boston, Mass, 1973)

Jennings, B., *The Irish Franciscan College of St. Anthony, Lovain* (Dublin, 1925)

—, 'The Irish Franciscans in Prague', *Studies* 28 (1939), 210–22

—, 'The Irish Franciscans of Boulay', *Archivium Hibernicum* 11 (1944), 118–53

—, 'The Irish Franciscans in Poland', *Archivium Hibernicum* 20 (1957), 38–56

Johnson, E.M., 'Problems common to both Protestant and Catholic churches in eighteenth-century Ireland' in MacDonagh, Mandle and Travers (eds), *Irish culture and nationalism, 1750–1950* (London, 1983)

Jones-Hughes, T., 'The origin and growth of towns in Ireland', *University Review* 2:7 (1960), 8–15

—, 'Society and settlement in nineteenth century Ireland', *Irish Geography* 5:2 (1965), 79–96

—, 'Village and town in mid-nineteenth century Ireland', *Irish Geography* 14 (1981), 99–106

—, 'Historical geography of Ireland from *c*.1700' in Herries Davies (ed.), *Irish geography* (1984), 149–68

—, 'Landholding and settlement in Co. Tipperary in the nineteenth century' in Nolan and McGrath, *Tipperary: history and society* (1985), 339–66

Kearney, H.F., 'The court of wards and liveries in Ireland, 1622–41', *PRIA* 57 (1955–6), 29–68

—, *Strafford in Ireland, 1633–41: a study in absolution* (Manchester, 1959)

—, 'Ecclesiastical politics and the Counter-Reformation in Ireland, 1618–48', *Journal of Ecclesiastical History* 2 (1960), 202–12

Kelly, J., '"The glorious and immortal memory": commemoration and Protestant identity in Ireland, 1660–1800', *PRIA* C 94 (1994), 25–52

Kennedy, L. (ed.), *Colonialism, religion and nationalism in Ireland* (Belfast, 1996)

Kennedy, L., 'The long retreat: Protestants, economy and society, 1660–1926' in L. Kennedy (ed.), *Colonialism, religion and nationalism, 1–34*

Kennedy, P.J., *The Clonmel charter school, 1747–1886* (Waterford, 1932)

◆Kerrigan, P.M., 'A return of barracks in Ireland, 1811', *Irish Sword* 15 (1982), 277–83

◆Kerrigan, P.M., 'Barracks in Ireland, 1847', *Irish Sword* 19 (1993–5), 227–32

—, *Castles and fortifications in Ireland, 1485–1945* (Cork, 1995)

Killen, W.D. (ed.), *A history of congregations of the Presbyterian Church in Ireland* (Belfast, 1886)

Kilroy, P., 'Sermons and pamphlet literature in the Irish reformed church, 1613–34', *Archivium Hibernicum* 33 (1975), 21–38

—, *Protestant dissent and controversy in Ireland, 1660–1714* (Cork, 1994)

King, C.S. (ed.), *A great archbishop of Dublin: William King DD 1650–1729* (London, 1906)

Kirtland, C., *A historical sketch of the Baptist denomination in Ireland* (London, 1868)

Klein, T., 'Minorities in central Europe in the sixteenth and early seventeenth centuries' in Hepburn (ed.), *Minorities in history: historical studies 12* (1978), 31–50

Knowles, A.K. (ed.), 'Historical GIS: the spatial turn in social science history', *Social Science History* 24:3 (2000), 451–70

◆Knox, I., 'The Revd Edward Bacon's register of baptisms, marriages and burials, part 1', *Irish Ancestor* 16:1 (1984), 35–48; part 2, *Irish Ancestor* 16:2 (1984), 96–115

◆Knox, I., 'Census of Protestants in the parishes of Shanrahan and Tulloghorton, Co. Tipperary in 1864–70', *Irish Ancestor* 16:2 (1984), 61–7

◆Knox, I., 'Census of Protestant parishioners in Clogheen union, Co. Tipperary in 1873, 1877 and 1880', *Irish Ancestor* 17:1 (1985), 25–9

◆Knox, S.J., *Ireland's debt to the Huguenots* (Dublin, 1959)

◆Laffan, T., 'Abstracts from the ancient records of the corporation of Cashel' *JRSAI* 14:34 (1904), 30–40

◆Laffan, T., 'Fethard, Co. Tipperary: its charters and corporation records', *JRSAI* 14:36 (1906), 143–553

◆Laffan, T., *Tipperary's families, being the hearth money records for 1665–6–7* (Dublin, 1911)

Lalor, H.J., 'Two collections of visitation reports in the library of Trinity College', *Hermathena* 13 (1905), 319–31

Large, D., 'The wealth of the great Irish landowners, 1750–1850', *IHS* 15 (1960), 21–47

Law, E., 'A Masonic burial in Fethard', *Tipperary Historical Journal* 10 (1997), 85

—, 'Amyas Griffith in eighteenth century Fethard', *Tipperary Historical Journal* 11 (1998), 215–22

Lecky, W.E.H., *A history of Ireland in the eighteenth century* (London, 1906)

Lee, G.L., *The Huguenot settlements in Ireland* (London, 1936)

Lees-Milne, J., 'Landed properties and proprietors' in Townend (ed.) *Burke's genealogy and heraldic history of the landed gentry* (London, 1965: 18th ed.)

◆Leet, A., *A directory to the market towns, villages, gentleman's seats and other noted places in Ireland* (Dublin, 1814)

Lenihan, P. (ed.), *Conquest and resistance: war in seventeenth century Ireland* (Boston, Mass., 2001).

Lenihan, P., *Confederate Catholics at war, 1641–49* (Cork, 2001)

Lennon, C., 'The Counter-Reformation in Ireland, 1542–1641', in Brady and Gillespie (eds), *Natives and newcomers* (1986)

—, *Seventeenth century Ireland: the incomplete conquest* (Dublin, 1994)

Lenox-Conyngham, M. (ed.), *Diaries of Ireland: an anthology, 1590–1987* (Dublin, 2000)

Leonard, H., 'Irish Catholic education, 1669–85', *Studies: An Irish Quarterly Review,* 58 (1969), 191–205; 309–21

◆Lewis, S., *A topographical dictionary of Ireland* (London, 1837: 2 vols)

Levistone-Cooney, D.A., *Asses' colts and loving people: the story of the people called Methodists on the Carlow circuit* (Carlow, 1998)

Lewis, C.S., *Hunting in Ireland: an historical and geographical analysis* (London, 1975)

◆Lidwell, J., *The history of the life and adventures of John Lidwell from his birth to his present age of nearly sixty years* (London, 1804)

Liechty, J., 'The popular Reformation comes to Ireland: the case of John Walker and the foundation of the Church of God, 1804' in Comerford (ed.), *Religion, conflict and co-existence* (1990), 159–87

Lindsay, D. and Fitzpatrick, D., *Records of the Irish Famine: a guide to local archives, 1840–55* (Dublin, 1993)

Linehan, D.C., 'Index to the manuscripts of military interest in the National Library of Ireland', *Irish Sword* 2 (1954), 33–9

Loeber, R., 'Irish country houses and castles of the late Caroline period: an unremembered past recaptured', *Bulletin of the Irish Georgian Society* 16: 1–2 (1973), 1–69

—, 'English and Irish sources for the history of Dutch economic activity in Ireland, 1600–89', *Irish Economic and Social History* 8 (1981), 71–81

—, *The geography and practice of English colonization in Ireland* (Athlone, 1991)

Lohan, R., *Guide to the archives of the Office of Public Works* (Dublin, 1994)

◆Loveday, J., *Diary of a tour in 1732 through parts of England, Wales, Ireland and Scotland* (Edinburgh, 1890)

Lotz-Heumann, U., 'The Protestant interpretation of history in Ireland: the case of James Ussher's *Discourse*' in B. Gordon (ed.), *Protestant history and identity in sixteenth century Europe: vol. 2, the later Reformation* (1998), 107–20

◆Lucas, R., 'General directory of the kingdom of Ireland, 1788', *Irish Genealogist* 3:11 (1966), 468–76

◆Luckombe, P., *A tour through Ireland* (London, 1780)

Luddy, M., 'Whiteboy support in Co. Tipperary, 1761–89', *Tipperary Historical Journal* 2 (1989), 66–79

Lynch, M., *Beyond Aherlow: the glen from Bansha to Galbally* (Piltown, Co. Kilkenny, 2002)

Lyons, M.C., *Illustrated encumbered estates of Ireland, 1850–1905* (Whitegate, Co. Clare, 1993)

◆MacCaffrey, J. (ed.), 'Report on the state of popery, 1731', *Archivium Hibernicum* 1 (1909), 10–27; 2 (1911), 108–56; 3 (1912), 124–59; 4 (1915), 131–77

◆MacCaffrey, J. (ed.), 'Irish Catholics licensed to keep arms, 1704', *Archivium Hibernicum* 4 (1915), 59–65

MacCarthy, R.B., 'Cahir church and parish', *Church yearbook for the united dioceses of Cashel, Emly, Waterford and Lismore for 1963* (Waterford, 1962)

—, 'The diocese of Lismore, 1801–69' (MA, UCC, 1965)

—, 'A scarce county for Protestants' in *The Nationalist Newspaper Centenary Supplement* (Clonmel, 1990), 106–09

—, *A short history of the Church of Ireland – ancient and modern* (Dublin, 1995)

MacCarthy-Morrogh, M., *The Munster plantation: English migration to southern Ireland, 1583–1641* (Oxford, 1986)

—, 'The English presence in early seventeenth century Munster' in Brady and Gillespie (eds), *Natives and Newcomers* (1986), 171–90

Maher, M., 'The local studies department of the county library', *Tipperary Historical Journal* 2 (1989), 119–22

Malcomson, A.P.W., 'Absenteeism in eighteenth century Ireland', *Irish Economic and Social History* 1 (1974), 15–35

—, *John Foster: the politics of the Anglo-Irish ascendancy* (Oxford, 1978)

—, *Archbishop Charles Agar: churchmanship and politics in Ireland, 1760–1810* (Dublin, 2002)

Malins, E. and The Knight of Glin, *Lost demesnes: Irish landscape gardening, 1660–1845* (London, 1976)

Marnane, D.G., *Land and violence: a history of west Tipperary from 1660* (Tipperary, 1985)

—, 'Land and violence in Tipperary in the 1800s', *Tipperary Historical Journal* 1 (1988), 53–89

—, 'The struggle for land in South Tipperary' in *The Nationalist Newspaper Centenary Supplement* (1990), 26–8

—, 'Land ownership in South Tipperary, 1849–1903' (PhD, UCC, 1991)

—, 'A Tipperary landlord's diary of the 1860s', *Tipperary Historical Journal* 4 (1991), 120–28

—, 'Samuel Cooper of Killenure (1750–1831): a Tipperary land agent and his diaries', *Tipperary Historical Journal* 6 (1993), 102–27

—, 'South Tipperary on the eve of the Great Famine', *Tipperary Historical Journal* 8 (1995), 1–53

—, 'Writing the past: Tipperary history and historians', *Tipperary Historical Journal* 10 (1997), 1–41

◆Marron, L. (ed.), 'Documents from the state papers concerning Miler Magrath', *Archivium Hibernicum* 21 (1958), 75–189

Martin, D., *The Longs of Longfield* (Toronto, 1998)

Martin, F.X., '"So manie in the very prime and spring of their youth, manie of them heirs of the land": the friars of the Irish Capuchin mission in northern France and the Low Countries 1591–1641' in B. Hayley and C. Murray (eds), *Ireland and France, a bountiful friendship: essays in honour of Patrick Rafroidi* (London, 1991), 7–16

—, 'The beatified martyrs of Ireland (12): William Tirry, OSA, priest', *Irish Theological Quarterly* 66:4 (2001), 383–9

◆Mason, W.S., *A statistical account or parochial survey of Ireland* (Dublin, 1814–19: 3 vols)

◆Mathews, G., *An account of the Regium Donum issued to the Presbyterian Church of Ireland* (Dublin, 1836)

Maxwell, C., *Irish history from contemporary sources, 1509–1610* (London, 1923)

—, *Country and town under the Georges* (Dundalk, 1949)

—, *The stranger in Ireland: from the reign of Elizabeth to the Great Famine* (Dublin, 1979)

McBride, I., 'The common name of Irishman': Protestantism and patriotism in eighteenth-century Ireland' in Claydon and McBride, *Protestantism and national identity* (1998), 236–64

McCarthy, M., *A Tipperary parish: a history of Knockavilla-Doniskeagh* (s.n., 1975)

McCormack, W.J., *The Dublin paper war of 1786–88: a bibliographical inquiry, including an account of the origins of the Protestant Ascendancy and its 'baptism' in 1792* (Dublin, 1993)

McCourt, M.P.A., 'The religious inquiry in the Irish census of 1861', *IHS* 21:82 (1978), 168–87

McCracken, J.L., 'The social structure and social life, 1714–60' in Moody and Vaughan (eds), *A new history of Ireland*, iv (1986), 31–56

—, 'The political structure, 1714–60' in Moody and Vaughan (eds), *A new history of Ireland*, iv (1986), 57–83

—, 'Protestant Ascendancy and the rise of colonial nationalism, 1714–60' in Moody and Vaughan (eds), *A new history of Ireland*, iv (1986), 105–22

—, 'The ecclesiastical structure, 1714–60' in Moody and Vaughan (eds), *A new history of Ireland*, iv (1986), 84–104

◆McCutcheon, R.G. (ed.), 'Elliott letters [1834–69]', *Irish Genealogical Research Society Newsletter* 4:1 (Nov. 2004)

McDowell, R.B., *Public opinion and government policy in Ireland, 1801–46* (Westport, Conn., 1975)

—, 'Colonial nationalism and the winning of parliamentary independence, 1760–82' in Moody and Vaughan (eds), *A new history of Ireland*, iv (1986), 196–235

—, 'Ireland in 1800' in Moody and Vaughan (eds), *A new history of Ireland*, iv (1986), 657–712

—, *Crisis and decline: the fate of the southern Unionists* (Dublin, 1997)

McGrath, C.I., 'Securing the Protestant interest: the origins and purpose of the penal laws of 1695', *IHS* 30:117 (1996), 25–46

McGrath, T., 'Interdenominational relations in pre-Famine Tipperary' in Nolan and McGrath (eds), *Tipperary: history and society* (1985)

McGuire, J.I., 'The Church of Ireland and the "glorious revolution" of 1688' in Cosgrove and McCartney, *Studies in Irish history: presented to R. Dudley Edwards* (Dublin, 1979), 137–49

—, 'Ireland, 1660–1800' in Lee, *Irish Historiography* (1981), 56–84

McGurk, J., *The Elizabethan conquest of Ireland: the 1590s crisis* (Manchester, 1997)

McKenny, K., 'The seventeenth century land settlement in Ireland: towards a statistical interpretation' in Ohlmeyer (ed.), *Ireland from independence to occupation* (1995), 181–200

McLoughney, M., *A bibliography of Tipperary history and antiquities* (Thurles, 1970)

McMillan, D., 'The Baptist Union of Ireland' in Richardson (ed.), *A tapestry of beliefs* (1997)

McParland E. et al., *The architecture of Richard Morrison (1767–1849) and William Vitruvius Morrison (1794–1830)* (Dublin, 1989)

McParland E., *A bibliography of Irish architectural history* (Dublin, 1989)

—, *Public architecture in Ireland, 1680–1760* (New York, 2002)

McRedmond, L., *To the greater glory: a history of the Irish Jesuits* (Dublin, 1991)

McVeigh, J. (ed.), *Richard Pococke's Irish tours* (Dublin, 1995)

Meagher, J.J., 'The beatified martyrs of Ireland (3): Dermot O'Hurley, archbishop of Cashel', *Irish Theological Quarterly* 64:3 (1999), 285–98

Meehan, C.P., *The rise and fall of the Irish Franciscan monasteries* (Dublin, 1872)

Meigs, S.A., '*Constantia in fide*: the persistence of traditional religion in early modern Ireland, 1400–1690', *Irish Economic and Social History* 21 (1994), 82–3

Miliband, R., *Capitalist democracy in Britain* (Oxford, 1984)

Miller, D., 'Irish Catholics and the great Famine', *Journal of Social History* 9 (1975), 81–98

Miller, K.A., *Emigrants and exiles: Ireland and the Irish exodus to North America* (New York, 1985)

—, 'No middle ground: the erosion of the Protestant middle classes in southern Ireland during the pre-Famine era', *Huntington Library Quarterly* 49 (1986), 295–306

Millett, B., 'Bonaventure Baron OFM, Hibernus Clonmeliensis' in O'Connell and Darmody (eds), *Siege of Clonmel commemoration* (1950), 41–6

—, *The Irish Franciscans, 1651–65* (Rome, 1964)

—, *Survival and reorganization, 1650–95: a history of Irish Catholicism* (Dublin, 1968)

◆Millett, B., 'Four letters of Father James White of Clonmel, 1668–79', *Collectanea Hibernica* 18 and 19 (1976–7), 7–18

◆Millett, B., 'Maurice MacBrien, bishop of Emly and the confiscation of his baggage, March 1578', *Collectanea Hibernica* 34 and 35 (1992–3), 10–14

—, 'The beatified martyrs of Ireland (1): Bishop Patrick O'Healy, OFM and Conn O'Rourke, OFM', *Irish Theological Quarterly* 64:1 (1999), 55–78

—, 'The Irish Franciscans and education in late medieval times and the early Counter-Reformation, 1230–1630', *Seanchas Ard Mhacha* 18:2 (2001), 1–30

—, 'The beatified martyrs of Ireland (11): John Kearney, OFM (priest)', *Irish Theological Quarterly* 66:3 (2001), 239–48

Mitchell, B., *A new genealogical atlas of Ireland* (Baltimore, 1986)

—, *A guide to Irish churches and graveyards* (Baltimore, 1990)

—, 'The ordnance survey memoirs: a source for emigration in the 1830s', *History Ireland* 4:4 (1996), 13–17

Moloney-Davis, H., *Sources for seventeenth century to nineteenth century historical studies in Special Collections, Boole Library, University College, Cork* (Cork, 1995)

Moody, T.W., F. X. Martin and F. J. Byrne (eds), *A new history of Ireland, iii – early modern Ireland, 1539–1641* (Oxford, 1976)

Moody, T.W. and W.E. Vaughan (eds), *A new history of Ireland, ix – maps, genealogies and lists – a companion to Irish history, part II* (Oxford, 1984)

—, *A new history of Ireland, iv – eighteenth century Ireland, 1691–1800* (Oxford, 1986)

Mooney, C., *The Irish Franciscans and France* (Dublin, 1964)

—, 'The Church in Gaelic Ireland, from the thirteenth century to the fifteenth century' in P.J. Corish (ed.), *A history of Irish Catholicism*, ii (Dublin, 1969), 14–17

Moran, P.F. (ed.), *Spicilegium Ossoriense: being a collection of original letters and papers illustrative of the history of the Irish Church from the Reformation to the year 1800* (Dublin, 1874–84: 3 vols)

— (ed.), *The analecta of David Rothe, bishop of Ossory* (Dublin, 1884)

Moran, P.F., *Historical sketch of the persecutions suffered by the Catholics of Ireland under the rule of Cromwell and the Puritans* (Dublin, 1907)

Morgan, H., 'Hugh O'Neill and the nine years war in Tudor Ireland', *Historical Journal* 36:1 (1993), 21–37

—, 'British policies before the British state', in Bradshaw and Morrill (eds), *The British problem* (1996)

— (ed.), *Political ideology in Ireland, 1541–1641* (Dublin, 1999)

Morris, T., 'The Butler archbishops of Cashel', *North Munster Antiquarian Journal* 7:2 (1955), 1–11

◆Morrice, T., *A collection of the state letters of the right honourable Roger Boyle, the first earl of Orrery, lord president of Munster of Ireland: containing a series of correspondence between the duke of Ormonde and his lordship, from the Restoration to the year 1668...by the Revd Mr Thomas Morrice, his lordship's chaplain* (Dublin, 1743)

Morrissey, J.M., 'Encountering colonialism: Gaelic Irish responses to New English settlement in early modern west Tipperary, c.1540–c.1641' (PhD, University of Exeter, 2000)

Murphy, D., *Our martyrs: a record of those who suffered for the Catholic faith under the penal laws in Ireland* (Dublin, 1896)

◆Murphy, D., *Triumphalia chronologica monasterii Sanctae Crucis in Hibernia: de Cisterciensium Hibernorum viris illustribus, 1640* (Dublin, 1895)

Murphy, D., *The two Tipperarys: the national and local politics – devolution and self-determination of the unique 1838 division into two ridings and the aftermath* (Nenagh, 1994)

Murphy, J.A., 'Inchiquin's change of religion', *JCHAS* 72:215 (1967), 58–68

—, 'The politics of the Munster Protestants, 1644–49', *JCHAS* 76:223 (1971), 1–20

◆Murphy, M.A. (ed.), 'Royal visitation of Cashel and Emly, 1615', *Archivium Hibernicum* 1 (1912), 277–311

Murphy, T.A., 'Father Nicholas Sheehy P.P. Clogheen' in O'Connell and Darmody (eds), *Siege of Clonmel commemoration* (1950), 47–50

◆Murray, R.H. (ed.), *The journal of John Stevens containing a brief account of the war in Ireland, 1689–91* (Oxford, 1912)

Myers, A.C., *Immigration of the Irish Quakers into Pennsylvania, 1682–1750, with their early history in Ireland* (Baltimore, 1985)

Neely, W.G., *Kilcooley: land and people of Tipperary* (Belfast, 1983)

—, 'The Protestant community of South Tipperary: 1660–1815, part I', *Tipperary Historical Journal* 4 (1991), 132–9; part II, *Tipperary Historical Journal* 5 (1992), 132–9

◆*New commercial directory for the cities of Waterford and Kilkenny, towns of Clonmel, Carrick-on-Suir, New Ross and Carlow* (Dublin, 1839)

Nicholls, K.W., 'Rectory, vicarage and parish in the western Irish dioceses', *JRSAI* 101 (1971), 53–84

◆Nicholson, A., *The Bible in Ireland: Ireland's welcome to the stranger, or excursions through Ireland in 1844 and 1845* (London, 1847)

Nolan, W., *Fassadinin: land, settlement and society in south east Ireland, 1600–1850* (Dublin, 1979)

—, *Tracing the past: sources for local studies in the Republic of Ireland* (Dublin, 1982)

— and T. McGrath (eds), *Tipperary: history and society – interdisciplinary essays on the history of an Irish county* (Dublin, 1985)

Nolan, W., 'Patterns of living in Tipperary, 1750–1850' in Nolan and McGrath, *Tipperary: history and society* (1985), 288–324

—, *The shaping of Ireland: the geographical perspective* (Cork, 1986)

Noonan, J.A., 'Baptists in Ireland, 1649–1798: a historical study, with particular reference to their involvement in educational endeavours' (MEd, UCC, 1972)

Noonan, K., '"The cruell pressure of an enraged barbarous people": Irish and English identity in seventeenth century policy and propaganda', *History Journal* 41:1 (1998), 151–78

North, J. S., *The Waterloo directory of Irish newspapers and periodicals, 1800–1900* (Waterloo, Ontario, 1986)

◆O'Byrne, E. (ed.), *The convert rolls* (Dublin, 1981)

Ó Cadhla, S., 'Captaen na bhFear mBán: Father Nicholas Sheehy in history/folklore', *Tipperary Historical Journal* 15 (2002), 69–89

Ó Caithnia, L.P., *Scéal na hIomána: ó thosagh ama go 1884 – the story of hurling from the beginning of time to 1884* (Dublin, 1980)

Ó Ciardha, É., *Ireland and the Jacobite cause, 1685–1766: a fatal attachment* (Dublin, 2000)

Ó Clerigh, N.B., 'Ownership of land in South Tipperary' in *The Nationalist Newspaper Centenary Supplement* (1990), 38

Ó Conbhuidhe, C., *Studies in Irish Cistercian history* (Dublin, 1998)

—, *The Cistercian abbeys of Tipperary* (Dublin, 1999)

O'Connell, B., 'The Nagles of Garnavilla', *Irish Genealogist* 3:1 (1956), 17–24

O'Connell, P. and W.C. Darmody (eds), *Siege of Clonmel commemoration: tercentenary souvenir record* (Clonmel, 1950)

O'Connell, P., *The Irish college at Alcalá de Henares, 1649–1785* (Dublin, 1997)

—, *The Irish college at Lisbon, 1590–1834* (Dublin, 2001)

O'Connell, W.D., 'Franciscan reorganization in Munster during the sixteenth century', *JCHAS* 44 (1939), 37–45

O'Connor, J., *A priest on the run: William Tirry OSA, 1608–54* (Dublin, 1992)

O'Doherty, D.J., 'Father Thomas White, founder of the Irish college, Salamanca', *Irish Ecclesiastical Record* 29 (1922), 578–97

O'Donnell, M., 'Life in Fethard in the 1800s', *Tipperary Historical Journal* 1 (1988), 22–37

O'Donoghue, J., 'The Scullys of Kilfeacle: Catholic middlemen of the 1760s', *Tipperary Historical Journal* 2 (1989), 38–51

O'Donoghue, P., 'Causes of the opposition to tithes, 1830–8', *Studia Hibernica* 5 (1965), 7–28

—, 'Opposition to tithe payments in 1830–1', *Studia Hibernica* 6 (1966), 69–98

◆O'Dwyer, C. (ed.), 'Archbishop Butler's visitation book, vol. i', *Archivium Hibernicum* 33 (1975), 1–90; vol. ii, *Archivium Hibernicum* 34 (1976–7), 1–49

Ó Fiaich, T., 'The registration of the clergy in 1704', *Seanchas Ard Mhacha* 6 (1971), 46–69

—, *The Irish colleges in France* (Dublin, 1990)

O'Flanagan, P., 'Markets and fairs in Ireland, 1600–1800: index of economic development and regional growth', *Journal of Historical Geography* 11:4 (1985), 364–78

—, *Rural Ireland, 1600–1900: continuity and change* (Cork, 1987)

— et al. (eds), *Rural Ireland, 1600–1900: modernization and change* (Cork, 1987)

O'Flanagan, P., 'Urban minorities and majorities: Catholics and Protestants in Munster towns, c.1659–1850' in Smyth and Whelan (eds), *Common ground* (1988), 124–48

Ohlmeyer, J.H. (ed.), *Ireland from independence to occupation, 1641–60* (New York, 1995)

—, *Political thought in seventeenth-century Ireland: kingdom or colony?* (Cambridge, 2000)

Ohlmeyer, J.H., 'For God, king or country?: political thought and culture in seventeenth-century Ireland' in Ohlmeyer, *Political thought in seventeenth-century Ireland* (2000), 1–34

O'Keeffe, D., '1798 in South Tipperary', *Tipperary Historical Society Journal* 3 (1990), 109–20

Olden, M., 'Counter-Reformation problems: Munster', *Irish Ecclesiastical Record* 104 (1965), 42–54

O'Reilly, M. (ed.), *Memorials of those who suffered for the Catholic faith in Ireland in the sixteenth, seventeenth and eighteenth centuries* (London, 1868)

O'Riordan, M., *The Gaelic mind and the collapse of the Gaelic world* (Cork, 1990)

—, 'Political poems in the mid-seventeenth century crisis' in Ohlmeyer (ed.), *Ireland from independence to occupation* (1995), 112–27

Orr, G.E., 'The Methodist Church in Ireland' in Richardson (ed.), *A tapestry of beliefs* (1997)

Ó Siochrú, M., *A kingdom in crisis: the confederates and the Irish civil wars* (Dublin, 2000)

—, *Kingdoms in crisis: Ireland in the 1640s: essays in honour of Donal Cregan* (Dublin, 2001)

O'Sullivan, D.J., *The Irish constabularies, 1822–1922: a century of policing in Ireland* (Dingle, 1999)

Ó Tuama, S. and T. Kinsella (eds), *An Dunaire, 1600–1900: poems of the dispossessed* (Mountrath, Co. Laois, 1981)

Palmer, S.H., *Police and protest in England and Ireland, 1780–1850* (Cambridge, 1988)

◆*Parliamentary Gazetteer of Ireland, 1844–5* (London, 1846)

Parish priests and churches of St Mary's, Clonmel (Clonmel, 1984)

◆Pender, S. (ed.), *A census of Ireland, c.1659, with supplementary material from the poll money ordinances of 1660–1* (Dublin, 1939)

Percival-Maxwell, M., *The outbreak of the Irish rebellion of 1641* (Dublin, 1994)

◆Pereira, H.P.E., 'A detail of the several regiments of dragoons and horse barracks in Ireland, 1729', *Irish Sword* 1 (1949–53), 142–4

◆Pereira, H.P.E., 'Quarters of the army in Ireland, 1769', *Irish Sword* 2 (1954–6), 230–1

◆Petty, W, *The political anatomy of Ireland, 1672: with the establishment for that kingdom, when the late duke of Ormond was lord lieutenant* (Dublin, 1691)

Phair, P.B., 'Seventeenth century regal visitations: an introduction', *Analecta Hibernica* 28 (1978), 81–102

Philips, W.A. (ed.), *History of the Church of Ireland from earliest times to the present day* (Oxford, 1933: 3 vols)

Phillimore, W.P.W. and G. Thrift, *Indexes to Irish wills* (Baltimore, 1970)

◆Pococke, R., *Pococke's tour in Ireland in 1752* (Dublin, 1891)

Pouchin-Mould, D.D.C., *The monasteries of Ireland: an introduction* (London, 1976)

Powell, A., 'Reflections on the landed gentry' in Townend (ed.) *Burke's genealogy and heraldic history of the landed gentry* (London, 1967: 18th ed.)

◆Power, P., 'Bishop Miler Magrath's visitation of Waterford and Lismore, 1588', *JWSEIAS* 12 (1909), 155–61

◆Power, P. (ed.), 'Notes from a Carrickman's diary, 1787–1809', *JWSEIAS* 14 (1913), 18–27

— (ed.), *A bishop of the penal times, being letters and reports of John Brenan, bishop of Waterford (1671–93) and archbishop of Cashel (1677–93): Irish historical documents* 3 (Cork, 1932)

Power, P., *Waterford and Lismore: a compendious history of the united diocese* (Cork, 1937).

—, *The placenames of Decies* (Cork, 1952)

Power, P.C., *Carrick-on-Suir and its people* (Dublin, 1977)

—, *History of South Tipperary* (Cork, 1989)

—, 'Converts' in Power and Whelan (eds), *Endurance and emergence* (1990), 1–20

—, 'Tipperary court-martials, 1798–1801', *Tipperary Historical Journal* 6 (1993), 135–47

◆Power, T.P., 'A minister's money account for Clonmel, 1703', *Analecta Hibernica* 34 (1987), 185–200

— and K. Whelan (eds), *Endurance and emergence: Catholics in Ireland in the eighteenth century* (Dublin, 1990)

Power, T.P., *Land, politics and society in eighteenth-century Tipperary* (Oxford, 1993)

Pratt, M.L., *Imperial eyes: travel writing and transculturalism* (London, 1992)

Prendergast, J.P., *The Cromwellian settlement of Ireland* (Dublin, 1922: 3rd ed.)

Prenderville, P.L., 'A select bibliography of Irish economic history, part two: the seventeenth and eighteenth centuries', *Economic History Review* 3:3 (1932), 402–16

◆Price, L. (ed.), *An eighteenth century antiquary: the sketches, notes and diaries of Austin Cooper, 1759–1830* (Dublin, 1942)

Proudfoot, L., 'Regionalism and localism: religious change and social protest, *c.*1700 to *c.*1900' in Graham and Proudfoot (eds), *Historical geography of Ireland* (1993), 185–218

—, 'Spatial transformation and social agency: property, society and improvement, *c.*1700 to *c.*1900' in Graham and Proudfoot (eds), *Historical geography of Ireland* (1993), 219–57

◆Publicola [T. Dawson], *A letter from a gentleman in the province of Munster to his Grace, the lord primate* (Cashel, 1741)

◆Quane, M., 'Tour in Ireland by John Harden in 1797', *JCHAS* 58:187 (1953), 26–32

Quinlan, M., 'History of devotion to the Sacred Heart 9: progress during the sixteenth and seventeenth centuries', *Irish Ecclesiastical Record* 59 (1942), 297–313

—, 'History of devotion to the Sacred Heart 12: the society of Jesus in the sixteenth and seventeenth centuries', *Irish Ecclesiastical Record* 61 (1942), 23–36

Quinlan, M., 'The Main Guard, Clonmel: the rediscovery of a seventeenth-century courthouse', *Bulletin of the Irish Georgian Society* 36 (1994), 4–29

Quinn, D.B., 'The Munster plantation: problems and opportunities', *JCHAS* 71:213–14 (1966), 19–40

—, *The Elizabethans and the Irish* (New York, 1966)

— and K.W. Nicholls, 'Ireland in 1534' in Moody, Martin and Byrne (eds), *A new history of Ireland*, iii (1976), 1–38

Reid, J.S., *History of the Presbyterian Church in Ireland* (Belfast, 1867)

Reid, N. (ed.), *A table of Church of Ireland parochial records and copies* (Dublin, 1994)

Rennison, W.H., *A succession list of the bishops, cathedral and parochial clergy of the united diocese of Waterford and Lismore* (Waterford, [1921])

Return of owners of land of one acre and upwards in the several counties, counties of cities and counties of towns in Ireland, 1876 (Baltimore, 1988)

Richardson, N. (ed.), *A tapestry of beliefs: Christian traditions in Northern Ireland* (Belfast, 1997)

Robinson, P.S., *The plantation of Ulster: British settlement in an Irish landscape, 1600–70* (Dublin, 1984)

Roberts, M., *Poetry and the cult of the martyrs: the Liber Peristerphanon of Prudentius Michael Roberts* (East Lansing, Michigan, 1993)

Rodgers, R.J., 'Presbyterian missionary activity amongst Roman Catholics in the nineteenth century in Ireland' (MA, QUB, 1968)

Rogal, S.J., *John Wesley in Ireland, 1749–89* (Dyfed, Wales, 1993: 2 vols)

Ronan, M.V., *The Reformation in Ireland under Elizabeth, 1558–80: from original sources* (London, 1930)

—, *The Irish martyrs of the penal laws* (London, 1935)

Rouse, S., *Into the light: an illustrated guide to the photograph collections in the National Library of Ireland* (Dublin, 1998)

Routledge, P., 'A spatiality of resistances: theory and practice in Nepal's revolution of 1990', in S. Pile and M. Keith (eds), *Geographies of Resistance* (London, 1997)

Ruane, J., 'Colonialism and the interpretation of Irish historical development' in Silverman and Gulliver (eds), *Approaching the past* (1992)

Rusling, G.W., *The schools of the Baptist Irish society* (London, 1968)

Russell, C., 'The British background to the Irish rebellion of 1641', *Bulletin of the Institute of Historical Research* 61:145 (1988), 166–82

Ryan, A., *Toemverig-Toom, Toem or Toemverig: now the modern parishes of Cappagh White-Hollyford* (Tipperary, 1992)

Ryan, J.G., *Irish records: sources for family and local history* (Dublin, 1988)

— (ed.), *Irish church records: their history, availability and use in family and local history* (Dublin, 1992)

Ryan, P., 'Miler Magrath, 1522–1622: archbishop of Cashel' (MA, UCD, 1962)

Sadleir, T.U., 'The pedigree of the Smith family of Kings County and Co. Tipperary, 1666–1881', *Journal of the Society for the Preservation of the Memorials to the Dead* 8 (1910–12), 208

◆Sadleir, T.U., 'Manuscripts at Kilboy, Co. Tipperary, in the possession of Lord Dunalley', *Analecta Hibernica* 12 (1943), 131–52

◆Sall, M., 'A letter about the massacre in Cashel cathedral, 14 September 1647: written by Father Andrew Sall, SJ', *Archivium Hibernicum* 6 (1917), 69–74

Savory, D.P., 'The Huguenot and Palatine settlements in the counties of Limerick, Kerry and Tipperary', *Huguenot Society Proceedings* 18:2 (1947), 214–31

◆Scale, B., *An Hibernian atlas or general description of the kingdom of Ireland* (London, 1809)

Senior, H., *Orangeism in Ireland and Britain, 1795–1836* (London, 1966)

◆Seward, W.W., *Topographia Hibernica, or the topography of Ireland, ancient and modern* (Dublin, 1811)

Seymour, S.J.D., *The succession of parochial clergy in the united diocese of Cashel and Emly: compiled from original sources* (Dublin, 1908)

◆Seymour, S.J.D., 'The chapter books of Cashel Cathedral', *JRSAI* 16 (1910), 328–39

Seymour, S.J.D., *The diocese of Emly* (Dublin, 1913)

—, 'Notes on a Tipperary parish [Donohill]', *JCHAS* 22:112 (1916), 145–56

—, *The Puritans in Ireland, 1641–61* (New York, 1921)

—, *Church plate and parochial records in the diocese of Cashel and Emly* (Clonmel, 1930)

Sharkey, C., 'Altar plate of the Franciscans' in O'Connell and Darmody (eds), *Siege of Clonmel commemoration* (1950)

Sharpe, J.A., 'Last dying speeches': religion, ideology and public execution in seventeenth-century England, *Past and Present* 107 (1985), 144–67

Shee, E.A. and S.J. Watson, *Clonmel – an architectural guide* (Clonmel, 1975)

Shee, W., *The Irish Church: its history and statistics: being a digest of the returns of the prelates* (London, 1863)

Silke, J.J., 'The Irish college, Seville', *Archivium Hibernicum* 24 (1961), 103–47

—, 'The Irish abroad, 1534–1691' in Moody, Martin and Byrne (eds), *A new history of Ireland*, iii (1976), 587–633

Silverman, M. and P.H. Gulliver, *In the valley of the Nore: a social history of Thomastown, Co. Kilkenny, 1840–1983* (Dublin, 1986)

—, *Approaching the past: historical anthropology through Irish case studies* (New York, 1992)

◆Simington, R.C., *The civil survey of Co. Tipperary, 1654–6* (Dublin, 1931)

Simms, A. and W. Nolan (eds), *Irish towns: a guide to sources* (Dublin, 1998)

Simms, J.G., 'The civil survey, 1654–6', *IHS* 9:35 (1955), 253–63

—, 'Irish Catholics and the parliamentary franchise, 1692–1728', *IHS* 12 (1960–1), 28–37

—, 'The Restoration, 1660–85' in Moody, Martin and Byrne, *A new history of Ireland*, iii (1976), 420–53

—, 'The war of the two kings, 1685–91' in Moody, Martin and Byrne, *A new history of Ireland*, iii (1976), 478–508

—, 'The establishment of the Protestant Ascendancy, 1691–1714' in Moody and Vaughan (eds), *A new history of Ireland*, iv (1986), 1–30

—, 'The Irish on the continent, 1691–1800' in Moody and Vaughan (eds), *A new history of Ireland*, iv (1986), 629–56

—, 'The Cromwellian settlement of Tipperary', *Tipperary Historical Journal* 2 (1989), 27–34

Skeats, H.S., *The Irish Church: a historical and statistical review* (London, 1868: 4th ed.)

◆Skehan, W.G., 'Extracts from the minutes of the corporation of Fethard, Co. Tipperary', *Irish Genealogist* 4:2 (1969), 81–92; 4:3 (1970), 183–93; 4:4 (1971), 308–22

—, *Cashel and Emly heritage* (Thurles, 1993)

◆Sleater, M., *Introductory essay to a new system of civil and ecclesiastical topography and itinerary of the counties of Ireland* (Dublin, 1805)

Smeltzer, M.R., *The Smeltzer's of Kilcooley and their Irish-Palatine cousins* (Baltimore, 1981)

Smiles, S., *The Huguenots: their settlements, churches and industries in England and Ireland* (London, 1876)

Smith, C., *The antient and present state of the county and city of Waterford, 1745–6* (London, 1746; rep. Cork, 1969)

Smyth, J., *The men of no property: Irish radicals and popular politics in the late eighteenth century* (Dublin, 1992)

—, 'Like amphibious animals': Irish Protestants, ancient Britons, 1691–1707', *History Journal* 36:4 (1993), 785–97

Smyth, W.J., 'Estate records and the making of the Irish landscape: an example from Co. Tipperary', *Irish Geography* 8 (1975), 39–49

—, 'The western isle of Ireland and the eastern seaboard of America: England's first frontiers', *Irish Geography* 11 (1978), 1–22

—, 'Land values, landownership and population patterns in Co. Tipperary for 1641–60 and 1841–50: some comparisons' in L.M. Cullen and F. Furet (eds), *Ireland and France* (Paris, 1980), 159–84

—, 'Landholding changes, kinship networks and class transformation in rural Ireland: a case-study from Co. Tipperary', *Irish Geography* 16 (1983), 1–20

—, 'Social geography of rural Ireland: inventory and prospect' in Herries Davies (ed.), *Irish Geography* (1984)

—, 'Explorations of place' in J.J. Lee (ed.), *Ireland: towards a sense of place* (Cork, 1985)

—, 'Property, patronage and population – reconstructing the human geography of mid-seventeenth century Co. Tipperary' in Nolan and McGrath (eds), *Tipperary: History and Society* (1985)

—, 'Society and settlement in seventeenth century Ireland: the evidence of the "1659 census"' in Smyth and Whelan, *Common ground* (1988), 55–83

—, 'The dynamic quality of Irish 'village' life: a reassessment' in *Campagnes et littoraux d'Europe: mélanges offert à Pierre Flatrès* (Lille, 1988), 109–13

— and K. Whelan (eds), *Common ground: essays on the historical geography of Ireland, presented to T. Jones Hughes* (Cork, 1988)

—, 'Towns and town life in mid-seventeenth century Co. Tipperary', *Tipperary Historical Journal* 4 (1991), 163–9

—, 'Making the documents of conquest speak: the transformation of property, society and settlement in seventeenth century Cos. Tipperary and Kilkenny' in Gulliver and Silverman (eds),
Approaching the past (1992), 236–90

—, 'The making of modern Ireland: agenda and perspectives on cultural geography' in Graham
and Proudfoot (eds), *Historical geography of Ireland* (1993), 399–438

—, 'The greening of Ireland: tenant tree-planting in the eighteenth and nineteenth centuries',
Irish Forestry 54:1 (1997), 55–72

—, 'Ireland, a colony: settlement implications of the revolution in military-administrative, urban
and ecclesiastical structures, *c.*1550–*c.*1730' in Barry (ed.), *A history of settlement in Ireland* (2000)

Somerville-Large, P., *The Irish country house: a social history* (London, 1995)

◆Spratt, H.D. (ed.), *The autobiography of the Revd Devereaux Spratt, who died at Mitchelstown, Co.
Cork, 1688* (London, 1886)

◆Stalley, R. (ed.), *Daniel Grose (c.1766–1838): the antiquities of Ireland* (Dublin, 1991)

Stevens, D., 'Differences and commonalities' in Richardson (ed.), *A tapestry of beliefs* (1997)

◆Storey, G.W., *A true and impartial history of the last two years* (London, 1691)

Swords, L., *Soldiers, scholars, priests: a short history of the Irish college, Paris* (Paris, 1985)

Taheny, L.J., 'The Dominicans in Clonmel' in O'Connell and Darmody (eds), *Siege of Clonmel
commemoration* (1950)

Tait, C.J., 'Harnessing corpses: death, burial, disinterment and commemoration in Ireland,
*c.*1560–1655' (PhD, UCC, 1999)

—, 'Adored for saints: Catholic martyrdom in Ireland, *c.*1560–1655', *Journal of Early Modern History*
5:2 (2001), 128–59

—, *Death, burial and commemoration in Ireland, 1550–1650* (Hampshire, 2002)

◆Taylor, G. and A. Skinner, *Maps of the roads of Ireland, surveyed 1777* (Dublin and London, 1788;
repr. Shannon, 1969)

Taylor, J., 'A dissuasion of popery to the people of Ireland' in E. Cardwell, *Tracts on points of issue
between the Church of England and Rome* (Oxford, 1852)

◆*The compleate Irish traveller* (London, 1788)

◆*The secret history and memoirs of the barracks of Ireland* (Dublin, 1759)

Thompson, J., 'The Irish Baptist association in the eighteenth century', *Irish Baptist Historical
Society Journal* 17 (1984), 18–31

—, 'Baptists in Ireland, 1792–1922: a dimension of Protestant dissent' (DPhil, Oxford University,
1992)

Tierney, M., 'A short title calendar of papers of Archbishop James Butler II in Archbishop's
House, Thurles, 1773–86', *Collectanea Hibernica* 18 and 19 (1976–7), 105–31; part II, '1787–91',
Collectanea Hibernica 20 (1978), 89–103

◆Trotter, J.B., *Walks through Ireland in 1812, 1814 and 1817* (London, 1819)

◆Twiss, R., *A tour of Ireland in 1775* (Dublin, 1776)

Valkenburg, A., *Two Dominican martyrs of Ireland* (Dublin, 1992)

—, 'The beatified martyrs of Ireland (10): Terence Albert O'Brien, OP, bishop of Emly', *Irish
Theological Quarterly* 66:2 (2001), 165–72

◆Wakefield, E., *An account of Ireland statistically and politically* (London, 1812: 2 vols)

Wall, M., *Catholic Ireland in the eighteenth: collected essays of Maureen Wall* (Dublin, 1989)

◆Walsh, H.D., 'Index to Irish wills in the Carrigan manuscripts', *Irish Genealogist* 4:3 (1970),
221–42

Walsh, R., 'Some of our martyrs', *Irish Ecclesiastical Record* 15 (1894), 301–14

◆Walsh, T.J., 'Some records of the Irish College at Bordeaux', *Archivium Hibernicum* 15 (1950),
92–141

—, *The Irish continental colleges movement: the colleges at Bordeaux, Toulouse and Lille* (Dublin, 1973)

Watson, S.J., *A dinner of herbs: the history of old St Mary's church, Clonmel* (Clonmel, 1988)

Whelan, K., 'The Catholic parish, the Catholic chapel and village development in Ireland', *Irish
Geography* 16 (1983), 1–15

—, 'The Catholic Church in Co. Tipperary, 1700–1850' in Nolan and McGrath, *Tipperary: history and society* (1985)

—, 'The regional impact of Irish Catholicism, 1700–1850' in Smyth and Whelan (eds), *Common Ground* (1988)

—, 'Catholic mobilization in Ireland, 1750–1850' in Bergeron and Cullen (eds), *Cultural and political practices in France and Ireland from the fifteenth to the eighteenth centuries* (Marseille, 1991), 235–58

—, 'United and disunited Irishmen: the discourse of sectarianism in the 1790s', in M. O'Dea and K. Whelan (eds), *Nations and nationalisms: France, Britain, Ireland and the eighteenth-century context* (Oxford, 1995), 231–47

—, 'The origins of the Orange order', *Bullán: An Irish Studies Journal* 2:2 (1996), 24–37

—, 'An underground gentry?: Catholic middlemen in eighteenth-century Ireland' in Donnelly and Miller, *Irish popular culture* (1998),118–72

—, 'Sectarianism and secularism in nineteenth-century Ireland' in P. Brennan (ed.), *La secularization en Irlande* (Caen, 1998), 71–90

—,'Settlement and society in eighteenth century Ireland' in Barry (ed.), *A history of settlement in Ireland* (2000)

Whelan, R. and C. Baxter (eds), *Toleration and religious identity: the implications of the edict of Nantes for France, Britain and Ireland* (Dublin, 2001)

Whelan-Richardson, R., 'The Salamanca archives' in A. Neligan (ed.), *Maynooth library treasures: the collections of St Patrick's College* (Maynooth, 1995)

◆Whelan-Richardson, R. (ed.), *The Salamanca letters: a catalogue of correspondence (1619–1871) from the archives of the Irish colleges in Spain in the library of St Patrick's College, Maynooth* (Maynooth, 1995)

◆White, R., 'Letter sent in 1617 from the east Munster (Ormond) 'residence' of the Jesuits', *JWSEIAS* 6 (1900), 69–74

Whitley, W.T., *A Baptist bibliography, being a register of the chief materials for Baptist history* (London, 1922)

Williams, G., *The Welsh Church from the conquest to the Reformation* (Cardiff, 1976)

Williams, T.D. (ed.), *Secret societies in Ireland* (Dublin, 1973)

◆Wilson, W., *The post-chaise companion or traveller's directory through Ireland* (Dublin, 1804)

Wood, H., *A guide to the Public Record Office of Ireland* (Dublin, 1919)

◆Woodward, R, *The present state of the Church of Ireland* (Dublin, 1787)

◆Woodward, R, *The unbiased Irishman: an answer to the publication on the state of the Established Church by Dr Woodward* (Dublin, 1808: 3rd ed.)

◆Wright, T. and J. Rutty, *A history of the rise and progress of the people called Quakers in Ireland, from the year 1653 to 1700 by T. Wright: revised, enlarged and continued to 1751 by John Rutty* (Dublin, 1818)

◆Wyse-Jackson, R., 'Queen Anne's Irish army establishment, 1704', *Irish Sword* 1 (1949), 133–5

Wyse-Jackson, R., 'Old church plate of Lismore diocese', *JRSAI* 85 (1955), 51–61

Yeoh, B.E.S., 'Historical geographies of the colonised world' in B.J. Graham and C. Nash (eds), *Modern historical geographies* (Harlow, 2000), 146–66

◆Young, A., *A tour in Ireland with general observations on the present state of the kingdom made in the years 1776, 1777 and 1778 and brought down to the end of 1779* (London, 1780: 2 vols)

Index

This index covers all parts of this book and the appendices. Where place names are not qualified with a county name, they are in Co. Tipperary. Locators followed by *n* indicate that the reference is in the footnotes. Locators followed by *t* indicate that the reference is in a table.

Castlelloyd 287

Catholic Relief Acts (1792–3) 238

census of Ireland (1831) 183

cess, parish 231

Chadwick family (Ballinard) 172

Chadwick, Richard (Ballinard) 218

Chancellorstown 167

chapels, building of 210–11, 212–17

chapels-of-ease 147, 210, 212

Charles I, King 60, 61n, 62

Charles II, King 96

Charleville (Co. Cork) 229n, 285

charter schools movement 166, 167–8, 171, 219, 241

Chearnley, Anthony (Burncourt) 113

Christian Brothers 208

church buildings, deterioration of 46, 52, 53–5, 58, 60, 128–9

church cess 231

church educational societies 240–1, 242, 260

church papists 52

church renovation and rebuilding 59, 189, 190, 192–3, 194–6, 207, 210–11, 212–17, 255, 262, 283

Church Temporalities Act (1833) 231, 245, 260

Cistercian order 37, 38, 42, 43, 145, 145n, 154, 163, 264, 269

civil survey 67, 69n, 70, 89, 259

Clanwilliam barony 17, 18, 65, 76, 78, 81, 89, 99, 114, 164, 165, 174

    distribution of Protestant population 68, 69, 70, 90t, 93t, 94, 164t, 250, 252, 273

    Ormond estate 111, 113

Cleghile 66

Clerihan 210, 275, 279, 282, 283, 284, 286 *see also* Ballyclerihan

Clocully 140

Clogheen 66, 76, 77, 78, 81, 85, 107, 110, 113, 122, 166, 170, 178, 183, 184t, 204, 208, 217, 219, 226, 261, 276, 277, 283

    barracks 284

    bridewell prison 234

    constabulary station 286

    district hospital 208

    fair patent 270

    garrison 95, 224, 226, 262

Clogheenfishoge 206

Clogher 48, 58, 70, 126n, 274, 275

Cloghkeating Baptist Church (nr. Cloughjordan) 154

Clonacody 107

Clonamiclon castle 108

Clonbeg 66, 129, 187, 187n, 273, 275, 281, 282, 288 *see also* Aherlow

Clonbrogan 112

Clonbullogue 48n, 173, 273

Cloneen 80, 126n, 157, 210, 270, 272, 275, 279, 282, 283

Clonkelly 233, 286

Clonmacnoise (Co. Offaly) 22

Clonmel 15, 24, 30, 37, 39, 40, 41, 43, 45, 51, 55, 58, 62, 97, 110, 142, 143, 144, 145, 147, 149–50, 151, 153, 163, 172, 204, 205, 208, 213, 221, 223, 224, 226, 241, 246, 258, 276, 282

    anti-tithe agitation 230

    army encampment 227

    Baptist congregation 86, 119, 154–5, 156, 196

    barracks 101–3, 105, 262, 284

    Bolton Street (Weavers Row) 117

    Carmelite priory 23, 269

    census returns (1766) 178–9

    charter school 166, 167, 168

    constabulary station 286, 287

    county gaol 234, 236

    Cromwellian campaign 85, 86, 87, 88, 89

    Cromwellian settlers 90, 119

    demolishing of citadel 98–9, 100

    district hospital 208

    disturbance at Gunpowder Plot commemoration 131

    estate colonies 259

    fair patent 270

    Flemish (Walloon) settlers 116

    flour milling industry 198

    Franciscan friary 29, 31, 49, 82, 145, 146, 153, 162, 269

    freeman parliamentary borough 122

    French settlers 115, 116

    garrison 96, 96n, 101, 224, 262

    Independent-Presbyterian congregation 119, 156, 158

    Irishtown 86, 90, 92, 131, 145

    Johnston Street (present Gladstone Street) 212

    Main Guard palatinate courthouse 154

Parker, John (Cullen) 79
parliamentary elections (1841) 256
parochial union 48
Patrician Brothers 208
patron dynasties 121
Peace Preservation Act (1814) 232
Peake 234, 286
Pearce, Sir Edward Lovett 110
Peel County, Toronto 182
penal laws 121, 146, 163, 164, 204, 205, 213,
  217, 221, 239
Pennefather family (Cashel) 110, 111, 122,
  123, 124, 174, 204, 233
Pennefather, Kingsmill 123, 133
Pennefather, Captain Matthew (MP for
  Cashel) 123
Pennefather, Richard 123
Peppardstown 126n
Percival, Sir Philip 70, 76, 83, 271, 272, 274
Percival, Richard 70
Perry family (Woodrooffe) 106, 108, 167,
  197, 204, 233
Perry, John (Woodrooffe) 114, 158
Perry, Richard (Knocklofty & Woodrooffe)
  107
Petty, Sir William 106, 259
pew politics 190
Phelan, Dr James (bishop of Ossory) 137
Philip II, King 34–6
Phillips, Thomas (Golden) 80
Pierce, Richard (bishop of Waterford and
  Lismore) 139
plantation, state 25, 60, 64, 65, 67, 69, 72–3
  New English colonists, transfer of power
    to 72–3
Plunkett, Archbishop Oliver 142, 149
Pococke, Bishop 168
Poe family (Harley Park) 233, 234
police barracks 244, 245
police force 232
Ponsonby-Barker estate (Kilcooley) 243, 256
popery acts 119, 120
potwalloping 121
Poulkerry 95
Powell, Robert (Fethard) 69, 271, 272
Power, Edmond (Garnavilla) 237
Power family (Newtownanner) 167
Powerstown 97, 212, 276, 277, 282, 283
  see also Kilgrant
Poynings' Law (1494) 163

Prendergast family (Ardfinnan) 204
Prendergast, Revd Gerard (Tullaghmelan)
  276
Prendergast, Revd William (vicar of
  Clonmel) 52
Presbyterian Church, Cork 172
Presbyterian congregations 15, 114, 120, 177,
  214, 261, 262
  Ulster Presbyterian textile workers 171
Presbyterian dissenters 48, 149, 150, 151, 153,
  155, 158, 169, 175, 199
Presbyterian-Baptist cooperation 155
Presentation Sisters 208
Price, Arthur (archbishop of Cashel) 164, 167
Price family (Ardmayle) 167
Primitive Wesleyan Methodist congregation
  196
Prince, Thomas 119
property laws 106, 258
Protestant Colonization Society of Ireland 255
Protestant dissenters 17, 119, 120–1, 149, 151,
  158, 175, 197, 199–200, 219
  emigration 252–5, 262–3
  estate colonies 180–1, 183–4, 259
  exhumation 82
  hegemonic supremacy 63, 71, 73, 83
  massacre, Cashel (1642) 43
  opposition to emancipation 244
  perceived decline in status 238
  population 17, 91, 92, 93, 176, 180, 183,
    196, 247, 252
  Reformation, failure of 26, 264
  'self-image' 62, 83, 134, 174, 219
  settlement 65, 66, 67, 69, 72–3, 76–8, 173,
    219
  siege mentality 74–5, 131, 232, 259, 260
  strategies to increase 64–5, 70–3, 169–70,
    259, 260
Protestantism, conversion to 170, 183n, 184,
  204–5
publications, contemporary 204
Pullin, Richard (Cullen) 79
Purcell, Patrick 78
Purefoy family (Greenfield) 233, 234
Purtill family (Killusty) 204
Pyke, John (Woodenstown) 114, 158, 187

Quaker dissenters 48, 149, 155–6, 178
Quakers 15, 112, 120, 177, 196, 197–8, 199n,
  215, 261, 262